PATRICK HENRY,
From the original portrait by Thomas Sully, in the
possession of his grandson,
William Wirt Henry, Richmond, Va.

1606.   1888.

VIRGINIA AND VIRGINIANS.

EMINENT VIRGINIANS.

Executives of the Colony of Virginia from Sir Thomas Smyth to Lord Dunmore. Executives of the State of Virginia from Patrick Henry to Fitzhugh Lee. Sketches of Gens. Ambrose Powell Hill, Robert E. Lee, Thos. Jonathan Jackson, Commodore Maury.

By DR. R. A. BROCK,
Secretary of the Virginia Historical Society.

HISTORY OF VIRGINIA.

From Settlement of Jamestown to Close of the Civil War.

Written by PROF. VIRGIL A. LEWIS.
Revised by DR. R. A. BROCK.

VOL. I.
WITH PORTRAITS AND ILLUSTRATIONS.

CLEARFIELD

Originally published
Richmond, Virginia, and Toledo, Ohio, 1888

Reprinted for Clearfield Company by
Genealogical Publishing Company
Baltimore, Maryland
1996, 2011

ISBN: Volume I: 978-0-8063-5516-0
ISBN: two-volume set: 978-0-8063-4633-5

Made in the United States of America

Contents of Volume I.

	PAGE.
EMINENT VIRGINIANS	7 to 270
Terms of the Executives of the Colony of Virginia	8 to 11
Terms of the Executives under the State Constitution	11 and 12
Sketches of the Executives of the Colony	12 to 65

These are given in the order of terms of service, as follows: Sir Thomas Smith, Edward Maria Wingfield, John Radcliffe, Captain John Smith, Captain George Percy, Lord De La Warr, Sir Thomas Gates, Sir Thomas Dale, Sir George Yeardley, Sir Samuel Argall, Captain Nathaniel Powell, Sir Francis Wyatt, Captain Francis West, Dr. John Pott, Sir John Harvey, Captain John West, Sir William Berkeley, Richard Kempe, Richard Bennet, Edward Digges, Colonel Samuel Matthews, Colonel Francis Morryson, Herbert Jeffreys, Sir Henry Chicheley, Lord Culpeper, Nicholas Spencer, Baron Effingham, Nathaniel Bacon, Sir Francis Nicholson, Sir Edmond Andros, Earl of Orkney, Edward Nott, Edmund Jenings, Robert Hunter, Alexander Spotswood, Hugh Drysdale, Robert Carter, Sir William Gooch, James Blair, Earl of Albemarle, John Robinson, Thomas Lee, Lewis Burwell, Robert Dinwiddie, Earl of Loudon, John Blair, Francis Fauquier, Sir Jeffrey Amherst, Lord Botetourt, William Nelson, Lord Dunmore.

Sketches of Executives of the State of Virginia	66 to 252

These are given in order of terms of service, as follows: Patrick Henry, Thomas Jefferson, William Fleming, Thomas Nelson, Benj. Harrison, Edmund Randolph, Beverly Randolph, Henry Lee, Robert Brooke, James Wood, James Monroe, John Page, William H. Cabell, John Tyler, George William Smith, Peyton Randolph, James Barbour, Wilson Cary Nicholas, James Patton Preston, Thomas Mann Randolph, James Pleasants, John Tyler, William Branch Giles, John Floyd, Littleton Waller Tazewell, Wyndham Robertson, David Campbell, Thomas Walker Gilmer, John Mercer Patton, John Rutherfoord, John Munford Gregory, James McDowell, William Smith, John Buchanan Floyd, Joseph Johnson, Henry Alexander Wise, John Letcher, Francis H. Pierpont, Henry H. Wells, Gilbert Carleton Walker, James Lawson Kemper, Frederick William Mackey Holliday, William Ewan Cameron.

Sketches of Ambrose Powell Hill, Robert Edward Lee, Thomas Jonathan Jackson, Commodore Maury	253 to 270
HISTORY OF VIRGINIA	271 to 408
Colonial Virginia	278 to 338
After the Revolution to 1861	338 to 346
In the War Between the States	246 to 406
Geographical and Physical View	406 to 408

Illustrations in Volume I.

PORTRAITS.

	PAGE.
Patrick Henry	Frontispiece.
Sir Thomas Smith	13
Peyton Randolph	21
Thomas West, Earl De La Warr	37
Captain George Percy	45
Lord Dunmore	61
Thomas, Lord Culpeper	77
Edmund Randolph	85
Robert Brooke	101
Alexander Spotswood	117
Lady Spotswood	125
George Sandys	149

	PAGE.
Lord Botetourt	157
Rev. John Buchanan	173
Rev. Miles Selden	189
Silhouette of Richard Channing Moore, D. D.	197
Gen. Robt. E. Lee	257
"Stonewall" Jackson	265
Pocahontas	273
Capt. John Smith	281
Robert Bolling	287
Merewether Lewis	331

MISCELLANEOUS ILLUSTRATIONS.

	PAGE.
Mace of the Borough of Norfolk	29
Drinking Cup made from the Silver Mace of the Speaker of the House of Burgesses (before the Revolution)	53
Autograph Bill of Patrick Henry	69
Scene in West Virginia	93
Chair of Speaker of House of Burgesses	109
Armorial Book Plate, Earl of Dunmore	133
Yorktown Monument	141
Old Valentine (1753)	165
St. John's Church, Richmond	181
Scene in Virginia	205
Blandford Church	213
John Randolph's Armorial Book Plate	221
View in West Virginia	229
View of the Capitol Building, Richmond	237

	PAGE.
Entrance to Hollywood Cemetery, Richmond	345
Ruins of Jamestown	291
Seal of Council Chamber, Colony of Virginia	297
Silver Medal King of Pamunkie	305
Silver Medal Queen of Pamunkey	313
Scene on the Great Kanawha	321
Revolutionary Relics—Grave of General Morgan	341
Broad Seal of Virginia Colony	351
Tomb of Mary, Mother of Washington	361
Seal of William and Mary College	371
Book Plate of Col. Wm. Byrd	377
Foley's Statue of "Stonewall" Jackson	383
Confederate States Seal	391
Tomb of Ex-President Monroe	401
View on Upper Potomac	407

EMINENT VIRGINIANS.

EXECUTIVES OF VIRGINIA, 1606–1889.

EXPLANATORY NOTE.

For a due understanding of the status of the several and successive executives of Virginia from its settlement, some explanation seems necessary. It may be thus concisely given : By the charter of the London Company for Virginia, from King James the First, of England, dated April the 10th, 1606, under which colonization was first effected, the chief direction of the affairs of the colony was vested in a Council in England, appointed by the King. They, in turn, named the resident Councillors in the Colony—each body electing its Executive or President. This plan was modified somewhat under a second charter granted the Company May the 23d, 1609, by which it was empowered to choose the Supreme Council in England, and under its instructions and regulations a Governor was provided, invested with absolute civil and military authority, with the title of "Governor and Captain General of Virginia." The resident Council was still retained. In the absence of the Governor-in-Chief, authority was vested in an appointed Deputy, or Lieutenant-Governor, or, in the absence of such officer, in the President of the Council. Upon the annulling of the charter of the London Company, and its dissolution July the 15th, 1624, the King henceforth appointed the Governor-in-Chief, who, however, but rarely resided in the Colony, his functions there being exercised by a Deputy, or Lieutenant-Governor. The resident Council was continued, being appointed by the King on the recommendation of the Governor, or Lieutenant-Governor. This mode obtained whilst Virginia remained a British Colony. The salary of the resident Governor in 1670, then Sir William Berkeley, was £1,200. In 1754 the salary of the Governor-in-Chief was £2,000, of which he retained £1,200, paying his Deputy, the Lieutenant-Governor residing in Virginia, £800. Upon the rupture with the mother country, Lord Dunmore, the last royal Governor, having fled from Williamsburg, the seat of government, in June, 1775, a recently dissolved Assembly met in Convention in the town of Richmond, July the 17th following, and organized a provisional form of government and plan of defence, with a Committee of Safety consisting of Edmund Pendleton, George Mason, John Page, Richard Bland, Thomas Ludwell Lee, Paul Carrington, Dudley Digges, James Mercer, Carter Braxton, William Cabell and John Tabb. A succeeding general Convention met by appointment at Williamsburg, May the 6th, 1776, and on the 29th of June following adopted a State Constitution which provided a Council of State, and a Governor, with a salary of £1,000, to be elected annually by a joint ballot of the Assembly. It is of interest to note in exhibition of the depreciation of the currency of the period that the salary of the Governor was successively increased until in October, 1779, it was made £7,500, and in May, 1780, because of the instability of the currency, was fixed in the primitive medium of Virginia and paid in 60,000 pounds of tobacco. In November, 1781, the amount was restored to £1,000, payable in specie, and this, or its equivalent in decimal currency—$3,333.33½—continued to be the salary until by act of the Assembly of June the 5th, 1852, it was increased to $5,000. In 1781 the term of the Governor was made three years. Under the amended Constitution of Virginia, of 1851, the Council of State was abolished and the Governor made elective by popular vote. Upon the surrender by General R. E. Lee, of the Confederate Army, April the 9th, 1865, Virginia was under martial law until May the 9th following, when, under proclamation of President Andrew Johnson, Governor Francis H. Pierpoint assumed the government, which he held, provisionally, until April the 16th, 1868, when he was superseded by Henry H. Wells, under the military appointment of General John M. Schofield, commanding the First Military District, comprising Virginia. A State Convention met at Richmond in December, 1867, and framed a new Constitution, which, having been adopted by a vote of the people on the 6th of July, 1869, the State was re-admitted to the Union, and a Governor—Gilbert C. Walker—elected, who took his seat January the 1st, 1870, for a term of four years.

EXECUTIVES.

1606, ... —Sir Thomas Smyth, or Smith, first President of the Council of the London Company, and its Treasurer.
1607, April 26—Captain Edward Maria Wingfield, President of the Council in Virginia.
1607, Sept. 10—Captain John Ratcliffe, President of the Council in Virginia.
1608, Sept. 7—Captain John Smith, President of the Council in Virginia.

(1609, May 23—Sir Thomas West, Earl De La Warr, or Delaware, appointed "Governor and Captain General;" did not reach the Colony until June 10th, 1610, the resident executives in the interim being as follows :)
1609, August —Captain George Percy, President of the Council in Virginia.
1610, May 23—Sir Thomas Gates, Lieutenant-General and Deputy Governor.
1610, June 10—Earl De La Warr, Governor and Captain General.
1611, Mar. 28—Captain George Percy, President of the Council.
1611, May 19—Sir Thomas Dale, "High Marshall" and Acting Governor.
1611, August —Sir Thomas Gates, Acting Governor.
1613, March —Sir Thomas Dale, Acting Governor.
1616, April —Captain George Yeardley, Deputy or Lieutenant-Governor.
1617, May 15—Captain Samuel Argall, Deputy or Lieutenant-Governor.
1619, April 9—Captain Nathaniel Powell, President of the Council in Virginia.
1619, April 19—Sir George Yeardley, who had been knighted and appointed Governor and Captain General, Nov. 18, 1618, arrived in the Colony.
1621, Nov. 8—Sir Francis Wyatt, Governor and Captain General.
1626, May 17—Sir George Yeardley (commissioned March 4th), Governor and Captain General. Died November, 1627.
1627, Nov. 14—Captain Francis West, President of the Council.
(1628, Mar. 26—Sir John Harvey, appointed Governor and Captain General, but did not arrive until later. In the interim, as follows :)
1629, Mar. 5—Doctor John Pott, President of the Council.
1630, March —Sir John Harvey, Governor and Captain General, "thrust out of his government" by the people, but re-commissioned by King Charles I., January 11, 1635. Until his arrival April 2, 1636, the executive was:
1635, April 28—Captain John West, President of the Council.
1636, April 2—Sir John Harvey, Governor and Captain General.
1639, Nov. —Sir Francis Wyatt, Governor and Captain General.
1642, Feb. —Sir William Berkeley, who had been commissioned Aug. 9, 1641, arrived as Governor and Captain General.

1644, June —Richard Kempe, President of the Council, Acting Governor during the absence of Sir Wm. Berkeley in England.
1645, June —Sir William Berkeley, Governor.
1652, April 30—Richard Bennet, Acting Governor under the Commonwealth of Cromwell.
1655, March —Edward Digges, President of the Council under the Commonwealth of Cromwell.
1658, Mar. 13—Captain Samuel Matthews, President of the Council under the Commonwealth of Cromwell until January, 1660, from which time the Colony was without a Governor until the election, by the Assembly,
1660, Mar. 23—Of Sir William Berkeley, as Governor. He was commissioned as such by Charles II., July 31, 1660.
1661, April 30—Col. Francis Morryson, Deputy or Lieutenant-Governor.
1662, fall of, —Sir William Berkeley, Governor.
(1675, July 8—Thomas Lord Culpeper appointed Governor and Captain General for life—died in 1719. Until his arrival:)
1677, April 27—Herbert Jeffreys, appointed Governor Oct. 9, 1676, (with Captain Robert Walter as his Deputy, who died Oct. 10, 1676); commissioned Lieutenant-Governor Nov. 11, 1676. Died Dec., 1678.
1678, Dec. 30—Sir Henry Chicheley, Deputy Governor.
1680, May 10—Thomas Lord Culpeper, Governor and Captain General.
1683, Sept. 17—Nicholas Spencer, President of the Council.
1684, April 16—Francis Lord Howard, Baron Effingham, Lieutenant-Governor; commissioned Sept 28, 1683.
1688, Oct. 20—Nathaniel Bacon, President of the Council.
1690, ...Sir Lionel Copley, Governor.
1690, Oct. 16—Col. Francis Nicholson, Lieutenant-Governor.
1693, Oct. 16—Sir Edmund Andros, who had been commissioned Governor March 1, 1693.
1698, Dec. 9—Col. Francis Nicholson, Lieutenant-Governor; commissioned July 20th, 1698.
(1704, ... —George Hamilton Douglas, Earl of Orkney, commissioned Governor-in-Chief; never came to Virginia; died July 29th, 1737.)
1705, Aug. 15—Edward Nott, Lieutenant-Governor; died Aug., 1706.
1706, August —Edmund Jenings, President of the Council.
(1707, April 4—Col. Robert Hunter, commissioned as Lieutenant-Governor, but being captured by the French on his voyage for Virginia, and conveyed to France, never acted.)
1710, June 23—Col. Alexander Spotswood, Lieutenant-Governor.

VIRGINIA AND VIRGINIANS.

1722, Sept. 27—Hugh Drysdale; died July 22, 1726.
1726, July 22—Robert Carter, President of the Council.
1727, Oct. 23—William Gooch (subsequently knighted), Lieutenant-Governor.
(1737, ... —William Anne Keppel, Second Earl of Albemarle; appointed Governor-in-Chief Sept. 6, 1737; died Dec. 23, 1754.)
1740, ... —Between Sept. 16th and Dec. 5th, as indicated by land patents, signed respectively by Sir Wm. Gooch and James Blair, D. D., the latter, as President of the Council, was Acting Governor during the absence of Sir Wm. Gooch in command of the expedition against Carthagena. The last patent signed by James Blair was on July 25, 1741.
1741, July —Sir William Gooch, Lieutenant-Governor.
1749, June 20—John Robinson, President of the Council.
1749, Sept. 5—Thomas Lee, President of the Council; died 1751.
1751, Feb. 12—Lewis Burwell, President of the Council.
1751, Nov. 20—Robert Dinwiddie, Lieutenant-Governor.
(1756, July —John Campbell, Earl of Loudon, appointed Governor-in-Chief, and though he came to New York, was never in Virginia.)
1758, January —John Blair, President of the Council.
1758, June 7—Francis Fauquier, Lieutenant-Governor; appointed Feb. 10, 1758.
(1763, ... —Sir Jeffrey Amherst appointed Governor-in-Chief.)
1767, Sept. 11—John Blair, President of the Council.
1768, Oct. 28—Norborne Berkeley, Baron de Botetourt, Governor-in-Chief; died Oct. 15, 1770.
1770, Oct. 15—William Nelson, President of the Council.
1771, August —John Murray, Earl Dunmore, Governor-in-Chief; appointed July, 1771; fled, June, 1775, from the seat of Government.

GOVERNORS UNDER THE STATE CONSTITUTION, ETC.

1776, June 29—Patrick Henry.
1779, June 1—Thomas Jefferson.
1781, June 12—Thomas Nelson, Jr.; resigned.
1781, Nov. 20—Benjamin Harrison.
1784, Nov. 29—Patrick Henry.
1786, Dec. 1—Edmund Randolph.
1788, Dec. 1—Beverley Randolph.
1791, Dec. 1—Henry Lee.
1794, Dec. 1—Robert Brooke.
1796, Dec. 1—James Wood.

1799, Dec. 1—James Monroe.
1802, Dec. 1—John Page.
1805, Dec. 1—William H. Cabell.
1808, Dec. 1—John Tyler.
1811, Jan. 11—James Monroe; appointed Secretary of State of the United States, Nov. 25, 1811.
1811, Nov. 25—George William Smith, Lieutenant-Governor, and Acting Governor; died Dec. 26, 1811.
1811, Dec. 26—Peyton Randolph, Senior Member of Council of State.
1812, Jan. 3—James Barbour, Governor.
1814, Dec. 1—Wilson Cary Nicholas.
1816, Dec. 1— James P. Preston.
1819, Dec. 1—Thomas Mann Randolph.
1822, Dec. 1—James Pleasants, Jr.
1825, Dec. 1—John Tyler.
1827, March —William B. Giles.
1830, March —John Floyd.
1834, March —Littleton Waller Tazewell; resigned April 30, 1836.
1836, April 30—Wyndham Robertson, Lieutenant-Governor.
1837, March —David Campbell.
1840, March —Thomas Walker Gilmer; resigned to take his seat as a Member of Congress.
1841, March —John Rutherfoord, Lieutenant-Governor.
1842, March —John M. Gregory, Lieutenant-Governor.
1843, January—James McDowell, Governor.
1846, January—William Smith.
1849, January—John B. Floyd.
1851, Jan. 1—Joseph Johnson.
1856, January—Henry Alexander Wise.
1860, January—John Letcher.
1864, January—William Smith.
1865, May 9—Francis H. Pierpoint.
1868, April 16—Henry H. Wells.
1870, Jan. 1—Gilbert C. Walker.
1874, Jan. 1—James L. Kemper.
1878, Jan. 1—Frederick W. M. Holliday.
1882, Jan. 1—William E. Cameron.
1886, Jan. 1—Fitzhugh Lee.

SIR THOMAS SMITH.

Sir Thomas Smith, an eminent merchant of London, and the chief of the assignees of the patents of Sir Walter Raleigh, was the first President of the Council of the London Company of Virginia, and its treas-

SIR THOS SMITH
First Treasurer of the Virginia Company.

urer until the close of the year 1618, when he was succeeded by Sir Edwin Sandys, who was succeeded by his brother, George Sandys, who came to Virginia and completed, on the banks of the James river, a translation of the *Metamorphoses* of Ovid, the first English book prepared in America, which was published in London in 1621. The portrait of George Sandys appears in this work. Sir Thomas Smith was a man of ability, and evidently an astute politician. He is stated by the historian, Rev. E. D. Neill, to have been embassador to Russia, but it is probable that the envoy was another of the same name and title, who died Nov. 28, 1609.

EDWARD MARIA WINGFIELD.

Edward Maria Wingfield, the first President of the Council in Virginia, was a man of gentle birth and honorable record, who had been a companion of Ferdinando Gorges in the European wars, subsequently served in the English army in Ireland, it is presumed with the rank of captain, as he is so designated in the "List of Adventurers," and, later, had been a merchant in London. Because of disagreements in the Colony, he returned to England in 1608. He wrote "A Discourse of Virginia," which was first printed in 1860 by the American Antiquarian Society, with an introduction and notes by Charles Deane, LL.D.

JOHN RATCLIFFE.

Captain John Ratcliffe was President of the Colony from September 10, 1607, to September 7, 1608, when, suffering from a wounded hand and enfeebled by sickness, he went to England, but returned in command of the "Diamond," with colonists, in July, of the following year.

CAPTAIN JOHN SMITH.

A biographical notice of Captain John Smith, President of the Colony from September 7, 1608, to August, 1609, will be found in the historical sketch of Virginia, in the second volume of VIRGINIA AND VIRGINIANS. He has been justly termed "the father of Virginia."

CAPTAIN GEORGE PERCY.

Captain George Percy, a younger brother of Henry, Earl of Northumberland, President of the Colony of Virginia from August, 1609, to May 23, 1610, and from March 28, 1611, to May 19, 1611, and sometime its faithful treasurer, was born September 4, 1586, and died, unmarried, in March, 1632. He was "a gentleman of honor and resolution," and had served with distinction in the wars of the Low Countries, and his soldierly qualities were evidenced in the Colony as a leader against the Indians, as well as his administrative ability as the successor of John Smith. The portrait of him given in this work is from a faithful copy of the original at Syon House, the seat of the Duke of Northumberland, made, in 1853, for the Virginia Historical Society. A mutilated hand in the portrait, it is said, was the result of a wound received in battle.

LORD DE LA WARR.

Sir Thomas West, third Lord De La Warr (or Delaware, as the name now obtains in America), the first resident Governor-in-Chief of the Colony of Virginia, and the descendant of a long line of noble ancestry, was born about the year 1579. His relatives and family connections, who were closely allied with royalty, were among the most active and influential agents of American colonization. The Virginia colony being in a languishing condition, the London Company obtained, May 23, 1609, a second charter, with enlarged privileges and territory, and, under it, Lord De La Warr received the appointment of "Governor and Captain General of Virginia" for life. He is contemporaneously characterized as "one of approved courage, temper and experience," and as "religious, wise, and of a valorous mind." The newly organized Company embraced an imposing representation of rank, wealth and influence, and to the "example, constancy and resolution" of Lord De La Warr is ascribed this revival of "that which was almost lifeless."

The new Governor arrived at Jamestown, June 10, 1610, and immediately instituted vigorous measures for the recuperation of the drooping settlement. The church at Jamestown was repaired and religious services regularly held; two forts were built on the Southampton river, and called after the King's sons, Henry and Charles, respectively. The administration of Lord De La Warr, though ludicrously ostentatious for so insignificant a dominion, was yet highly wholesome, and under his judicious discipline the settlement was restored to order and contentment. His health failing, Lord De La Warr sailed March 28, 1611, for the Island of Mevis, for the benefit of the warm baths, leaving his colony in the charge of Captain George Percy. His health improving somewhat, he desired to return to his government in Virginia, but was overruled by medical advice, and sailed for England instead. His generous exertions for the welfare of the Colony here continued were most assiduous, and were largely instrumental in the frequent procurement for it of new supplies, and in securing a third and yet more advantageous charter for the Company, which was granted by the King, March 12, 1611-12. Lord De La Warr set sail from England to return to Virginia some time in March or April, 1618, but unfortunately died in or near Delaware Bay, on the 7th of June following, sealing his devotion to the Colony with his life, after having dissipated his fortune in the advancement of its interests. The portrait of Lord De La Warr given in this work is from a photograph of the original at Buckhurst Park, in the county of Sussex, England, the seat of the present Earl De La Warr, and was furnished by Hon. L. S. Sackville West, a younger brother of the Earl and the present British minister at Washington, D. C. He prepared a "*Relation*" of the planting of his Colony in Virginia, which was published at London in 1611. It was reprinted (50 copies) in 1859, and again by R. W. Griswold (20 copies) in 1868. A letter from Lord De La Warr, July 7, 1610, from the Harleian manuscript, is printed in the Hakluyt Society's edition of Strachey, p. xxiii.

SIR THOMAS GATES.

Sir Thomas Gates, a patentee named in the first charter to the Virginia Company, was a Captain in the English army, and, by leave, served in the United Netherlands in 1608. He sailed for Virginia with the title of Lieutenant-General, accompanied by his wife and daughters, June 1, 1609, in the "Sea Venture," with colonists and supplies. The vessel being shipwrecked on the Bermudas, they were detained there some months, during which the wife of Gates died. He arrived at Jamestown May 23, 1609, and assumed the government of the Colony until the arrival of Lord De La Warr on the 10th of June following. Gates was sent to England the same year, and returned to the Colony with supplies in August, 1611. He remained as Governor until March, 1613, when he finally departed for England. He is mentioned subsequently as being present at a meetimg of the Virginia Company, held in London, July 13, 1619.

SIR THOMAS DALE.

Thomas Dale, a soldier of distinction in the Low Countries, was knighted by King James the First in June, 1608, as Sir Thomas Dale of Surrey. He sailed with the appointment of "high marshall" from England, for Virginia, March 17, 1611, arrived at Jamestown on the 19th of May following, and superseded Captain George Percy in the government of the Colony. The States-General soon after gave him a three years' leave of absence, which, in 1614, was extended. Under an extraordinary code of "Lawes, Divine, Morall and Martial," compiled by William Strachey, Dale inaugurated vigorous measures for the government and advancement of the Colony. He planted a new settlement at Henrico, remedied to some extent the pernicious system of a community of property by allotting to each settler three acres of land to be worked for his individual benefit; planted "comon gardens for hemp and flaxe, and such other seedes," and conquered the Appomattox Indians and took their town. He was superseded by Sir Thomas Gates in August, 1611, but continued to take an active part in the affairs of the Colony; and on Gates' return to England in March, 1613, he resumed the government. It was under his auspices that the marriage of John Rolfe and Pocahontas was consummated, and this politic example he singularly attempted to follow himself, though he had a wife living in England. He sent Ralph Hamor (who had been Secretary of the Council under Lord De La Warr) to Powhatan, with a request for the younger sister of Pocahontas, a girl scarce twelve years of age, but his overtures were disdainfully rejected.

Dale returned to England in April, 1616. He was in Holland in February, 1617, and in January, 1619, was made Commodore of the East Indian fleet, and had an engagement with the Dutch near Bantam. His health gave way under the climate and he died early in 1620.

SIR GEORGE YEARDLEY.

Captain George Yeardley, as President of the Council, was left by Dale as his Deputy in the government of Virginia, upon the departure of the latter for England in April, 1616. Yeardley was superseded by Captain Samuel Argall, May 15, 1617, and returned to England. Upon the intelligence of the death of Lord De La Warr, Yeardley, who was knighted on the occasion, was appointed to succeed him. He arrived in the Colony April 19, 1619, and assumed the government. On July 30th following the first representative legislative assembly ever held in America was convened at Jamestown. Yeardley was superseded November 18, 1621, by Sir Francis Wyatt, but resumed the government May 17, 1626. He died in November following. During his administration many important improvements were made, and the power, population and prosperity of the Colony much enhanced.

He is reported in January, 1622, as having built a windmill, the first erected in America. He left a widow, Lady Temperance, and two sons, Francis and Argall, the first of whom remarkably instanced individual enterprise, effecting, in 1654, discoveries in North Carolina, and purchasing from the natives at a cost of £300, "three great rivers and all such others as they should like Southerly," which country he took possession of in the name of the Commonwealth. Sir George Yeardley has representative descendants of the name in the United States, but it is not known to the writer that such exist in Virginia.

SIR SAMUEL ARGALL.

Captain Samuel Argall, born at Bristol, England, in 1572, was a relative of Sir Thomas Smith, the Treasurer of the Virginia Company. He first arrived in Virginia at Jamestown in July, 1609, with a ship-load of wine and provisions to trade on private account, and to fish for sturgeon contrary to the regulations of the Company. The colonists, suffering for provisions, seized his supplies. Argall remained in the Colony until June 19, 1610, when he sailed in the "Discovery" for the Bermudas for provisions for the Colony, in company with the vessel of Sir George Somers, from whom, however, he was soon separated in a violent storm. Being driven northward, he came to anchor in a great bay, which he named Delaware Bay. He soon made his way back to Jamestown, and about Christmas, sailing up the Potomac to trade with the natives, recovered from Jopassus, a brother of Powhatan, a captive English boy, Henry Spelman, who afterward wrote a narrative of his captivity, which was printed from the original manuscript by J. F. Hunnewell in 1872.

In February, 1611, Argall attacked the chief of the Warroskoyaks for a breach of contract, and burned two of his towns. Early in 1613 he bribed Jopassus with a brass kettle to deliver Pocahontas into his hands, designing to hold her for a ransom.

In 1614, under orders from Sir Thomas Dale, Argall broke up the French settlement at Mt. Desert, on the coast of Maine, causing a war between the French and English colonists. He also destroyed the French settlements at St. Croix and Port Royal. He now sailed for England, where he arrived in June, 1614. He returned to Virginia as Deputy Governor, May 15, 1617, with a purpose to traffic in violation of the laws he was to administer. He found "the market place, streets, and other spare places in Jamestown planted in tobacco," so alluring to the colonists was the profit yielded by the weed. He enacted severe sumptuary laws, and by his arbitrary conduct rendered himself odious. He was recalled, and Sir George Yeardley appointed in his place, but, before the arrival of the latter, Argall secretly stole away from the Colony. Called to account for his misconduct, he was shielded from punishment by his trading partner, the Earl of Warwick. In 1620 he was a captain in the expedition against the Algerines; was knighted by James I. in 1623, and in 1625 was engaged in Cecil's expedition against the Spanish. He died in 1639. An account of his voyage from Jamestown in 1610, and his letter respecting his voyage to Virginia in 1617, are preserved in Purchas. After the death of Lord De La Warr, Argall took charge of his estate; and letters of Lady De La Warr are in existence accusing him of the most flagrant and barefaced peculation

CAPTAIN NATHANIEL POWELL.

Captain Nathaniel Powell, of the Council, was Acting Governor of the Colony from the departure of Argall, April 9, 1619, until the 19th inst., when Governor Yeardley arrived. Powell, with his wife and eleven others, was slain at his plantation, "Powle Brooke," by the savages, in the memorable massacre of March 22, 1622.

SIR FRANCIS WYATT.

The father of Sir Francis was George Wyatt, and his mother was a daughter of Sir Thomas Finch. His sister Eleanora married Sir John Finch; and his wife was a daughter of Samuel Sandys. Sir Francis arrived in Virginia in October, 1621, with an appointment to relieve Governor Yeardley (whose term expired November 18th) at the request of the latter. Sir Francis was accompanied by his brother, Rev. Hunt Wyatt, Dr. John Pott, physician (afterward Acting Governor of the Colony), William Claiborne (subsequently prominent, and designated in history as "the rebel") as surveyor, and George Sandys, treasurer, who during his stay translated the *Metamorphoses* of Ovid and the First Book of Virgil's *Æneid*. This first Anglo-American poetical production was published in London in 1626. Sir Francis brought with him a new constitution for the Colony, granted July 24th, by which all former immunities and franchises were confirmed. Trial by jury was first secured, and an annual assembly provided. During the administration of Wyatt, which was judicious, occurred the Indian massacre of March 22, 1622, in which three hundred and forty-seven of the colonists fell victims; and on the 16th of June, 1624, the charter of the Virginia Company was annulled. The death of his father, Sir George Wyatt, in 1626, calling Sir Francis to Ireland to attend to his private affairs, he was succeeded in the government of Virginia by Sir George Yeardley. Sir Francis was re-appointed Governor in November, 1639, but was relieved by Sir William Berkeley in February, 1642. He died at Bexley, Kent, England in 1644.

CAPTAIN FRANCIS WEST.

Captain Francis West, a younger brother of Lord De La Warr, arrived in the Colony in September, 1608. He is said by the historian Neill to have married a widow in the Colony; no issue is mentioned. He was long a member of the Council, and in 1622 held the appointment of Admiral of New England. He owned lands near "Westover," James River, famed as the seat of the Byrds. He was Acting Governor of Virginia from the death of Sir George Yeardley, November 14, 1627, until his departure for England, March 5, 1629, when he was succeeded by Dr. John Pott. He must have returned to Virginia, as his name appears as a member of the Council in 1632-3. By a tradition in the family he is said to have been drowned; when, it is not stated.

VIRGINIA AND VIRGINIANS.

DOCTOR JOHN POTT.

Doctor John Pott, who accompanied Sir Francis Wyatt to Virginia as physician, arriving in October, 1621, as President of the Council succeeded Captain Francis West in the Government of Virginia upon the departure of the latter for England. Pott was superseded by the arrival of Sir John Harvey in March, 1630, and in July following by a strange mutation of fortune, the late Governor was tried for cattle-stealing and convicted. This was the first trial by jury in the Colony.

SIR JOHN HARVEY.

John Harvey was commissioned Governor of the Colony March 26, 1628, and knighted soon after. He had been one of the Commissioners sent in 1623 to procure evidence to be used against the Virginia Company to secure the annulling of the charter, and was a member of the provisional government in 1625. He arrived in Virginia in March, 1630. He was one of the most rapacious, tyrannical and unpopular of the royal governors, and in the contest of Colonel William Claiborne with George Calvert, of Maryland, for the possession of Kent Island, Harvey—actuated, it was charged, by motives of private interest—sided with Maryland in the disputes, and rendered himself so obnoxious that an assembly was called for the 7th of May, 1635, to hear complaints against him. Before it met, however, he consented to go to England to answer the charges. He was reinstated by Charles I. as Governor, by commission dated April 2, 1634, but in November, 1639, was displaced by Sir Francis Wyatt.

CAPTAIN JOHN WEST.

Captain John West, a younger brother of Lord De La Warr, and long a member of the Council, succeeded Sir John Harvey when the latter was "thrust out of his Government" April 28, 1635. He was superseded by Sir John Harvey, April 2, 1636. He remained in Virginia, and has many worthy descendants in Virginia in honored family names. In March 1659–60, the House of Burgesses passed an act acknowledging "the many important favors and services rendered to the country of Virginia by the noble family of the West, predecessors to Mr. John West, their now only survivor."

SIR WILLIAM BERKELEY.

Sir William Berkeley, the son of Sir Maurice, and brother of Lord John Berkeley of Stratton, was born near London about 1610. He graduated M. A., at Oxford, in 1629, traveled extensively in Europe in

PEYTON RANDOLPH,
First Speaker of the Continental Congress.

From the original in the possession of Peyton
Johnston, Esq., Richmond.

1630, and returned an accomplished courtier and cavalier. He was commissioned Governor of Virginia, August 9, 1641, and arrived in the Colony in February, 1642, and by some salutary measures as well as by his prepossessing manners, rendered himself acceptable to the colonists. On the 18th of April, 1644, a second Indian massacre occurred in the Colony. The number of the victims has been variously stated as three and five hundred. During a visit of Berkeley to England from June, 1644, to June, 1645, his place was filled by Richard Kempe, a member of the Council, and who had been its Secretary. During the civil war in England, Berkeley took the royal side, and Virginia was the last of the English possessions which acknowledged the authority of Cromwell. He manifested shrewdness as well as courage when the fleet of parliament appeared in James River in 1651, and made terms satisfactory to both parties. He was superseded in the Government, according to Hening, April 30, 1652, by Richard Bennet, but there are grants of land of record in the Virginia Land Registry, signed by Bennet in January, 1652.

He was re-elected Governor by the Assembly March 23, 1660, and commissioned by Charles II., July 31, 1660. He was sent, April 30, 1661, by the Colony to England to protest against the enforcement of the Navigation Act, Colonel Francis Morrison acting as Governor until Berkeley's return in the fall of 1662.

Berkeley lost popularity with the colonists by his extreme severity towards the followers of Nathanial Bacon, whose so-called "rebellion" had been occasioned by Berkeley's own faithlessness and obstinacy. Twenty-three of the participants were executed, and Berkeley was only restrained from the further shedding of blood by the remonstrance of the Assembly.

Charles II. is reported to have said: "The old fool has taken more lives in his naked country than I have taken for my father's murder." Through the influence of the planters, Berkeley was recalled, and died at Twickenham, July 9, 1677, before he could have an interview with the King. Berkeley in his reply to commissioners, sent to inquire into the condition of the Colony, said, "Thank God! there are no free schools or printing presses, and I hope there will be none for a hundred years; for learning has brought disobedience and heresy and sects into the world, and printing has divulged these and other 'libels.'" He wrote two plays, and is the author of "A Description of Virginia," folio, 1663. His widow, Lady Frances Berkeley, who had before been Dame Stephens, and whose maiden name was Culpeper, married thirdly, Philip Ludwell of "Green Spring," Virginia, long the secretary of the Colony.

RICHARD KEMPE.

Richard Kempe appears as a Member of the Council of Virginia in 1642, and as its President, in June, 1644, upon the departure of Sir

VIRGINIA AND VIRGINIANS. 23

William Berkeley for England, became the acting Governor of the colony. It is notable that during his incumbency the first fast and thanksgiving days in the Colony of which any record is preserved, were ordered. "Att James Cittye the 17th of February, 1644–5," it was " enacted by the Governour, Counsell and Burgesses of this present Grand Assembly, for God's glory and the publick benefit of the collony to the end that God might avert his heavie judgments that are now vpon vs, That the last Wednesday in every month be sett apart for a day of ffast and humiliation, And that it be wholly dedicated to prayers and preaching;" also, "That the eighteenth day of April be yearly celebrated by thanksgivings for our deliverance from the hands of the Salvages." [Referring to the recent massacre by the Indians.] (*Hening's Statutes*, I., pp. 289, 290.)

Sir William Berkeley, returning in June, 1645, resumed the government of Virginia, but Richard Kempe continued to serve the colony as a member of the Council until 1648, and perhaps later, latterly as the Secretary of the body. He died sometime before 1678. William Kempe, probably a kinsman, was a Burgess from Elizabeth City County in 1630. The name is a highly respected one in Virginia, and the parish records of Middlesex county present frequent representatives among the lists of vestrymen.

RICHARD BENNET.

Richard Bennet, who is mentioned as being "one of Lord Arlington's family," was a merchant, and appears as a Burgess from "Warrosquoyeake" in October, 1629. He was a Member of the Council in 1642. A Puritan in religious belief, he fled into the province of Maryland in 1643 to escape persecution. From thence he went to London, and in September, 1651, returned to Virginia with the appointment from the Parliamentary Government as one of the Commissioners to effect the reduction of the royal colony of Virginia, the remaining Commissioners being Captain Robert Dennis, Thomas Stegge (an uncle of the first William Byrd, of "Westover"), and Colonel William Claiborne, "the rebel." Bennet was elected Governor of the Colony by the Assembly, April 30, 1652, and was continued in office until March 30, 1655, when he was sent to England as the Agent of Virginia to rep resent its interests before Parliament. In 1666 he commanded the militia of three of the four military districts into which Virginia was divided, with the rank of Major-General. The remaining district was commanded by the Governor, Sir William Berkeley. In 1667 Major-General Bennet served as a Commissioner to Maryland to regulate the cultivation of tobacco. He was a member of the Council as late as 1674, and is presumed to have died soon after this period. He owned the plantations "Weyanoak" and "Kicotan," on James River. His daughter Anne (died November, 1687) married Theodrick Bland, of

"Westover," (born January 16, 1629; died August, 1669) and their descendants, in the honored names of Randolph, Lee, Harrison, Beverley and others, have been and are among the most worthy people of Virginia.

EDWARD DIGGES.

Edward Digges, a younger son of Sir Dudley Digges, of Chilham, County Kent, England, Knight and Baronet, and Master of the Rolls in the reign of Charles the First, was born in 1620. He was appointed a member of the Council November 22, 1654, and was elected by the Assembly Governor of Virginia March 30, 1655, to succeed Governor Bennet, and served until March 13, 1658, when he was sent to England as one of the agents of the colony. He married Elizabeth Bray, and died March 15, 1675. In the epitaph upon his tomb at the family seat, "Bellefield," distant eight miles from Williamsburg, he is described as "a gentleman of most considerable parts and ingenuity, and the only promoter of the silk manufacture in this colonie, and in everything else a pattern worthy of all pious imitation." He left six sons and seven daughters, whose blood now intermingles in the best esteemed families of the State. Several of his sons were prominent in the affairs of the colony, one of them, Dudley, being long a member of the Council, as was also his grandson, Cole Digges.

COLONEL SAMUEL MATTHEWS.

Samuel Matthews, who is termed "an ancient planter," was a member of the Council as early as 1629. In March, 1630, he built the fort at Point Comfort, James River. He served continuously in the Council, or Assembly, and latterly as County-Lieutenant of Warwick County, deriving thence his title of Lieutenant-Colonel. In 1656 he was sent as one of the agents of the colony to England, and on March 13, 1658, was elected by the Assembly Governor to succeed Edward Digges. He was an honest, energetic and capable servant of the colony, and his death, which occurred in January, 1660, was universally lamented. The colony was now without a Governor until the 23d of March, when Sir William Berkeley was elected by the Assembly. There are highly esteemed descendants of Governor Matthews in Virginia, one of them being James M. Matthews, Esq., of Richmond, late the able Reporter of the Court of Appeals of the State.

COLONEL FRANCIS MORRYSON, OR MORRISON.

Major Francis Morryson, or Morrison, embarked from London with his brother loyalists, Colonel Henry Norwood and Major Richard Fox, for Virginia, September 23, 1649, and arrived in the colony in November following. They were kindly received by Sir William Berkeley, the Governor, whe gave Morrison the command of the fort at Point Comfort. He became a member of the Council, and it is presumed County-Lieutenant of James City County, since his later designation was Colonel. He was Speaker of the House of Burgesses in 1656, and from April 30, 1661, to sometime in the fall of the following year (during the absence of Sir William Berkeley in England), Governor of Virginia. March 26, 1663, he was sent to England as the agent of the colony, with an annual salary of £200. The records do not evidence that he ever returned to Virginia. He married Cecilia, the sister of Giles Rawlins, who died during her residence in Virginia, and she petitioned afterward for a share in the distribution of his estate.

HERBERT JEFFREYS.

Colonel Herbert Jeffreys was commissioned Governor of the Colony of Virginia, October 9, 1676, and Captain Robert Walter appointed his Deputy the following day, but the latter died without entering upon office, and Jeffreys was recommissioned Lieutenant-Governor, November 11, 1676. He entered upon his office, April 27, 1677. He effected a treaty of peace with the Indians (who had long held the Colony in terror) by which each town agreed to pay three arrows for their land, and twenty beaver skins annually for protection. Jeffreys died December 30, 1678, and was succeeded by Sir Henry Chicheley.

SIR HENRY CHICHELEY.

Sir Henry Chicheley is first mentioned in Virginia in November, 1649, as the guest of Captain Ralph Wormeley, of "Rosegill," Middlesex County (afterwards Clerk of Lancaster County), whose widow, Agatha, he married sometime before 1667. In 1656 he was a Burgess from Lancaster County, and in 1674, a member of the Council. In March, 1676, he was appointed commander of the forces to be sent against the Indians, but the forces were disbanded before marching by Sir William Berkeley. He became Deputy Governor of Virginia, December 30, 1678, upon the death of Governor Herbert Jeffreys, under a commission dated February 28, 1674, and served until the arrival of Lord Culpeper, March 10, 1680, but he continued to act as Deputy Governor during the absence of Lord Culpeper until 1683. Sir Henry Chicheley died sometime after 1692, and was buried at Christ Church in Middlesex County. His descendants intermarried with the Corbin, Thacker, and other families, and there are representatives of his own name, as well, in Virginia at the present day.

LORD CULPEPER.

Thomas, Lord Culpeper, Baron of Thorsway, who had been one of the Commissioners for Plantations, was on July 8, 1675, appointed by Charles II., Governor of Virginia for life. He is described as "an able, but artful and covetous man." Regarding his office doubtless a sinecure, he lingered in England until a reproof from the King impelled his departure. He came over to Virginia in 1680, and was sworn into office May 10th. He brought with him several bills ready prepared for the consideration of the Assembly, and procured the passage by that body of several popular acts, including one of "free and general pardon, indemnitie, and oblivion" for all participants in the recent movement known as "Bacon's Rebellion."

He had the address, withal, to have the import of two shillings per hogshead made perpetual, and instead of being accounted for to the Assembly, as formerly, to be disposed of as his Majesty might deem fit.

He also, notwithstanding the impoverished condition of the Colony, contrived the enlargement of his salary from one thousand pounds to upwards of two thousand, besides perquisites amounting to eight hundred more. He went over to England in August, 1680, leaving Sir Henry Chicheley as Deputy Governor of the Colony. An act of the Assembly requiring tobacco for shipment to be laden at established towns, having created much popular commotion and riotous destruction of tobacco plant beds, to quell the disaffection Culpeper was commanded to return to Virginia. He arrived in November, 1682, and as a result of his measures taken, several of the ring-leaders in the riots were hanged. One of them, Major Robert Beverley, clerk of the House of Burgesses, and the father of the Virginia historian of the same name, endured a lengthy and rigorous imprisonment, and was disfranchised. Culpeper returned to England September 17, 1683, leaving his kinsman, Nicholas Spencer, as the executive of the Colony.

Thus, again, quitting his government in violation of his orders, he was arrested immediately upon his arrival in England, and being found guilty, also, of receiving presents from the Assembly, a jury of Middlesex found that he had forfeited his commission. He died in 1719. He was in 1669 a co-grantee with Henry, Earl of Arlington, of the extensive territory between the Rappahannock and Potomac Rivers, Virginia, known as the "Northern Neck." By purchase, he became sole proprietor; his daughter, Catherine, sole heiress, married Thomas, fifth Lord Fairfax and Baron Cameron, and the proprietary descended to their son Thomas, sixth Lord Fairfax, who established his seat, in Virginia, at "Greenway Court," Frederick County, where he lived in much state, dispensing a liberal hospitality. He was the friend and patron of Washington, whom, at the age of sixteen, in 1748, he employed to survey his lands

VIRGINIA AND VIRGINIANS.

west of the Blue Ridge. Lord Fairfax died December 12, 1787, aged 90 years ; his barony and immense domain of 5,282,000 acres descending to his only brother Robert, seventh Lord Fairfax, but as the latter was in the possession of Lord Thomas during the Revolution, it was confiscated. The portrait of Lord Culpeper in this work is from a photograph of a copy in the collections of the Virginia Historical Society, at Richmond, Va., of the original at Leeds Castle, England, painted by Andr. Hennemorn in 1664.

NICHOLAS SPENCER.

Colonel Nicholas Spencer, a kinsman of Lord Culpeper, who had been a member of the Council and its Secretary from 1679, as President became the acting Governor of Virginia upon the departure of Lord Culpeper for England, September 17, 1683. He was superseded April 16, 1684, by Lord Effingham. Spencer was still Secretary of the Colony in 1689, and perhaps served later.

FRANCIS HOWARD, BARON EFFINGHAM.

Francis Howard, Baron Effingham, son of Sir Charles Howard, succeeded to his title in 1681. He was commissioned Governor of Virginia, September 28, 1683, and arrived in the Colony and entered upon the duties of his office, April 16, 1684. He was instructed to prevent the use of the printing press in Virginia. Owing to the incursions of the Five Nations upon the frontier of Virginia, it was deemed expedient to treat with them through the Governor of New York; and for this purpose, Lord Effingham sailed for Albany the 23d of June, and in July effected a treaty with the chiefs of the warlike tribes. During Effingham's absence from Virginia, the Government was administered by Nathaniel Bacon, Senior, President of the Council.

Effingham, no less avaricious and unscrupulous than his predecessor, Culpeper, had been, by his tyranny and rapacity aroused a general spirit of indignation. He prorogued and dissolved the Assembly; created a new Court of Chancery, making himself a petty lord chancellor; multiplied fees, and stooped to share them with the clerks, silencing the victims of his extortions by arbitrary imprisonment. The prayers for relief of the groaning colonists were at length heard, and Effingham was recalled, embarking for England, October 20, 1688, leaving Nathanial Bacon, Senior, President of the Council, in the Government. Lord Effingham died in England, March 30, 1694.

NATHANIEL BACON.

Nathaniel Bacon, Senior, of the lineage of the celebrated Francis Bacon, Lord Verulam, and a cousin of Nathaniel Bacon, Junior, known in history as "the rebel," was born in 1620. He was prominent in the affairs of the Colony, and held various offices of distinction and trust. He was County-Lieutenant, or "Commander-in-Chief" of the County of York; long the auditor of the Colony, and, as his epitaph recites, a member of the Council "for above forty years." As President of the body, he was the acting Governor of Virginia from the departure of Lord Effingham, October 20, 1688, until the arrival of Francis Nicholson, October 16, 1690. He died March 16, 1693. His wife was Elizabeth, daughter of Richard Kingsmell, a name corruptly perpetuated in Kingsmill Wharf, York County, James River. The tombs of Nathaniel Bacon and his wife, massive marble tablets with armorial insignia, remained a few years since in the ancient burial ground near the mouth of King's Creek, York County.

Nathaniel Bacon, Senior, bequeathed his estate to his niece Abigail (nee Smith), wife of Major Lewis Burwell, as he left no issue. But of his chivalric kinsman, "the rebel," there are claimed representative descendants of the present generation.

SIR FRANCIS NICHOLSON.

Colonel Francis Nicholson was by profession a soldier. Lieutenant-Governor of the Colony of New York under Sir Edmund Andros, he was at the head of the administration there in 1687–1689, but was driven thence by a popular outbreak. He came from England to Virginia as its Lieutenant-Governor in 1690, and relieved President Nathaniel Bacon, October 16. Courting popularity, he instituted athletic games, and offered prizes to those who should excel in riding, running, shooting, wrestling and fencing. He also proposed the establishment of a post-office, and recommended the erection of a college, heading, with the Council, a private subscription by which £2500 were raised, and the result was the charter in February, 1692, of the ancient seat of learning, William and Mary College.

Nicholson was relieved October 15, 1693, by Sir Edmond Andros, Governor-in-Chief. Nicholson was now appointed Governor of Maryland, serving as such until December 9, 1698, when he relieved Sir Edmond Andros as Governor of Virginia, under a commission, dated July 20th preceding. Nicholson entertained a plan to form the several colonies into a Confederacy, of which he aspired to be made viceroy. Disappointed in his aims, he displayed ultimately such freaks of caprice, and such audacity in misrule, as to call in question his sanity. Becoming passionately attached to a daughter of Lewis Burwell, Jr., and failing to win her favor, or that of her parents, he exhibited furious manifestations, and persisted Quixotically for years in his

MACE
Of the Borough of Norfolk,
Presented by Gov. Dinwiddie,
1754.

futile attentions to the lady, venting threats against her father, brothers and others. He became involved, also, in contentions with the clergy. For a more healthy location, Governor Nicholson removed the seat of Government from Jamestown to Middle Plantations (subsequently named Williamsburg) in 1698. Upon the complaint of the clergy and Council, Governor Nicholson was recalled to England in August, 1705, and on the 15th of that month, succeeded by Edward Nott as Lieutenant-Governor. In 1710 Nicholas was appointed General and Commander-in-chief of the forces sent against Port Royal, in Acadia, which was surrendered to him October 2. He returned to England to urge another attempt upon Canada, taking with him five Iroquois Indians, who were presented to Queen Anne. He commanded the unsuccessful expedition against Canada in 1711. From October 12, 1712, to August, 1717, he was Governor of Nova Scotia. He was knighted in 1720, and served as Governor of South Carolina from 1721 to June, 1725, when, returning to England, he was made a Lieutenant-General. Bancroft describes him as "an adept in colonial governments; trained by long experience in New York, Virginia, and Maryland; brave and not penurious, but narrow and irascible; of loose morality, yet a fervent supporter of the church." He was the author of "An Apology or Vindication of Francis Nicholson, Governor of South Carolina," London, folio, 1724, and of "Journal of an Expedition for the Reduction of Port Royal," London, 4to, 1711. He died in London, March 5, 1728.

SIR EDMOND ANDROS.

Edmond Andros was born in London, December 6, 1637. Bred a soldier, he distinguished himself in the war with the Dutch, which closed in 1667, and in 1672 was appointed a major in Prince Rupert's Dragoons. In the year 1674, upon the death of his father, he succeeded him as bailiff of Guernsey. He was appointed Governor of the Colony of New York, where he had previously served in a military capacity in 1678, and continued governor until 1681, being principally employed there in passing grants to the subjects, and in presiding in the Court of Sessions. Appointed Governor of New England, he arrived in Boston December 21. There his administration was to the utmost degree arbitrary and tyrannical. He interfered with the liberty of the press, levied enormous taxes without authority, and required the proprietors of lands to obtain from him new titles at great expense. In October, 1687, he demanded, at the head of his troops, the surrender of the charter of Connecticut, but it was successfully concealed in the famous Charter Oak, at Hartford. His wife died and was buried at Boston, February 10, 1687–8, in King's Chapel burying ground. In 1688 he caused an Indian war by his aggressions on the Penobscot tribe. At last, under the weight of his oppressions, the people of Boston deposed and imprisoned him. The abdication of James the Second prevented any consequent trouble with the British Government, because of this summary assertion of popular prerogative, and no judicial decision was rendered regarding Andros. He was commissioned Governor of Virginia March 1, 1693, and arrived in the colony October 16th, following, relieving Colonel Francis Nicholson in the government. He was kindly received by the Virginians, whose solicitations to King William for warlike stores he had promoted. He soon gave some offence, however, by ordering ships to cruise against vessels engaged in contraband trade, yet his administration was a salutary and prosperous one for Virginia, and by his conduct here he is considered by some to have largely condoned his previous lawless career. During his term of office the ancient seat of learning, William and Mary College, was established, and in 1693 an act was passed for organizing a post-office department for Virginia, with a central office and sub-offices in each county, with fixed rates of postage, and Thomas Neale as Postmaster-General. Andros's love of order carried him into the public departments, and finding the documents and papers in great confusion, torn, soiled and moth-eaten, he ordered their reparation, and pressed reform with vigor. He encouraged manufactures, incited the planters to the cultivation of cotton, and gave his assent to an act establishing the first fulling-mills ever known in the settlement. Invested with the power of Ordinary, or representative of the King and the Bishop of London, his acts brought him in collision with commissary James Blair, President of William and Mary College, who, in 1694, preferred charges to the King against him as an enemy to religion, the church, and the college, and occasioned, thus, his removal from office. He was succeeded, December 9, 1698, by Colonel Francis Nicholson. Andros was Governor of Guernsey from 1704 to 1706. He died at London, February 27, 1713–14, honored and respected. The narrative of his proceedings in New England was published in 1691, and republished in 1773. The "Andros Tracts," edited by William H. Whitmore, were published by the Prince Society, Boston, 1868, 2 vols. 4to.

EARL OF ORKNEY.

George Hamilton, Earl of Orkney, a member of a distinguished family, was appointed Governor-in-chief of Virginia in 1697, and enjoyed it as a pensionary sinecure for forty years, all the while residing in England, and out of the annual salary of £2,000 receiving £1,200. George Hamilton entered the army in his youth, was made a colonel in 1689, and, in 1695, was created Earl of Orkney, in consideration of his gallantry. He was present at the battles of the Boyne, Athlone,

Limerick, Aghrim, Stimkirk, Landen, Namur, and Blenheim, and was a great favorite with King William the Third. In the first year of Queen Anne's reign he was made a major-general, and shortly afterwards a Knight of the Thistle, serving with distinction in all the wars of her reign. As one of the sixteen peers of Scotland, he was a member of the House of Lords for many years. He married, in 1695, Elizabeth, daughter of Sir Edward Villiers, Knight, (Maid of Honor to Queen Mary,) sister of Edward, Earl of Jersey, by whom he had issue three daughters: Lady Anne, who married the Earl of Inchequin; Lady Frances, who married Sir Thomas Sanderson (brother to the Earl of Scarborough), and Lady Harriet, who married the Earl of Orrery. He died January 29, 1737, and, on September 6 of that year, was succeeded as Governor-in-chief of Virginia by the Earl of Albemarle. The nephew of the Earl of Orkney, the celebrated Sir William Hamilton, the husband of the famous beauty, Lady Emma Hamilton, whose name is connected with that of the heroic Lord Nelson, of the Nile, was, in 1772, an unsuccessful applicant for the resident governorship of Virginia.

EDWARD NOTT.

Edward Nott, born in 1654, succeeded, August 15, 1705, as the deputy of the Earl of Orkney, Francis Nicholson, in the resident government of Virginia.

Governor Nott procured the passage, in October, 1705, by the assembly, of an act for the building of a palace for the governor, with an appropriation of £3,000, also an act establishing the general court, but the last was disallowed by the British Board of Trade. During Governor Nott's administration the College of William and Mary was destroyed by fire. Governor Nott died, greatly lamented by the Colony, August 23, 1706, and in the epitaph upon the handsome tomb to his memory, still standing in the church yard of Old Bruton Church, in Williamsburg, the regard in which he was held is thus testified: " In his private character he was a good Christian, and in his public a good Governor. He was a lover of mankind and bountiful to his friends. By the prudence and justice of his administration he was universally esteemed a public blessing while he lived, and when he died it was a public calamity. * * * In grateful remembrance of whose many virtues, the General Assembly of this Colony have erected this monument."

EDMUND JENINGS.

Edmund Jenings, son of Sir Edmund Jenings, of Ripon, Yorkshire, England, Member of Parliament, is first mentioned in Virginia annals, August 1, 1684, as Attorney-General of the Colony. Captain Peter Jenings, of Gloucester county, probably a relative, was an "Adjutant-

General" and a burgess in 1660, and then, or later, Attorney-General. He died in 1671. John Jenings appears as a grantee of land in James City county in 1649. Edmund Jenings married Frances (died in London, November 22, 1713), daughter of Henry Corbin, emigrant ancestor from England of the family of his name in Virginia. Jenings was, in 1696, Deputy Secretary of Virginia, and, a little later, the agent of the proprietary of the Northern Neck. He was long a member of the council, and, as its president, upon the death of Governor Nott, became, August 23, 1705, the executive of Virginia. He was one of the commissioners the same year for laying off the city of Williamsburg. His daughter Ariana became the wife of John Randolph, Attorney-General of Virginia, and their son, Edmund Randolph, became the Governor of Virginia and Attorney-General of the United States under Washington. Another daughter of Edmund Jenings married William Hill, of the family of the Marquis of Downshire. The blood of Edmund Jenings has intermingled with that of the worthiest families of Virginia, comprising the honored names of Randolph, Carter, Lee, Ludwell, Meade and others. Jenings continued the executive of Virginia until the arrival of Lieutenant-Governor Spotswood, June 23, 1710.

ROBERT HUNTER.

Robert Hunter was appointed Lieutenant-Governor of Virginia, April 4, 1707, and his commission from George, Prince of Denmark, consort of Queen Anne, and Lord Admiral, is preserved in the cabinet of the Virginia Historical Society. It is a huge vellum document, measuring two feet by two feet six inches, closely covered with Latin script, and is probably the only example in Virginia of the commissions of her governors in colonial times; and yet Hunter, being captured by the French, then at war with England, on his voyage to Virginia, never acted as her executive, being conveyed as a prisoner to Paris by his captors. It appears that, soon after this, a plan having been proposed to reduce the Spanish West India Islands, Hunter was proposed, by the Duke of Marlborough, to command it. During Hunter's detention in Paris, he corresponded with Dean Swift, who, it appears, had been suspected of being the author of the famous letter concerning enthusiasm, usually printed in Lord Shaftesbury's *Characteristics*, but which was really written by Hunter. Returning to England, Hunter was made Governor of New York, and was sent thither in 1710, with 2,700 expatriated Palatines, to settle that colony. He returned to England in 1719. On the accession of George the Second, he was reinstated in the government of New York and New Jersey. The climate not agreeing with him, he obtained the government of Jamaica instead, arriving there in February, 1727. He died March 31, 1734. He was a friend of Addison, as well as of Swift; was a wit and scholar, and, in addition to the letter mentioned, wrote a farce called "Androboros."

ALEXANDER SPOTSWOOD.

Colonel Alexander Spotswood, who arrived, June 23, 1710, in Virginia, as the deputy or lieutenant of George Hamilton, Earl of Orkney, the Governor and Commander-in-chief of the Colony, was descended from the ancient Scottish family of Spottiswoode, a local surname assumed by the proprietors of the lands and barony of Spottiswoode in the parish of Gordon and county of Berwick, at the earliest period when surnames became hereditary in Scotland; but his lineage is yet more nobly avouched in the virtue, learning, ability and courage of its representatives through centuries of succession. The traditional account of the family is, that the male line of the ancient barons of Spottiswoode, failing in the reign of Alexander II., a younger son of the illustrious house of Gordon, which was then seated in the same county, married the heiress and was obliged to take upon himself the name of Spottiswoode; but he retained the boar's head of the Gordons, which his successors, the barons of Spottiswoode, carry to this day. The immediate progenitor of this family was Robert de Spotswoods, born during the reign of Alexander III., who succeeded to the crown of Scotland in 1249. Seventh in descent from Robert was John Spotiswood; born, 1510; died 1585; superintendent of Lothian, a zealous Protestant divine and one of the compilers of "The First Book of Discipline and of the Confession of Faith." His son, John Spotswood, of Spotiswoode, born in 1595, became archbishop of Glasgow and one of the privy counsel of Scotland in 1635. He suffered from the popular indignation at the attempt, discouraged by him, to impose a liturgy on the Scottish Church, and was deposed and excommunicated by the Assembly which met at Glasgow in November, 1638. He retired to London, where he died November 26th, 1639. He was the author, among other works, of "The History of the Church and State of Scotland." His second son, Sir Robert Spottiswoode, president of the Court of Sessions, author of "The Practicks of the Laws of Scotland," a man of distinguished learning and merit, was born in 1596, and met his death at the hands of Parliament, January 17th, 1646, as an adherant of the royal cause. The son of the last Robert Spotswoods, who died in 1688, married a widow, Catharine Elliott, who had by her first marriage a son, General Elliott, whose portrait is in the State Library at Richmond, Virginia. The only child of Robert and Catherine (Elliott) Spotswood, Alexander, the subject of this notice, was born in 1676, at Tangier, then an English colony, in Africa, his father being then resident surgeon to the governor of the island, the Earl of Middleton, and to the garrison there. Alexander Spotswood was literally bred in the army from his childhood and, uniting genius with courage, served with distinction under the Duke of Marlborough. He was dangerously wounded in the breast by the first fire of the French on the Confederates at the battle of Blenheim, during the heat of which sanguinary encounter he served as deputy quartermaster-general, with the rank of colonel. Though Virginia enjoyed tranquillity and the voice of faction was hushed at the time of the arrival of Spotswood, yet the condition of the colony was not prosperous. Her defenseless coasts were invaded by privateers and pirates, and through the decline of her staple commerce, because of the quantities of tobacco procured from Germany by the Dutch, the surreptitious shipment of it from the colony, and the greed of the English factors, there was a just complaint of the scantiness of essential supplies of English manufactures. Spotswood was hailed with acclamation by the colonists, because he brought with him the invaluable benefit of the *habeas corpus* act, which had been denied by the late ministers when their representatives endeavored to extend it by their own authority. But while the assembly regarded the recent favors granted, they could not, October, 1710, be persuaded to see the defenseless condition of the colony, since the certain expense of protection appeared more immediate than distant danger; nor did the fear of a threatened French invasion the following summer, appeal any more effectually. They refused to pay the expense of collecting the militia or to discharge the debt due, because, as Spotswood informed the Ministry, " they hoped by their frugality to recommend themselves to the populace."

They would only consent to levy £20,000 by duties laid chiefly on British manufactures, and insisted on discriminating privileges to Virginia owners of vessels, in preference to British subjects, upon the plea that the exemption had always existed. The governor declined the proffered levy, dissolved the assembly, and in anticipation of an Indian war, was obliged to secure arms and supplies from England. By prompt and energetic measures he quelled in the neighboring province of North Carolina, an insurrection which threatened to subvert all regular government there; and later, in the war with the Tuscarora Indians (commenced by a massacre on the frontier of North Carolina, in September, 1711), by a conciliatory course, prevented the tributary Indians from joining the enemy, with whom, in January, 1714, he concluded a peace, and blending humanity with vigor, he taught them that while he could use violence, he commiserated their fate. When a new Assembly was called by Spotswood, in 1712, they did more than he expected, and discharged most of the debts of the Colony, when he demonstrated that the standing revenue had been so defective during the previous twenty-two years as to have required £7,000 from the monarch's private estate to make up the deficiencies in governmental expenses. The frontier of the Colony being no longer subjected to Indian incursions, the expenditure of government was reduced to one-third of what had been previously required, and under the able administration of Spotswood, Virginia advanced in commerce, population and wealth more rapidly than any of her sister colonies. A settlement of German Protestants was also effected under the auspices of the Governor, on the Rapid Anne river, which was called after the name of his residence, Germanna. A profitable trade was established with the West Indies, in the exchange of corn, lumber and salted provisions, for sugar, rum and wine. In 1715 the population of Virginia was 72,500 whites and 23,000 negroes, it being of the American colonies second in number only to Massachusetts, which was only one thousand greater. The slave population of Virginia was, during the reign of George I., increased by 10,000. The colony now comprised twenty-five counties, represented by fifty-two burgesses. The government was administered by a governor (appointed by the king), who nominated inferior magistrates and officers; and also by twelve councilors, also created by the royal mandate. The energy and discipline of Spotswood soon ran counter to the economical spirit of the Assembly, whom he further offended by his haughtiness. Anonymous letters were constantly transmitted against him to the board of trade, who gave him an opportunity of vindicating, in the vigor of his replies, the wisdom and beneficence of his administration. As zealous a churchman as he is proven to have been, he yet, in the exercise of the right of induction of ministers, incurred the animosity of the Bishop of London's commissary, James Blair, who laid formal complaint against him before the king. Colonel William Byrd was also sent over by the colony in 1719, to represent its grievances, but being unsuccessful in his embassy, he begged the board of trade " to recommend forgiveness and moderation to both parties." A more harmonious season ensued, and the Governor, Council and the Assembly concurred in measures for the public welfare and prosperity.

The pirates who infested the coast were subdued, and the frontiers were extended to the foot of the Blue Ridge mountains, a passage across which had been discovered by an expedition made under the leadership of Spotswood in 1716, and composed of some of the first gentlemen in the Colony. Upon its return, the governor presented each of his companions with a golden horseshoe (some of which are said to have been covered with valuable stones, resembling heads of nails), bearing the inscription: *"Sic juvat transcendere montes."* In the year 1720, two new counties, Spotsylvania and Brunswick, were established. Spotswood urged upon the British Government the policy of establishing a chain of posts beyond the Alleghanies, from the lakes to the Mississippi, to restrain the encroachments of the French. His wise recommendation was at first unheeded, and it was not until after the treaty of Aix-la-Chapelle that it was adopted. He was the author of an act for

THOMAS WEST, EARL DE LA WARR.
From the original in the possession of the
present Earl Delaware, England.

improving the staple of tobacco, and making tobacco notes the medium of circulation. Being a master of the military art, he kept the militia under admirable discipline. He was a proficient in mathematics; built the octagon magazine at Williamsburg (still standing), rebuilt William and Mary College (which had been burnt) and made improvements in the governor's house (then called palace) and gardens. He was an excellent judge on the bench. At his instance a grant of £1,000 was made by the governors and visitors of the college, in 1718, and a fund established for instructing Indian children in Christianity, and he erected a school for that purpose on the southern frontier, at Fort Christiana, established on the south side of the Meherrin river, in what is now Southampton county. The Rev. Charles Griffin had charge of the school in 1715, at which time there were seventy-seven Indian children under instruction. Spotswood was styled the "Tubal Cain of Virginia," and he was, indeed, the first to establish a regular iron furnace in North America. But, despite his momentous services to the Colony, intrigue, as his friends urge, at length effected his removal as governor, in September, 1722. His character and administration are thus warmly eulogized by Chalmers: "There was a utility in his designs, a vigour in his conduct, and an attachment to the true interest of the kingdom and the colony, which merit the greatest praise. Had he attended more to the courtly maxim of Charles the Second, 'to quarrel with no man, however great might be the provocation, since he knew not how soon he should be obliged to act with him,' that able officer might be recommended as the model of a provincial governor. The fabled heroes who had discovered the uses of the anvil and the axe, who introduced the labors of the plow, with the arts of the fisher, have been immortalized as the greatest benefactors of mankind. Had Spotswood even invaded the privileges, while he only mortified the pride of the Virginians, they ought to have erected a statue to the memory of the ruler who gave them the manufacture of iron and showed them by his active example that it is diligence and attention which can alone make a people great." In the county of Spotsylvania, Spotswood had, about the year 1716, founded on a horse-shoe peninsula of four hundred acres, on the Rapid Anne, the little town of Germanna, so called after the Germans sent over by Queen Anne, and settled in that quarter, and at this place he resided after his retirement. A church was built there, mainly at his expense. Possessing an extensive tract of forty-five thousand acres of land, which abounded in iron ore, he engaged largely, in connection with Robert Cary of England, and others in Virginia, in the iron manufacture. In the year 1730, he was made deputy postmaster-general for the American Colonies, and held the office until 1739; and it was he who promoted Benjamin Franklin to the office of postmaster for the province of Pennsylvania. He married, in 1724, Anne Butler, the daughter of Richard Brayne, Esq., of Westminster, England. She derived her middle name from James Butler, Duke of Ormond, her godfather. Her portrait in this work is from one in oil in the library of the State of Virginia, at Richmond, and now first engraved. She had issue: John, Robert, Anne Catharine and Dorothea. John Spotswood married, in 1745, Mary, daughter of William Dandridge, of the British navy, and their issue was two sons: General Alexander and Captain John Spotswood, of the Army of the Revolution, and two daughters, Mary and Anne. Robert, the younger son of the governor, and an officer, under Washington, in the French and Indian war, was slain by the Indians. Anne Catharine, the elder daughter of Governor Spotswood, married Bernard Moore, Esq., of "Chelsea," in the county of King William, Va. Dorothea, the younger daughter, married Captain Nathaniel West Dandridge, of the British navy, son of Captain William Dandridge, of Elson Green.

Promoted Major-General, and on the eve of embarking with troops destined for Carthagena, Spotswood died at Annapolis, Maryland, on the 7th of June, 1740. There is reason to believe that he lies buried at "Temple Farm," his country residence near Yorktown, and which was so called from a sepulchral building erected by him in the garden there. It was in the dwelling-house at "Temple Farm" (called the Moore House) that Lord Cornwallis signed the articles of his capitulation. The widow of Governor Spotswood surviving him, and continuing to reside at Germanna, married, secondly, November 9, 1742, the Rev. John Thompson of Culpeper County, a minister of the Episcopal Church, and of exemplary character. The descendants of Governor Spotswood in Virginia are now represented, in addition to the family names already given, in those of Aylett, Braxton, Brooke, Berkeley, Burwell, Bassett, Chiswell, Carter, Campbell, Callaway, Cullen, Claiborne, Dandridge, Dangerfield, Dabney, Fairfax, Fontaine, Gaines, Gilliam, Kemp, Kinlock, Lloyd, Lee, Leigh, Macon, Mason, Manson, Marshall, Meriwether, McDonald, McCarty, Nelson, Parker, Page, Randolph, Robinson, Smallwood, Skyring, Talaferro, Temple, Thweatt, Taylor, Walker, Waller, Wickham, Watkins, and others, scarce less esteemed. The portrait in this work is from a contemporaneous portrait in oil, in the possession of the eminent sculptor, Edward V. Valentine, Richmond, Va., whose late estimable wife was of the lineage of the Governor.

HUGH DRYSDALE.

Hugh Drysdale succeeded Spotswood as Lieutenant-Governor of Virginia, September 27, 1722. He was a man of but mediocre capacity, and his administration was not marked with any event of importance. It may be noted, however, that to relieve the people of Virginia from a poll-tax, a duty was laid by the Assembly on the importation of liquors and slaves, but owing to the opposition of the African Company and interested traders in England, the act was annulled by the British Board of Trade. Thus did Great Britain, and later the New England States, foster the institution of slavery so long as the importation of slaves was profitable to them, though the Southern Colonies repeatedly and ineffectually enacted laws prohibiting further importation. Drysdale, dying July 22, 1726, Colonel Robert Carter, President of the Council, succeeded to the government of the Colony.

ROBERT CARTER.

Robert Carter, born in 1667, was the son of John Carter, an emigrant from England, who settled in upper Norfolk County, which he represented in the House of Burgesses in 1642; later for a number of years the representative of Lancaster County; Commander-in-chief of the forces sent against the Rappahannock Indians, and who died in 1669. Robert Carter was long the agent of Lord Fairfax, proprietor of the Northern Neck grant, and by the extent of his landed possessions, thus acquired, obtained the sobriquet of "King Carter."

He was speaker of the House of Burgesses for six years, treasurer of the Colony, for many years a member of the Council, and, as President of that body, he was at the head of the government of Virginia from the death of Governor Drysdale, July 22, 1726, until the arrival of Governor William Gooch, October 13, 1727. Robert Carter built a fine church on the site of one formerly built by his father, near his seat, "Corotoman," on the Rappahannock River, in Lancaster County, and it is still standing, in good preservation. Robert Carter, by his two wives, Judith Armistead and a widow whose maiden name was Betty Landon, left many children, who are now represented by a legion of names of the most worthy people of Virginia. He died August 4, 1732, and lies beneath a handsome tomb with a long and eulogistic Latin epitaph, near the east end of Christ Church, before mentioned as having been built by him.

SIR WILLIAM GOOCH.

William Gooch was born at Yarmouth, England, October 21, 1681. He was an officer of superior military abilities, and had served under Marlborough, and in the Revolution of 1715. He arrived in Virginia October 13, 1727, relieving President Robert Carter in the government. The council, without authority, allowing Gooch three hundred pounds out of the quit-rents in augmentation of his salary, he in return resigned, in a great measure, the helm of government to them, and so insinuating was he in his diplomacy and so facile in accommodating himself doubly to the home authorities and to the people of Virginia that he greatly endeared himself to them, and he is said to have been the only Colonial Governor in America against whom there was never any complaint, either from inhabitant or merchant abroad.

Owing partly to his address, and partly to a well-established revenue and the enforcement of a rigid economy, the Colony enjoyed prosperous repose during his long administration. During the year 1728, the boundary line between Virginia and North Carolina was run by Colonel William Byrd and Messrs. Fitzwilliam and Dandridge, Commissioners in behalf of Virginia, and others on the part of North Carolina, and the transaction is most entertainingly detailed in the "Westover MSS." of Colonel Byrd. In 1740, troops for the first time were transported from the Colonies to co-operate with the forces of the mother country in offensive war. An attack upon Carthagena being determined on, Gooch raised four hundred men as the quota of Virginia, and the Assembly voted £5,000 for their support. Major-General Alexander Spotswood, who had been appointed to the command of the four battalions raised in the Colonies, dying June 7, 1740, at Annapolis, on the eve of embarkation, Governor Gooch assumed the command of the expedition. During his absence the government of Virginia devolved on Commissary James Blair, President of the Council. During the administration of Gooch, the settlement of the fertile valley of Virginia was effected, first in 1734, twelve miles from the present town of Woodstock. In May, 1746, the Assembly appropriated £4,000 to the raising of Virginia's quota of troops for the invasion of Canada. They sailed from Hampton in June; the expedition, however, proved abortive. Governor Gooch, who had been appointed Commander, but declined, was created a Baronet during the year, and in 1747 was made a Major General. He returned to England in 1749, leaving John Robinson, President of the Council, as the Acting Governor of the Colony. Sir William Gooch died December 17, 1751. The press in 1878 chronicled the unhappy estrangement of his descendant, Sir Thomas Gooch, the eighth baronet, from his childless wife, Lady Anne (Sutherland), because of an attempt to deceive him with a spurious heir. Broken in spirit and health, the sorrowful wife, in her death the following year, expiated her offense.

It may be of interest to note that another of the lineage of Governor Gooch, and bearing the same Christian name, preceded him as a resident of the Colony. At "Temple Farm," a seat of Governor Spotswood, near Yorktown, Va., within the structure known as the "Temple" is the tomb of Major William Gooch (who died October 29, 1655, aged twenty-nine), bearing the arms of Gooch of Norfolk (of which family was the Governor) as follows: Paly of right ar. and sa. a chev. of the first betw. three dogs of the second spotted of the field. Crest—A greyhound passant ar. spotted sa. and collared of the last. This William Gooch was a Burgess from York County, in 1654, and it is claimed there are those of the name, of his lineage in Virginia now.

COMMISSARY JAMES BLAIR.

James Blair, D.D., was born in Scotland about the year 1655. Having graduated from the University of Edinburgh, he was admitted to orders in the Established Church of England, and commenced his ministry in Scotland, but finding his usefulness obstructed by popular prejudice, he went to London, and was sent by its bishop in 1685 as a missionary to Virginia. He served here first as rector of Henrico parish for nine years. His ability and great zeal displayed in furtherance of the cause of religion, procured him, in 1689, the appointment of Commissary of the Bishop of London. He removed his residence to Jamestown to prosecute plans for the founding of an institution of learning in the Colony. Meeting with much encouragement, he proceeded to England, where, having secured a subscription of £2,500, he obtained from the King in February, 1692, a charter for William and Mary College, with a grant of twenty thousand acres of land for its support. The King himself subscribed £2,000 towards its building out of the quit-rents. Seymour, the Attorney General of Great Britain, having received the royal commands to prepare the charter of the college, remonstrated against the liberality of the King, urging that the nation was engaged in an expensive war; that the money was needed for better purposes, and that he did not see the slightest occasion for a college in Virginia. Commissary Blair, in reply, represented to him that its intention was to educate and qualify young men to be ministers of the Gospel; and begged that the Attorney-General would consider that the people of Virginia had souls to be saved as well as the people of England. "Souls!" exclaimed the imperious Seymour, "damn your souls!—make tobacco!" The college was erected according to a design by Sir Christopher Wren, at Williamsburg, in 1694, with five professorships of Greek and Latin, the mathematics, moral philosophy, and two of divinity, with Dr. Blair as President, which position he held during life. In 1710, Commissary Blair became rector of Bruton Parish at Williamsburg. He was long a member of the Council, and, as the President of this body, was the Acting Governor of Virginia during the absence of Governor Gooch in command of the Carthagena expedition from June 1740 to July 25, 1741, and perhaps later. Commissary Blair in 1727 assisted John Hartwell and Edward Chilton in compiling "The State of His Majesty's Colony in Virginia," and one hundred and seventeen of his "Sermons and Discourses" expository of the Sermon on the Mount, were published in four volumes 8vo at London in 1742. He died August 3, 1743, aged 88, and was buried at Jamestown, where his tomb with a long epitaph in Latin was still standing, though in a damaged condition, just prior to our late war. By his will Commissary Blair bequeathed his library and £500 to William and Mary College.

THE EARL OF ALBERMARLE.

William Anne Keppel, second Earl of Albermarle, was born at Whitehall in 1702, and received his second Christian name from Her Majesty Queen Anne, who in person and as sponsor graced his baptism. He succeeded George Hamilton, Earl of Orkney, as the Governor-in-chief of Virginia, after the death of the latter, September 6, 1737. Appointed August 25, 1717, by George I. a captain in the British army, he was continuously promoted, and on February 20, 1743, was made a Lieutenant-General, and distinguished himself June 2d in that year at the battle of Dettingen in the Netherlands. In 1744 he made the campaign with Marshall Wade, and in 1745, under the Duke of Cumberland, at the battle of Fontenoy, he was wounded. On April 16, 1746, he commanded the right wing at the battle of Culloden, and succeeded to the command in chief, as General, August 23d. Distinguished himself July 2, 1747, at the battle of Vall; was ambassador to France in 1748; was created a Knight of the Garter, July 12, 1750; was made a member of the Privy Council, July 12, 1751, and on March 30, 1752, one of the Lords Justices during the absence of the King in his German dominions. He married, in 1722, Anne, daughter of Charles, first Duke of Richmond, and who was one of the ladies of the bed-chamber of Queen Caroline. The issue of this marriage was eight sons and seven daughters. The portrait of Lord Albermarle, with those of Sir Charles Wager; Charles Montague, first Earl of Halifax; Colonel Daniel Parke, Governor of the Leeward Islands, whose daughter Lucy was the wife of the second Colonel William Byrd: the third Earl of Orrery; the Earl of Egremont; the second Duke of Argyll; Peggy Blount, the favorite of the poet Alexander Pope; Sir Robert Walpole, Lady Betty Cromwell, Sir Wilfred Lawson, Sir Robert Southwell, and others of colonial distinction, with those of the second William Byrd, and of members of his family, from a gallery formerly at "Westover," are now preserved at the hospitable seat of the Harrison family, "Lower Brandon," on James River. Lord Abermarle died at Paris, December 22, 1754, and was succeeded in the title by his eldest son George, the third Earl. Admiral Augustus Keppel, of the British Navy, was his second son. The name of Lord Albermarle is commemorated in a sound on the coast of North Carolina and in a county in Virginia.

JOHN ROBINSON.

The ancestor of the distinguished family Robinson in Virginia, was Christopher Robinson, of Cleasby, in Yorkshire, England, who settled about the year 1666, at "Hewick," near Urbanna, in Middlesex County. He was the brother of the Right Reverend John Robinson (born 1650, died 1722), a distinguished prelate and statesman, who was Bishop of London as well as embassador for many years to Sweden, and who represented England as First Plenipotentiary at the Congress of Utrecht in 1712.

Christopher Robinson was born in 1645; married, first, Agatha Bertram, secondly, Catharine, daughter of Theodore Hone, and widow of Robert Beverley, of Virginia. John Robinson, their second son, was born in 1683. As President of the Council, he was Acting Governor of Virginia from June 20th to his death in September, 1749. He married, first Catherine, daughter of Robert Beverley, and, secondly, Mrs. Mary Welsh, of Essex County, Va. His descendants through intermarriage have been connected with nearly all of the old Virginia families, and the name Robinson itself has had many worthy and valued representatives in the annals of the Colony and State.

THOMAS LEE.

Thomas Lee, the fourth son of Richard and Lettice (Corbin) Lee, and descended in the third generation from Richard Lee, who emigrated from Shropshire, England, and settled in Westmoreland county, Virginia, in 1641, was born about the year 1680. He married in 1721, Hannah, daughter of Philip Ludwell, and granddaughter of Lady Berkeley (widow of Sir William), who married, thirdly, in 1680, Philip Ludwell. Thomas Lee was long a member of the House of Burgesses and of the Council, and as President of that body after the death of John Robinson, became the Acting Governor of Virginia, and but for his death, which occurred in the early part of 1751, it was presumed, from the influence of his connections in England, that he would have received the appointment of Deputy or Lieutenant-Governor, for which, it is said, a commission had been executed. He had been also the recipient of royal bounty, it is said, upon the destruction of his residence by fire, being then aided from the privy purse of Queen Caroline towards the building of the famous "Stratford" mansion.

He was a member of the historical Ohio Company, and was a man of great enterprise and sagacity. Rarely has a sire been so distinguished in his offspring as was Thomas Lee, the father of six sons, severally eminent among the lustrous patriots of the Revolution. The names of Philip Ludwell and Thomas Ludwell Lee are indelibly engraven on the pages of the history of Virginia, whilst the fame of Richard Henry and of Francis Lightfoot Lee (signers of the instrument of American Free-

CAPT. GEORGE PERCY,
Treasurer of the Colony of Virginia, and
Governor in 1609.

From the original at Syon House, England, seat of
the Earl of Northumberland.

dom) and of William and Arthur Lee, is food for national pride. The grand hero, Robert Edward Lee, was a descendant in the third generation of Henry Lee, the brother of Governor Thomas Lee.

LEWIS BURWELL.

The Burwell family is "of very ancient date upon the borders of England and Scotland." It was settled at Berwick-upon-Tweed as early as the year 1250. The names Minion Burrell and William Burrell appear in the list of adventurers for Virginia. The ancestor of the family in the Colony was Major Lewis Burwell, who settled on Carter's Creek, in Gloucester County, in 1640. In 1646 he was a member of the deputation sent to invite Charles the Second to come to Virginia as its King. He married Lucy, daughter of the "valiant Captain Robert Higginson, one of the first commanders who subdued the country of Virginia from the power of the heathen." Of the issue of this marriage, Major Nathaniel Burwell, the fourth son, born about 1680, married Elizabeth, eldest daughter of "King" Robert Carter, who, after his death in 1721, married Dr. George Nicholas, and was the mother of Robert Carter Nicholas, long the Treasurer of Virginia. The eldest son of Major Nathaniel and Elizabeth (Carter) Burwell, Lewis Burwell, known by the name of his seat, as of "The Grove," Gloucester County, was born about the year 1710. He matriculated at Caius College, Cambridge, England, in 1731, and was a man of genius and learning. He married in October, 1736, Mary, daughter of Colonel Francis and Ann Willis. He was a Burgess from Gloucester County as early as 1736, a little later became a member of the Council, and as the President of that body, after the death of Thomas Lee, was, on February 12, 1751, acting Governor of Virginia. He was relieved by the arrival of Lieutenant-Governor Robert Dinwiddie, November 20, 1751, and died in 1752.

ROBERT DINWIDDIE.

The period of the accession of Robert Dinwiddie as the executive of the Colony of Virginia, was one of anxiety and momentous presage in its history, and the dignity of Lieutenant-Governor at this critical exigency was conferred on him in royal recognition of the singular ability, zeal and fidelity exhibited by him in previous positions of governmental trust. The Dinwiddie is an ancient Scotch family of historic mention. On the "Ragman's Roll," A. D. 1296, appears the name of Alleyn Dinwithie, the progenitor, it is said, of the Dinwiddies who were long seated as chief proprietors on lands called after them, in the parish of Applegarth, Annandale, Dumfries-shire. The immediate ancestors of Governor Dinwiddie were denizens of Glasgow, and had been, for some generations probably, merchants in honorable esteem, as was his father, Robert Dinwiddie. His mother was of an old Glasgow family of the same calling. She was Sarah, the daughter of Matthew Cumming, who was Baillie of the city in 1691, 1696 and 1699. The son, Robert Dinwiddie, was born in 1693, at Germiston, his father's seat. He was disciplined in the counting house, and was probably for a time a merchant in Glasgow. He was appointed, December 1, 1727, a collector of the customs in the Island of Bermuda, which position he held under successive commissions, until April 11, 1738, when, in acknowledgment of his vigilance and zeal in the discharge of official duty, in the detecting and exposing a long practiced system of fraud in the collection of the customs of the West India Islands, he received the appointment of "Surveyor General of the customs of the Southern ports of the Continent of America."

He was named, as his predecessor had been, a member of the respective Councils of the American Colonies. This mandate was recognized by Governor Gooch, of Virginia (in which colony Dinwiddie appears to have fixed his chief residence), but was resisted by the Councillors, who, jealous of interference with their prerogatives, refused to allow him to sit with them, and transmitted a remonstrance to the King for his exclusion. The controversy was decided by the Board of Trade in May, 1742, advising that the royal purpose should be enforced, in opposition to claims dangerous because they were new. Dinwiddie was specially commissioned, August 17, 1743, with the designation of "Inspector General," to examine into the duties of the Collector of Customs of the Island of Barbadoes, and, in the discharge of this trust, exposed to the English Government an enormous defalcation in the revenues there. In 1749, he appears to have resided in London as a merchant, engaged in trade with the colonies. He was appointed Lieutenant-Governor of Virginia, July 20, 1751, and with his wife Rebecca (*nee* Affleck) and two daughters, Elizabeth and Rebecca, arrived in the Colony November 20th following. He was warmly welcomed with expressions of respect and regard, but in a little while gave offence by declaring the dissent of the King to certain acts which his more insinuating predecessor, Gooch, had approved. Governor Dinwiddie finding that the regulations governing the patenting of lands were but little regarded, and that a practice had long prevailed of securing the possession and use of lands by warrants of survey without the entering of patents, by which more than a million of acres of land were unpatented, and the royal revenue from the quit-rents of two-shillings annual tax upon every fifty acres, seriously defrauded—with the advice of the Council, in an endeavor to correct the abuse, and by the exaction of a fee of a pistole (about $3.60 in value) on every patent issued, incurred yet greater animosity. The House of Burgesses unavailingly remonstrated against this exercise of the royal prerogative, and, in 1754, sent Peyton Randolph (then Attorney-General of the Colony and ultimately distinguished as the first President of the Continental Congress) to England, as its agent, with a salary of £2500, and bearing a petition to the King for relief from the fee. The decision of the Board of Trade was virtually in favor of Governor Dinwiddie, though their instructions were at first singularly indefinite. This difference, when harmony in Council and concert in action were so essential, was unfortunate. The aggrandizing policy in North America of the French—who asserted their claim to the whole Mississippi Valley, in virtue of primal rights of discovery and occupation under the explorations of Marquette, La Salle, and others—was a constant menace to English colonization. In every treaty between the two competing powers, the territorial limits of France had been left undecided. To that fatal treaty between Charles I. and Louis XIII., by which "was restored to France, absolutely and without demarcation of limits, all the places possessed by the English, in New France, Lacadie and Canada, particularly Port Royal, Quebec and Cape Breton," holds McPherson, may be ascribed the subsequent troubles with France. From 1690, the colonies from New Hampshire to Georgia were engaged in almost unremitting hostilities with the savages on their borders, instigated by the French in the North and the Spaniards in the South. The intent of the French to link their possessions in Louisiana and on the St. Lawrence by a chain of forts on the Ohio, was manifest. Governor Dinwiddie, viewing with alarm their encroachments, at the close of October, 1753, dispatched Major George Washington, then only twenty-one years of age, to M. Le Gardeur de St. Pierre, the Commandant of the fort on the Ohio, to demand by whose authority an armed force had crossed the lakes, and to urge a speedy and peaceable departure. The mission, accomplished under many hardships, was ineffectual, and Governor Dinwiddie immediately instituted the most energetic and widespread efforts for defense. His vigilance, zeal and activity were signal. Though suffering from the debilitating effects of a stroke of paralysis, his personal activity for the public good would have been creditable to one of physical capacity the most favored. He promptly reported the impending danger to the English government, and to the Executives of the several Colonies, urging immediate and effectual measures of resistance, and praying their assistance. He had but meager response in America, but in the course of the year 1754 was aided with a grant of £20,000, arms and ordnance stores from Great Britain. The money was ordered to be reimbursed from the export duty of two shillings per hogshead on tobacco. The English Ministry perceiving, from the unfortunate events of 1754, that expedients were fruitless, and that no effective conjoined action of the American Colonies could be hoped for, determined on an offensive policy by sea and land, and early in 1755, Admirals Boscawen and Mostyn were sent with a powerful fleet into the North American seas, to intercept the reinforcements of France; and General Braddock, with the appointment of Commander-in-chief, was sent to Virginia with two regiments from the regular army. This last was a succor which had been persistently solicited by Governor Dinwiddie, but which now, unfortunately, availed not. However, the disastrous defeat of Braddock inspired the colonists with such alarm that their reviving martial spirit found expression in the organization of companies for defense. Their ardor was stimulated from the pulpit, and several of such stirring appeals from the eloquent Samuel Davies, " the father of the Presbyterian Church in Virginia," are incorporated in his published sermons. The Assembly voted £40,000 for the service, and the Virginia regiment was enlarged to sixteen companies, and the command given to Washington. He had scarcely completed a tour of inspection of the mountain outposts before he was called to arrest the horrors of a savage invasion of the frontiers of Augusta County. The terror inspired by the atrocities committed, influenced the Assembly, in 1756, to direct the building of a line of forts from the Potomac River through the Alleghany Mountains to the borders of North Carolina. The construction of these, with the constantly demanded service of the Virginia troops in the protection of the frontiers from the Indians, debarred them for a time from participation in the campaigns in the North against the French, and the futile expedition under Major Andrew Lewis against the Indian towns on the west of the Ohio, known as the Sandy Creek expedition, was the most pretentious offensive operation of the Colony during the year. Among the officers in this expedition were Captains Peter Hog, William Preston, John Smith, Archibald Alexander, Obadiah Woodson, James Overton, and David Stewart, Commissary. It was accompanied by a party of friendly Cherokees under Captain Richard Pearis.

The Earl of Loudon arrived in America in July, with the appointment of Governor of Virginia, and a commission as Commander-in-chief of the British forces in America, but he was never in the Colony, and Dinwiddie continued in the control of its affairs. He appears to have so met the varied and onerous duties of his trust as to have commanded repeatedly the thankful commendation of the colonial clergy and Assembly, and of the English Ministry.

The year 1757 was as uneventful in Virginia as its predecessor had been, and at its close, Governor Dinwiddie, worn out with fatigue, was at his own request relieved from his arduous station. He sailed for England in January, 1758, after receiving voted testimonials of the regard of the Council and of the municipal authorities of Williamsburg, the seat of government. By the Council, also, he was charged with the delivery to the great Pitt, then at the head of the English Ministry, of an address of thanks for his generous course towards the colonies, and with the negotiation of some important interests of Virginia.

The administration of Governor Dinwiddie had been a peculiarly trying one. His disputes with the Assembly, and his difficulties with Washington, have, through the prejudicial representations of some writers, left an unpleasant impression on the American mind, which has been allowed to veil virtues which would otherwise have commanded undivided esteem and regard. An attempt has been made to stigmatize his memory with the crime of dishonesty in the charge of misappropriation to his own use of funds intrusted to him for the public service—a calumny which rests alone upon the unsupported allegations of his enemies. In all public expenditures he appears to have acted in conjunction with, and by authority of, a committee appointed by the colonial Council, and his reports of the disposition of the funds received from England were systematically regular. It should not be forgotten that the government of Virginia was bestowed on him as the meed of singular integrity and vigilance in previous stations; that he was the warm friend of religion, and, withal, entirely tolerant of all mere differences of creed ; that he sought the enforcement of morality, and was the patron of knowledge and of education. The library of the ancient seat of learning, William and Mary College, until its destruction by fire, during our late internecine war, preserved many tokens of his generosity, each marked with his armorial book-plate. Another memorial still exists in Virginia—the silver mace presented by him to the corporation of Norfolk in 1754, an engraving of which is presented in this work. The faithful services of Governor Dinwiddie appear to have been duly recognized in Great Britain ; and Chalmers, the authoritative colonial annalist, warmly and repeatedly commends his " vigilant " and " able " administration in Virginia. James Abercromby, the agent of the Colony in Virginia, whose letter-books are in the possession of the present writer, in a letter dated London, March 6, 1758, to Richard Corbin, Receiver-General of the Colony, a member of the Council, and the friend and patron of Washington, says, " Your good opinion of your late Governor is fully confirmed by the kind reception he has met with from the Ministry." He makes use of similar expressions also to John Blair, President of the Council, and who was the Acting Governor of the Colony until the arrival, on the 7th of June, 1758, of Governor Fauquier.

Abercromby also makes frequent later acknowledgments of essential aid received by him from Governor Dinwiddie, in his solicitations of the English Ministry in behalf of the Colony. These services, and many others for his personal friends in Virginia, were continuously rendered by the amiable and benevolent old man when his infirmities had become such that all physical exertions were painful. He died at Clifton, Bristol, whither he had gone for the benefit of the baths, July 27, 1770, and was interred in the parish church there with much " pomp and circumstance." The curious bill of his funeral expenses is given in the *Dinwiddie Papers*, Vol. I., published by the Virginia Historical Society. The honorable and stainless record of Governor Dinwiddie was publicly attested.

John Dinwiddie, a brother of the Governor, a merchant on the Rappahannock River, married a granddaughter of George Mason, and a sister, Mary, the Rev. Andrew Stuart, of Pennsylvania. Their descendants in the honored names of Fowke, Phillips, Johnston, Ficklen, Mason, Peyton, Stuart and others, are quite numerous in the United States. To the campaign of 1758, under Forbes, Virginia contributed 2,000 men, in two regiments, with Washington in chief command as Colonel of the first, and Wm. Byrd (the third of the name in lineal succession in Virginia) of the second. These troops nobly sustained the reputation which they had valorously earned in the ill-fated expedition of Braddock, and it was largely due to their bravery, admits Chalmers, that the French were driven from Fort Duquesne, which was taken possession of November 25th, repaired, and re-named Fort Pitt, in compliment to the Prime Minister.

In a preliminary engagement with the French of a reconnoitering party under Major Grant, a detachment of one hundred and sixty-two Virginians, in command of Major Andrew Lewis, gallantly participated. Of their number, sixty-two were killed and two wounded; and of the eight officers present, five were slain, a sixth wounded and the seventh captured. Captain Thomas Bullitt, the remaining officer (Major Grant, the commanding officer, having fallen into the hands of the enemy), with fifty Virginians, defended the baggage with great valor, and was instrumental in saving the remnant of the force. The war was prosecuted at the North with vigor, and in the succeeding summer of 1759, Niagara and Crown Point fell into the possession of the British crown, and on the 18th of September, Quebec surrendered to the gallant Wolfe. The treaty of Fontainebleau, in November, 1762, put an end to the war (which it is estimated had cost the British empire the loss of the lives of more than twenty thousand adults), and the English were supreme in North America.

THE EARL OF LOUDON.

John Campbell, son of Hugh, Earl of Loudon, was born in 1705, and succeeded his father in the title in November, 1731. In July, 1756, he arrived in New York with the appointment of Governor-in-chief of Virginia, and also with the commission of Commander-in-chief of the British forces in America, but, proving inefficient, returned to England in 1757. He was made Lieutenant-General in 1758, and General in 1770. He died April 27, 1782. He was succeeded by Norborne Berkeley, Baron de Botetourt, as Governor of Virginia, in 1768.

JOHN BLAIR.

John Blair, the son of Dr. Archibald Blair, and a nephew of Rev. James Blair, D.D., President of William and Mary College, was born at Williamsburg, Va., in 1689. He was a member of the House of Burgesses from James City County as early as 1736, and a little later became a member of the Council, of which as President he was Acting Governor of Virginia from the departure of Lieutenant-Governor Robert Dinwiddie for England, in January, 1758, until the arrival on June 7th following of Lieutenant-Governor Francis Fauquier, and again from the death of the latter, March 3, 1768, until October following, when he was relieved by Lord Botetourt. During the trying period of the incumbency of President Blair, his ability, vigilance and discretion were signally displayed in protecting the frontier of the colony from Indian invasion. He served for some years from 1752 as Deputy Auditor of the Colony, and from 1758 to 1761, was a visitor of William and Mary College. From a MS. diary kept by him and now in the collections of the Virginia Historical Society, it is manifest that his life was one of manifold usefulness. An extract regarding the rebuilding of the Capitol at Williamsburg, which was built in 1699, and destroyed by fire in 1746, is of interest. President Blair records, December 12, 1752: "This afternoon I laid the last top brick on the capitol wall, and so it is now ready to receive the roof; and some of the wall plates were raised and laid on this day. I had laid a foundation brick at the first building of the capitol about fifty years ago, and another foundation brick in April last." President Blair died November 5, 1771. His sister Harrison was the third wife of Dr. George Gilmer of Williamsburg, a skilled physician and the ancestor of the distinguished Gilmer family of Virginia. One son of President Blair, Archibald Blair, was the Secretary of the Patriot Convention of 1776, and another, John Blair, was nationally distinguished. The last, born in 1732, after graduating from William and Mary College, studied law at the Temple, London, being here a protege of Governor Dinwiddie. Returning to Williamsburg, he rose to the first rank as a lawyer and enjoyed a lucrative practice, and was prominent in public affairs. He was a member of the House of Burgesses as early as 1765, and on the dissolution of that body in 1769, he, with Washington and other patriots, met at the Raleigh tavern, Williamsburg, and drafted the non-importation agreement. He was one of the committee which in June, 1776, drew up the plan for the government of the State; was a member of the Council in 1779, was made chief justice of the general court, and upon the death of Robert Carter Nicholas in 1780, he was appointed a judge of the high Court of Chancery; and by virtue of both stations, was a judge of the first Court of Appeals of the State.

Two Views of Drinking Cup made from the bowl of the Silver Mace of the Speaker of the House of Burgesses of Virginia, before the Revolution.
(Original in the Cabinet of the Virginia Historical Society.)

Upon the formation of the Grand Lodge of Ancient Free and Accepted Masons of Virginia, Judge Blair was elected, October 13, 1778, the first Grand Master of the State. In 1787, he was a member of the convention which framed the Federal Constitution, and in 1788, was a member of that which ratified it. In 1789, he was appointed by Washington a Judge of the Supreme Court of the United States, but resigned the office in 1796. He died at Williamsburg, August 31, 1800.

FRANCIS FAUQUIER.

Francis Fauquier, born in 1703, was appointed Lieutenant-Governor of Virginia to succeed Dinwiddie, February 10, 1758, and arrived in the Colony on June 7th following. He was generous and elegant in his manners and an accomplished scholar, but brought with him the frivolous tastes and dissipated habits of a man of fashion; he was addicted to gaming and by his example diffused in the Colony a passion for gaming. Notwithstanding these charged frailties, he was, in the opinion of Mr. Jefferson, the ablest of the Governors of Virgnia. It is noteworthy that the odious and portentous stamp act was attempted to be enforced during his administration, a measure which had the happy effect of encouraging domestic manufactures in Virginia and of inducing an abstinence from luxuries. Governor Fauquier died March 3, 1768, and until the arrival of Botetourt in October following, the government devolved on John Blair, President of the Council. Fauquier was the author of a pamphlet: "Raising Money for the Support of the War," 8vo, published at London in 1757. Fauquier County, Va., was named in his honor.

SIR JEFFREY AMHERST.

Sir Jeffrey Amherst was born in Kent, England, January 29, 1717. He was page to the Duke of Dorset while Lord Lieutenant of Ireland; became an ensign in the army in 1731; was aide to Lord Ligonier at Dottingen, Fontenoy, and Roncoux, and afterwards to the Duke of Cumberland at Laffaldt. He was made Major General in 1756, and in 1758 was given the command of an expedition against Louisburg. Landing there June 8th, a lodgment was effected July 26, and the place surrendered, as did also St. Johns and other French strongholds. He was appointed Commander-in-chief of the British army in America, September 30, 1758, and the surrender of Quebec to Wolfe's forces, and that of Fort Niagara to Townsend and Johnson, was followed by that of Crown Point, July 26th, and that of Ticonderoga, August 4, 1759, to Amherst in person. Obtaining the naval supremacy on Lake Champlain, Fort Nevis and Isle Aux Noix fell into his hands; and Septem-

VIRGINIA AND VIRGINIANS. 55

ber 8, 1760, Montreal and the whole of Canada became a British possession. Amherst was rewarded with the thanks of Parliament, with the insignia of the Order of a Knight of Bath, and was made Governor-in-chief of Virginia in 1763. When in 1768 it was desired by the Ministry that he should reside in the Colony, he resigned, and was succeeded in July by Lord Botetourt. General Amherst was appointed Governor of Guernsey in 1771; created a baron in 1776; was commander of the British army from 1778 to 1795, and was made a Field Marshal in July, 1796. He died August 3, 1797. His brother, William Amherst, was Lieutenant-General and Colonel of the 32d Foot and Governor of St. Johns, New Foundland. He was aide-de-camp to Sir Jeffrey Amherst in America, and was at the capture of Louisburg. He died May 13, 1781. Amherst County, Va., was named in honor of Sir Jeffrey Amherst.

LORD BOTETOURT.

Norborne Berkeley, Baron de Botetourt, son of John Symes Berkeley, was born in 1718. He was Colonel of the North Gloucestershire Militia in 1761; represented that shire in Parliament; and in 1764 was raised to the peerage. He was the second of Lord Talbott in a duel with John Wilkes in 1762, and was Constable of the Tower of London in 1767. The accession of Lord Botetourt to the vice-royal government of Virginia, occurred at a period rife with discontent among the American Colonies, and pregnant with swiftly approaching and momentous events. The brilliant Horace Walpole, writing to Sir Horace Mann, August 14, 1768, after alluding to the disquiet in America, says: " Virginia, though not the most mutinous, contains the best heads and the principal *boutes-feux*. It was thought necessary that the Governor should reside there. It was known that Sir Jeffrey Amherst would not like that; he must besides have superseded Gage. At the same time, Lord Botetourt, a court favorite, yet ruined in fortune, was thought of by Lord Hillsborough."

To this bit of cabinet history, the relentless Junius personally adds of Botetourt, " Having ruined himself by gambling, he became a cringing, bowing, fawning, sword-bearing courtier." It would appear from the subsequent career of this best beloved of our colonial viceroys that the character so pitilessly drawn by the stern censor was hardly merited. He received the appointment of Governor (succeeding Sir Jeffrey Amherst) in July, 1768, though he did not arrive in the Colony until sometime in October following. A contemporary presents a foil to the venomously drawn picture of Junius. Edmund Randolph, in a MS. history of Virginia, in the collections of the Virginia Historical Society, says of Lord Botetourt: " If from birth and education he had not been a courtier, his dependence on the Crown for the revival of an extinguished title, must have generated habits to conciliate and please. He came hither, not only with the grace of polished life, but also with the predilections of the people, who were proud in being no longer governed by a deputy. His predecessors, Fauquier, Dinwiddie, Gooch, Spotswood, Nicholson and Drysdale, had been the vehicles of sinecures to some principals who never cast an eye or thought on Virginia. Through Botetourt, the Colony was assured by the King, that as a mark of honor to it, the residence of the chief Governor there should never be dispensed with in the future. Always accessible on business, adhering without a single deviation to the resolution of sleeping every night in the metropolis, affable to the humblest visitor in social circles, easy himself, and contributing to the ease of others, he was sincerely and universally beloved. In his public functions, his purity and punctuality confirmed the attachment which his qualities as a gentleman had begun. By his patronage, he inspired the youth of William and Mary with ardour and emulation, and by his daily example in the observance of religion, he acquired a kind of sacred ascendancy over the public mind."

Solicitous to serve the Virginians, Botetourt pledged his life and fortune to extend the boundary of the Colony on the west to the Tennessee River, on the parallel of $36\frac{1}{2}$ degrees. On the 11th of May, 1769, when the Assembly was convened, the Governor, attended by a numerous retinue of guards, rode from the palace to the capitol in a luxurious state-coach drawn by six milk-white horses—a present from George III.—and the insignia of royalty was displayed with unusual pomp. On that day and the one following, he entertained fifty-two guests at dinner. The Assembly, however, on the 16th instant following, venturing upon the assertion of certain colonial prerogatives by the passage of resolutions against parliamentary taxation, and the sending of accused persons to England for trial, was dissolved by him. But this exercise of arbitrary power was speedily condoned by an action of cordial conciliation. Botetourt, having received from the Earl of Hillsborough, Secretary of State for the Colonies, assurance that it was not the intention of the Ministry to propose any further taxes, and that they intended to advocate a repeal of those already complained of, called the Assembly together, and communicated these assurances, pledging himself to every exertion in his power towards the redressing of the grievances of the colonists, and the promotion of every measure tending to their advancement and prosperity, which led to an interchange of cordial greeting between the colonial legislative bodies and the Governor, and the inauguration of that warm sentiment of esteem and affection already so graphically portrayed. But the generous-minded Botetourt, soon finding that the promises held out to him by the Ministry were utterly faithless, and indignant at the deception practiced upon him, demanded his recall. Shortly after this, on October 15, 1770, he fell a victim to an attack of bilious fever. He appears to have met death with the calm fortitude of the philosopher and the confiding trust of the Christian. The pure-minded and deeply pious Robert Carter Nicholas, the Treasurer of the Colony, with whom he was on terms of the strictest friendship, having during one of his visits to the Governor observed that he thought that the latter would be very unwilling to die, "because," as he said, " you are so social in your nature, and so much beloved, and you have so many good things about you, that you must be loth to leave them," his lordship made at the time no reply; but a short time after, being on his death-bed, he sent in haste for Colonel Nicholas, who lived near the palace, and who instantly repaired thither to receive the last sight of his dying friend. On entering his chamber he asked his commands. "Nothing," replied his lordship, " but to let you see that I resign these good things which you formerly spoke of with as much composure as I enjoyed them;" after which he grasped his hand with warmth, and instantly expired. His death was deeply lamented by the colony, and the funeral ceremonies incident upon his burial were conducted with great state, the ostentation exhibited being unprecedented in the country. A verification of the display, being copies of bills presented against his estate (inclusive of those for the funeral expenditures) lies before the writer.

The originals, lately in his possession, have been returned to their owner, Miss Sarah Nicholas Randolph, of "Edgehill," Abermarle County, Va., the great grand-daughter of Thomas Jefferson. The expenses aggregate about £700 sterling, and the items are stated with great minuteness. The remains appear to have been enclosed in three several coffins—one of lead, furnished by one Joseph Kidd; an "inside coffin," and one of black walnut, by one Joshua Kendall. The "inside coffin" was laid with "Persian fully ornamented," and the "outside coffin," covered with "crimson velvet," ornamented in the best manner. There were "eight silver handles and sixteen escutcheons for his lordship's coffin," and "one large silver plate engraved, a lute-string shroud, mattress, pillow and cap." The church was hung with black cloth, and it and the hearse were ornamented with "escutcheons." "Sixteen books of silver leaf," and "one dozen books of Dutch metal," also appear as charges. Staffs were borne by, and cloaks furnished the mourners. There were "streamers for the horses," and an extensive list of articles for the costuming of the numerous attendants upon the obsequies.

The interment did not take place until the 20th of October, if it was not later, as numerous items of the incidental expense were entered on that date. The body was deposited in one of the vaults beneath the chapel of William and Mary College, and a beautiful marble statue of Botetourt was erected at the expense of the Colony in 1774 in front of the old capitol. It now stands, much mutilated, in front of William and Mary College, whither it was removed in 1797.

The pedestal is inscribed with a glowing tribute to the merits and virtue of the beloved viceroy. In the parish church of Stoke Gifford, Gloucestershire, England, a long monumental inscription also commemorates his worth. Lord Botetourt gave to the College of William and Mary a sum of money, the interest of which was sufficient to purchase annually two gold medals—one to be given to the best classical scholar, and the other to the best scholar in philosophy. This medal was annually awarded until the Revolution. In *Howe's Historical Collections of Virginia*, an account is given of the joyous and impressive reception of Lord Botetourt by the colonists, together with an ode, recited and sung with an accompaniment of music on the occasion.

On the evening of the 22d of February, 1876, there was held at the theater in the city of Richmond, Va., a ball, in commemoration of the the vice-regal court of Williamsburg, as it appeared during the government of Lord Botetourt. The participants, in most instances the lineal descendants of distinguished men and courtly dames who formed the society of the colonial capital, Williamsburg, reproduced the attire of that day in all of its original resplendance and impressive concomitants. Many were the treasured memorials, transmitted heirlooms, jewels, swords, fans, rich brocades and satins, and costly laces—which were drawn forth from careful and jealous keeping for the occasion. The stage of the theater was fitted up for the brilliant tableaux, the body of the building being filled to overflowing with spectators. This memorable occasion was the accomplishment of a number of patriotic ladies who desired to celebrate appropriately the birthday of Washington, and at the same time earn money with which to improve the condition of the Virginia room at Mount Vernon.

The name of Botetourt is commemorated in that of one the counties of Virginia.

The portrait of the Governor given in this work is from a very rare print, of which probably the copy in the collections of the Virginia Historical Society is the only one in America.

WILLIAM NELSON.

The progenitor of the Nelson family in Virginia was Thomas (distinguished in the traditions of the family as "Scotch Tom"), the son of Hugh and Sarah Nelson, of Penrith, Cumberland County, England, who was born February 20, 1677, and emigrated to the Colony in early manhood. He settled as an importing merchant at Yorktown, then the chief seaport of Virginia. Here he died, October 7, 1745. He married twice; first, Margaret Reed, and secondly, Mrs. Francis Tucker *nee* Courteney. He had issue by his first wife, two sons and a daughter, and by the last a daughter. Some notice of each of his sons may here be appropriately given in virtue of their important association with the history of Virginia and because the second has been conflicted in the minds of some with his more eminent nephew of the same name. William Nelson, the eldest son of the emigrant "Scotch Tom," was born in 1711, and died November 19, 1772. He followed in the respected career of his father as a merchant, adding largely by his honest gains to the ample estate which he inherited. It is claimed in evidence of his enterprise that he imported goods to supply the then incipient marts of Baltimore and Philadelphia, as well as for Virginia consumption. He was long a member of the Council of Virginia and often its presiding officer. Hence the designation of President Nelson, by which he was commonly called. On the death of Lord Botetourt, October 15, 1770, President Nelson, in virtue of his office, was invested with the Government of the Colony, which he administered until the arrival of the Earl of Dunmore, early in 1772. He married in February, 1737, Elizabeth, daughter of Nathaniel and Elizabeth (Carter) Burwell, and had issue five sons and one daughter. Three of these sons, one of whom was General Thomas Nelson, Jr., distinguished themselves in the American Revolution. The tombs of both, Thomas Nelson, the emigrant, and of his son President William Nelson, with elaborately wrought marble slabs with the arms of the family, are in the old church-yard at Yorktown. This epitaph of the last is a glowing recitation of public service and personal worth:

[Nelson arms—Per pale, argent, and sable, a chevron between 3 fleur de lis counter-changed. Crest—a fleur de lis.]

Here lies the body of the

HONORABLE WILLIAM NELSON, Esq.,

Late President of His Majesty's Council in this Dominion, in whom the
love of man and the love of God so restrained and enforced each other
and so invigorated the mental powers in general as not only to
defend him from the vices and follies of his country, but also to
render it a matter of difficult decision in what part of laud-
able conduct he most excelled: whether in the tender
and endearing accomplishments of domestic life, or in
the more active duties of a wider circuit, as a
neighbour, a gentleman, or a magistrate, whether in the graces of
hospitality or in the exercises of charity or of piety.
Reader, if you feel the spirit of that excellent ardour, which
aspires to that felicity of conscious virtue, animated
by those consolations and divine admoni-
tions, perform the task and
expect the distinction of
the righteous man.

He died the 19th of November, Anno Domini 1772,
Aged 61.

The second son of "Scotch Tom," the emigrant, Thomas Nelson, Jr., as he subscribed himself, was born in 1716, and died at Yorktown in 1786. He occupied a seat in the Virginia Council for thirty years, during which protracted period he also acted as its Secretary. This was an office of important trust and of emolument, it being charged with the preservation of the records of all public acts, and of the land office. Secretary Nelson, as he was known in virtue of his office, married Lucy, daughter of John and Martha (Burwell) Armstead, by whom he had issue ten children, among whom were three sons who served with distinction in the army of the Revolution.

The noted Nelson House, which attracted so much attention in the Centennial observances at Yorktown in 1881, is a large two-storied brick structure with corners of hewn stone, "built on the old English model," and stands on the main street of Yorktown, fronting the river. The time of its erection, according to the gentle annalist Bishop Meade, may be fixed at 1712, since he narrates that "the corner stone of it was laid by old president Nelson (born 1711), when an infant, as it was designed for him. He was held by his nurse, and the brick in his apron, was passed through his little hand." The good bishop whose ancestors were among the occupants of its spacious halls, thus enthusiastically apostrophizes the old mansion: "It was long the abode of love, friendship, and hospitality.

> Farewell, a prouder mansion I may see,
> But much must meet in that which equals thee!"

As one said of modern Italy, "Our memory sees more than our eyes in this place." What Paulding said of Virginia, may emphatically be said of York:

> "All hail, thou birthplace of the glowing west!
> Thou seem'st like the ruined eagle's nest."

The Nelson mansion descended to the eldest son of President Nelson, the glorious patriot, General Thomas Nelson, Jr., and was his residence until the threatened dangers of the prospective siege of York prompted the removal of his family to "Offley," in Hanover county. The headquarters of Lord Cornwallis during the siege were first in the mansion of Secretary Thomas Nelson, which was destroyed by the fire of the patriot army. The Nelson House, described, and still standing, was also occupied by Cornwallis or portions of his staff subsequent to the destruction of the mansion of Secretary Nelson, and while thus the shelter of the foe, General Nelson loftily exemplified his patriotism. Having command of the first battery which opened upon Yorktown, he

LORD DUNMORE
Last Royal Governor of Virginia.

pointed the first gun against his own dwelling, and offered to the gunner a reward of five guineas for every bombshell that should be fired into it. The marks of their effects are visible to this day.

Among the illustrations of our work is a delineation of the commemorative Yorktown monument proposed to be erected by the nation.

LORD DUNMORE.

John Murray, fourth Earl of Dunmore, the last royal Governor of the Colony of Virginia, was born in 1732. He was descended in the female line from the royal house of Stuart, and succeeded to the peerage in 1756. He was appointed Governor of New York in January, 1770, and of Virginia in July, 1771. He arrived in the Colony early in 1772, and found that he had already incurred suspicion on account of the appointment of Captain Edward Foy as his clerk or private secretary, with a salary of five hundred pounds, which was to be derived from newly created fees to be exacted from the colonists. The Governor, however, relinquished the objectionable fees, and thus conciliated so cordial a feeling that the Assembly expressed their gratitude in terms of warmth and affection. They also endeavored to permanently honor the family titles of Lord Dunmore and of his eldest son George, Lord Fincastle, in creating from Frederick County those of Berkeley and Dunmore, and from Botetourt that of Fincastle, by acts passed in February, 1772. The flood of patriotic resentment, incident upon the struggle for freedom, caused them subsequently, in October, 1776, to obliterate Fincastle County, by dividing it into the counties of Kentucky, Washington, and Montgomery, and to change, in October, 1777, the name of Dunmore to "Shanandoa," now rendered Shenandoah. Captain Peter Hog, a gallant soldier of the French and Indian War, an intimate friend of Washington, was appointed Deputy Attorney-General of Virginia for the county of Dunmore, by Lord Dunmore, April 10, 1772. Captain Hog became distinguished in the practice of law, and his descendants in the name of Hoge, Hogg, Hall, Blair, Blackley, Hawkins, McPherson, and others, are numerous in Virginia and West Virginia, and are held in high social estimation. Fincastle, the county-seat of Botetourt, is said by Howe (*Historical Collections of Virginia*, p. 202) to have been named after the seat of Lord Botetourt in England; but it is probable that it was a revival of the name of the obliterated county.

The Assembly of February, 1772, passed also several important acts for the promotion of internal improvements, in making roads and canals, and clearing the navigation of the Potomac and Matapony rivers. The Assembly was prorogued to the 10th of June. Dunmore, notwithstanding his recent complaisance, evinced his regal proclivities and jealousy of popular assemblies, by proroguing the Virginia Burgesses from time to time, until at last a forgery of the paper currency of the Colony compelled him to call the Assembly together again by proclamation, March 4, 1773. The political horizon of America was again darkening by gathering clouds. A British armed revenue vessel having been burned in Narragansett Bay, an act of Parliament was passed, making such offenses punishable by death, and authorizing the accused to be transported to England for trial. Virginia had already, in 1769, remonstrated against this last measure. Patrick Henry, Jefferson, Richard Henry Lee, Francis Lightfoot Lee, Dabney Carr, and others were at this gloomy and threatening period in the habit of meeting together in the evening in a private room in the old Raleigh Tavern, to hold consultations on the state of affairs. In conformity with an agreement entered into by them, Dabney Carr, the brother-in-law of Jefferson, on the 12th of March, moved a series of resolutions, recommending a committee of correspondence, and instructing them to inquire in regard to the newly constituted court in Rhode Island. Richard Henry Lee and Patrick Henry made speeches of memorable eloquence on this occasion. Mr. Lee was the author of the plan of inter-colonial committees of correspondence; and Virginia was the first Colony to adopt it. The resolutions passed without opposition, and Dunmore immediately dissolved the House of Burgesses. These resolutions "struck a greater panic into the ministers" than any thing that had taken place since the passage of the Stamp Act. The Committee of Correspondence appointed were Peyton Randolph, Robert Carter Nicholas, Richard Bland, Richard Henry Lee, Benjamin Harrison, Edmund Pendleton, Patrick Henry, Dudley Digges, Dabney Carr, Archibald Cary, and Thomas Jefferson. On the day after the dissolution of the Assembly, the Committee addressed a circular to the other American Colonies.

In the Summer, Dunmore visited the frontiers of the Colony, on a tour of observation. He remained some time at Pittsburg, and endeavored, with the aid of Dr. John Connolly, to extend the bounds of Virginia in that quarter. Late in April, 1774, the Countess of Dunmore and her family, George, Lord Fincastle, the Honorables Alexander and John Murray, and the Ladies Catharine, Augusta, and Susan Murray, arrived in Williamsburg, accompanied by Captain Foy and his wife. A younger daughter of Lord Dunmore, born subsequently and during his residence in the Colony, named Virginia, was formally adopted by the Assembly as the daughter of the Dominion, with provision for her life support. After the Revolution she reminded the State Assembly of its spontaneously assumed obligations, and later in life, in the present century, she petitioned the United States Congress in mediation or by its own act to secure to her some provision, being infirm and in indigent circumstances; but her prayers were unheeded. The visit to this country of the present representative of the earldom of Dunmore during the past year is fresh in the memory of the public. The three sons of Lord Dunmore were students in the College of William and Mary in 1774. Captain Foy had served with distinction in the battle of Minden, and, subsequently, as Governor of New Hampshire. The arrival of the family of Lord Dunmore was celebrated with an illumination of the city of Williamsburg, and the people with acclamations welcomed them to Virginia. When the Assembly met in May following, the capital presented a scene of unwonted gayety, and a court-herald published a code of etiquette for the regulation of the society of the vice-regal court. At the beginning of the session, the Burgesses, in an address, congratulated the Governor on the arrival of his Lady, and agreed to give a ball in her honor on the 27th of the month; but the horizon was again suddenly overcast by intelligence of the act of Parliament shutting up the port of Boston. The Assembly made an indignant protest against this act, and set apart the 1st of June, appointed for the closing of the port, as a day of fasting, prayer, and humiliation, in which the divine interposition was to be implored to protect the rights of the Colonies and avert the horrors of civil war, and to unite the people of America in the common cause. On the next day Dunmore dissolved the Assembly. The Burgesses repaired immediately to the Raleigh Tavern, and in the room called "the Apollo" adopted resolutions against the use of tea and other East India commodities, and recommended an annual congress of representatives of the Colonies. Notwithstanding the ominous aspect of affairs, Washington dined with the Governor on the 25th of May, and attended the ball, which was given, as proposed, to Lady Dunmore on the 27th. The Burgesses, remaining in Williamsburg, on the 29th of the month held a meeting, at which Peyton Randolph presided, and they issued a circular, recommending a meeting of deputies to assemble in convention there on the first of August following. In April, 1774, the Indians renewed their hostilities upon the frontiers of Virginia. In September, Dunmore, with two regiments under Colonels William Fleming and Charles Lewis, marched to the relief of the inhabitants. General Andrew Lewis later marched with eleven hundred men. Dunmore concluded a peace with the Delawares in October; but a band of Delawares, Mingoes, Cayugas, Iowas, Wyandots, and Shawnees, under the Chief Cornstalk, had determined to surprise the camp of Lewis with an attack. An engagement, known as the battle of Point Pleasant, took place on the 10th of October, in which the Virginians lost between forty and seventy-five in killed and one hundred and forty wounded. The loss of the savages was unascertained. Dunmore, later, concluded a treaty with the several Indian tribes. Logan, the Cayuga chief, assented to the treaty, but, still indignant at the murder of his wife in the preceding spring, refused to attend the camp. In the charge by Jefferson, in his *Notes on Virginia*, that this tragic event was instigated or committed by Captain Michael Cresap, when it was known to him that one Greathouse was the author of the bloody deed, he most unworthily maligned the memory of a brave soldier, a useful pioneer, and an honorable man. In the beginning of 1775, the people of Virginia were still in a state of anxious suspense, expecting civil war. The second convention assembled at Richmond on the 20th of March. Here, in the venerable St. John's Church, Patrick Henry sounded the tocsin of liberty. Militia, called minute men, were established. On the 20th of April, Lord Dunmore caused the removal of the powder from the magazine at Williamsburg to an English ship. This proceeding produced great excitement, the people took arms under Patrick Henry, and Dunmore was forced to compromise the affair by paying for the powder. June 6th, he fled with his family, and took refuge on board the "Fowey" man-of-war. Rallying a band of tories, runaway negroes, and British soldiers, he collected a naval force, and carried on a petty warfare, plundering the inhabitants along the James and York rivers, and carrying off their slaves. December 9th, 1775, his followers suffered a severe defeat at the battle of Great Bridge, near Norfolk; and on the following night Dunmore took refuge on board his fleet. January 1st, 1776, he set on fire and destroyed Norfolk, then the most flourishing and populous town in Virginia. Continuing his predatory warfare, he established himself early in June on Gwynn Island, in the Chesapeake Bay, whence he was dislodged by the Virginians, July 8th, being wounded in the leg by a splinter. He shortly afterward returned to England, and in 1786 was appointed Governor of Bermuda. He died at Ramsgate, England, in May, 1809. He was a man of culture, and possessed a large and valuable library, volumes from which frequently appear in auction sales of books. The armorial book-plate from one of these is reproduced in the illustrations in this work. His portrait, which we also present, is from the portrait in oil in the State library at Richmond, and has never before been engraved. It may be trite to notice also, in connection with the last royal Governor of Virginia, the chair of the Speaker of the Colonial House of Burgesses, now also preserved in the State library at Richmond, and of which we present a faithful semblance from a photograph specially made for us. It has never before been pictured. According to a statement by Edmund Randolph in a MS. and unpublished History of Virginia, in the collections of the Virginia Historical Society, the Speaker's chair was originally richly decorated with various insignia of royalty, of which it was denuded in the beginning of our struggle for independence by the hasty hands of fervent patriots, to whom all tokens of royalty were obnoxious.

PATRICK HENRY.

In vigor of intellect, in its varied exemplifications, in true manhood, and in illustrious and material service in church, state and the army, in the one sex, and in the typical exhibition of the sweet graces and exalted virtues characteristic of Virginia and the Southern States, in the other and gentler, no citizen of the Old Dominion, within its annals or traditions, has been more honored in his descendants, including the present generation, than John Henry, a native of Aberdeen, Scotland, and son of John Henry and his wife Jane, the sister of William Robertson, D.D., the divine, scholar and historian. He was a cousin of David Henry, the publisher of the *Gentleman's Magazine*, and through Dr. Robertson, the cousin of the distinguished Lord Brougham. The late British Premier, William Ewart Gladstone, is also of the same lineage. John Henry settled in Virginia some time prior to 1730. He enjoyed the friendship and patronage of Governor Robert Dinwiddie, who introduced him to the acquaintance of Colonel John Syme, of Hanover county, who dying, his widow, *née* Winston, John Henry in time married. John Henry was a most useful citizen of Hanover county, serving as Colonel of militia, surveyor, and presiding magistrate for many years. He had been liberally educated, was well grounded in the classics, and, withal, was endowed with an excellent judgment and a vigorous mind. He executed a map of Virginia, which was published in London, in 1770. A copy of it was in the possession of Joseph Horner, Esq., Warrenton, Virginia, a few years since. Charles Campbell (*History of Virginia*, p. 521), says that "appended to it is an epitome of the state and condition of Virginia. The marginal illustration is profuse and, like the map, well executed." Soon after the settlement of Colonel John Henry in Virginia, Patrick, a minister of the Church of England followed him, and in April, 1733, by his brother's interest, became rector of St. George's parish in the county of Spotsylvania. He was subsequently rector of St. Paul's parish, in Hanover county. The wife of Colonel John Henry, says Wirt, "possessed in an eminent degree, the mild and benevolent disposition, the undeviating probity, the correct understanding and easy elocution," for which the ancient family of Winston is distinguished. Her brother, William Winston, an officer in the French and Indian war, is said to have been noted for his oratorical powers. The grave of Colonel Henry, and presumably that of his wife, is at "Studley," their latest residence in Hanover county. Patrick, the second son and the youngest of the family of nine children, of Colonel John and Sarah (Winston-Syme) Henry, was born at "Studley," May 29, 1736. Under the tuition of his father he received the basis of a sound English education, with a knowledge of mathematics, and of the Greek and Latin, a well-thumbed copy of the Testament, in the former language, which was through life a prized possession, being still preserved by a descendant. The pecuniary circumstances of Colonel Henry impelled him to qualify his sons at an early age to support themselves. With this view, Patrick was placed, at the age of fifteen, with a country merchant. In the year following, his father was encouraged by his apparent qualifications to purchase for his two sons, William and Patrick, a small adventure of goods, to "set them up in trade." The chief management of this mercantile venture devolved upon Patrick, whose levity of disposition, and proclivities for the chase and for social gatherings, illy comported with his responsibilities. The result was a very natural one; one year put an end to the business of the store, but Patrick was engaged for two or three years following, in winding up the disastrous experiment. Notwithstanding his misfortunes, at the early age of eighteen he married Sarah Shelton, the daughter, it has been said, of the keeper of a house of entertainment at the county seat of Hanover. By the joint assistance of their parents the young couple were settled on a small farm, and Mr. Henry, with the assistance of one or two slaves, again essayed the struggle for a livelihood, but his want of agricultural skill and his aversion to systematic labor, drove him, necessarily, after a trial of two years, to abandon this pursuit. Selling out for cash, at a sacrifice, his little possessions, he resumed his inauspicious mercantile pursuits, which he continued until some time in the year 1759, as evidenced by the memorial illustration in this work—reduced fac-similes from the originals, of an account in his autograph, and of a quaint pair of iron-framed spectacles, said to have been possessed and worn by him in advanced life. The second mercantile venture was more unfortunate than the first, involving him in absolute bankruptcy. His situation was indeed lamentable; penniless, with an increasing family, and with the resources of his friends exhausted, nevertheless he was sustained by innate fortitude and buoyancy of heart. Jefferson, who first made the acquaintance of Mr. Henry after his disasters in the winter of 1759-60, states that they were "not to be traced either in his countenance or conduct," and that his passion was "music, dancing and pleasantry." Mr. Henry now determined on the study of law, "and at last found the path for which he was designed, and into which he had been driven by the severe but kindly discipline of Providence." Within the alleged, but absurdly inadequate time of six weeks only in preparation, he obtained a license to practice at the age of twenty-four. According to Wirt, Mr. Henry was but little employed in his profession for several years; his family was chiefly maintained during this period by his father-in-law, Mr. Shelton, who kept a tavern at Hanover Court House, Mr. Henry lending his assistance in the entertainment of the guests, and that his talent remained unknown until it blazed forth like a meteor, as the advocate of the people in the famous "Parson's Cause," tried at the November term, 1763, of Hanover Court. The opposing counsel was Peter Lyons, subsequently of the Supreme Court of Appeals, of the State.

The story is a winning one, but Mr. Wirt was mistaken as to the facts. Patrick Henry came to the bar in the latter part of 1760. His fee books, now in the possession of his family, show that his practice was extensive from the beginning. They disclose, according to a recent publication by his grandson, William Wirt Henry, that "from the September of 1760, when he came to the bar, to the 31st of December, 1763," Patrick Henry charged fees in 1,185 suits, besides many fees for preparing papers out of court, indicating that his success was remarkable and his talents appreciated. In 1764 Mr. Henry removed his family to the county of Louisa, residing at a place called "Roundabout." In the fall of that year he had the opportunity of a new theater for his genius, as the advocate before the House of Burgesses, at Williamsburg, of Nathaniel West Dandridge, who contested the seat in that body, on the charge of bribery and corruption, of James Littlepage, who had been returned from Hanover County. Here Mr. Henry "distinguished himself by a copious and brilliant display on the great subject of the rights of suffrage, superior to any thing that had been heard before within those walls." The same year, 1764, is memorable as that of the passage of the Stamp Act, and for the origination of the great question which finally led to American Independence, to which, says Jefferson, " Mr. Henry gave the first impulse." On the 1st of May, 1765, Mr. Henry entered the House of Burgesses as the representative from Louisa County. His first address to the House was upon the proposition for a public Loan Office, devised by John Robinson, the Speaker, to allow the public money to be loaned out to individuals, on security. It was a scheme to hide certain misappropriations, which Robinson, as Treasurer, had made and wished to conceal. Henry opposed it with such vigor and eloquence that it was lost on the first vote. On the 20th he was added to the committee for courts of justice. A few days afterward his celebrated resolutions on the Stamp Act were offered. The original, hastily written upon the fly-leaf of an old law book, is now in the possession of Mr. William Wirt Henry. In the stormy debate which ensued, Patrick Henry vehemently exclaimed : " Cæsar had his Brutus; Charles the First, his Cromwell, and George the Third"—"Treason!" cried the Speaker; the cry was echoed from every part of the House—" may profit by their example!* If this be treason, make the most of it." The resolutions were carried, the last by a majority of one only.

---

* In a MS. History of Virginia, by Edmund Randolph, who was present on this memorable occasion, he renders the final clause of this memorable menace so as to greatly diminish its strength, reporting instead, "may he never have either."

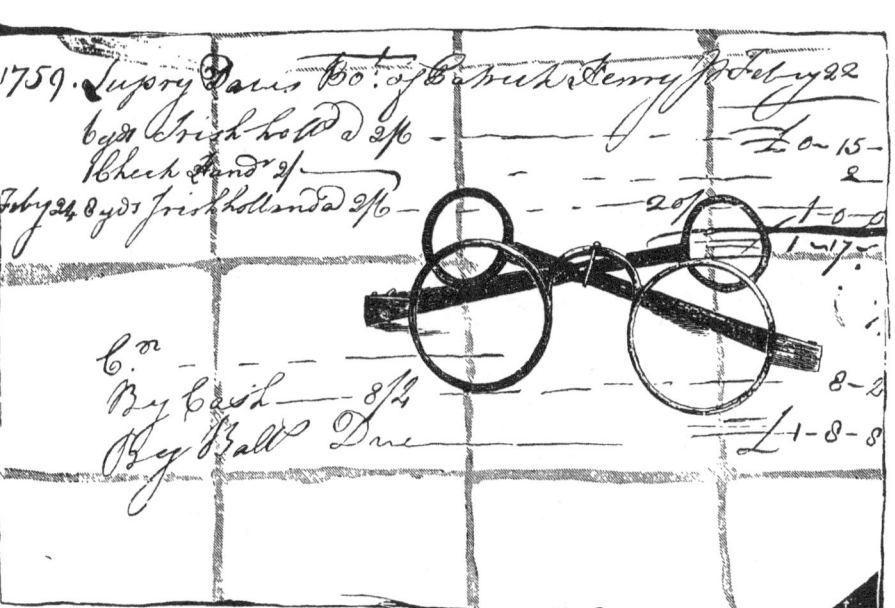

AUTOGRAPH BILL OF PATRICK HENRY, WHILE A SHOPKEEPER,
With massive iron spectacles worn by him, from the original in the possession of R. A. Brock, Secretary of the Virginia Historical Society.

Henry left the capital that morning for his home, and the next day, the defeated leaders, taking advantage of his absence, succeeded in having expunged, the fifth, last and most obnoxious of the resolutions, which claimed "that the Assembly had the sole right to levy taxes, and that the vesting such power in any other person whatsoever, had a manifest tendency to destroy British as well as American freedom." In 1769 Mr. Henry was admitted to the bar of the General Court, where he came into competition with the most eminent characters in the colony, some of whom had been educated at the Temple, London, and the names of a majority of them are historical. Here his wonderful powers of oratory were pre-eminent. His reputation was such that in January, 1773, Robert Carter Nicholas, who had enjoyed the first practice at the bar, being forced to relinquish it by accepting the office of Treasurer of the Colony, committed to him by public advertisement, his unfinished business. Mr. Henry removed from Louisa to his native county, Hanover, in 1767, but was continued a member of the House of Burgesses. The exactions and odious inflictions of Great Britain continued, and the storm of Revolution was gathering strength. Every act of resistance on the part of the Colonial Assemblies, was met by the royal Governors by a prompt dissolution. Thus matters progressed for several years; when, in 1774, the Virginia House of Burgesses, having been suddenly dissolved by Lord Dunmore, for their spirited resentment of the Boston Port Bill, the members met at the Raleigh Tavern, and recommended the first call of a Congress of all the friends of liberty. By the Convention at Williamsburg, shortly afterward, Mr. Henry was elected a delegate to the Continental Congress which met at Philadelphia, September 4, 1774. He was the first to address this body, in an address of such surpassing eloquence, that great as was his reputation, he seemed to exalt himself to the magnitude of the occasion. His extraordinary powers astonished all listeners, and he took rank as the greatest orator of America. In the Virginia Convention, which on the 20th of March, 1775, reassembled at Richmond, in the venerable St. John's Church (of the exterior and interior of which, before alteration, accurate representations from photographs are given in this work), to take further steps in the cause of liberty. Mr. Henry, on the 23d, moved the organization of militia and that the "Colony be immediately put in a state of defense." The bold proposal roused the resistance of many of the firmest friends of the colonial cause, and the debate was fierce in the extreme. But the genius of Henry rose to the full demands of the occasion, and as the last thrilling exclamation, "give me liberty, or give me death!" fell on the ear of the House, all were infused with the spirit of the orator; the bill passed, and the colony was at once placed in an attitude of defense. Lord Dunmore, on the 20th of April following, having clandestinely removed all the powder from the public magazine at Williamsburg, to a sloop of war lying in York river, Henry placed himself at the head of the company of Captain Samuel Meredith (who resigned in his favor), of Hanover county, marched upon Williamsburg and forced the Governor to give him an order on the Receiver-General of the Colony, for the value of the powder. In June, Henry was appointed to the Colonelcy of the First Virginia regiment, and the command-in-chief of all the forces of the Colony. Colonel Henry at once went into camp at Williamsburg and ardently began the recruitment and disciplining of the troops. But the act of the Virginia Committee of Safety, in intrusting to Woodford, the second colonel in rank, the duty of arresting the ravages of the motley band of Dunmore, drove Henry, who had solicited the enterprise, from the military service back into the councils of state. Mortified by this disregard of his prerogative of rank, and being wounded further by the promotion over him, in the Continental line, to the rank of Brigadier-General, of two Colonels, to whose appointments his own was prior, he resigned his commission. The action of the convention excited universal condemnation, and nearly produced a mutiny in the army.

Ninety officers united in an address to Henry, regretting his loss to the service and applauding his spirited resentment. With exalted unselfishness, Henry exerted himself to quiet the discontent of his soldiers, and having accomplished this, retired to his home.

Immediately upon the resignation of his commission as Colonel, he was elected a delegate to the Convention from the county of Hanover. The session of that body which was approaching, was pregnant with importance. Dunmore had abdicated the government, and the royal authority in the Colony was seen and felt no longer except in acts of hostility. The Convention met at Williamsburg on the 6th of May, 1776. On the 29th of June, a plan of government having been adopted, Patrick Henry was elected Governor of Virginia under its new constitution for a term of twelve months, at a salary of one thousand pounds per annum, Virginia currency, equivalent in value to $3,333.33⅓ in our present currency. His competitors for the office were Thomas Nelson and John Page, the latter of whom was subsequently Governor of Virginia. Shortly after the election of Mr. Henry as Governor, Lord Dunmore was driven from Gwinns Island and from the State, to return to it no more. The autumn of the year 1776 was one of the darkest and most dispiriting periods of the Revolution, and of which Thomas Paine, in his *Crisis*, used the memorable expression, "These are the times that try the souls of men." For a time the courage of the country fell. Washington alone was undaunted. Even the heroism of the Virginia Legislature gave way, and in a season of despair, the mad project of a dictator was seriously meditated. Mr. Henry is said to have been thought of for this office, but there is no evidence that the project was ever countenanced by him, and his firm and unselfish patriotism, so abundantly evidenced, irrefragably refutes bare suspicion even. That the Virginia Assembly entertained no doubt of him is manifest in the fact that he was unanimously re-elected Governor for another annual term on the 30th of May, 1777.

The "Father of his Country," even, did not escape the insidious attacks of those who were basely envious of him. One of these anonymous letters was received by Mr. Henry in January, 1778, filled with the grossest imputations of the incapacity and dishonesty of Washington, and suggesting Gates, Lee, or Conway as Commander-in-chief instead. Mr. Henry at once inclosed the letter to his loved and revered friend. Mr. Henry having completed a third term as Governor, retired from the office, being inelegible to re-election under the constitution. His administration had been able, vigilant and effective. The wife of Mr. Henry died in 1775. He soon after sold the farm in Hanover, called "Scotch Town," on which he had resided, and purchased about ten thousand acres of land in Henry County, formed in 1776 from Pittsylvania county and named in his honor, as was subsequently the neighboring county of Patrick carved from Henry county in 1791. In 1777 he married, secondly, Dorothea Dandridge, granddaughter of Governor Alexander Spotswood, and daughter of Nathaniel West Dandridge, a descendant of Captain John West, the brother of Lord Delaware—both early Governors of Virginia. Soon after the expiration of the governmental office of Mr. Henry, he removed with his family to his newly acquired estate in Henry county, called "Leatherwood," and resumed the practice of law. In 1780, he was again in the State Assembly and one of the most active members in the House. He continuously served in this body until November, 1784. Mr. Henry gave an endearing exhibition of his generous sensibility, in the winter session of 1780, in the resolution which he moved expressing sympathy with General Gates in his unfortunate defeat at Camden, and giving him assurance of continued regard and esteem upon the entrance into Richmond of the retreating General. In November, 1784, to conciliate the Indians on the borders of Virginia, and to avert the danger of hostility from them, Mr. Henry introduced a remarkable resolution, providing for the intermarriage of the white with the Indian race, and investing the offspring of such alliances with all the rights of citizenship. It was rejected. Washington visited Richmond on the 15th and Lafayette on the 17th of the month, and they were received with public demonstrations. On the 17th of November, 1784, Mr. Henry was again elected Governor of Virginia; his term of three years to commence on the 30th of the month. The necessities of his family compelled his resignation of his office on the 29th of November, 1786, declining re-election for another year, as constitutionally provided. On the 4th of December in the same year, George Washington, Patrick Henry, Edmund Randolph, John Blair, James Madison, George Mason and George Wythe were appointed by the Virginia Assembly delegates to the convention to be held in May following in Philadelphia for the adoption of the Federal Constitution, but Henry was debarred by his pecuniary circumstances (being oppressed with debt) from obeying this honorable call. Of the Virginia Convention to decide the relations of the State to the newly proposed Federal Constitution, Mr. Henry was elected a member from Prince Edward county. In this body, composed of the grandest intellects in the Old Dominion, and which met in Richmond on the 2d of June, 1788, in a quaint old edifice subsequently known as the African Church (and now displaced by another church with a colored membership of nearly 4,000 members), Mr. Henry opposed the ratification of the instrument of compact with all the eloquence and vigor of his nature. He feared that the final result would be the destruction of the rights of the sovereign States. His faculties rose to the altitude of the occasion, and during his whole brilliant career he had never before appeared to greater advantage. But, for almost the only time in his life, he failed to carry his point. The opposing array of intellectual giants, backed by predominant popular sentiment, were not to be overcome. His opposition, however, was not fruitless. He secured the passage of a Bill of Rights and a variety of amendments, afterward incorporated into the Constitution. The Constitution having been adopted, the government organized, and Washington elected President, the repugnance of Mr. Henry measurably abated. The chapter of amendments considerably neutralized his objections; but it is believed that his acquiescence resulted more from the consideration of his duty as a citizen, his confidence in the chief magistrate and a hopeful reliance on the wisdom and virtue of the people, than from any material change in his opinions. In 1794, he retired from the bar with an ample estate, and removed to his seat, "Red Hill," in Charlotte county. In 1794 he was elected United States Senator, and in 1796 Governor of the State, but declined both offices, as he did, in 1795, the appointment by Washington as Secretary of State, to succeed Jefferson, and subsequently that of Minister to France by Adams.

From a letter of General Henry Lee, still preserved in the original, it appears that Washington, in December, 1795, after the declination of the office of Secretary of State, desired the acceptance by Mr. Henry of the Chief Justiceship of the Supreme Court of the United States. In 1798, the strong and animated resolutions of the Virginia Assembly in opposition to the Alien and Sedition Laws called again for his services in the councils of Virginia, and he presented himself as a candidate, at the spring election of 1799, for the House of Delegates. His speech on this occasion before the polls were opened was the last effort of his eloquence. As he finished, he literally descended into the arms of the uncontrollable throng and was borne about in triumph; whereon the eminent Presbyterian Divine, John H. Rice, D. D., touchingly exclaimed, "The sun has set in all his glory."

It is memorable that the brilliant and erratic John Randolph (who subsequently designated himself as "of Roanoke") offered himself on the same occasion at Charlotte Court House as a candidate for Congress, and undaunted replied to Mr. Henry with cutting satire and caustic crimination of the Federal party. His effort was received with loud huzzas. This was a new experience to Mr. Henry, unaccustomed to rivalry, to be confronted by a beardless boy, for such was the youthful appearance of Mr. Randolph. Mr. Henry returned to the rostrum, and in a second address soared above his wonted passionate and majestic eloquence. He unstintingly complimented the rare talents of his competitor, whilst he deprecated the youthful errors of his political zeal, and by his pathos wrought himself and audience to tears. In these efforts of Mr. Henry, as attested by two of his audience, Colonels Robert Morton and Clement Carrington, of Charlotte county, in 1837, in statements published by the late Charles Campbell in 1867, Mr. Henry did not approve the Alien and Sedition Laws (which he apprehended tended to civil war), and patriotically endeavored to quiet the minds of the people and to avert the apparent impending dissolution of the Union. He said: "Let us all go together, right or wrong. If we go into civil war, your Washington will lead the Governmental armies; and who, I ask, is willing to point a bayonet against *his* breast?"

Mr. Henry and Mr. Randolph were each elected severally to the stations for which they offered, but Mr. Henry, whose health had been visibly declining for several years, died on the 6th of June, 1799, a few months before Washington, and before the meeting of the body to which he had been elected. His remains and those of his second wife rest side by side beneath massive and ornate marble tablets in the family cemetery at "Red Hill," which seat is now owned by his grandson, William Wirt Henry.

The following obituary of Patrick Henry, which appeared contemporaneously in the Virginia newspapers, and was written by General Henry Lee, is a touching plaint and merits perpetuation here·

"MOURN, VIRGINIA, MOURN.

"Your Henry is no more! Ye friends of Liberty in every clime, drop a tear! No more will his social feelings spread delight through his happy home. No more will his edifying example dictate to his numerous offspring the sweetness of virtue and the majesty of patriotism. No more will the sage adviser, guided by zeal for their common happiness, impart light and utility to his caressing neighbors. No more will he illuminate the public councils with sentiments drawn from the Cabinet of his own mind, ever directed to the public good, clothed with eloquence sublime, delightful and commanding. Farewell, great and noble patriot, farewell!

"As long as our rivers flow and mountains stand, so long will your excellence and worth be the theme of our homage and endearments; and Virginia, bearing in mind her loss, will say to rising generations, IMITATE HENRY."

The affectionate reverence in which Patrick Henry was held is evidenced in the commitment to memory of this lament by numerous admirers and its oral transmission in some instances to the present day.

The distinguished orator and theologian, Rev. Archibald Alexander, D. D., a repeated personal witness, thus lucidly and satisfactorily analyzes the springs of the oratorical genius of Patrick Henry:

"The power of Henry's eloquence was due, first, to the greatness of his emotion and passion, accompanied with a versatility which enabled him to assume at once any emotion or passion which was suited to his ends. Not less indispensable, secondly, was a matchless perfection of the organs of expression, including the entire apparatus of voice, intonation, pause, gesture, attitude, and indescribable play of countenance. In no instance did he ever indulge in an expression that was not instantly recognized as nature itself; yet some of his penetrating and subduing tones were absolutely peculiar, and as inimitable as they were indescribable. These were felt by every hearer, in all their force. His mightiest feelings were sometimes indicated and communicated by a long pause, aided by an eloquent aspect, and some significant use of the finger. The sympathy between mind and mind is inexplicable. Where the channels of communication are open, the faculty of revealing inward passion great, and the expression of it sudden and visible, the effects are extraordinary. Let these shocks of influence be repeated again and again, and all other opinions and ideas are for the moment absorbed or excluded; the whole mind is brought into unison with that of the speaker; and the spell-bound listener, till the cause ceases, is under an entire fascination. Then perhaps the charm ceases, upon reflection, and the infatuated hearer resumes his ordinary state. Patrick Henry, of course, owed much to his singular insight into the feelings of the common mind. In great cases, he scanned his jury, and formed his mental estimate; on this basis he founded his appeals to their predilections and character. It is what other advocates do, in a lesser degree. When he knew there were conscientious or religious men among the jury, he would most solemnly address himself to their sense of right, and would adroitly bring in scriptural citations. If this handle was not offered, he would lay bare the sensibility of patriotism. * * *

A learned and intelligent gentleman stated to me that he once heard Mr. Henry's defense of a man arraigned for a capital crime. So clear and abundant was the evidence that my informant was unable to conceive any grounds of defense, especially after the law had been ably placed before the jury by the attorney for the Commonwealth. For a long time after Mr. Henry began, he never once adverted to the merits of the case or the arguments of the prosecution, but went off into a most captivating and discursive oration on general topics, expressing opinions in perfect accordance with those of his hearers, until having fully succeeded in obliterating every impression of his opponent's speech, he obliquely approached the subject, and as occasion was offered, dealt forth strokes which seemed to tell upon the minds of the jury. In this case, it should be added, the force of truth prevailed over the art of the consummate orator."

The descendants of Colonel John Henry and of his eminent son Patrick Henry, comprise the distinguished family names of Meredith, Madison, Lewis, Bowyer, Christian, Pope, Bullitt, Campbell, Russell, Wood, Preston, Armistead, Garland, Carrington, McDowell, Breckenridge, Floyd, Hampton, Johnston, Southall, Venable, Hughes, Michel, Fontaine, Roane, Lyons, Dandridge, Crenshaw, Granberry, Bailey, Scott, and others, and embrace authors, divines, educators, governors, generals, jurists, scientists, statesmen, etc.

A portrait of Patrick Henry, painted by Thomas Sully, and pronounced by his contemporaries an admirable likeness, is in the possession of his grandson, William Wirt Henry, a distinguished practitioner of the law, and the Vice-President of the Virginia Historical Society. From this portrait has been engraved the illustration in our work.

THOMAS JEFFERSON.

Upon the resignation of Patrick Henry, Thomas Jefferson, by election of the General Assembly, succeeded him as Governor of Virginia, June 1st, 1779. During his administration, in January, 1781, the traitor Arnold invaded Virginia, leaving ravage in his wake. At Richmond, the public stores fell a prey; private property was plundered, and several houses were burned. Many of the public archives were also destroyed. Lieutenant-Colonel Simcoe, of his command, commanding the Queen's Rangers, proceeded to Westham, six miles above Richmond, and destroyed the foundry, magazine, arms, and military supplies there. Arnold now retired to Portsmouth, where he rested until April, when General William Phillips, succeeding to the command, paid another visit of desolation to Manchester. In May came Lord Cornwallis with his victorious army from the South, driving every thing before him. The 7th of May was the day appointed by law for the meeting of the Assembly at Richmond. A quorum not being in attendance, the house adjourned from day to day until the 10th, when, upon the approach of the enemy, they adjourned to the 24th, to meet at Charlottesville. The house did not proceed to business until the 28th. Eight days after, they again fled before the rapid approach of the rapacious Tarleton. All the machinery of government for a time was in confusion, the Governor, Assembly, and the Council, save a single member, Colonel William Fleming, as it appears, being in flight before the enemy. Governor Jefferson resigned June 1st, and was succeeded by General Thomas Nelson, Jr., on the 12th of the month. An extended sketch

THOMAS LORD CULPEPER,
Governor of Virginia,

From a portrait in oil in the possession of the Virginia
Historical Society.

of the life of Thomas Jefferson will be found in the second volume of VIRGINIA AND VIRGINIANS.

WILLIAM FLEMING.

William Fleming emigrated from Scotland to Virginia in early manhood. By tradition he was of noble extraction, and he had received a liberal education. He is believed to have had a knowledge of medicine, and to have served in a medical and military capacity in the French and Indian war, with the rank of Lieutenant, in 1755 and 1756, and perhaps longer. He was of a bold and adventurous spirit, and was among the earliest settlers in the portion of Augusta County which now forms Botetourt County, taking up large tracts of land, which, enhancing in value, made him a man of wealth. In 1774 he raised a regiment, which he gallantly and effectively commanded in the sanguinary battle of Point Pleasant, in which he received a wound from which he never fully recovered. He was a member of the Council of Virginia in 1781, and for a time in the month of June was the executive of the Colony, as is evidenced by the following resolution of the Virginia Assembly (*Hening's Statutes*, Vol. X, p. 567):

"It appearing to the General Assembly that Colonel William Fleming, being the only acting member of the council for some time before the appointment of the Chief Magistrate, did give orders for the calling out the militia, and also pursued such other measures as were essential to good government, and it is just and reasonable that he should be indemnified therein,

"*Resolved, therefore,* That the said William Fleming, Esq., be indemnified for his conduct as before mentioned, and the Assembly do approve of the same. "JOHN BECKLEY, C. H. D.
"1781, June 23d.
"Agreed to by the Senate. WILL. DREW, C. S."

Colonel Fleming, in 1788, represented the county of Botetourt in the Virginia Convention which ratified the Federal Constitution—an eminent body.

Colonel Fleming married and left a family. One of his daughters, Anne, became the wife of Rev. George A. Baxter, D. D., Rector in 1798 of Liberty Hall Academy (the beginning of the present Washington and Lee University). He was also Professor of Mathematics, Natural Philosophy, and Astronomy in that institution, and Minister of the New Monmouth and Lexington Presbyterian Churches.

THOMAS NELSON.

Thomas Nelson, the eldest son of President William Nelson, of the Virginia Council, and his wife Elizabeth Burwell (granddaughter of Robert "King" Carter), was born at Yorktown, December 26th, 1738. After having been under the tuition of Rev. William Yates, of Gloucester, afterward President of William and Mary College, he was sent, at the age of fourteen, to England, to finish his education, remaining seven years. He enjoyed there the superintending care of the celebrated Dr. Beilby Porteus, afterward Bishop of London, who subsequently sent to his former ward in Virginia a volume of his sermons in token of remembrance. Thomas was first at the school of Dr. Newcombe, at Hackney; then at Eton. Graduated with distinction from Trinity College, Cambridge, he returned to Virginia in his twenty-second year. Whilst on his voyage, from respect to his father, he was elected a member of the House of Burgesses. He married, in 1762, Lucy Grymes, of Middlesex County, the eldest daughter of Philip and Mary (Randolph) Grymes, the elder, of "Brandon." He was associated as a merchant with his father, from whom, at the death of the latter, he received a portion of £40,000 sterling (the equivalent of $200,000 in our present currency, and when, too, the relative value in purchasing capacity was several times greater than now).

Thomas Nelson was a member of the Virginia Conventions of 1774 and 1775, and displayed extraordinary boldness in resisting British tyranny. He was elected by the Convention, in July, 1775, Colonel of the Second Virginia regiment, which post he resigned on being elected to the Continental Congress the same year. He was a conspicuous member of the Virginia Convention of 1776, which framed the Constitution of Virginia. He was a member of the Committee on Articles of Confederation, and July 5th, 1776, signed the Declaration of Independence. Restless for active service in the field, he resigned his seat in Congress in May, 1777, and in August following was appointed Commander-in-chief of the State forces of Virginia. He soon after raised a troop of cavalry, with which he repaired to Philadelphia. Resuming his duties in the Virginia Legislature, he strongly opposed the proposition to sequestrate British property, on the ground that it would be an unjust retaliation of public wrongs on private individuals. He was again elected to Congress, in February, 1779, but was obliged, by indisposition, to resign his seat. In May he was called upon to organize the State militia, and repel an invading expedition of the enemy. A loan of $2,000,000 being called for by Virginia in June, 1780, which, in that period of despondency and distrust, being difficult to obtain, General Nelson, by strenuous endeavors, and on his own personal security, raised a large portion of the amount. He also advanced money to pay two Virginia regiments ordered to the South, which refused to march until arrearages due them were paid. In the then critical aspect of affairs, upon the resignation of Governor Jefferson, a military executive being deemed a necessity, General Nelson was, June 12th, 1781, elected to succeed him, opposing in person, with what militia he could command, with sleepless vigilance and untiring energy, the enemy who were ravaging the State, anticipating the wants of the service with remarkable comprehensive forecast, and a provision wonderful in view of the difficulties which beset him. His gallantry and nobility of soul, as evinced at the siege of Yorktown, have already been noted in the sketch of his father, President William Nelson.

General Nelson died at his seat, "Offley," in Hanover County, January 4th, 1789, leaving as a legacy to his family naught but an imperishable record—sublime in its lofty aims and disinterested patriotism; for his advances to Virginia had impoverished him, and the claims of his remaining creditors literally beggared them. An effort was made in 1822, by the late Hon. St. George Tucker, before the Virginia Assembly, for indemnity to the heirs of General Nelson for advances made by the latter during the Revolution, which, after various contemptuous delays, was at last referred to a select committee, who rendered "an eloquent report, setting forth in glowing language" the merits, etc., of General Nelson, and concluding with the words, "That a just regard for the character of the State requires that some compensation should be made to his representatives for the losses sustained." The report was adopted by the House of Delegates, and, on motion, the committee was discharged from the duty of bringing in a bill in conformity thereto. The matter remained dormant until 1831, when, being again brought up, it was referred to the First and Second Auditors of the State, who reported against the claim.

The heirs finally petitioned Congress on the 10th of December, 1833, when, after vexatious delays, it was finally reported on, and *unfavorably.* Never before in the history of nations have patriotic services so eminent and so essentially vital, and sacrifices personally so absolute, been more ungratefully requited. The disease which carried off General Nelson was asthma, occasioned by exposure incident to his military services. His remains were conveyed to Yorktown, and buried at the foot of the grave of his father. *No stone marks the spot.* His grandson, Philip Nelson, presented, December 7th, 1839, a petition to the General Assembly of Virginia for the payment of the claims of General Nelson, which, after various delays, in sheer hopelessness of success, was withdrawn in September, 1840. A fort built at Louisville, Kentucky, in 1782, was named Fort Nelson in honor of General Nelson, as was also Nelson County, Virginia, formed in 1807 from Amherst County. His statue in bronze is one of the six which adorn the Washington monument in the public square at Richmond, Virginia. A representation of this grand and much admired work of art, in connection with the Capitol building, is given in this work. The only portrait of General Nelson, for which he ever sat, is preserved in the State Library of Virginia.

VIRGINIA AND VIRGINIANS. 81

It was painted by Chamberlain, in London, in 1754, whilst the subject was a student at Eton. It represents him as a handsome, ruddy-cheeked, brown-haired youth, with oval contour of face and a most engaging expression of countenance.

BENJAMIN HARRISON.

Benjamin Harrison succeeded Thomas Nelson as Governor of Virginia, upon the resignation of the latter, from ill-health, November 30th, 1781. He served for three years, when he was succeeded, November 29th, 1784, by Patrick Henry. An extended sketch of the life of Benjamin Harrison will be found under the head of "The Declaration of Independence and its Signers," in another portion of this work.

EDMUND RANDOLPH.

Edmund Randolph was born in Williamsburg, the capital of the Colony of Virginia, August 10, 1753. He was of distinguished lineage. His father, John Randolph, was Attorney-General of the Colony, and the son of Sir John Randolph, who had filled the same office and received the honor of Knighthood for eminent services to the Crown, and was the fifth son of the emigrant ancestor of the family in Virginia, William Randolph, born in Yorkshire, England; died at his seat, "Turkey Island," James River, April 11, 1711. The mother of Edmund Randolph was Ariana, daughter of Edmund Jenings, Attorney-General of Maryland and of Virginia, and at one time the Acting Governor of the last. Peyton Randolph, the first President of the Continental Congress, was his uncle.

Educated at William and Mary College, Edmund Randolph early determined on the profession of law, which his ancestors, paternal and maternal, had so eminently adorned. But his career was temporarily interrupted by the exciting occurrences of 1775, when ardently enlisting in the cause of the "rebellious" colonists, he was disinherited by his father, who remained "loyal" to the Crown, and sailing with Lord Dunmore for England, subsequently died there. Upon the appointment of Washington as Commander-in-chief of the Continental Army, then investing Boston, Edmund Randolph became a member of his staff and secretary, remaining in such capacity during the greater part of the siege. But having been adopted by his uncle, Peyton Randolph, who owned several large plantations in Virginia, whose public duties precluded his attention to them, and who died in October, 1775, he was compelled by his extended interests to return to Virginia, to civil life. He combined with the management of his estates the practice of law, in which he was eminently successful.

On the 29th of August, 1776, he married Elizabeth, daughter of Robert Carter Nicholas, Treasurer and Speaker of the House of Burgesses of Virginia, and granddaughter of Robert "King" Carter. In the same year he was a delegate from Williamsburg to the Convention which adopted the first constitution of the State, and before the close of the year was elected Mayor of the same city. He was appointed by the Convention Attorney-General under the new constitution, with an annual salary of £200, and at a subsequent session of the General Assembly he was elected its clerk, an office which has been filled by such men as George Wythe and William Wirt. In 1779 he was a delegate to the Continental Congress, of which he remained a member until 1782. Upon the resignation of Patrick Henry as Governor of Virginia, he succeeded him in the office by the election of the General Assembly, December 1, 1786, and was chosen by the same body one of the seven delegates to the Convention at Annapolis, and in the following year, in 1787, a member of the convention that formed the Federal Constitution, and introduced what was called the "Virginia plan." In 1788, he was returned by the county of Henrico, being then a resident of Richmond, to the convention which was called to decide upon the Federal Constitution. December 1, 1788, Edmund Randolph was succeeded as Governor of Virginia by his kinsman, Beverley Randolph. In 1784 he was appointed Deputy Grand Master of the Grand Lodge of Ancient Free and Accepted Masons of Virginia, and in 1786 was elected Grand Master of the same body, "when he was pleased to appoint the Honorable John Marshall as his Deputy." They served in their respective positions until 1788. It is of interest to note that the Masons' Hall in Richmond, a large wooden structure on the south side of Franklin, near Eighteenth Street, the oldest building for Masonic purposes in America, was erected in 1785, during the term as Grand Master of James Mercer and whilst Edmund Randolph was Deputy Grand Master. The name of Edmund Randolph is masonically perpetuated in that of the Richmond Randolph Lodge, No. 19, chartered October 19, 1787. In 1790 he was appointed by Washington the first Attorney-General of the United States, and on the 2d of August, 1794, he succeeded Jefferson as Secretary of State, which office he held until the 19th of August, 1795, when he withdrew to private life and resumed the practice of law. His person and his eloquence are vividly embalmed by Wirt in the pages of his *British Spy*. Hugh Blair Grigsby, another masterful delineator, in his *Virginia Convention of 1776*, says of Edmund Randolph's service in the Federal Convention of 1787, "His career in that body was surpassingly brilliant and effective, * * * nor was his course in the Virginia Convention of Ratification less imposing." The withdrawal of Edmund Randolph from the Cabinet of Washington, in 1795, was made the occasion, and the causes of it, of misrepresentations and calumnies by his political enemies, which he ably refuted and effectively silenced by the "Vindication," then published by him, and which was republished with a preface by his grandson, Peter V. Daniel, Jr., in 1855. Edmund Randolph died in Frederick County, Va., September 12, 1813. His daughter Lucy married Peter Vivian Daniel, born in Stafford county, Va., 1785; appointed, March 3, 1841, Justice of the United States Supreme Court; died at Richmond, May 31, 1860. His son, Peter V. Daniel, Jr., long President of the Richmond, Fredericksburg and Potomac Railroad, is a prominent member of the Richmond Bar. A MS. history of Virginia, by Edmund Randolph, which is several times quoted from in these sketches, is in the collections of the Virginia Historical Society.

BEVERLEY RANDOLPH.

Beverley Randolph, the son of Colonel Peter and Lucy (Bolling) Randolph of "Chatsworth," Henrico County, James River, Va. ("Surveyor of Customs of North America" in 1749, and long a member of the House of Burgesses), and third in descent from William Randolph, of "Turkey Island," was born at his father's seat in 1754. He graduated from William and Mary College in 1771, and was, during the Revolution, a member of the Virginia Assembly. He succeeded Edmund Randolph as Governor of Virginia, December 1, 1788, and served until December 1. 1791, when he was succeeded by Henry Lee. He married Martha Cocke, and their descendants are represented also in the names of Randolph, Fitzhugh, and others equally worthy. Governor Randolph died at his seat, "Green Creek," in February, 1797.

HENRY LEE.

Henry Lee, popularly known as "Light-Horse Harry Lee" from his gallant and efficient service during the Revolutionary War, was born, January 29th, 1756, at "Leesylvania," which is situated on a point of land jutting into the Potomac River, three miles above Dumfries, then the county seat of Prince William. He was the son of Henry and Lucy (Grymes) Lee, and fifth in descent from Richard Lee, of Shropshire, England, the emigrant ancestor of the family in Virginia, and combined also in his descent the blood of the historic Corbin, Ludwell, and Bland families. He was the second cousin of the distinguished brothers— Philip Ludwell, Thomas Ludwell, Richard Henry, Francis Lightfoot, William, and Arthur Lee. His youngest brother, Charles Lee, was Attorney-General in the second cabinet of Washington. Henry Lee was educated at Princeton College, New Jersey, graduating thence in 1773. Intending the profession of law, he was about to embark for England to pursue his studies under the direction of his relative, Bishop Porteus, of London, when the commencement of hostilities with the mother country changed his destiny. In May, 1776, he was appointed by the Virginia Convention a captain in the cavalry regiment of Colonel Theodrick Bland, Jr., and in September, 1777, joined the main army. By the stern discipline which he introduced, he was enabled to move with celerity and effect, and his rapid and daring system of tactics made "Lee's Legion" highly efficient. Besides being present at other important actions in the Northern Department, he was at the battles of Brandywine, Germantown, and Springfield. He early became a favorite of Washington, who selected his company as a bodyguard at Germantown. In the difficult and critical operations in Pennsylvania, New Jersey, and New York, 1777-1780, Lee was always placed near the enemy, intrusted with the command of outposts, the superintendence of scouts, and such like service, for which his skill, daring, and self-possession pre-eminently fitted him. In January, 1778, Lee, with only ten men, was attacked in a stone house by two hundred British troopers, whom he repulsed. He was soon after promoted to the rank of major, with the command of an independent corps of two companies of horse, afterward increased to three, and a body of infantry. He co-operated, as far as cavalry could act, in General Wayne's attack upon Stony Point, and procured the intelligence upon which it was projected. July 19, 1779, he surprised the garrison of Paulus Hook, and took one hundred and sixty prisoners. For his "prudence, address, and bravery" in this affair Congress voted him a gold medal.

Promoted to the rank of Lieutenant-Colonel, November 6th, 1780, Lee joined the Southern Army under General Nathaniel Greene, in January, 1781. He was at once detached toward the Santee River, in South Carolina, to co-operate with the famous "Swamp-fox" Marion, and these officers were speedily engaged in the successful surprise of Georgetown. During the retreat of Greene before Cornwallis, Lee's Legion formed the rear guard. Whilst watching the movements of Cornwallis in North Carolina, he fell upon the Tory Colonel Pyle (who was leading four hundred men to Cornwallis), and killed and captured most of his command. At the battle of Guilford Court House, Lee encountered the boastful and truculent Tarleton and drove him back with loss, afterward held his ground obstinately on Greene's left wing, and finally covered the retreat. It was by the advice of Lee that Greene adopted the daring policy of not following Cornwallis into Virginia, but of leaving that province to its fate, and marching south to end the conflict in South Carolina and Georgia. The result fully vindicated the expediency of this policy. Lee with his Legion joining the partisan forces of Marion, by a series of vigorous operations reduced Forts Watson, Motte, and Granby. While on his way to join Colonel Pickens he surprised and took Fort Galphin. Augusta was taken after a siege of sixteen days. He was also at the unsuccessful siege of Fort Ninety-six. At the battle of Eutaw his gallantry contributed greatly to the successful result. Lee's impetuous charge, causing the retreat of

EDMUND RANDOLPH,
Governor of Virginia, 1786–8.

the British left wing, probably saved the army from defeat. In the extensive sweep which Lee's Legion made from the Santee to Augusta, embracing from the 15th of April to the 5th of June, this corps, acting in conjunction first with Marion, afterward with Pickens, and sometimes alone, had constituted the principal force which carried the British posts, and made upward of 1,100 prisoners—about four times its own number.

The health of Colonel Lee under his incessant and arduous service gave way, and from the effects of disease his spirits, too, became depressed, and led to his retirement from a most brilliant and effective career in the army, in January, 1782. His commander, General Greene, in a letter dated January 27th, 1782, expresses the deepest concern at this determination of Colonel Lee, and acknowledges to him "the greatest obligations—obligations which I can never cancel," for "substantial service" of "lasting reputation," which are "the best panegyric that can be given of your actions." He continues: "I have the highest opinion of you as an officer, and you know I love you as a friend."

Very soon after the return of Colonel Lee to Virginia, he visited "Stratford," the seat of his kinsman, Colonel Philip Ludwell Lee, in Westmoreland County, on the bluffs of the Potomac, and in a short time was happily married to Matilda, the eldest daughter of his host. In the midst of his happiness he did not forget the brave men he had left in Carolina. His correspondence with General Greene, continued to the end of the war, is filled with evidences of the solicitude he felt for his soldiers. In 1786, Colonel Lee was elected to represent Westmoreland County in the House of Delegates of Virginia, and was a representative in the Continental Congress, 1786-1788, and in the latter year was a member of the Virginia Convention to decide upon the Federal Constitution, of which compact he was a prominent advocate. He succeeded Beverley Randolph as Governor of Virginia, December 1st, 1791, serving until December 1st, 1794. After the disastrous defeat of General St. Clair in the Northwest, in 1791, which moved Washington to a profane outburst of passion, Lee is said to have been the preference of the President to succeed St. Clair; but a question of policy and of precedency in rank prevailed, and General Anthony Wayne was appointed instead. General Lee, however, in 1794, was commissioned a Major-General, to command the forces raised to quell the "Whisky Insurrection" in Western Pennsylvania, and, advancing at the head of 15,000 men, speedily silenced all tumult. In 1799, General Lee was again in Congress, in which body he voiced the grief of the American Nation upon the death of Washington, in the appealing eulogy in which occurs the enduring sentiment, "*First in war, first in peace, first in the hearts of his countrymen.*" In 1809, General Lee wrote his "Memoirs of the War in the Southern Department of the United

States," which was republished in 1827, with additions by his son, Major Henry Lee, and again in 1869, with revisions and a biography of the author, by his son, General Robert E. Lee. In 1811, General Lee removed with his family to Alexandria, for the purpose of educating his children. In the second war with England, after the first disastrous campaigns in Canada, he was offered and accepted a Major-General's commission in the army. Whilst making his arrangements to enter the service, business called him to Baltimore, and, being an inmate of the house of Mr. Hanson when the riot connected with the *Federal Republican* newspaper occurred, he received injuries at the hands of the mob, from which he never recovered. The results of that night were fatal to General Lingan. The injuries of General Lee nearly deprived him of sight, and were otherwise so severe as to prevent his taking any part in the war of 1812, and eventually terminated his life. It was thought that a voyage to the West Indies and the influence of the mild climate there might restore him. Here he remained until 1818, when, despairing of recovery, he prepared to return home. He intended first to land at Savannah, Georgia, but only reached Cumberland Island on the coast, where he was received at the home of Mrs. Shaw, the daughter of General Greene. Here he died, March 25th, 1818, and was buried on the island. In person, General Lee was about five feet nine inches in height, well proportioned, of an open, noble, and benignant countenance, and a dark complexion. His manners were frank and engaging, and his disposition generous and hospitable. He was twice married. By his first wife, as stated, he had issue a son, Major Henry Lee, diplomatist and author of ability, and a daughter, Lucy, who married Bernard Carter. By his second wife, Anne Hill, daughter of Charles Carter, of "Shirley," James River, whom he married June 18th, 1794, General Lee had issue: Charles Carter, author and poet; Commodore Sidney Smith, of the United States and Confederate States navies; and General Robert Edward Lee, the peerless hero; and two daughters, Anne Carter and Mildred, who married respectively William L. Marshall and Edward Childe—the latter of Boston, Massachusetts.

Of the military talents of General Henry Lee, General Greene said, "No man in the progress of the Southern campaign had equal merits with Lee;" and the "love and thanks" expressed to Lee in Washington's letter, in 1789, show the affection which his generous qualities had inspired. In these sketches of the eminent men of Virginia it will be observed that the connection of many of them with the philanthropic and beneficent fraternity of Free Masons, of the period of the Revolution and subsequent thereto, is noted. It has been asserted that nearly every general officer in the Continental army, from Washington down, was a Mason. From a report submitted to the Grand Lodge of Virginia in 1867, by a venerable brother, Peyton Johnston, Esq., of Richmond, it is evidenced that General Lee was an earnest Mason, and that on the red field of war he practiced "Relief and Brotherly Love" in saving the life of Colonel Broun, a British officer, whom he recognized masonically as a brother of the "Mystic Tie." Lee County, formed in 1792 from Russell, was named in honor of General Lee.

ROBERT BROOKE.

Robert Brooke, the grandfather of the subject of this sketch, a native of England, of gentle descent and of classic education, accompanied Robert Beverley, the historian, and Governor Spotswood, to Virginia in 1710. He was a skilled and probably a professional surveyor. He must have been appointed surveyor of the Colony immediately upon or very soon after his arrival. He accompanied Governor Spotswood in his famous expedition across the Blue Ridge Mountains, which set out from Williamsburg, August 20, 1716, and on the 5th of September following, drank the health of King George I. on the summit of the Appalachian range, and returning, the party reached "Germanna," the seat of the Governor, on the Rappahannock River, on the 10th instant following. Robert Brooke was decorated with one of the horseshoe badges described in the preceding sketch of Governor Spotswood. In 1736, Robert Brooke was one of the surveyors in behalf of His Majesty, George II., to determine the disputed boundaries of the Northern Neck Proprietary of Lord Fairfax.

The commissioners in behalf the Crown were William Byrd, John Robinson and John Grymes; Lord Fairfax being represented by William Fairfax, William Beverley and Charles Carter. Robert Brooke had several sons, the youngest of whom, Richard, married a Miss Taliaferro, who brought him as a dowry the seat and estate "Smithfield," on the Rappahannock, about four miles below Fredericksburg. By tradition, the estate was so called after Captain John Smith, the pioneer settler of Virginia. As mythical as this may appear, it is yet recorded that Smith ascended the Rappahannock with an exploring party in July, 1608, and that Richard Featherstone, a "gentleman" of the party, dying, he was buried on the banks of the river near where Fredericksburg now stands. Richard Brooke left four sons and a daughter by his wife as stated, and a fifth son by a second marriage. He died in 1792, aged sixty years. The two eldest sons, Laurence and Robert (under notice), were sent to the University of Edinburg to be educated for the two learned professions, Medicine and Law, and did not return until the American Revolution was in progress.

Going over first to France, Dr. Laurence Brooke was appointed, through the influence of Benjamin Franklin, surgeon of the American privateer, the "Bonhomie Richard," commanded by the celebrated John Paul Jones, and was in the engagement with the "Serapis" and all other actions of that memorable cruise. Robert Brooke was captured on his voyage to America and carried to New York, from whence he was sent back to England by Lord Howe, the British Admiral. From England, Robert Brooke went into Scotland and from thence again got over to France, and returned to Virginia in a French frigate that brought the arms supplied the continentals by the French government. Burning with patriotic ardor, he joined at once a volunteer troop of cavalry commanded by Captain Larkin Smith, was captured in January, 1781, in a charge of dragoons by a Captain Loller, of Simcoe's Queen's Rangers at Westham, six miles above Richmond (which raid is mentioned in the preceding sketch of Governor Jefferson); but was soon exchanged, returning to the service. After the war he entered upon the practice of his profession, in which he soon acquired distinction. In 1794 he represented the county of Spotsylvania in the House of Delegates of Virginia, and in the same year was elected Governor of the State by the Legislature, entering upon his duties December 1st and serving until December 1, 1796, when he was succeeded by James Wood. In 1795 he was elected Grand Master of the Grand Lodge of Ancient Free and Accepted Masons of Virginia (having previously served as Deputy Grand Master), and served until 1797. In 1798 he was elected Attorney-General of Virginia over Bushrod Washington, the nephew of George Washington, and who was afterward a Justice of the Supreme Court of the United States. Robert Brooke died in the office of Attorney-General in 1799, aged thirty-eight years. His grandson, Robert T. Brooke, Esq., an estimable citizen of Richmond, is the Treasurer of the Virginia Historical Society. The county of Brooke, formed in 1797 from Ohio county, commemorates the name of the Governor. The third son of Richard Brooke, John, was a Lieutenant in the Revolution and a pensioner of the State for gallant service. The fourth son, Francis T. (born August 27, 1763), at the age of sixteen was appointed a first Lieutenant in Colonel (afterward General) Charles Harrison's Regiment of Artillery, serving first in the campaign of General Lafayette during the invasion of Lord Cornwallis. He was soon after placed in command of the Magazine and Laboratory at Westham, six miles above Richmond, with a force of seventy-five men. Although so young an officer, Captain Brooke acquitted himself with skill and gallantry throughout the war, winning encomiums uniformly from his several Generals, Harrison, Lafayette and Greene. In 1788 he commenced the practice of Law in the counties of Monongalia and Harrison, and was soon appointed Attorney for the Commonwealth of the District Court of Morgantown. In 1790 he removed to Essex county, which county he represented subsequently in the House of Delegates, and in 1791 married Mary Randolph, the daughter of General Alexander Spotswood and a grand niece of General Washington. Mrs. Brooke died in 1803, leaving four children, and

Captain Brooke married secondly Mary Champe Carter, by whom he had two children. Captain Brooke was a member of the State Senate in 1800, and in 1804 Speaker of that body, and in the latter year was elected a member of the General Court of Virginia. In 1811 he was elected Judge of the Supreme Court of Appeals, of which he was long President. By successive promotions he was appointed General of the first Brigade of the State forces in 1802. He was the last Vice-President and presiding executive of the Virginia Branch of the Order of Cincinnati, the funds of which, some $20,000, ultimately went, by the vote of the few surviving members of the Order, about the year 1820, to the endowment of Washington College, now Washington and Lee University, Lexington, Va. Judge Brooke died March 3, 1851, widely revered for his sterling worth, and deeply lamented. A scarce little memorial, "A Narrative of my Life; For my Family, by Francis T. Brooke," privately printed in 1849, has furnished many of the facts in this sketch. The name Brooke is of much earlier dating in Virginia than as above stated. Nicholas Brooke, "the younger, merchant," being a patentee of 500 acres in Middle Plantations, York county, August 13, 1646.

The names of Henry, Humphrey, Paulin and George Brooke subsequently appear as grantees of land, and the name has been frequently represented in the Legislative bodies of Virginia and in the army and navy of America. It has been asserted that all of the name of Brooke as severally represented in Virginia, and by Roger Brooke in Maryland, the ancestor of the eminent jurist, Roger Brooke Taney, are of the same lineage from the parent stock in England.

JAMES WOOD.

James Wood, the son of Colonel James Wood, the founder of Winchester, Virginia, was born about the year 1750, in Frederick County, which he represented in the Virginia Convention of 1776, which framed the State Constitution. He was appointed by that body, Nov. 15, 1776, a Colonel in the Virginia line, and rendered gallant service in the cause of Freedom, as well as in the defence of the frontiers of Virginia from the Indians. He was long a member of the State Council, and by seniority in that body, Lieutenant-Governor of Virginia. He was elected Governor of the State, December 1, 1796, serving until December 1, 1799, when he was succeeded by Governor James Monroe. Governor Wood was subsequently commissioned a Brigadier-General of State troops. He was also, for a time, President of the Virginia branch of the Order of Cincinnati. He died at Richmond, June 16, 1813. The county of Wood, formed in 1799 from Harrison county, was named in commemoration of his patriotic services. The wife of General Wood, who was Jean, daughter of Rev. John Moncure, a Huguenot refugee, who fled from religious persecution to Virginia, early in the eighteenth century, and was long the rector of Overwharton parish, Stafford county, survived her husband several years. Mrs. Wood was a lady of great benevolence of character, and was gifted with both poetic and musical talents. Of her poetry, examples are preserved in the *Southern Literary Messenger*. She also frequently contributed to the newspaper press, and left in MS. a volume of unpublished poetry and sketches. Mrs. Wood spent the close of her life in pious works of charity and usefulness. A noble monument to her philanthropy, is a society for the assistance of indigent widows and children, which she founded with the assistance of Mrs. Samuel Pleasants, and a Mrs. Chapman. It was styled the "Female Humane Association of Richmond," and was incorporated by the Legislature of Virginia, in 1811. Mrs. Wood was the first President of the Society, and untiringly performed the somewhat arduous duties of that responsible station until her death, in 1825, at the age of sixty-eight years. Her grave is in the cemetery of the Robinson family, a little beyond the western limits of Richmond, near the banks of James river. Soon after the death of Mrs. Wood, the Rev. John H. Rice, President of Hampden-Sydney College, instituted an association of ladies for the purpose of working for the benefit of poor theological students of the College, and which, in compliment to Mrs. Wood, he called the Jean Wood Society.

JAMES MONROE.

James Monroe succeeded James Wood as Governor of Virginia, December 1, 1799, and served until December 1, 1802, when he was succeeded by John Page. He was again governor from January 4, 1811, to December 5th following, when he was succeeded by George William Smith, Lieutenant-Governor of the State. An extended account of the career of James Monroe will be found in Volume II. of this work, in the serial of biographical sketches of presidents of the United States.

The period of the first service of James Monroe as Governor of Virginia was, however, marked by an event, tragical in its sequence, which though frequently referred to as "Gabriel's Insurrection," but few of the present generation have any definite knowledge of, as there has been no circumstantial account of it published, since that which contemporaneously appeared in the newspapers, of which but few files have been preserved, and they are practically inaccessible to the public. Some notice of it, therefore, in these pages, can not but prove interesting.

In a message of Governor Monroe to the General Assembly of Virginia, dated December 5, 1800, he states that on the 30th of August preceding, about two o'clock in the afternoon, Mr. Mosby Shepherd, a reputable citizen of Henrico county, who resided about three miles north of the city of Richmond, beyond a small stream known as the Brook, called upon him and informed him that he had just received advice from two of his slaves that the negroes in the neighborhood mentioned intended to rise that night, kill their masters and their families, and proceed to Richmond, where they would be joined by the negroes there, and would seize all the public arms and ammunition, murder the white inhabitants and take possession of the city. Thereupon Governor Monroe took immediate measures to avert the threatened fell design by stationing guards at the state penitentiary, where the public arms were deposited; at the magazine, and at the state capitol, and by disposing the city troop of cavalry (commanded by Captain Moses Austin, then conducting a shot tower in the city of Richmond, and who was subsequently noted as a Texan pioneer) in detachments to patrol the several routes leading to the city from the suspected neighborhood. "The close of the day, however, was marked by one of the most extraordinary falls of rain ever known in our country. Every animal sought shelter from it." The brook was in consequence so swollen in its volume as to be impassable, thus interposing a bar to the execution of the plan of the negroes. Nothing occurred during the night of the alarming character suspected, to disturb the tranquillity of the city, and the only unusual circumstance reported by the patrolling troopers in the morning following, was, that all negroes passed on the road, in the interval of the storm, were going from the city, whereas it was their usual custom to visit it on that night of the week (Saturday), which circumstance was not unimportant, as it had been reported that the first rendezvous of the negroes was to be in the country. The same precautions being again observed the succeeding night without developments of the alleged design, Governor Monroe was on the point of concluding that the alarm was groundless, when from further information from Major William Mosby and other gentlemen, residents of the suspected neighborhood, he was fully satisfied that the insurrection had been planned by the negroes, and that they still intended to carry it into effect. He therefore convened the Executive Council of the State, on Monday, September 1, who took such measures that in the afternoon of the same day twenty of the negro conspirators were apprehended on the estate of Colonel Thomas H. Prosser, a prominent and influential gentleman, and from those of others in the suspected neighborhood, and brought to Richmond. "As the jail could not contain them, they were lodged in the penitentiary." The ringleaders, or chiefs, had fled and were not then to be found.

Every day now threw light on the diabolical plot and gave it additional importance. In the progress of the trials of the conspirators, it was satisfactorily demonstrated that a general insurrection of the slaves in the State was contemplated by the originators of the plot. A species of organization had taken place among them, and at a meeting held for the purpose, they had elected a commander, one Gabriel, the slave of Colonel Prosser, and to whom they had given the title of General. They had also appointed subordinate officers, captains, sergeants, etc.

SCENE IN WEST VIRGINIA.

They contemplated a force of cavalry, as well as of infantry, and had formed a plan of attack on the city, which was to commence by setting fire to the wooden buildings in the lower portion of it, called Rocketts, with the expectation of attracting the inhabitants thither whilst they assailed the penitentiary, magazine and capitol; intending, after capturing these and getting possession of arms and ammunition, to meet the people on their return and slaughter them. The accounts varied as to the number who were to inaugurate the movement. According to the testimony adduced in the trials of the conspiring wretches, it was variously stated at from five hundred to ten thousand. It was manifest, however, that it embraced a majority of the slaves in the city of Richmond and its neighborhood, and that the combination extended to the adjacent counties of Hanover, Caroline, Louisa, Chesterfield, and to the neighborhood of Point of Fork in Fluvanna County, and there was good cause to believe that the knowledge of the project pervaded other portions, if not the whole of the State. It was suspected "that the design was prompted by others who were invisible, but whose agency might be powerful." To meet such contingency, Governor Monroe called into service the 9th, 19th and 23d, and a portion of the 33d regiments of the State Militia, which were chiefly stationed in Richmond and the adjacent town of Manchester. The military force was gradually diminished, until, on the 18th of October following, the residue was discharged.

The judicial disposition of the ring-leaders of the plot was summary, five of them were executed on the 12th of September, and five more on the 15th thereafter. "General" Gabriel, the sable chief, was apprehended on the 27th of the same month, in the city of Norfolk, and suffered death in January following. The savage disposition of Gabriel, according to the records of Henrico County Court, had, a year previous to his final heinous conception, subjected him to punishment and lengthy imprisonment for biting off the ear of a fellow slave. In the testimony given by the witnesses (who were all negroes), in the trials of the conspirators, there were some curious as well as characteristic communications made. The whole plot was stupidly conceived, with a provision ludicrously trifling. The entire armament captured, consisted of twelve rude swords which had been manufactured from scythe blades by one of the conspirators, Solomon, the brother of "General" Gabriel, a blacksmith, and the slave, also, of Colonel Prosser. A broken pistol was also owned by one of the conspirators, and it was stated by some of the witnesses at the trial, that "General" Gabriel had provided also six guns, ten pounds of gunpowder, and five hundred bullets, which he had moulded. It was evidently the expectancy of the bloody-minded wretches to secure, primarily, arms from the residences of their masters, whose households were to be the unsuspecting victims of midnight assassination. As in the case of Nat. Turner, the leader in the subsequent and more serious insurrection which occurred in Southampton County, in August, 1831, religious fanaticism seems also to have been a factor in Gabriel's insurrection, as it was urged by Martin, one of the prime instigators, that God had said in the Bible, "If we will worship him, we should have peace in all our land, five of you shall conquer an hundred, and a hundred, a thousand of our enemies." A piece of silk, for a flag, was to be provided, with the motto "*Death or Liberty*" inscribed upon it. "None of the whites were to be spared except Quakers, Methodists and French people, unless they agreed to the freedom of the blacks, in which case they would at least cut off one of their arms." It was also designed to send a messenger to the nation of Catawba Indians in North Carolina, and to request their co-operation. The immunity stated as having been designed the Quakers, might have been actuated by a consciousness of the active philanthropy of that society towards the negroes, but why Methodists should be spared is less satisfactorily comprehended. Perhaps there were many followers of that church among the negroes. The coincidence of the mercy to the French, and the proposed mission to the Catawba Indians is strikingly curious, and affords grounds for the supposition that a tradition had lingered in the minds of the benighted negroes of the dread French and Indian War of some fifty years previous. The Indians of North Carolina, it may be added, had given the colonists much trouble some forty years earlier, even in the administration of Governor Spotswood. The matter is one to engage interest and speculative thought. An exemplification of the characteristic superstition of the negro is afforded in the desire of the conspirators to "enlist the *outlandish* (*i. e.*, foreigners) people, because they were supposed to deal with witches and wizards, and of course useful in armies, to tell when any calamity was to befall them." Monroe County, now in West Virginia, formed in 1799 from Greenbrier County, was named in honor of Governor, afterwards President, Monroe.

JOHN PAGE.

No patriot among the worthies who have illumined the annals of the Old Dominion could boast a more widely honored lineage and more influential family connections than the distinguished subject of this sketch, John Page, of "Rosewell," Gloucester county, Virginia. John Page, the first of the family in the Colony, a relative of Sir Gregory Page, baronet of Greenwich, County Kent, England, was born in England, about the year 1627; emigrated to Virginia in 1650; married in 1656, Alice Luckin, of County Essex, England; became a member of the Colonial Council; died January 23, 1692, in the county of York, and was buried in Bruton parish churchyard, Williamsburg, Virginia. A chaste and substantial monument was erected over his remains in 1878, by Dr. R. C. M. Page, of New York City, a descendant. A MS. legacy of pious instructions from Hon. John Page, to his children, was published in 1856, under the title of a "Deed of Gift," by the late Bishop Wm. Meade, of Virginia. Matthew, the second son of Hon. John Page, was born in 1659, and died January 9, 1703, at his seat, "Rosewell," in Gloucester county. He was also a member of the Council, and one of the members of the original board of trustees of William and Mary College. He married, in 1689, Mary, only child and heiress of John and Mary Mann, of "Timberneck," Gloucester county. Of their children, Mann was the only survivor, born in 1691; member of the Council; died January 24, 1730, at "Rosewell," the imposing mansion at which seat, still standing, he completed the year of his death; his tomb is also there. He was twice married; first, in 1712, to Judith, daughter of Hon. Ralph Wormeley, secretary of the Colony, and secondly, in 1718, to Judith, second daughter of Hon. Robert ("King") Carter. Mann, the eldest child of the second marriage, born about 1718; married first in 1743, Alice, daughter of Hon. John Grymes, of Middlesex county, a member of the Council; married secondly, about 1748, Anne Corbin, daughter of Hon. John Tayloe, of "Mount Airy," Spotsylvania county, a member of the Council. John Page, the eldest child of the first marriage, and the subject under notice, was born at "Rosewell," April 17, 1743 (old style). After private tuition under the Rev. William Yates, and one learned and worthy William Price, he entered the grammar school of William and Mary College in 1760, and graduated from that institution in 1763, with distinction. His classical attainments brought him under the favorable notice successively of the Colonial Governors Dinwiddie, Fauquier, Lord Botetourt, and the Earl of Dunmore. He was appointed a Visitor of William and Mary College in 1768, and in 1773 represented it in the House of Burgesses, and was also a member of the Council, and by his opposition in that body, in 1775, to the measures of Lord Dunmore, incurred his displeasure, particularly in boldly advising him to give up the gunpowder which the Governor had seized. Continuing in the Virginia Assembly, he was distinguished by his talents and patriotism, and as a member of the Committee of Safety, in 1775, and of the First Council under the Constitution, in 1776, and as Lieutenant-Governor of the Commonwealth, he rendered important services in the Revolutionary struggle. He also contributed freely from his private fortune to the public cause, and served as colonel of militia from Gloucester county in 1781. In the midst of exacting public service, and the exciting events of the period of the incipiency of the American Revolution, John Page yet found time for investigations in natural and in physical science, of which evidences in his MS. of Meteorological Observations have been preserved, one of them being in the possession of the present writer. In testimony of his attainments, John Page was, June 16, 1774, elected the first president of the "Society for the Advancement of Useful Knowledge," in Virginia. In 1784 he served with Bishop James Madison and Robert Andrews, of Virginia, and Andrew Ellicott, of Pennsylvania, in ascertaining and fixing the boundary line between the two states. In 1785 he was a lay deputy from the convention of the Protestant Episcopal Church in Virginia, with Rev. Dr. David Griffith and Rev. Samuel S. McCroskey, D.D., in the National Convention held in New York City. In 1789 he was elected one of the earliest representatives in Congress from Virginia, upon the adoption of the Federal Constitution—the seat of government being at that time in the city of New York—and continued to act in that capacity until 1797. In 1794 he served as lieutenant-colonel commandant of a regiment from Gloucester county in the suppression of the "Whiskey Insurrection" in western Pennsylvania. In 1796 and 1799 he published Addresses to the People, and in 1800 was a Presidential elector. December 1, 1802, he succeeded James Monroe as Governor, filling the office most acceptably, and by two successive annual re-elections, under the provisions of the state constitution, serving until December 1, 1805, when, not being eligible again until after an interval of four years, he was succeeded by William H. Cabell. In 1806 Governor Page was appointed by Jefferson United States Commissioner of Loans for Virginia, and acted in that capacity until his death at Richmond, October 11, 1808. He was buried in the churchyard of the venerable sanctuary of St. John, at Richmond, and his grave, in the eastern portion of the grounds, was unmarked until 1881, when Dr. R. C. M. Page, of New York, reverently placed over his remains a handsome tomb of Carrara marble. Governor Page was twice married, first, about 1765, to Frances, daughter of Colonel Robin and Sarah (daughter of "Scotch Tom" Nelson) Burwell, who dying in 1784, aged thirty-seven years, Governor Page married secondly in 1789, in New York City, Margaret, daughter of William Lowther, of Scotland. By the first marriage he had twelve children, nine of whom survived; of these nine, five married sons and daughters of their illustrious kinsman, General Thomas Nelson. Of eight children, the issue of the second marriage, only two married. The descendants of Governor Page comprise the worthy names of Nelson, Smith, Digges, Pendleton, Meade, Berkeley, Blair, Anderson, Saunders, and others.

The county of Page, formed from those of Rockingham and Shenandoah, in 1831, was named in honor of Governor Page. The following is a just tribute to his worth: "Hon. John Page was, from his youth, a man of pure and unblemished life. He was a patriot, a statesman, a philosopher, and a Christian. From the commencement of the American Revolution to the last hour of his life he exhibited a firm, inflexible, unremitting, and ardent attachment to his country, and rendered her very important services. His conduct was marked by uprightness in all the vicissitudes of life—in the prosperous and calamitous times through which he passed—in seasons of gladness and affliction. He was not only the patriot, soldier, and politician, the well-read theologian and zealous churchman—so that some wished him to take orders, with a view to being the first bishop of Virginia—but he was a most affectionate domestic character."

There are two original portraits of Governor Page in existence. One representing him as a handsome youth, at the age of fourteen years, said to have been painted by the celebrated Benjamin West, and now in the possession of his descendant, Dr. R. C. M. Page, of New York City, who generously presented the State of Virginia, in October, 1880, with a copy by G. P. A. Healey, of New York City, and which copy is in the State Library at Richmond, Virginia. The other, by Charles Wilson Peale, is in the Museum of the Independence Hall building, Philadelphia.

WILLIAM H. CABELL.

The ancestry of William H. Cabell unites several of the worthiest of the families of the Old Dominion, whose qualities are avouched in an extensive connection which it is believed now links almost every family of prominence in the State, and numbers honored representatives throughout our Union. His paternal ancestor, William Cabell, born March 1, 1687, at Warminster, Wiltshire, England, of an ancient family (said to have been originally from Spain, and thus indicated in the family arms, and name, originally Caballos), was a surgeon in the British navy, and settled in Virginia about 1724, acquiring extensive landed possessions which enriched his descendants. Two brothers, the heads of an estimable family in Virginia, Joseph (founder of the historic seat "Powhatan," near Richmond), and William Mayo, of the family of Poulshot, England, who came to Virginia in 1728, after having made some stay at Bridgetown, Barbadoes, were near relatives of Dr. Cabell, their mothers being sisters. William Mayo ran the dividing line between Virginia and North Carolina in 1728, under Colonel William Byrd, laid out the cities of Richmond and Petersburg, and was the surveyor of Goochland County when it embraced both sides of James River to the Appomattox River, on the south, and from Henrico and Chesterfield counties, respectively, to the Blue Ridge. Of the issue of the first marriage of Dr. Cabell with Miss Elizabeth Birks, of one daughter and four sons, Nicholas, the youngest, of "Liberty Hall," born October, 1750, died August 18, 1806, was the father of the subject of the present sketch, who may be deemed to continue satisfactorily this narrative in a brief autobiography which has been kindly supplied the writer by his friend Alexander Brown, Esq., a worthy representative of the family: "I was born December 16, 1772, at 'Boston Hill,' about five miles distant from Cartersville, in Cumberland County, Virginia, the residence of my maternal grandfather, Colonel George Carrington, whose wife was Anne, daughter of William Mayo, of Powhatan County. I am the eldest son of Colonel Nicholas and Hannah (Carrington) Cabell. From the spring of 1782 to the spring of 1783 I attended school from my father's [Liberty Hall, Nelson County, Virginia,] to George Lambert, a teacher of English. From March, 1784, to Christmas following, I went to school at my maternal grandfather's, in the county of Cumberland, to Mr. James Wilson, where I commenced the study of the Latin language. In February, 1785, I entered Hampden-Sidney College, where I continued until September, 1789. In February, 1790, I entered William and Mary College, where I continued until July, 1793 [graduating, then, B. L.]. In the fall of 1793 I went to Richmond to complete the study of the law, and remained there till June 13, 1794, when, after examination by Judges Joseph Prentis, James Henry, and William Nelson, I was licensed to practice law. On the 9th of April, 1795, I married [Rev. Mr. O'Neal officiating] Elizabeth, youngest daughter of Colonel William Cabell, of 'Union Hill' [his father's brother], in whose family I lived until his death in 1798, and afterwards with his widow, at 'Union Hill,' till the 29th of January, 1801, when I moved to my own home at 'Midway.' My first wife died November 5, 1801, and was buried at 'Union Hill.' Shortly after this I went to Charleston, South Carolina. I returned the following spring. I had been elected to the Assembly [from Amherst county] in the spring of 1796. I was also in the Assembly of 1798, and voted for the famous resolutions of that session. I was an elector at the first election of Mr. Jefferson, and filled the same office again [at his second election]. I was a member of the Assembly in the years 1802, 1803, 1804. On the 11th of March, 1805, I was married to Agnes Sarah Bell [born August 22, 1783; died February 15, 1863], eldest daughter of Col. Robert Gamble, of Richmond [a native of Augusta County, who having creditably served throughout the Revolution, particularly distinguishing himself as an officer with Lieutenant James Gibbon, in leading the memorable forlorn hope at Stony Point, settled, after the war, in Richmond, and amassed in mercantile pursuits a handsome competence. He was killed by a fall from his horse in the streets of Richmond, April 12, 1810, in the fifty-sixth year of his age. His tomb is in the churchyard of the venerable St. John's, at Richmond. The wife of Colonel Gamble was Catharine, a daughter of Major Robert Grattan, of the lineage of the celebrated leader of the Irish Parliament, and who built the first stone mill in the Shenandoah Valley, and from its manufacture contributed to the two hundred barrels of flour sent by the people of Augusta County to the distressed city of Boston, during the British siege of 1776. The second daughter of Colonel Gamble, Elizabeth Washington, born January 30, 1784, became, in 1802, the second wife of the celebrated William Wirt, Attorney-General of the United States, etc. She was the author of *Flora's Dictionary*, published in

Baltimore in 1829, and died at Annapolis, Maryland, January 24, 1857. The relations between Governor Cabell and William Wirt, thus closely established, were ever afterwards the most intimate, touching, and confidential. The commodious stuccoed residence of Colonel Gamble is still standing, unchanged in appearance, on the hill designated by his name in Richmond, and overlooks the famed Tredegar Iron Works]. In April, 1805, I was again elected to the Assembly, and attended as a member, but within a few days (December, 1805) after the commencement of the session, I was elected Governor, in which office I continued for three years, until December, 1808, when I was elected by the Legislature a Judge of the General Court, being commissioned by Governor John Tyler, December 15, 1808, which office I held till April, 1811, when I was elected a Judge of the Court of Appeals, being appointed March 21, 1811, by Governor Monroe and the Privy Council, and qualifying April 3, 1811. I was elected also by the Legislature, December 7, 1811, and then commissioned by Governor George William Smith. After the adoption of the new constitution of Virginia [1830] I was again reelected a Judge of the Court of Appeals, April 11, 1831, and commissioned by Governor John Floyd. And on the 18th of January, 1842, I was elected president of that court, and commissioned by Lieutenant-Governor John Rutherfoord, and qualified and took my seat January 20, 1842." It may be added that Judge Cabell continued to serve as President of the Court of Appeals until 1851, when he retired from the bench. He died at Richmond, January 12, 1853, widely revered for his virtues and deeply lamented, and was interred in Shockoe Hill Cemetery. At a called meeting of the Court of Appeals and bar of Virginia, held in Richmond, January 14, glowing resolutions in testimony of the singular purity of character and excellences of Judge Cabell were passed, which were published in the *American Times* of January 19, 1853. From thence the following is extracted:

"*Resolved*, That we cherish, and shall ever retain, a grateful remembrance of the signal excellence of the Honorable William H. Cabell, as well in his private as in his public life. There were no bounds to the esteem which he deserved and enjoyed. Of conspicuous ability, learning and diligence, there combined therewith a simplicity, uprightness and courtesy, which left nothing to be supplied to inspire and confirm confidence and respect. It was as natural to love and honor him; and both loved and honored was he by all who had an opportunity of observing his unwearied benignity or his conduct as a judge. In that capacity wherein he labored for forty years in our Supreme Court of Appeals, having previously served the State as Governor and Circuit Judge, such was his uniform gentleness, application and ability; so impartial, patient and just was he; of such remarkable clearness of perception and perspicuity, precision and force in stating his convictions, that he was regarded with warmer feelings than those of merely official reference. To him is due much of the credit which may be claimed for our judicial system and its literature. It was an occasion of profound regret, when his infirmities of age, about two years since, required him to retire from the bench, and again are we reminded, by his death, of the irreparable loss sustained by the public and the profession."

ROBERT BROOKE,
Governor of Virginia, 1794-6.

The General Assembly of Virginia also passed a series of resolutions in testimony of the eminent worth of Judge Cabell, and eulogies delivered in that body alike warmly exhibit the profound regard in which he was held.

It may be noted that it was during the incumbency of Judge Cabell as Governor of Virginia, that the serious disputes with England began, first in the wrangles on the subject of naturalization and protection of British seamen, which gave rise, in June, 1807, to the attack on the frigate "Chesapeake," by the British sloop-of-war "Leopard," one of the preliminary instigations to the war of 1812.

Another event in the administration of Governor Cabell served to make it memorable—the examination and trial of Aaron Burr, at Richmond, before Chief Justice John Marshall, in the spring and summer of 1807, for treason in an alleged design to found an empire in the western part of America. Messrs. John Wickham, Edmund Randolph, and Benjamin Botts, eminent lawyers, residents of Richmond, and the celebrated Luther Martin, of Maryland, were the counsel of Burr. Alexander McRae and George Hay, of Richmond, and the brilliant William Wirt, were associated with Cæsar Rodney, the Attorney-General of the United States, in the prosecution. Colonel Edward Carrington, a distinguished soldier of the Revolution, was foreman of the jury which sat in the case, and which had been formed with much difficulty by repeated venires, summoned from all portions of the State.

So high had been the official position of the accused, and with so much interest was his character and alleged designs invested, and such was the legal talent engaged, that the trial attracted to Richmond distinguished visitors from various portions of the Union, among them the future President, the famous Andrew Jackson, who journeyed from Tennessee on horseback. The result, as is well known, was the acquittal of Burr, but the suspicion of which he was prevailingly the subject, seemed to attend him through the remainder of his life, and utterly blasted all of his cherished hopes for political preferment. He led a precarious existence henceforth, and died in squalor and neglect on Staten Island, New York, September 14, 1836, in the eighty-first year of his age.

By the first marriage of Judge Cabell he had issue three children : Nicholas Carrington, born February 9, 1796, lawyer, died October 13, 1821, unmarried; Louisa Elizabeth, born February 19, 1798, married, May 23, 1820, Harry Carrington, of Charlotte County, Va., died January 8, 1865; Abraham Joseph, M.D., born April 24, 1800, died October, 1831, in Florida, unmarried. Of the issue of his second marriage, Doctors Robert G., and J. Grattan Cabell, distinguished physicians, and

Colonel Henry Coalter Cabell, a gallant officer of artillery in the Confederate Army, in the late war, and a prominent member of the bar, are well-known citizens of Richmond. Another son, Edward Carrington Cabell, at one time a member of Congress, resides in the State of Missouri.

The county of Cabell, formed in 1809 from Kanawha County, was named in honor of Governor Cabell.

JOHN TYLER.

To the golden worth of the subject of the present sketch the great statesman, Henry Clay, publicly bore the following ardent testimony: "I knew the father of the President, Judge Tyler, of the Supreme Court of Virginia, and a purer patriot or a more honest man never breathed the breath of life. I am one of those who hold to the safety which flows from honest ancestors and the purity of blood" (*Congressional Globe*, Vol. VIII, p. 345). Some interesting communications regarding early representatives of the name Tyler in England, and its curious etymological changes, are presented in a correspondence, held in 1852, between President John Tyler and Rev. William Tyler, of Massachusetts, as to their common lineage. It is conjectured there that the first of the name who settled in England was of Norman origin, and accompanied thither William the Conqueror, and assisted him to throw off the Saxon power which went down with Harold, and who was a beneficiary in the parceling out of lands in 1202, under the name of Gilbert *de Tiler*; which, in 1233, was rendered *de Tyler*, then *le Tyler* when the race became more numerous—being represented in Parliament by Thomas le Tyler in 1311—and finally Tyler, a numerous family, including Knights, Baronets, Admirals in the Navy, Members of Parliament and distinguished Divines; but the subject of our sketch, regardless of titles, was prouder of the tradition which declared him a veritable descendant of Wat Tyler, the great blacksmith of English history, who in the reign of Richard II., led the glorious rebellion which forced the reconfirmation of Magna Charta; bearing testimony to his sincerity in the name of his first born son, Wat Henry, called after the two greatest rebels in English history, Wat Tyler and Patrick Henry. The received tradition is that the ancestor of the family in Virginia, Henry Tyler, was one of three brothers from Shropshire, England, the other two settling severally in Massachusetts and Rhode Island. Henry Tyler first appears in the records of Virginia, January 7, 1652, as a patentee of lands in James City County, at "The Middle Plantations," where Williamsburg now stands. He was a man of station and influence. When, after the destruction of the State House at Jamestown by fire, Governor Nicholson, in 1699, removed the seat of government to Middle Plantations, the General Assembly by act laid off the city of Williamsburg, as the new capital, on the lands of Henry Tyler, " Gentleman." He was named with the Governor, Edmund Jenings, Philip Ludwell, Thomas Ballard, Lewis Burwell, Philip Ludwell, Jr., John Page, James Whaley and Benjamin Harrison, Jr., trustees and directors to carry the same into effect. He retained lands for the site of a residence for himself, adjoining the Governor's "palace," and was on terms of friendship with Governor Nicholson. Henry Tyler served as sheriff of York County, and died in 1710, leaving with other issue two sons, Francis and John. The latter settled in James City County; was a vestryman of Bruton parish; married Elizabeth Tyler, and died about 1737, leaving issue a daughter, Joanna, who married Dr. William McKenzie, of an ancient Scotch family; and three sons, John, Henry and William. John Tyler, the eldest son, married Anne, daughter of Dr. Louis Contesse, a Huguenot refugee from religious persecution, and a distinguished physician; he was marshal of the Vice Admiralty Court, and died August 26, 1773, at his ancestral home in James City County, leaving issue: Elizabeth, who married John Greenhow; Rachel, who married, first, William Drummond, and secondly, Colonel Stith Hardyman, of Charles City County; Louis Contesse; Anne Contesse, who married Dr. Anthony Tucker Dixon, and Joanna, who married Major Wood Bouldin, of Charlotte County. Of the above, John Tyler, the subject of this sketch, was born February 28, 1747. He entered the grammar school of William and Mary College, in the eighth year of his age, and graduated from the college in due course. He then studied law for five years in the office of Robert Carter Nicholas, in Williamsburg. Jefferson, four years his senior in age, was a student there, also, at the same time, with George Wythe. Alike devoted to popular right, and both lovers of the fiddle, as many other eminent Virginians have been, there was early cemented between these ardent youths a friendship which endured with their lives. Together they tested their musical skill, to the discomfiture of the future author of the Declaration of Independence, who so envied the bow arm of young Tyler, that he declared were that arm his own he would yield to no man living in the excellence of his performance. Together they listened to Patrick Henry, the "forest born Demosthenes," in his famous philippic against George III., with like enkindling emotions. So earnestly were the sympathies of young Tyler enlisted in the cause of colonial rights, and so outspoken were his sentiments, that they led him into contentions with his father, to whose loyal sensibilities such utterances were all but impious. His remonstrances being futile, he would dubiously shake his head and depreciatingly say to his rebellious son: "Ah, John! they will hang you yet! They will hang you yet!" Mr. Tyler, having been duly licensed, for a time practiced his profession in James City, but in 1772 removed to Charles City, probably as offering a less crowded field to a young aspirant, but there was another reason amply alluring. In a MS. volume of poetical essays by him, still extant, there are some lines, dated 1774, in which the charms of a daughter of the "County of Presidents," are glowingly portrayed. This lady, Mary, the daughter of Robert Armistead (a descendant from William D'Armstadt of Hesse, who settled in Virginia about 1650), at the age of sixteen became the wife of John Tyler, in 1776, at "Weyanoke," the seat of Colonel Samuel Harwood, on James River. The mother of Mrs. Tyler was the daughter of Colonel Samuel Shield, a worthy representative of a family of sterling virtues.

At a meeting of the freeholders of Charles City County, held December 17, 1774, Benjamin Harrison was appointed chairman of a committee consisting of John Tyler, William Acrill, Francis Eppes, Samuel Harwood, David Minge, John Edloe and some others, who were charged with the duty of looking to the observance of the regulations of an association lately recommended to Congress, to prevent the use of merchandise shipped from Great Britain and Ireland. The march in April, 1775, of Patrick Henry, to recover the powder removed by Dunmore from the magazine at Williamsburg, kindled the martial spirit of the colonists to fiercest heat. They were everywhere eager to rush to the standard of Henry. Tyler, at the head of a company from Charles City County, was among the first to thus organize, but the ready indemnity offered by the terrified Dunmore, gave him no opportunity for immediate service. On September 11th following, deputies from the district of which Charles City was a county, assembled at Williamsburg, to take into consideration the military aspect of affairs. A battalion was resolved on with the following officers: Colonel, Champion Travis; Lieutenant-Colonel, Hugh Nelson; Major, Samuel Harwood; and of one of two companies from Charles City, John Tyler was made captain. But the abilities of Mr. Tyler were needed in another sphere. He was appointed by the Virginia Convention, July 5, 1776, one of the judges of the High Court of Admiralty. In the spring of 1778, he was called by the voice of Charles City, to represent it in the House of Delegates, of which body he was Speaker from 1781 to 1786. In this body also he moved, and secured the passage of the bill which convened the famous Assembly at Annapolis, Maryland, in 1786, and which, not having a quorum from the several States, adjourned to meet at Philadelphia the year following, and there framed the new Federal Constitution.

In the year 1780 he was appointed a member of the Council of State. A reminiscence of his experience in this station, which would have aptly illustrated the preceding sketch of Patrick Henry, still deserves preservation here. In May, 1781, Mr. Tyler was in attendance upon the Assembly, which, as already narrated in the sketch of Thomas Jefferson, had adjourned before British pursuit to Charlottesville. Thither the noted Colonel Tarleton followed them with his regiment, with the intention of capturing the leading members. Receiving through one Jewett, by dint of hard riding, the appalling intelligence, the fugitive legislators betook themselves again to their saddles. Late in the day Patrick Henry, John Tyler, Benjamin Harrison, and Colonel William Christian, who had fled together, fatigued and hungry, stopped their horses at the door of a small hut in a gorge of the Blue Ridge, and asked for refreshments. A woman, the sole occupant of the hut, inquired of them who they were, and where from. "We are members of the Legislature," said Mr. Henry, "and have just been compelled to leave Charlottesville on account of the approach of the enemy." "Ride on, then, ye cowardly knaves," replied the old woman, violently indignant; "here my husband and sons have just gone to Charlottesville to fight for ye, and you are running away with all your might. Clear out; ye shall have nothing here." "But," Mr. Henry rejoined, in an expostulating tone, "we were obliged to fly. It would not do for the Legislature to be broken up by the enemy. Here is Mr. Speaker Harrison; you don't think he would have fled had it not been necessary?" "I always thought a great deal of Mr. Harrison till now," the old woman answered; "but he'd no business to run from the enemy," and she was about to shut the door in their faces. "Wait a moment, my good woman," again interposed Mr. Henry; "you would hardly believe that Mr. Tyler or Colonel Christian would take to flight if there were not good cause for so doing?" "No, indeed, that I wouldn't," she replied. "But Mr. Tyler and Colonel Christian are here," said he. "They here! Well, I never could have thought it," and she stood a moment as if in doubt, but finally added, "No matter; we love those gentlemen, and I didn't suppose they would ever run from the British; but since they have, they shall have nothing to eat in my house. You may ride along." As a last resort, Mr. Tyler then stepped forward and said: "What would you say, my good woman, if I would tell you that Patrick Henry fled with the rest of us?" "Patrick Henry! I would tell ye that there wasn't a word of truth in it," she answered, angrily; "Patrick Henry would never do such a cowardly thing." "But this *is* Mr. Henry," rejoined Mr. Tyler, pointing him out. The old woman was manifestly astounded. After a moment's consideration, and a convulsive twitch or two at her apron string, by way of recovering her scattered thoughts, she said: "Well, then, if that's Patrick Henry, *it must be all right.* Come in, and ye shall have the best I have in the house."

Perhaps, says Abeel, in his life of President Tyler, from which the above is extracted, no higher compliment was ever paid to the patriotism of Patrick Henry than this simple tribute, expressive of the sentiment with which he was regarded by the people of Virginia. Throughout the Revolution Mr. Tyler devoted himself unceasingly and untiringly to its success. A bold, free, and elegant speaker, his voice was never silent when it could avail aught for the great cause in which he was enlisted. In 1786 Mr. Tyler was again appointed a Judge of the Court of Admiralty, and was consequently a member of the first Court of Appeals of the State. He was appointed a Judge of the General Court in 1788, and served in this capacity until December 1, 1808, when he was elected Governor of Virginia. From the last station he was called, by the appointment of Mr. Madison, to the judgeship of the District Court of the United States for Virginia; which office he held until his death at his seat, "Greenway," in Charles City County, January 6, 1813 —the period of the second war with Great Britain. As a judge, the first prize case—the capture of the privateer Globe—was passed upon by him, and so ardent was his individuality as a Republican, that his repeated utterance on the fatal bed of sickness is memorable: "My only regret," he would feebly say, "is, that I can not live long enough to see that proud English nation once more humbled by American arms." The eminent Daniel Call, in his *Reports* (Vol. IV, p. 23), says of Mr. Tyler: "In all his public situations he maintained an independence of character which was highly honorable to him. * * * He was very attentive to young lawyers upon their first coming to the bar; and did every thing in his power to put them at ease and inspire them with confidence. His conversation was familiar, his heart benevolent, and his friendship sincere."

Mr. Tyler left three sons, Wat Henry, a skilled and popular physician of Hanover County, Virginia; John, 10th President of the United States; and William; and five daughters, Anne Contesse, married the learned James Semple, long the Judge of the General Court of Virginia, and Professor of Law at William and Mary College; Elizabeth, married John Clayton Pryor, of Gloucester county; Maria Henry, married John Boswell Seawell, of Gloucester county; Martha Jefferson, married Thomas Gunols Waggaman, of Maryland, a brother of United States Senator Waggaman, of Louisiana, and Christiana, who became the wife of Dr. Henry Curtis, an accomplished and highly successful physician and surgeon of "Puccoon," Hanover County, Virginia, who was of the same lineage as the distinguished New England family of that name, both deriving from Sir Henry Curtis of England.

Of the person of Governor Tyler the writer has been furnished the following description by a grandson, Lyon G. Tyler, Esq., of Richmond, Va., who has recently prepared for publication a meritorious account of his progenitors—the President and the Governor—*The Life and Letters of the Tylers:* "Governor Tyler did not exceed five feet ten inches in stature. He was lightly built and somewhat round-shouldered. His complexion was fair, nose aquiline, hair brown, inclining to auburn, and eyes light blue."

There is an expressive portrait of Governor Tyler in the State Library at Richmond, which seemingly denotes the virtues and characteristics which so adorned his life.

The County of Tyler, formed, in 1814, from Ohio County, commemorates the name of Governor Tyler.

GEORGE WILLIAM SMITH.

The familiar patronymic Smith has been most worthily represented in Virginia from its settlement. The capital figure in the line, doughty Captain John Smith, "the father of the Colony," however, returned a bachelor to England. The next prominent representative of the name in the annals of "ye Ancient Dominion," is Major Lawrence Smith, who was designated by the Assembly, in 1674, as the "chiefe commander" of a "ffort" to be built near the falls of Rappahannock River, and to be garrisoned by "one hundred and eleven men out of Gloucester County." This fort was built in 1676, and in April, 1679, Major Lawrence Smith and Captain William Byrd were allowed to seat lands at the head of Rappahannock and James Rivers. Major Larkin Smith was a gallant officer of the Revolution, and the same name was meritoriously represented in the war of 1812, and also in the recent great internecine strife. John Augustine Smith, M. D., distinguished author and president of William and Mary College, 1814–26, and subsequently, for a lengthy period, lecturer on anatomy in the College of Physicians, New York, was a native of Virginia, and a graduate of William and Mary College in 1800. Governor William Smith, statesmen, and Major-General of the Confederate States Army, of whom due notice anon, should not be forgotten here. Major Lawrence Smith, as above, it is thought due investigation will establish as the original ancestor in Virginia of the subject of our sketch. His immediate progenitor was Merewether Smith, born about the year 1730, at the family seat, "Bathurst," in Essex County, Virginia, and whose Christian name is indicative of descent from another worthy line. The mother of Merewether Smith was a daughter of Launcelot Bathurst, a patentee of nearly 8,000 acres of land in New Kent County, Virginia, in 1683, and who is said to have been of the family of the Earl of Bathurst, whose arms are: Sa. two bars ermine in chief, three crosses pattie or. *Crest*, a dexter arm embowed; habited in mail, holding in the hand all ppr. a spiked club or. Launcelot Bathurst was "learned in the law," and the records of Henrico evidence that he was appointed August 1, 1684, by Edmund Jenings, the Attorney-General for the Colony, his deputy for the said county. The name Bathurst appears as a continuously favored Christian name in the Stith, Buckner, Jones, Skelton, Smith, Randolph, Hinton and other families. Merewether Smith married twice: first, about 1760, Alice, daughter of Philip Lee, third in de-

THE CHAIR OF THE SPEAKER
of the House of Burgesses of the Colony of Va.

scent from the emigrant Richard Lee, and widow of Thomas Clarke; and, secondly, September 29, 1769, Elizabeth, daughter of Colonel William Dangerfield, of Essex County, member of the House of Burgesses in 1758. Merewether Smith served Virginia with zeal and distinction through a long series of years and in important stations. He appears as a signer to the articles of the Westmoreland Association, of February 27, 1766, which, in opposition to the odious Stamp Act, was pledged to use no articles of British importation, and on May 18, 1769, was a signer also of the resolutions of the Williamsburg Association, which met at the old Raleigh Tavern, in that city, and who bound themselves to abstain from the use of the proscribed British merchandise, and to "promote and encourage industry and frugality, and discourage all luxury and extravagance." In 1770 he represented Essex County in the House of Burgesses. He was a member of the Conventions of 1775 and 1776, and family tradition affirms that in the latter body he prepared the first drafts of both of the noble instruments, the Bill of Rights and the Constitution, which were offered by George Mason. It is stated that the late President John Tyler was in possession of documentary evidence, derived from his father, Governor John Tyler, substantiating the claim, but which Lyon Gardiner Tyler, Esq., the son of the President, thinks was destroyed by a casualty during the late war. The original drafts, it is said, were in the possession of the grandson of Merewether Smith, the late John Adams Smith, cashier of the Farmers' Bank, at Richmond, and having been deposited by him for safe keeping in the vault of the bank, were destroyed in its burning, April 3, 1865, incident upon the evacuation of Richmond. Merewether Smith was a representative of Virginia in the Continental Congress, from 1778 to 1782. He represented Essex County in the House of Delegates, in 1786 and 1787, and in 1788 was a member of the Convention which ratified the Federal Constitution. He died January 25, 1790; his wife, Mrs. Elizabeth Smith, surviving him, died January 24, 1794. They were both buried at "Bathurst." George William Smith, the issue of the first marriage of his father, was born at "Bathurst" about 1762. He married February 7, 1793, Sarah, fourth daughter of Colonel Richard Adams, the elder, a member of the Convention of 1776, an ardent patriot throughout the Revolution, and one of the most enterprising, public spirited, wealthy and influential citizens of Richmond. Colonel Adams was a large property holder, and the Assembly seriously considered for a time the erection of the State capitol upon a site on Richmond Hill owned by him and proffered as a gift to the State.

In 1794 George William Smith represented the county of Essex in the House of Delegates. Soon thereafter he made Richmond his residence, and in the practice of his profession of the law speedily took high rank and enjoyed a lucrative practice. He represented the city in the legislature from 1802 to 1808 inclusive, and in 1810 was appointed a member of the State Council, and as senior member of that body, or

Lieutenant-Governor, upon the resignation of Governor James Monroe to accept the position of Secretary of State in the Cabinet of President Madison, succeeded him, December 5, 1811, as the Executive of the State. His term was lamentably brief, he being one of the victims of the memorable calamity, the burning of the Richmond Theater, on Thursday night, December 26th following. The winter had opened with unusual gaiety in Richmond; brilliant assemblies followed each other in quick succession; the theater was sustained by high histrionic talent; the fascinations of the metropolis had drawn thither the young, the beautiful, the gay, and the distinguished from every portion of the state. On the lamentable occasion of the catastrophe the theater was crowded. Six hundred persons, embracing many of the *élite*, the wealthy, the honored, and the influential of the State, had assembled within the frail wooden building. A new drama was to be presented for the benefit of Henry Placide, a favorite actor; and it was to be followed by the pantomime of "The Bleeding Nun," by Monk Lewis, founded on the wild legend of that name. The regular piece had been played; the pantomime had commenced; the curtain had risen upon its second act, when sparks of fire were seen to fall from the scenery on the back part of the stage, and supposed to have been communicated by one of the chandeliers improperly raised. A moment after, Mr. Robertson, one of the actors, ran forward, and waving his hand towards the ceiling, called aloud, "The house is on fire!" His voice carried a thrill of horror through the assembly. All rose and pressed wildly to the doors of the building. The spectators in the pit escaped without difficulty; the passage leading from it to the outer exit was broad, and had those in the boxes descended by the pillars many would have been saved. Some who were thrown down by violence were thus preserved. But the crowd from the boxes pressed into the lobbies, and it was here, among the refined and the lovely, that the scene became the most appalling. The building was soon wrapped in flames; volumes of dense vapor penetrated every part and produced suffocation; the fire leaping with awful rapidity encircled with flame those nearest to it, and piercing shrieks rose above the sound of the mass of frantic human beings struggling for life. The weak were trampled under foot, and strong men in the desperation of fear passed over the heads of all before them, in their way towards the doors or windows of the theater. The windows even of the upper lobby were sought; many who sprang from them perished by the fall; many were seen with garments on fire as they descended, and died soon afterwards from their injuries; few who were saved by this means escaped entirely unhurt. But in the midst of terrors which roused the selfishness of human nature to its utmost strength, there were displays of love in death which invoke profound sensibility. Fathers were seen rushing back into the flames to save their children, mothers were calling in frenzied tones for their daughters, and were with difficulty dragged from the building; husbands and wives and lovers refused to leave each other, and met death together; even friends sacrificed their lives in endeavoring to save those under their care. The fate of Lieutenant James Gibbon, of the United States Navy, a son of the hero of the "forlorn hope" at Stony Point, and his betrothed bride, the lovely Miss Conyers, who died interlocked in the embrace of each other, was most touching. Governor Smith had reached a place of safety without the burning building, but returning to the rescue of his little son, John Adams, already mentioned, and who had been separated from him by the throng, he became a victim. Benjamin Botts, an eminent lawyer and the father of the late statesman John Minor Botts, had gained the door, but his wife was left behind. Hastily returning to save her, they both perished. Seventy persons are known to have perished in this horrible holocaust, but it was thought that the victims were much more numerous from among the many strangers present. Richmond was shrouded in mourning; hardly a family had escaped affliction from among its members, connections, or friends. And the stroke was not felt alone at home, but fell upon hearts far from the immediate scene of the catastrophe. Indeed, the horror quite sped the globe, and the clergy of varying creeds alike vented it as a thunderbolt of God's manifest displeasure at such and like exhibitions and exemplifications of the sinfulness of worldly and pleasure-loving flesh—to a whilom damning of the noble drama. On the 30th of December, intelligence of the calamity was communicated to the Senate of the United States, and a resolution adopted that the Senators would wear crape on the left arm for a month. A similar resolution was adopted in the House of Representatives, having been introduced in a feeling address by the Hon. William Dawson, of Virginia. The Monumental Church (Episcopal), a handsome octagonal edifice, was erected in 1812 upon the site of the ill-fated theater. The remains of the unfortunate victims are buried in the portico of the church, beneath a marble monument inscribed with their names. A son of the late John Adams and Lucy (Williams) Smith, and grandson of Governor Smith, Bathurst L. Smith, Esq., is a prominent merchant of Memphis, Tennessee.

PEYTON RANDOLPH.

Upon the lamentable death of Governor George William Smith, in the burning of the Richmond Theater, December 26, 1811, Peyton Randolph, the senior member of the Council of State, was the acting executive of Virginia until January 3d, following, when, by election of the Assembly, then in session, James Barbour, of Orange County, was inaugurated as Governor.

VIRGINIA AND VIRGINIANS.

Peyton Randolph, the son of Governor Edmund Randolph, graduated from William and Mary College in 1798. Inheriting the genius of his progenitors in successive generations, he became early distinguished in the practice of his chosen profession of law. In 1821 he became the reporter of the Supreme Court of Virginia, but in the midst of his increasing usefulness, with the most brilliant prospects before him, he fell in the prime of manhood, a victim to pulmonary disease, dying at Richmond, December 26, 1828, widely lamented by numerous friends to whom his virtues and worth had endeared him. His successor as reporter was the eminent Benjamin Watkins Leigh. The result of Mr. Randolph's labors—"Report of Cases argued and determined in the Court of Appeals of Virginia, 1821–1828," were published in 6 volumes, 8vo, Richmond, 1823–1832. A son of Mr. Randolph, Edmund Randolph, died in California during our late war.

JAMES BARBOUR.

The Barbour family of Virginia, it is claimed, is of Scottish origin, and to be of the lineage of John Barbour,* one of the earliest Scotch poets and historians; archdeacon of Aberdeen as early as 1357, and who died in 1396. A national work of his, still extant, called *The Bruce*, is a metrical chronicle of the warlike deeds of Robert the First (1306–1329) in his efforts for the independence of his beloved country. Barbour also composed another book, setting forth the genealogical history of the kings of Scotland, and deducing their origin from the Trojan colony of Brutus. He was a favorite author with Sir Walter Scott, who frequently quotes his lines, which are remarkable, also, for their intelligibility to the modern reader. In the Land Records of Virginia the name of William Barber appears as a patentee of lands in Hampton parish, York County, May 6, 1651. William Barber speedily became a man of mark and influence, since in 1656 he is found again as a patentee with the title of Lieutenant-Colonel or County-Lieutenant of York. In October, 1660, the Governor, Sir William Berkeley, with Colonel William Barber,† Colonel Gerard Fowke, Colonel Kendall, Thomas Warren, Rawleigh Traverse, and Thomas Lucas were the superintendents for the erection of the State House at Jamestown. There are subsequent grants of land in Rappahannock County to William and to Richard Barber. Thomas Barbar appears as a patentee in New Kent County in 1714. William Barber was a Burgess from York County in 1718, and Charles Barber from Richmond County in 1723. But the definite ancestor of the subject of our sketch was James

---

* His name is also variously rendered, Barber, Barbere, and Barbar.
† Tradition accredits William Barber as a son of the Baron of Mulderg.

Barbour,* who appears as a grantee of lands in St. George's parish, Spottsylvania County, June 26, 1731, and again, in 1733, of lands in St. Mark's parish in the same county. He was one of the first vestrymen of this latter parish, at its organization at Germanna, in 1731, and served in that office until the division of the parish in 1740, which threw him into the new parish of St. Thomas, in Orange County, in which division he lived. Among his children was James Barbour, who represented the county of Culpeper in the House of Burgesses in 1764, was colonel and commander-in-chief of the militia of the county in 1775, and was the father of Mordecai, Thomas, Richard, and Gabriel Barbour, the last three of whom emigrated to Kentucky. Mordecai Barbour married a daughter of John Strode, of "Fleetwood," Culpeper County, and was the father of the late Hon. John Strode Barbour, statesman and lawyer, and grandfather of Hon. John Strode Barbour, a present representative of Virginia in the National House of Representatives, and whose material and political services to the State have gained him enduring regard. Thomas Barbour, another son of James Barbour, the settler in what is now Orange County, was a member of the House of Burgesses in 1769, when it issued the first protest against the Stamp Act. He was again a Burgess in 1775, and was a member of the "Committee of Public Safety," of Orange County, in the same year. He married Isabella Thomas, granddaughter of Philip Pendleton.† Their third son was the Hon. Philip Pendleton Barbour, Speaker of Congress and of the Virginia Convention of 1829–30, and a Justice of the United States Supreme Court. He married Frances Todd, daughter of Benjamin Johnson, Burgess, of Orange County, and had issue: Philippa, married Judge Richard H. Field; Elizabeth, married John J. Ambler, of "Jacqueline Hall," Madison County; Thomas, M. D., married Catharine Strother; Edmund Pendleton, married Harriet, daughter of Colonel John Stuart, of King George County; Quintus, married Mary, daughter of James Somerville, of Culpeper County; Sextus, and Septimus. Justice Barbour died in 1841, and his wife, aged eighty-five, in April, 1872. James Barbour, the subject of this sketch, the fourth son of Thomas Barbour, was born in Orange County, June 10, 1775. His

* The name is rendered Barber in the State Land Records, and from a seal ring lately in the possession of the family, the arms displayed were those of the family of Staffordshire, England: Gules, three mullets argent, within a bordure ermine. *Crest*—A passion cross on three steps, gules. The motto, *Nihilo nisi cruce*, seems to indicate an origin in the days of the Crusaders.

† Philip Pendleton, grandson of Henry Pendleton, of Norwich, England, and whose descendants include the names of Clayton, Taylor ("John Taylor, of Carolina," a grandson), Gaines, Strother, Ragland, Browning, Beverley, Byrd, Dudley, Burk, Ellis, Slaughter, Hoge, Shackleford, Williams, Spotswood, and others equally worthy.

education was limited, and chiefly obtained while he was acting as a deputy sheriff, but his tutor for a time was the celebrated James Waddell, commemorated as the "Blind Preacher," by William Wirt, in his *British Spy*. James Barbour entered the service of the State at the age of twenty-four years, as a member of the memorable Assembly of 1799. His colleague from the county of Orange was James Madison (afterwards President of the United States), and he looked forward with eager expectancy to a conflict in debate of that able intellect with Patrick Henry, also a member elect of the Assembly. But he was disappointed in the death of the great orator of the Revolution, in June, 1799, before the body convened. James Barbour participated in every debate, ably vindicated the famous resolutions of Mr. Madison, and was the proposer of the anti-duelling law—one of the most stringent and effective legislative acts ever passed. While still a member of the Assembly, he was elected by it, January 3, 1811, Governor of Virginia, to succeed George William Smith, who was one of the victims of the awful burning of the Richmond Theater, on the 26th of December preceding. The administration of James Barbour, covering the important period of the second conflict with Great Britain, was signally able, vigilant, and patriotic. He was emphatically the "War Governor," and in pledging his personal means to sustain the credit of Virginia, takes honorable rank with Governor Thomas Nelson, of the Revolution.

Virginia nobly demeaned herself in the War of 1812. Many of her sons highly distinguished themselves in the combats by sea and land, and she suffered from the invasion of the enemy. In May, 1813, Admiral Cockburn with a British fleet entered Chesapeake Bay, and commenced a series of depredations on private property, which far eclipsed those which had made the name of Dunmore infamous in the War of Independence. An English fleet of four line-of-battle ships with twelve frigates was collected in the bay, near the capes and Lynhaven Bay. They carried a large land force under Sir Sydney Beckwith, the naval commander being Admiral Warren. They were closely watched from Norfolk and Hampton. The harbor of Norfolk was chiefly defended by the armament of Mr. Jefferson's famous "Gunboat System," but for the threatened emergency, large bodies of militia, from the upper counties of the State, had been ordered to the seaboard. Unused to the malaria of the summer season in lower Virginia, a large number of them were prostrated with sickness and many of them died. General Robert Barraud Taylor, of the State line, commanded the military district, and Commodore Cassin, of the United States Navy, directed the sea defences. On the 20th of June, the advance of the English frigate "Junon," upon Norfolk, was gallantly checked by our immature American Navy. Some movements on the following day among the British shipping, which had moved near Newports News, seemed to indicate an early attack upon Craney Island, near the mouth of Elizabeth River, and which commands the approach from Hampton Roads to Norfolk. Its defence was therefore all-important. The forces on the island consisted of about 400 infantry of the line, 50 riflemen from Winchester, under Captain Roberts, 91 artillery in two companies, one from Portsmouth, Captain Arthur Emerson, and the other from one of the upper counties, commanded by Captain Richardson; the whole force being under the command of Lieutenant-Colonel H. Beatty, assisted by Major Wagner of the infantry, and Major Faulkner of the artillery service. Of this force 43 were on the sick-list. On the evening of the 21st, they were reinforced by order of General Taylor, by Captain Pollard of the United States Army, with 30 of his company from Fort Norfolk; Lieutenant Atkinson from Culpeper County, with 30 volunteers of the militia of Isle of Wight County, and by 150 seamen and marines, under Lieutenants Neale, Shubrick and Saunders, from the frigate "Constellation," Captain Tarbell. On the morning of the 22d, the enemy landed about 2,500 troops, under Sir Sydney Beckwith, with the view to approach from the west side of the island, across the water in that direction, which at low water was passable by infantry. Soon after they landed, there approached about 50 boats filled with men, which directed their course to the north side of the island. Here two twenty-four-pounders and four six-pounders had been advantageously posted by Major Faulkner. These were gallantly and effectively served by Captain Emerson and Lieutenants Parke G. Howle and Godwin, aided by Lieutenant Neale and his command. A galling fire was opened upon the approaching foe, and the guns were trained with such fatal precision that five of their barges were sunk, and one of them literally cut in twain. The other boats hauled off in discomfiture and the valorous Virginians had to speedily succor the drowning wretches thus left struggling in the water. Admiral Warren's own barge, the "Centipede," 52 feet long, and working 24 oars, stranded and was taken with 22 men, a brass pounder and numbers of small arms. In the meanwhile the landed detachments were attempting to cross the narrow inlet in front of the battery, but were grievously harassed at long shot, and when they came nearer the havoc was so fearful that they precipitately retreated. So eager were the Virginians for the fray, that the Winchester riflemen pursued the foe into the water, hoping to reach them with their bullets. The loss of the enemy was fully 200, besides the prisoners named, and 50 deserters, whilst on the American side not a man was lost. In transmitting the report of Colonel Beatty to the Secretary of War, General Taylor justly remarks of this brilliant feat: "The courage and constancy with which this inferior force, in the face of a formidable naval armament, not only sustained a position in which nothing was complete, but repelled the enemy with considerable loss, can not fail to command

ALEXANDER SPOTSWOOD,
Governor of Virginia.
From a copy in oil, in the State Library of Virginia.

the approbation of their government and the applause of their country," and adds: "It has infused into the residue of the army a general spirit of competition, the beneficial effects of which will, I trust, be displayed in our future conflicts." The heroic defence of Craney Island filled the enemy with rage and shame. They abandoned their designs upon Norfolk, and Hampton was the next point of attack, led by Cockburn in person, on the 25th of June. Invested with the small force of 400 artillery and infantry, under Major Stapleton Crutchfield, he was unable to withstand the furious assault of a foe, by sea and land, ten times his number. The enemy took possession of Hampton and committed the most revolting deeds. A wanton destruction of private property took place, and the degraded soldiery and the negro slaves, who had been enticed from their owners, were allowed to riot in every species of brutality. The militia of the country, however, collecting in formidable numbers for an attack, the British evacuated the town on the 27th of June, and soon after the invading fleet left the Chesapeake, and prepared for a descent upon North Carolina. It is noteworthy that the patriotic ladies of the city of Richmond, early in 1812, contributed, by the sale of their jewels, towards the building and equipping of a vessel of war called the "First Attempt," the command of which was given to Captain Isbon Benedict.

In 1815, Mr. Barbour was elected by the Virginia Assembly to the United States Senate, and served continuously for ten years, until 1825. In this body he took an important part in the discussion on the Missouri question, and his speeches on the abolition of imprisonment for debt elicited great applause and commendation throughout the Union. He was chairman of the committee on foreign affairs, the District of Columbia and other important committees, and frequently President *pro tem.* of the Senate. In 1825, upon the invitation of President John Quincy Adams, he became a member of his cabinet, as Secretary of War, and served in that capacity until May 26, 1828, when he was appointed Envoy Extraordinary and Minister Plenipotentiary to Great Britain. His brief sojourn in England was a season of unalloyed pleasure to him. The bitterness of the (then) recent conflict between the two countries had measurably passed away, and Great Britain was beginning to cherish a sentiment of pride in the lusty Republic, which she had long regarded as a rebellious child of her own. James Barbour was everywhere received with the utmost cordiality. A commanding physique and noble mien (in which he was, in the estimation of many, the peer of the majestic statesman, Daniel Webster), added to wondrous colloquial powers, in which pathos, humor and eloquence were charmingly blended with a sunny geniality of manner, united in a personal magnetism which claimed the regard of all in every circle which he entered. His ready wit and patriotic impulse were happily exhibited in his reply to the good old Bishop of Bath and

Wells. They were chance companions at a large dinner party, and after some brilliant manifestation of the rare colloquial powers of Mr. Barbour, the good old Bishop naively inquired, "How long, sir, have you been in this country?" "About two months," was the reply. "You astonish me," said the Bishop, "for you speak the English language remarkably well, considering your brief sojourn here." "Why, sir," said Mr. Barbour, "I represent a country where we flatter ourselves that we have preserved the English language in greater purity than you have in England." A visit to Mr. Coke of Holkham (subsequently created Earl of Leicester), is referred to in a brief diary kept by Mr. Barbour, as one of rare enjoyment to him. Holkham was a striking manifestation of what agriculture, under the combined influence of skill, capital and perseverance, can accomplish, for these had rendered fertile and bounteously productive, thousands of acres of the sandy lands of Norfolk County, which the merry monarch, Charles the Second, had sarcastically said, was only fit to be cut up into roads for the remainder of his kingdom. Mr. Coke recited to Mr. Barbour many interesting anecdotes relating to the revolt of the American Colonies, at which period he was a Member of Parliament, and was wont, he said, in the greatest throes of the struggle, with Edmund Burke and others, in the luncheon room (with hand over the mouth) to drink "Success to America!" Another reminiscence, recorded by Mr. Barbour, is so remarkable that it is deemed worthy of preservation here. He narrates with manifest satisfaction, that Mr. Coke had the rare privilege and exquisite delight of seeing a vessel launched at Woolwich, which was composed in large part from the timber of trees which he had himself planted when a youth.

Mr. Barbour was recalled by President Jackson, in September, 1829. He now retired to the enjoyments of private life, from which he only again emerged in obedience to the impulses of duty and the claims of friendship. In the Convention for the nomination of President, held at Harrisburg, Pennsylvania, in December, 1839, Mr. Barbour presided. He was brilliantly conspicuous in his advocacy of the claims of General William Henry Harrison, and prominent and effective in the campaign which resulted in his election as President. Soon after this the disease which was ultimately fatal manifested itself. He died at his seat, Barboursville, June 7, 1842, within three days of the anniversary of his birth. Within half an hour of his decease he said to his son, present at his bed-side, "If any thing is put over me, let it be of the plainest granite, with no other claim than this:

"HERE LIES JAMES BARBOUR,
ORIGINATOR OF
THE LITERARY FUND
OF VIRGINIA."

The following reminiscence, with which the present writer has been kindly furnished by the venerable statesman, the Hon. Alexander H. H. Stuart, Staunton, Virginia, evidences the just esteem in which Mr. Barbour was held by those who were favored in the opportunity to know his worth. Mr. Stuart writes: "In the greater part of my service in Congress, from 1841 to 1843, I was a member of the Committee on Foreign Affairs, of which John Quincy Adams was chairman. During the warm season of the year, Mr. Adams was in the habit of going, immediately after breakfast, to the committee room, which was a spacious and airy apartment in the upper story of the southern wing of the Capitol, where he occupied himself in writing until the committee assembled. As my family were with me, I also found it convenient to go at an early hour to the committee room, to examine my morning mail and to reply to such letters as required prompt attention. In this way it happened that Mr. Adams and I met in the committee room almost every day, an hour or two before the time appointed for the meeting of the committee. And, as it not unfrequently occurred that the other members of the committee failed to attend, Mr. Adams and I were the only occupants of the room from eight to twelve o'clock. This close association often led to very interesting conversation between us in regard to the early political history of our country, and the statesmen who bore a prominent part in it. In these interviews I always found Mr. Adams exceedingly affable, and I need hardly add, interesting and instructive. On one occasion, on entering the room, with my newspapers and letters in my hand, I found Mr. Adams sitting at the table engaged in writing. Not wishing to interrupt him, after exchanging salutations with him, I withdrew to a window to look over my morning mail. I was shocked to see, in the Richmond papers, the announcement of the death of my venerable and honored friend Governor James Barbour. With some strong ejaculation expressive of surprise and grief, I announced the fact to Mr. Adams, who seemed as painfully impressed by the news as I had been. Without uttering a word, he pushed back the papers which were before him, and folding his arms on the table, rested his head on them for some time, as if lost in thought. Then slowly raising his head, he turned his face toward me, and in a voice tremulous with emotion, said: 'Mr. Stuart, I have been connected with this government, in one way or another, almost from its foundation to the present hour. I have known personally nearly all the great men who have been connected with its administration, and I can safely say that I have rarely known a wiser, and never a better man than James Barbour.' Such a noble tribute, coming fresh and spontaneously from the heart of its illustrious author, made an impression on my mind which can never be erased, especially as my own relations to Governor Barbour enabled me to recognize and appreciate its justice. On other occasions I have heard Mr. Adams speak in the most cordial terms of Mr. Barbour, and refer to incidents which occurred while he was Secretary of War in Mr. Adams' administration, which illustrated his integrity and manly independence of character." In an "Eulogium upon the Life and Character of James Madison," by Mr. Barbour, 8vo, Washington, 1836, the paternal affection in which the illustrious subject ever held the reverential eulogist is touchingly manifested. A like dutiful tribute was rendered to the exalted worth of Mr. Barbour by his warm personal friend, Hon. Jeremiah Morton, but the writer has been unable to obtain a copy of it.

Mr. Barbour married, October 29, 1792, Lucy, daughter of Benjamin Johnson, of Orange County, a member of the House of Burgesses. The surviving issue of this congenial marriage are: Hon. Benjamin Johnson Barbour, of Barboursville, Virginia, born June 14, 1821, and married, November 17, 1844, Caroline Homoesel, daughter of Dr. George Watson, a distinguished physician of Richmond, Virginia. Mr. Barbour inherits the rare gifts of his eminent father in a marked degree, and is a gentleman of profound culture. His addresses, historical, literary, political, and agricultural, on various occasions, are alike chaste and felicitous. In 1865 he was elected to the United States Congress, but the representatives of unreconstructed Virginia were not allowed in that year to take their seats.

Lucy, daughter of Governor Barbour, married, in 1822, John Seymour Taliaferro, who was, unhappily, drowned in 1830. Another daughter, Frances Cornelia Barbour, is the wife of William Hardy Collins, a distinguished lawyer of Baltimore, Maryland.

A portrait of Governor Barbour is in the attractive gallery of the governors and distinguished men of Virginia in the State Library at Richmond. Barbour County, now in West Virginia, formed in 1843 from the counties of Harrison, Lewis, and Randolph, perpetuates the name of the distinguished Barbour family.

WILSON CARY NICHOLAS.

The ancestry of Wilson Cary Nicholas embraces several of the most worthily represented families in the Old Dominion. The founder of the distinguished Nicholas family of Virginia was Dr. George Nicholas,*

---

* The arms of the family, as given the writer, appear to be those of the families of London, Ashton-Keynes, and Ryndway, County Witts, England, as follows: Az. a chev. engr. betw. three owls or. *Crest*—On a chapeau az. (another gu.) turned up erm. an owl with wings expanded or.

of County Lancaster, England, a surgeon in the British Navy, who settled in the Colony about the beginning of the eighteenth century, and married, about 1722, Elizabeth, widow of Major Nathaniel Burwell, and daughter of Robert "King" Carter. Their issue was: Robert Carter, born about 1723; John, married Martha, daughter of Colonel Joshua Fry; and George Nicholas. Robert Carter Nicholas, statesman, jurist, and patriot, familiarly known as Treasurer Nicholas in colonial annals, from having long and honorably filled that important office, married, in 1754, Anne, daughter of Colonel Wilson and Sarah (Blair —grandniece of the Commissary) Cary (second in descent from Colonel Myles Cary, the emigrant ancestor of the family in Virginia, who was born in Bristol, England, in 1620; died in Virginia, June 10, 1667, and was fourth in descent from William Cary, Mayor of Bristol in 1546, and who lineally descended from Adam de Kari, Lord of Castle Cary, in Somerset, in 1198).† Robert Carter and Anne (Cary) Nicholas had issue five sons and three daughters: John, married Anne Lawson; member of Congress 1793–1801, removed to Geneva, New York, where he has numerous descendants; George, married the daughter of the Hon. John Smith, of Baltimore, Maryland, and was the father of Judge Samuel Smith Nicholas, who published a masterly plea for the *Habeas Corpus* when it was suspended by President Lincoln, during our late war; Wilson Cary; Lewis; and Philip Norborne Nicholas, many years Attorney-General of Virginia, President of the Farmers' Bank of Richmond, Member of the Virginia Convention of 1829–30, and a Judge of the General Court of Virginia. He was associated with William Wirt and George Hay in an able defence of James Thompson Callender, who was tried in Richmond in May, 1800, before Judge Samuel Chase, of the United States Supreme Court, for publishing a pamphlet entitled "The Prospect before Us," in which the character of President John Adams was infamously libelled. The prosecuting attorney was Thomas Nelson, son of General Thomas Nelson, Jr., of the Revolution. The zeal of Judge Chase in directing the prosecution subjected him to the charge of having transcended his powers, and occasioned his famous trial for impeachment before the United States Senate. Judge Philip Norborne Nicholas was twice married; first, to Mary Spear, of Baltimore, Maryland (and had issue three sons, of whom only one— John Spear Nicholas, of Baltimore, survives); and, secondly, to Maria Carter, daughter of Thomas Taylor and Mary Anne (daughter of William Armistead) Byrd, of Clarke County, Virginia, and granddaughter of the third Colonel William Byrd, of Westover, James River. The issue of the second marriage of Judge Nicholas was Philip Cary (a well known member of the bar of Richmond, and long the efficient

---

† The descendants of Colonel Myles Cary, in the first five generations, intermarried with the Milner, Wills, Wilson, Scarborough, Barbour, Blair, Selden, Whiting, Scarbrook, Jacqueline, Randolph, Bell, Spiers, Fairfax, Nicholas, Taylor, Page, Bolling, Kingcade, Carr, Nelson, Peachy, Curle, Snowden, Herbert, and other families of worth.

librarian of the State Law Library of Virginia), Sydney Smith, and Miss Elizabeth Byrd Nicholas, an accomplished lady, foremost in the art and literary circles of Richmond, and who was a leading originator in the Colonial Court Ball, mentioned in the preceding sketch of Lord Botetourt as having been held in Richmond, February 22, 1876, the pecuniary proceeds of which were patriotically devoted to the furnishing of the Virginia Room in the Mount Vernon mansion. Of the three daughters of Robert Carter and Anne (Cary) Nicholas, Sarah, married John Hatley Norton; Elizabeth, married Governor Edmund Randolph; and Mary, died unmarried. Wilson Cary Nicholas, the subject of this sketch, the third son of Robert Carter and Anne (Cary) Nicholas, was born January 31, 1761, in the city of Williamsburg, Virginia, which continued to be the residence of his father until the opening of the Revolutionary War in 1775, when he removed his family to a country seat, called "The Retreat," in Hanover County, and at which he died in 1780. The year following, Cornwallis, in the route of his invasion of Virginia, stopped at "The Retreat." Mrs. Nicholas, being apprised of the approach of the British troops, had taken the precaution to conceal her plate and jewels in the chimney. One of her children betraying the place of deposit, Lord Cornwallis begged, with a bland smile, that she would give herself no uneasiness as to their fate, and indeed demeaned himself with courtly consideration throughout his brief visit. The visible apprehension of Mrs. Nicholas had a more serious cause of excitement. Her maternal instincts were keenly upon the rack for the fate of her eldest born, John, whose flight under hot chase by the British dragoons, she witnessed through the open door with eager eyes and tumultuous heart. Happily the superior fleetness of his horse enabled him to escape his pursuers. After this intrusion, Mrs. Nicholas, in her unprotected situation, deemed it prudent to remove her residence to Albemarle County, where her husband had purchased an extensive estate on James River. Wilson Cary Nicholas was a student at William and Mary College, which he left in 1779, at the age of eighteen, to enter the army. His gallantry met with deserved promotion, and he was the commander of Washington's Life Guard until its disbandment in 1783, when he returned to Albemarle County and took possession of his estate there, called "Warren." In the same year also he married Margaret, daughter of John Smith, of Baltimore, and the sister of the wife of his brother George. It was a happy union, and Mr. Nicholas was fortunate in the possession of a companion and helpmate who united the gentle graces of womanhood with rare judgment and fine intellectual powers. Sent from Baltimore in early girlhood to avoid the dangers to which a seaport was necessarily subjected in time of war, she was yet cognizant of many of the stirring events of the Revolution. In her place of refuge in Carlisle, Pennsylvania, she was apprised of

the dangers daily incurred by her father as the active chairman of the
Committee of Ways and Means of the State of Maryland. She saw her
three brothers arm in defence of their beloved country, one of them to
return home to die from the effects of a severe winter campaign, and
another as the laurelled defender of Fort Mifflin—and whose subsequent
long, useful, and honored career is instantaneously identified in the historic name of General Samuel Smith, defender of Baltimore in 1812, and
statesman. At Carlisle, too, in her father's family, was the accomplished and hapless Major André domesticated, whilst a prisoner on
parole, and who engaged her childish affections by his many genial
graces, yet she was the patriot even to recognize the necessity of his stern
fate. In her, it is said, "love of country was no mere sentiment. It
was a principle inculcated in early childhood, and fixed by the study
and reflection of riper years. When at the age of eighty she was erroneously informed that her son, Colonel Robert Carter Nicholas, of
Louisiana, had changed his politics, she rose from her chair, and raising
her hand, with her eyes brilliant as in youth, and her voice tremulous
with emotion, said, 'Tell my son, as he values the blessing of his old
mother, never to forsake the faith of his Fathers!'" With such a mother,
such a wife, it is not to be wondered that the distinguishing trait in the
character of Mr. Nicholas was an intense devotion to his country. His
public services commenced in 1784, as the representative of Albemarle
County in the House of Delegates of Virginia. In first offering for their
suffrages he made the acquaintance of every freeholder in the county.
This was done by domiciliary visits which were never repeated, and he
rarely attended the county courts, the ordinary propitiatory hustings
of the aspiring politician. During the legislative sessions of 1784 and
1785 Mr. Nicholas, though so youthful and inexperienced, was zealous
and prominent in the advocacy of the bill securing religious freedom,
and in the suppression of parish vestries, and for the remandment of
the property of the Episcopal Church in glebes, to support of the poor
in the several counties. Drawn by domestic ties, Mr. Nicholas, at the
close of the session of 1785, returned to private life, from which he was
recalled by the strenuous opposition made to the adoption by Virginia
of the Federal Constitution. After a warm contest, he and his brother
George were returned to represent the county of Albemarle in the
Convention of 1788. Mr. Nicholas was conspicuous in his advocacy of
the adoption of the Constitution. He served in the House of Delegates in 1789 and 1790, and again from 1794 to the autumn of 1799,
when he was elected by the Assembly to the United States Senate, in
which body he at once became a leader of the Republican party. In
1801, upon the accession of Mr. Jefferson as President, Mr. Nicholas,
who was his warm personal and confidential friend, zealously and ably
supported his administration. The questions brought before the Senate
at this period were highly important. The new organization of the

LADY SPOTSWOOD,
Wife of Governor Spotswood.
From the original in oil in the State Library of Virginia.

courts and of the financial system, the repeal of the bankrupt law, the amendment of the Constitution as to the election of President and Vice-President, the attempt to make war on Spain, together with many other questions, all highly exciting, were not to be decided in a body where parties were so nearly equally divided, without engendering intemperate discussion and bitterness of feeling. Mr. Nicholas, however, passed through the ordeal of this political cauldron most creditably, in the full confidence of those with whom he acted, and winning the esteem and respect of his opponents. All the measures projected by the Republican party having been accomplished, and the dispute about the right of the deposits at New Orleans adjusted without a war with Spain, by the acquisition of Louisiana, Mr. Nicholas deemed that he might, without any dereliction of duty, resign his seat in the Senate, which he did in 1804. It was a step which the state of his private affairs imperatively demanded, as he had become seriously embarrassed. To the reparation of his fortunes he now devoted himself with great assiduity, his success in agriculture bearing witness to the skill and energy with which his operations were conducted. In 1806 he declined a special mission to France, to ratify, under the auspices of Napoleon, the treaty with Spain. But, in 1807, the necessity of a champion " whose talents and standing taken together would have weight enough to give him the lead " in the National Council, brought on him such urgent appeals to his political convictions and patriotism, that he was forced to yield. He became a candidate for Congress and was elected without opposition. "The period was momentous and highly critical. The aggressions of England in the attack on the 'Chesapeake,' and the extension of the orders of the King in council, and afterwards the application by France of the Berlin and Milan decrees to our commerce, imposed upon us the necessity of resistance. But pursuant to the pacific policy which had governed our councils during a period of most unparalleled aggression on the part of Great Britain, a period extending as far back as 1793, our government proposed an embargo. The government was at that time in a wholly defenceless state. We had but the skeleton of an army, few or no ships in commission, no military stores, with an immense value of property afloat, and our whole seaboard from north to south open to attack." Under these circumstances, Mr. Nicholas united cordially in the support of the embargo, being willing to try its efficacy for awhile as a coercive measure, but relying on it more as giving us time to prepare for other measures. In 1807 he assured his constituents that in the event of the failure of the embargo to produce some speedy change in the policy of France and Great Britain, the only alternative offered was a base and abject submission or a determined resistance. In his printed circular to them, as well as from his seat in Congress, he urged the necessity of raising men and money, and the immediate provision of every requisite of war. In the autumn of 1808 he wrote to Mr. Jefferson, urging him, unless there was a certainty of a favorable change in the affairs of the nation, before the meeting of Congress, to announce to the body in his message, that the great object in laying the embargo had been effected. That nothing more was to be expected from it, and that it should be raised, and other measures which the vindication of the national honor demanded, resorted to; that our people would not much longer submit to the burdensome restrictions of the embargo, and that we could not and ought not to think of abandoning the resistance which we so solemnly pledged to make. In 1809 Mr. Nicholas was re-elected to Congress, and served in the spring session, during which the agreement of our government with Mr. Erskine produced for a time a delusive calm. In the autumn of the same year, on his way to Washington, he experienced so violent an attack of rheumatism, that he was compelled to resign his seat, and was closely confined to his room for a period of four months. He was now so thoroughly convinced of the impracticability of enforcing any commercial restrictions; of their demoralizing influence on the people, and exhausting effect on the finances of the country, that he frequently avowed his intention never again to vote for any similar measure, except as preparatory to war, and for the briefest duration. In the month of December, 1814, the gloomiest period of the war, and when Virginia especially, but the remaining States as well, were chiefly left to their own resources, Mr. Nicholas was elected Governor of the State, an unthankful office, which yet his patriotism would not allow him to decline. The happy announcement of peace in the spring of the following year, gave but little opportunity for the exhibition of administrative capacity, which emergency, with his attested characteristics, would have enlisted. The defence of the State depending chiefly upon the militia, who could not be kept constantly in the field, an appropriation was made by the Assembly to enable him to erect telegraphic stations, and to raise a corps of videttes to be so distributed at his discretion, as to transmit his orders throughout the State with the utmost dispatch possible. But peace rendered needless the carrying into execution this well digested provision.

The great confidence reposed in Governor Nicholas by the State Legislature, was evinced in their enactment, in great haste, at the close of the spring session of 1815, of a statute for the raising of forces for the defence of the State, the execution of which, in almost every particular, was dependent on such instructions as the discretion of the Governor might deem advisable. Loans, which were necessary to equip and pay this force, were provided by the Governor, under terms the most reasonable, with a just condition not originally specified by the Legislature, but which that body, to its honor, duly authorized at its next session. Peace having been declared, every duly audited claim against the State was promptly paid. The militia were discharged in a manner the most gratifying to them. They were fully paid for their term of service, provision was made for their return home, and for the care of the sick until they could be safely removed. All military stores of a perishable nature were sold. The remaining supplies, including tents and other camp equipages, sufficient for an army of ten thousand men, were deposited in the State Arsenals. The closing of the accounts for the expenses of the war, was pushed with all dispatch consistent with the interest of the State, in their after adjustment at Washington with the National Government. It had been the determination of the Governor, in the event of the continuance of the war, to urge all men of talent and ability with whom he might take the liberty, to offer for election to the ensuing Assembly, that the State might have the benefit of their counsel in her time of need. The return of peace did not prevent this application, but the motive was different. Foreseeing that the State would have command of considerable funds, he deemed it to be important that an early effort should be made to induce the Assembly to apply the proceeds to the great purposes of internal improvement and education. This application, it is believed, was not without effect, as in the two succeeding Assemblies there appeared many gentlemen of conspicuous ability, who had not served in the body for some years before. At the commencement of the autumn session of 1815, Governor Nicholas zealously pressed these subjects upon their attention. They were acted upon, and means severally placed at the disposal of the Board of Public Works, and of the President and Directors of the Literary Fund, to be devoted to the respective objects. The foundation was thus laid of systems which have fostered and infused education, as well as expanded the wealth and fructified the material prosperity of the State. Upon a review of the messages of Governor Nicholas, it will be found that most of the objects recommended by him were acted upon by the Legislature, and that they are all strongly marked by an intimate knowledge of the needs and capacity of Virginia. The first act of the second term of the Governor, was an effort to adjust the claims of the Commonwealth against the United States, all previous attempts having proved abortive. After reflection, he devised a plan, which was finally adopted by the Council, and an additional agent being appointed, a speedy adjustment ensued. As the President of the Board of Public Works and of the Literary Fund, Governor Nicholas displayed the industry and wise foresight which uniformly characterized his administration in every department of the Government. In every contract made by him for the State, the utmost economy was observed, and every caution used to protect and conserve the public interest. A remarkable proof of this was given in the execution of a law providing for a complete survey of the State within justifiable limits. This desirable accomplishment he hesitated to authorize in a general contract, fearing that the expense would exceed the provision contemplated. Finally, under specific instructions to the several county courts of the State, the survey was accomplished in districts at an aggregate cost by which fully $100,000 was saved to the State. After the expiration of his second term as Governor, Mr. Nicholas served for a few months as President of the branch of the United States Bank at Richmond. In the spring of 1819 he returned to "Warren," his country-seat.

His constitution had always been delicate, and the physical fatigue and mental anxiety which he had undergone in his later years of public service had seriously impaired his health. A journey on horseback was advised as salutary by his physician. He accordingly thus set out from home, but upon reaching "Montpelier," the residence of ex-President Madison, in Orange County, he found himself too feeble to proceed, and returned to "Tufton," the residence of his son-in-law, Thomas Jefferson Randolph, the grandson of Thomas Jefferson. Here he lingered, each day hoping to be well enough to return to his own home. Mr. Jefferson and Mr. Madison (the latter being then on a visit at "Monticello"), with both of whom his relations had always been of the warmest personal friendship and confidence, visited him frequently, and all was done which affection could suggest for his recovery, but without avail. On the 10th of October, 1820, he suddenly expired whilst in the act of dressing.

The popularity and success of Governor Nicholas were the just results of intrinsic worth and of conscientious purpose. His style in conversation, as well as on the hustings or in debate, was deliberate, sententious, and impressive. It was effective through the justness of his conclusions and the cogency of his reasoning, and borrowed nothing from the meretricious arts of the popular orator, whose devices, indeed, he held in contempt. Though ever ready, at the sacrifice of his private interests, to serve his country, he was singularly modest in his personal claims, and shunned instead of seeking political preferment. The successive positions occupied by Mr. Monroe, previous to his election as President, and which proved the stepping-stones to that exalted station, were all declined by Mr. Nicholas before they were offered to Mr. Monroe. Mr. Jefferson, his life-long friend, saw in the pecuniary embarassments in which he became unfortunately involved, the only obstacle to his election to the highest post in the gift of the country, and which, he maintained, the wisdom, purity of purpose, and varied talents of Wilson Cary Nicholas would have eminently adorned.

JAMES PATTON PRESTON.

Scarce another American family has numbered as many prominent and honored representatives as that of the yeoman founded Preston descent, with its collateral lines and alliances.

John Preston, its *propositus*, a ship-carpenter, was born in Londonderry, Ireland, where he married Elizabeth Patton, a sister of Colonel James Patton, of Donegal, with whom he removed to Virginia, and settled in the summer of 1735 in that portion of Orange County from which Augusta County was erected in 1738. Colonel Patton had for some years commanded a merchant ship trading to Virginia, and was a man of property, enterprise and influence. He obtained an order from the Council of Virginia under which patents were issued to him and his associates for 120,000 acres of the best lands lying beyond the Blue Ridge. He was killed by the Indians at Smithfield, Virginia, in 1753. He left as issue two daughters, one of whom married Captain William Thompson, and the other Colonel John Buchanan. From the last were descended John Floyd and John B. Floyd, Governors of Virginia, Hon. James D. Breckinridge, of Louisville, Ky., and Colonel William P. Anderson, of the United States Army. John Preston settled first at Spring Hill, but in 1743 he purchased a tract of land, adjoining Staunton, on the north side of the town. He died soon after, and was buried at the Tinkling Spring Meeting-House. His widow died in 1776, aged seventy-six years. They had issue five children: Letitia, who married Colonel Robert Breckinridge; Margaret, who married Rev. John Brown; William, who married Susanna, daughter of Francis Smith, of Hanover County, Virginia, and who was a member of the House of Burgesses and a prominent patriot in the American Revolution; Ann, who married Francis Smith; and Mary, who married John Howard.

Colonel William and Susanna (Smith) Preston had issue twelve children: i. Elizabeth, married William S. Madison, the second son of John Madison, and the brother of Rev. James Madison (President of William and Mary College), of Thomas Madison, who married the youngest sister of Patrick Henry, and of George Madison, Governor of Kentucky, who married Jane Smith, the niece of Colonel Preston's wife; ii. General John, member of the Assembly, and long treasurer of Virginia; married twice, first to Mary, daughter of William Radford, and secondly, to Mrs. Elizabeth Mayo, *née* Carrington; iii. Francis, lawyer; member of Virginia Senate, and of Congress, and brigadier-general in the war of 1812; married Sarah B. Campbell, a niece of Patrick Henry and daughter of General William Campbell, the hero of King's Mountain; iv. Sarah, married Colonel James McDowell, of Rockbridge County, an officer of the war of 1812, and had issue Governor James McDowell and two daughters: Susan S., who married Hon. William Taylor, of Virginia, and Elizabeth, who married Hon. Thomas H. Benton, of Missouri; v. Anne, died at the age of thirteen years; vi. William, Captain in the United States Army under Wayne; married Caroline, daughter of Colonel George Hancock; of their issue, Henrietta, married General Albert Sydney Johnston, of the United States and

Confederate States Armies; and William, statesman, diplomate and soldier, was a Major-General in the Confederate States Army; vii. Susanna, married Nathaniel Hart, of Woodford County, Kentucky; viii. James Patton; ix. Mary, married John Lewis, of Sweet Springs, Virginia; x. Letitia, married John Floyd, Governor of Virginia; xi. Thomas Lewis, lawyer, member of the Virginia Assembly and Major in the war of 1812; married Edmonia, daughter of Governor Edmund Randolph, and had issue: Elizabeth R., who married William A. Cocke, of Cumberland County, Virginia; and John Thomas Lewis, Colonel in the Confederate States Army, and Professor in the Virginia Military Institute, who married Margaret Junkin, Virginia's sweet poetess; xii. Margaret Brown, married Colonel John Preston, of Walnut Grove, Virginia, a distant relative. James Patton Preston, the subject of the present sketch, and the eighth of the children of Colonel William and Susanna (Smith) Preston, as enumerated, was born at Smithfield, June 21, 1774. He enjoyed early advantages of education, under one Palfrenan, a poet and scholar, who having, in a drunken frolic, been inveigled into a disreputable marriage in London, shipped himself to Virginia, under articles of service for his passage. Upon his arrival at Williamsburg he was purchased by Colonel William Preston, and employed by him as a tutor in his family. Palfrenan was the friend and correspondent of the poetess Elizabeth Carter, an English lady of great learning and acquirements. Colonel Preston also possessed a fine library which had been selected for him in London by Gabriel Jones, a learned and able lawyer, who is said to have been an early partner in the practice with Thomas Jefferson. James Patton Preston appears from the catalogue of William and Mary College to have been a student in that institution for some time during the period 1790–1795. He probably graduated thence about the year last stated. Tradition affirms him to have been a merry youth; and a distinguished jurist, in a recent letter to the writer, accredits him with the perpetration, whilst a student, of a feat of equivocal distinction. In the preceding sketch of Lord Botetourt, it will be recollected that it is stated that the statue of him erected by order of the House of Burgesses, had been much mutilated by the college students. Its graceless decapitation is stated to have been a frolicsome freak of the embryo legislator and chief executive of the Commonwealth of Virginia.

James Patton Preston was elected to the State Senate of Virginia in 1802; was appointed Lieutenant-Colonel of the 12th Infantry, United States Army, March 19, 1812, and for gallantry was promoted, August 15, 1813, to the rank of Colonel, and assigned to the command of the 23d Regiment of Infantry. He participated in the battle of Chrystler's Field, November 11, 1813, and was so severely wounded in the thigh that he was crippled for life. Peace having been declared, his command was disbanded, and he was honorably discharged from service, August 18, 1815. In recognition of his patriotic service he was elected, by the General Assembly, Governor of Virginia, to succeed Wilson Cary Nicholas, December 1, 1816, and served in that capacity by annual re-election until December 1, 1819. It is noteworthy that in the last year of his incumbency, on the 25th of January, the law was passed establishing the University of Virginia, in Albemarle County, upon a site near Charlottesville which had previously belonged to Central College, which was purchased. Fifteen thousand dollars per annum were appropriated from the Literary Fund to meet expenses of building and of subsequent endowment. The institution was to be under the direction of seven visitors, appointed by the Governor and Council, and from their number these visitors were to elect a rector to preside and give general superintendence. Thomas Jefferson was elected the first rector and retained the office until his death. He drew all the plans for the buildings, which were so nearly completed in 1824 that preparations were made for opening the schools the following year. This was done with professors chiefly obtained from Europe. Only the chairs of law, chemistry and ethics were filled from the United States. In the year 1819, also, a revision of the Code of Virginia was made.

Subsequent to his gubernatorial service, Mr. Preston was for several years postmaster of the city of Richmond. He finally retired to his patrimonial inheritance, the homestead "Smithfield," in Montgomery County, where he died May 4, 1843. The county of Preston, now in West Virginia, formed in 1818, from Monongalia County, was named in his honor.

He married Ann Taylor, the second daughter of Robert Taylor, a prominent merchant of Norfolk, Virginia, and the sister of General Robert Barraud Taylor, of Virginia, and left issue three sons and three daughters: i. William Ballard Preston, a member of the Virginia Conventions of 1850-1 and 1861, Secretary of the Navy in the Cabinet of President Taylor and Confederate States Senator; married Lucy Redd, and left issue; ii. Robert Taylor Preston, Colonel Confederate States Army, married Mary Hart, of South Carolina, and left issue; iii. James Patton Preston, Jr., Colonel Confederate States Army, married Sarah Caperton, and left issue; iv. Susan Preston, died unmarried; v. Virginia Preston, died unmarried; and vi. Jane Grace Preston, married Judge George Gilmer.

In support of the claim made in the opening paragraph of this sketch, it may be said of "the Preston family" that it has furnished the National Government a Vice-President (the Hon. John Cabell Breckinridge), has been represented in several of the Executive Departments, and in both branches of Congress. It has given Virginia five Governors—McDowell, Campbell, Preston, and the two Floyds—

ARMORIAL BOOK-PLATE OF JOHN MURRAY
EARL OF DUNMORE,
Last Royal Governor of Virginia.

and to Kentucky, Missouri, and California, one each—severally in Governors Jacobs, B. Gratz Brown, and Miller; Thomas Hart Benton, John J. Crittenden, William C. and William Ballard Preston, leading moulders of public sentiment; the Breckinridges, Dr. Robert J. and William L., distinguished theologians of Kentucky; Professors Holmes, Venable, and Cabell of the University of Virginia, besides other distinguished educators. Nor is their battle-roll less glorious. It is claimed that more than a thousand of this family and its connections served in the contending armies in our late civil war. Among the leaders were Generals Wade Hampton, Albert Sydney Johnston, Joseph Eggleston Johnston, John Buchanan Floyd, John Cabell Breckinridge, and John S. and William Preston. When it is stated that besides the names enumerated, the family is connected with those of Baldwin, Blair, Bowyer, Brown, Buchanan, Bruce, Cabell, Carrington, Christian, Cocke, Flournoy, Gamble, Garland, Gilmer, Gibson, Grattan, Hart, Henry, Hughes, Howard, Lee, Lewis, Madison, Marshall, Mason, Massie, Mayo, Parker, Payne, Peyton, Pleasants, Pope, Radford, Randolph, Read, Redd, Rives, Siddon, Sheffey, Taylor, Thompson, Trigg, Venable, Watkins, Ward, Watts, Winston, Wickliffe, among many others as well esteemed, some idea may be formed of its mental characteristics and social influence.

THOMAS MANN RANDOLPH.

Thomas Mann Randolph, the eldest son of Thomas Mann and Anne (Cary) Randolph, was born at "Tuckahoe," the family seat, in Goochland County, Virginia, in the year 1768. His father, a member of the Virginia Convention and of the Committee of Safety of 1775, and frequently afterwards of the State Assembly, was the son of Thomas and Anne (daughter of Tarleton Fleming) Randolph, and the grandson of the emigrant William Randolph, of "Turkey Island." His mother was Anne, daughter of Colonel Archibald Cary, of "Ampthill," Chesterfield County, an ardent patriot of the Revolution, whose uncompromising resistance to British rule gained him the sobriquet of "Old Iron." The wife of Colonel Cary was Mary, daughter of Richard Randolph, of "Carles," and his wife Jane, daughter of John Bolling, of "Cobbs," who was fourth in descent from Pocahontas and John Rolfe.

Thomas Mann Randolph, the subject of this sketch, after a preliminary course at William and Mary College, completed his education at the University of Edinburgh, and visited Paris in 1788, where Thomas Jefferson was then residing as the Minister from the United States, having with him his daughter Martha. The young people were second cousins, and had been attached to each other from childhood.

Young Randolph in person and mind exhibited marked traces of both lines of his descent. "He was tall, lean, with dark expressive features and a flashing eye, commanding in carriage, elastic as steel, and had that sudden sinewy strength which it would not be difficult to fancy he inherited from the forest monarchs of Virginia." His education was a finished one. His reading was extensive and varied. His fortune was ample, and would have been immense but for the change effected in the Virginia statutes of descent. Few young men had attracted more attention abroad. He received marked attentions in the Scottish capital, and made friends, too, among the grave and learned. Thomas Mann Randolph and Martha Jefferson were married at "Monticello," February 23, 1790. The young couple for a time lived at "Varina," a few miles below Richmond, in Henrico County, noted as having been the county seat, the residence of Rev. William Stith, the historian, and as the point of exchange of Confederate and Federal prisoners during the late war. Thomas Mann Randolph served as a member of the Virginia Senate in 1793 and 1794. He removed soon after this period to "Edge Hill," Albemarle County, where he continued to reside until 1808, when his family was domesticated with Mr. Jefferson, at "Monticello." He was a representative from Virginia in the United States Congress from 1803 to 1807. On the last day of the session of 1806, misapprehending an expression in a speech made by his brilliant and eccentric kinsman, John Randolph "of Roanoke," he rose and passionately resented the supposed reflection in bitter denunciation. The calmer counsels of friends, however, convinced him of his error, which he with due manliness admitted in the House, regretting his expressions, and disclaiming any "disposition to wound the feelings of any gentleman who did not intend to wound his." A duel, however, for a time seemed imminent, and Mr. Randolph repaired to Richmond with the expectancy of a hostile meeting, but reason prevailed and the matter was ended. The sentiments of two eminent men, elicited by this affair, are worthy of transmission. They are extracted from the original letters, before the writer. Mr. Jefferson writes from Washington, June 23, 1806: "I had fondly hoped that the unfortunate matter between yourself and John Randolph, the last evening of Congress, had been stifled almost in the moment of its birth;" and, in reference to the wife and children of Mr. Randolph: "is it possible that your duties to those dear objects can weigh more lightly than those to a gladiator? Be assured this is not the opinion of the mass of mankind, of the thinking part of society, of that discreet part whose esteem we value. If malice and levity find sport in mischief, rational men are not therefore to exhibit themselves for their amusement. But even the striplings of fashion are sensible that the laws of dueling are made for them alone, for lives of no consequence to others; not for the fathers of families or for those charged with other great moral concerns. The valuable part of society condemns in their hearts that knight-errantry which, following the *ignis fatuus* of an imaginary honour, bursts asunder all the ligaments of duty and affection." Mr. Jefferson, writing again, July 13th, says: "I find but one sentiment prevailing (and I have that from very many)—that the thing may stop where it is with entire honour to yourself, and with no other diminution of it to the other party, than showing that he has not that ravenous appetite for unnecessary risk which some had ascribed to him; and which indeed is the falsest of honour, as a mere compound of crime and folly. I hope, therefore, that the matter is at an end, and that great care will be taken not to revive it. I believe that will be the case on his side, for I think you have been mistaken in supposing he meant to try any experiment on your sensibility. Of this he is acquitted, I find, by all who had opportunities of observing his selection of characters to be the subjects of his sarcasms." The celebrated John Taylor, "of Caroline," writing from Fredericksburg, June 26, 1806, to Wilson Cary Nicholas, says: "The two Randolphs are preparing, I see, to cut each other's throats—the devil having made such men mischievous in society as would imbibe vice, could only rob it of those who would not be wicked by a stratagem. Therefore he invented a delusion called 'honour,' concealing the epithet of 'false,' which ought to belong to the inscription upon all his manufactures. * * * Nothing can, in my view, be more ridiculous than the controversy which may eventually rob the State of one or of two of her most valuable citizens. * * * And pray, for be assured it will be a good action, stop where it is, the progress of this 'affair of his majesty's honour.'"

Mr. Randolph now, in deference to the desire of his wife, withdrew from public life, and devoted himself to agricultural pursuits at "Edge Hill," riding thither daily from "Monticello." He possessed a restless and vehement energy—but it was not sufficiently accompanied with that degree of perseverance which is the basis of important and continued success. He corresponded widely with leading agriculturists in the United States and England—in the latter with Sir John Sinclair, who was also a correspondent of Washington. The claims of his beloved State, invaded by the enemy in the war with Great Britain in 1812, met with instantaneous response in the ardent patriotism of Mr. Randolph. He was among the first to raise a command and rush to her defence. He gallantly participated in the engagements of the sea-board, and was soon promoted to the rank of Lieutenant Colonel, and placed in command of the 1st Light Corps. On the 20th of March, 1813, he became the Colonel commandant of the 20th United States Infantry, and performed efficient service on the Canada line. December 1, 1819, by election of the Assembly, he succeeded James P. Preston as Governor of Virginia, and thus served by annual re-election until December 1,

1822. Returning to his farm he resumed his private pursuits, but becoming pecuniarily involved, he resigned his affairs to the charge of his eldest son, Thomas Jefferson Randolph, and applied for a commission from the Government to run the boundary line between Georgia and Florida. But the precarious condition of his health necessitated the relinquishment of the proposed employment and his return home. He died at "Monticello," June 20, 1828, aged sixty years. His characteristics are thus recited by Randall, in his *Life of Jefferson* (Vol. I, p. 558): "He was brilliant, versatile, eloquent in conversation, impetuous and imperious in temper, chivalric in generosity, a knight-errant in courage, in calm moments a just, and at all times a high toned man." His son, the late Thomas Jefferson Randolph, was wont to apply to him the lines of Scott, in the *Lay of the Last Minstrel*, describing William of Deloraine:

"Alike to him were time and tide,
December's sleets or July's pride.
Alike to him were tide or time,
Moonless midnight or matin prime."

The range of scientific attainment of Governor Randolph has been alluded to. His only surviving child, Mrs. Meikleham, of Washington, D. C., has kindly communicated the following in relation thereto: "The Abbe Corria, who was sent by the Portuguese government to study the flora of America, who was called in Paris 'the learned Portuguese,' and who was ranked by De Candolle with, if not above Cuvier and Humboldt, spent the summers and autumns during his visit, at 'Monticello.' He and my father spent hours every day wandering, in company with each other, through the woods and fields, and he was thus fully able to pronounce judgment upon the proficiency of one branch at least of the scientific attainments of my father, whom he affirmed to be the best botanist with whom he had met in America."

Of the issue of Governor Randolph his son, Thomas Jefferson Randolph, who married Jane, the daughter of Governor Wilson Cary Nicholas, served frequently in the Virginia Assembly, and edited the papers of his grandfather, Thomas Jefferson, published in four volumes, 8vo, in 1828. Another son, George Wythe Randolph, a lawyer of distinction—a conspicuous member of the Virginia Convention of 1860-1, which passed the ordinance of secession—entered the Confederate service as Major of the Howitzer Battalion, of Richmond, and for gallantry at the battle of Bethel was made a brigadier-general. He was Secretary of War of the Confederate States from March 17 to November 17, 1862. Resuming the practice of law, he in December, 1863, went to France as the agent of the Confederate Treasury Department, and returned home in September, 1865, with shattered health. He died at Richmond,

Virginia, April 4, 1867, in the forty-ninth year of his age. Of the daughters of Governor Randolph, Anne Cary, married Charles Bankhead; Eleanora, married Joseph Coolidge, of Boston, Mass.; Virginia, married Nicholas P. Trist; and Septimia, married David Meikleham. Congress has recently granted Mrs. Meikleham a pension. A daughter of Thomas Jefferson Randolph, Miss Sarah Nicholas Randolph, is favorably known as the authoress of *Home Reminiscences of Thomas Jefferson*, and other works of merit. She has been associated for some years with her sisters in the conduction of an admirable female school at "Edge Hill." Among his daughters, Margaret, married William Randolph; Martha Jefferson, married J. C. R. Taylor; Cary Anne, married Colonel Frank G. Ruffin, a vigorous writer, and favorably known in the agricultural and political annals of Virginia; Maria Jefferson, married Charles R. Mason; Jane H., married Major R. G. H. Kean, a prominent member of the Lynchburg bar; Ellen W., married William B. Harrison. Of his two sons, Dr. Wilson Cary Nicholas Randolph, a successful physician, married Miss Holladay, and Lewis Meriwether Randolph, Major Confederate States Army, married Miss Daniel. The last died a few years since.

JAMES PLEASANTS.

The founder of the excellent Pleasants family of Virginia, John Pleasants, was a member of the pacific, prudent and upright Society of Friends, and many of his descendants have consistently held the same tenets to the present day. He was a native of Norwich, England, from whence, in 1665, in the twenty-fifth year of his age, he emigrated to the colony of Virginia, settling in Henrico County, on James River, in 1668. During the period 1679-1690 he received grants of nearly five thousand acres of land. He married Jane, widow of Samuel Tucker, and died at his seat, "Curles," May 12, 1698. He had issue: i. John, who married Dorothea Cary, was a patentee of nearly ten thousand acres of land, and February 17, 1752, was appointed one of the trustees of the town of Richmond, Virginia; ii. Elizabeth, married James Cocke, and their numerous descendants number the names of Harrison, Poythress, and many others equally estimable; iii. Joseph, patented nearly two thousand acres of land, married Martha Cocke.

Of the issue of four sons and three daughters of Joseph and Martha (Cocke) Pleasants, the second son, John, of "Pickanockie," married Susanna, the sixth child of Tarleton* and Ursula (Fleming†) Woodson.

---

* His mother was Judith, daughter of Stephen Tarleton, who is said to have been of the family of Colonel Banastre Tarleton, the famous British partisan ranger of the Revolution.

† The daughter of Charles Fleming, of New Kent County, Virginia, who was said to be descended from Sir Tarleton Fleming, second son of the Earl of Wigton, who married in England, Miss Tarleton; emigrated to Virginia in 1616, landing at Jamestown, but settling afterwards in New Kent County, where he died. He

of the fourth generation in descent from John Woodson, of Dorsetshire, England, who accompanied Sir John Harvey to the colony of Virginia in 1624, according to tradition, "in the capacity of surgeon to a company of soldiers." Of the issue of six sons and two daughters of John and Susanna (Woodson) Pleasants, the third son, James, of "Contention," married Anne, widow of John P. Pleasants and Isham Randolph, of "Dungenness," Goochland County, who was the son of the emigrant William Randolph, of "Turkey Island," James River, Virginia. Of the issue of two sons and four daughters of James and Anne (Pleasants-Randolph) Pleasants, James, the subject of this sketch, was the first child. He was born in 1769, and after a well grounded common school education, studied law with the distinguished Judge William Fleming, and entered on the practice with considerable success. In 1796 he was elected to represent Goochland County in the House of Delegates of Virginia, and in 1803 was chosen the clerk of the body, which latter position he filled most acceptably until some time during the year 1810, when he was elected a member of the United States House of Representatives, in which body he faithfully and efficiently served from 1811 to 1819. December 1, 1822, by election of the General Assembly of Virginia, he succeeded Thomas Mann Randolph as Governor of Virginia, and thus served by annual re-election, with great acceptability, until December 1, 1825, when, being by the constitution no longer eligible, he was succeeded by John Tyler. Mr. Pleasants subsequently served as a member of the distinguished and important State Constitutional Convention of 1829–1830. This was his last public service, for though twice appointed to judicial position, such was his rare modesty that he declined acceptance from a distrust of his qualifications. He died November 9, 1836, in Goochland County, universally esteemed for his public and private virtues. Governor Pleasants married Susanna Lawson, second daughter of Colonel Hugh Rose,* of "Geddes," and his

had issue three sons: Tarleton, John and Charles (as above), and several daughters. Tarleton Fleming married Miss Bates, of Williamsburg (Edward Bates, of Missouri, was of the same family), and had three sons, of whom Tarleton married Mary, sister of Thomas Mann Randolph, Sr., of "Tuckahoe," Virginia. Of this Fleming family was Colonel John Fleming, of the Revolution, and the distinguished jurist, William Fleming, of the Supreme Court of Appeals of Virginia.

* He was the second son of Rev. Robert Rose, and his wife Anne, daughter of Henry Fitzhugh, of Stafford County, Virginia. Rev. Robert Rose was the son of John and Margaret (Grant) Rose, of Wester Alves, Scotland, deduced in the twelfth generation from Hugh Rose, of Esther Geddes, 1302. He migrated to Virginia early in the eighteenth century, and was a man of varied usefulness, sometime rector of St. Anne's parish, Albemarle County, Virginia. He had no mean knowledge of surveying, medicine and surgery, conducted milling, was an extensive planter, not unskilled in mechanics, and was a merchant withal. He

wife, who was Caroline Matilda Jordan, of "Seven Islands," Buckingham County, Virginia.
The issue of Governor James and Susanna (Rose) Pleasants was:
i. Marianna, married Granville Smith; ii. Caroline, married Thomas Curd, M. D.; iii. John Hampden, a journalist of conspicuous talents, who founded the Richmond *Whig*, and was its chief editor for twenty-two years. He was a poignant thorn in the side of the Democracy, and a fearless antagonist of the Richmond *Enquirer*, its organ, which was founded and conducted by the famous Thomas Ritchie, "the father of the Democratic party." His trenchant pen led to a duel between himself and Thomas Ritchie, Jr., in which he was fatally wounded, dying February 25, 1846, in the prime of manhood, in the midst of usefulness and the full assurance of the most brilliant career. His death was profoundly deplored, and his friends have never ceased to deprecate the agencies instrumental to it. It was regarded, as was the death of Alexander Hamilton at the hands of Aaron Burr, as an immolation upon the altar of partisan spirit; iv. Marella, married Marcellus Smith; v. Susanna Lawson, married John Morris, M. D., of "Green Springs," Louisa County, Virginia; vi. Hugh Rose, a distinguished journalist, long connected with the press of Richmond, died April 27, 1870; vii. Charles James; and viii. Anne Matilda, married Dr. Ealam, of Chesterfield County, Virginia. John Hampden Pleasants was twice married; first to Ann Irving, and secondly to Mary Massie. He had issue: James Pleasants, a prominent lawyer of Richmond, and Ann Eliza, who married Douglas H. Gordon. The descendants of John Pleasants, the founder of the family in Virginia, are so numerous and so widely connected with the prominent families of the State and Union as to render any enumeration of names injudicious here.

JOHN TYLER.

John Tyler (whose descent has been deduced in a preceding sketch), the second son of Governor John and Mary (Armistead) Tyler, was born at "Greenway," his father's seat in Charles City County, Virginia, March 29, 1790. As a mere child he was of an unusually studious habit, and early exhibited a passion for books, particularly for works of history. Entering William and Mary College as a student at the age of twelve years, he soon attracted the notice of Bishop James Madison, the venerable president of that institution; and during his entire collegiate course young John Tyler was, in an especial degree,

was the executor of Governor Spotswood, and died June 30, 1751, and rests beneath a massive marble tomb in the grounds of the venerable St. John's Church, at Richmond, Virginia. He left a landed estate of nearly 30,000 acres, and his descendants include the names of Turpin, Garland, Cabell, Claiborne, Walker, Scott, Lewis, Carter, Price, Taliaferro, Roane, Coleman, Irving, Whitehead, Berry, Brooke, Redd, Dox, Eubank, and of many others of the highest esteem, scattered throughout the United States.

YORKTOWN MONUMENT.

the favorite of that distinguished man. Generous in his disposition, with pleasing and conciliating manners, and an open, frank and hearty spirit—these characteristics, by which he was distinguished through life, and which were so largely conducive to his public success, then endeared him to his fellow-students, and he was not less their favorite than that of his teacher. Having completed the courses, he graduated at the age of seventeen, and delivered on the occasion, an address on the subject of "Female Education," which was pronounced by the college faculty as singularly creditable. He now devoted himself to the study of the law, which he had already commenced during his collegiate course, and passed the next two years in reading, first with his father, and latterly with Edmund Randolph, a former Governor of Virginia and one of the most eminent lawyers in the State. Aided by the counsels of two such preceptors, his progress in this, as in his previous studies, was most rapid. At the age of nineteen he appeared at the bar of his native county as a practicing lawyer, a certificate having been given him without inquiry as to his having attained the prerequisite years of manhood. Such was his speedy success, that it is said that ere three months had elapsed there was scarcely a disputable case on the docket of the court in which he was not retained. At the age of twenty he was offered a nomination as the delegate from Charles City County in the State Assembly, but he declined the proffered honor until the following year, when, having attained his majority a short time before the election was held, he was chosen almost unanimously a member of the House of Delegates. He took his seat in that body in December, 1811. The breaking out of the war with Great Britain, with its incidental exciting measures, and the public solicitude involved, afforded a fine scope for the improvement of his powers of oratory. Like the brilliant Charles James Fox, he spoke often with the view of increasing them, and was encouraged by the attention which his speeches commanded. About this period, Messrs. Giles and Brent, then Senators from Virginia, disobeying an instruction from the State Assembly to vote against the chartering of a United States Bank, Mr. Tyler introduced a resolution of censure in the House of Delegates, animadverting severely upon the course of the Senators, and laying it down as a principle to be adhered to undeviatingly thereafter, that any person accepting the office of United States Senator from Virginia tacitly bound himself to obey, during the period of his service, the instructions he might receive from its Legislature. Later in his public life he consistently exhibited his adherence to a principle thus early inculcated, in resigning his seat in the United States Senate rather than record a vote alike repugnant to his judgment and his sense of conscientious duty. Mr. Tyler continued a member of the Legislature by re-election for five years successively. His popularity in his native county is instanced in the fact that on one occasion, during this period, when seven candidates offered themselves, Mr. Tyler received all the votes polled in the county but five. Some years later, when a candidate for Congress, of the two hundred votes given in the same county, he received, with a strong and distinguished competitor, all but one. He zealously supported the administration during the war, and raised a volunteer company when Richmond was threatened, but they were not brought into action. During the session of 1815–1816, whilst still a member of the House of Delegates, Mr. Tyler was elected a member of the Executive Council, and acted in this capacity until November, 1816, when he was elected to fill a vacancy in the representation in Congress, from the Richmond district, occasioned by the death of Hon. John Clopton, and took his seat in the month following. In the debate in this body on the rate of compensation to be allowed its members, and in which Calhoun, John Randolph, Grosvenor, Henry Clay, Southard and other prominent statesmen participated, Mr. Tyler eloquently replied to Mr. Calhoun, advocating a return to the former per diem rate of six dollars, and consistently maintaining his early enunciated principles of the rights of constituents and the duty of their representatives. Said he: "You have no robes of office here to bestow, no stars or garter to confer, but the proudest title which we can boast, and the only one worthy of being boasted of, is that which is to be read in the applause of our contemporaries and the gratitude of posterity. * * * If a member of this body *is not* a representative of the people, what is he? and if he *is*, how can he be regarded as representing the people when he speaks, not their language, but his own? He ceases to be their representative when he does so, and *represents himself alone.* Is the creature to set himself in opposition to his creator? Is the servant to disobey the wishes of his master? From the very meaning of the word representative, the obligation to obey instructions results. The Federal Constitution was submitted to conventions of the different States for adoption. Suppose the people had instructed their representatives in convention to have rejected the Constitution, and their instructions had been disobeyed, would this be called a government of the people adopted by their choice? * * * The gentleman from South Carolina mentioned the name of Edmund Burke. I venerate the talents of that distinguished orator as highly as any man; and I hold in high respect the memory and virtues of the illustrious Chatham; but, highly as I esteem the memories of those great statesmen, they will suffer no disparagement by a comparison with the immortal Sidney. I prefer to draw my principles from the father of the Church, from the man who fell a martyr in the cause of freedom, who consecrated his principles by his blood, from the fountain from which has flowed the principles of the very Constitution under which we act." Mr. Tyler also in the same session ably opposed the resolution, introduced by Mr. Pickens, of South Carolina, proposing an amendment to the Constitution, which provided for the establishment of a uniform mode of electing representatives in Congress and electors of President and Vice-President throughout the United States, by the division of the several States into districts for those purposes. After much discussion, the proposition was laid on the table near the close of the session, not again to be revived. In the fifteenth Congress Mr. Tyler voted against the provision offered by Mr. Clay for a minister to the provinces of the Rio la Plata, holding that it would be a virtual acknowledgment by the United States of their independence. He also opposed all internal improvements by the General Government, and the recharter of the United States Bank, which he held to be unconstitutional. In the lengthy debate on the resolutions censuring General Jackson for his arbitrary course in the Seminole War, in the execution of the prisoners Arbuthnot and Ambrister, Mr. Tyler warmly participated, urging the adoption of the resolutions, but they were finally negatived. In the sixteenth Congress he opposed the prominent measures of a revision of the tariff for protection, and the Missouri Compromise, the latter upon the ground that it restricted the diffusion of slaves, which he held to be the surest means towards their ultimate emancipation. Mr. Tyler, by re-election, continued to serve in Congress until near the close of the term of 1821, when ill-health necessitated his resignation, and he retired to his farm, "Sherwood Forest," in Charles City County, possessing the respect of each of the great political parties. He did not long remain in private life. In 1823 he was again elected a member of the Virginia Legislature, and took the lead in all matters of public utility which occupied that body; many of the most beneficial of the internal improvements of the State being the result of his zealous and untiring labors. In 1825 he was elected by the Assembly Governor of Virginia, succeeding James Pleasants, December 1st. He was re-elected the following year by a unanimous vote, but being elected January 18, 1827, to succeed John Randolph in the United States Senate, he resigned the office of Governor on the 4th of March, and was succeeded by William Branch Giles. The claims of the soldiers of the Revolution had ever been warmly maintained by Mr. Tyler, and during his service in Congress he had strenuously resisted every effort to reduce the pittances which had been provided for them by the nation. In a communication to the General Assembly, whilst Governor, he insisted that the claims of the Revolutionary patriots of the Virginia State Line, which had with flagrant injustice, been discriminated against, should be pressed upon the attention of the General Government. He urges that: "The claims of our soldiers have ever been listened to with an attentive ear by the constituted authorities of this State, and would long since have been fulfilled to the very letter of promise but for the magnificent donation made by Virginia to the Federal Government of all her northern lands. It may be confidently asserted that in making that cession this Commonwealth never intended that the claims of any part of her hardy veterans should in any manner have remained unprovided for. The fact of the omission of all mention of her troops on State establishment in the compacts entered into by her with the Government of the United States must have been an omission resulting purely from accident. * * * The fact is, that the Virginia troops on State establishment are as much entitled to the liberality of Congress as those who served on Continental establishment. Those of the State Line who were entitled to land bounty, enlisted for a period not less than three years, and were found fighting by the side of the Continental troops, from one extremity of the Confederacy to the other. Their services in the achievement of our independence equally entitle them to the nation's gratitude. Why, then, should not Congress interfere in their behalf? While we present to the National Government an occasion for the exercise of its liberality, we present also a claim sanctioned by every principle of justice; and we might reasonably indulge the anticipation that our application would be listened to with attention and crowned with success." Mr. Tyler also strenuously recommended to the Assembly the organization of a system for the general instruction of the masses of the people. The year 1826 was marked by an event which threw the whole American nation into mourning—the deaths of Thomas Jefferson and John Adams. That two of three only survivors of the signers of the Declaration of Independence should breathe their last upon the same day, and that day the anniversary of the promulgation of that grand instrument, was a coincidence the most remarkable. Mr. Jefferson died at "Monticello," just fifty years after the Declaration, at the very recurrent hour of the day, it is said, at which the immortal work of his hands was read in the Congress of the United States. On the receipt of the intelligence at Richmond, Governor Tyler was requested to deliver a commemorative address, and accordingly on the 11th instant, after scarce three days of preparation, pronounced at the Capitol square, in Richmond, a funeral oration, profoundly touching in its beauty and impressive eloquence. Mr. Tyler took his seat in the United States Senate in December, 1827. In that body he voted against the tariff bill of 1828, and was a firm supporter of General Jackson on his accession to the Presidency, but ever maintained an independence of action. He was frank in the avowal of his opinions, which were sometimes at variance with those of the President. Whilst thus efficiently representing Virginia in the Supreme Council of the nation, Mr. Tyler also rendered service in her important and illustriously composed Constitutional Convention of 1829–30. During the session of 1831–1832 he opposed the recharter of the United States Bank, maintaining, as on a previous occasion, that it was an unconstitutional measure. He also voted against the tariff bill of 1832; but in the course of a speech in the

Senate, he enunciated the principles of concession upon which, and at his instance, Mr. Clay, in 1833, predicated his famous compromise act. Mr. Tyler in a speech of much eloquence avowed his sympathy with the nullification movement in South Carolina, in 1832, and in consequence of the proclamation of President Jackson, withdrew his support from him. When the movement was made in the Virginia Assembly, in 1832, for the emancipation of slaves, William H. Brodnax, John Randolph "of Roanoke," John Marshall, Philip A. Bolling, Thomas Jefferson Randolph, James McDowell, and William H. Roane, being among its prominent supporters, Mr. Tyler, then a member of the Senate Committee on the District of Columbia, drew with his own hands, and inserted in the code prepared for the District, but which was not acted on, a bill providing for the abolition of slavery in the District, thus anticipating by eighteen years a similar provision inserted in the Compromise of 1850. In 1833 he was re-elected to the Senate for six years, and opposed the removal of the Government deposits from the United States Bank. His independent course separated him from the President's friends in Virginia, who subsequently supported Mr. Van Buren.

In 1836 the Legislature of Virginia instructed its Senators, Mr. Tyler and Benjamin Watkins Leigh, to vote for expunging from the journals of the Senate the resolution of Mr. Clay censuring the President for his assumption of unjustifiable authority in removing the bank deposits. As Mr. Tyler approved of the resolution, and believed the proposition to expunge to be in violation of the Constitution, he could not conscientiously obey instructions, and, true to his avowed principles, he resigned his seat February 10th, and was succeeded by William Cabell Rives. His colleague, Mr. Leigh, however, refused to obey the will of the Legislature, and held his seat; and though locally lauded and complimented, with Mr. Tyler, by the Whigs of Richmond (his residence), with a public dinner, yet his course, in the sequel, was proved to be an injudicious one, as weighed in the scale of his public interests, for, notwithstanding his pure character and great intellect, his error was irredeemable. He was henceforth barred from political preferment. In the spring of 1838 Mr. Tyler was elected by the Whigs of James City County to the Virginia Assembly, and in 1839 he was elected a member of the Whig Convention that met at Harrisburg, Pennsylvania, to nominate a candidate for President of the United States. He was chosen Vice-President of the Convention, and warmly supported Mr. Clay for the nomination. The choice of the Convention, however, was General William H. Harrison for President, with Mr. Tyler for Vice-President, and in 1840 they were both elected, and were inaugurated on the 4th of March, 1841; but the former dying April 4th, after an administration of only one month, Mr. Tyler, in accordance with the provisions of the Constitution, became President of the United States.

He retained the Cabinet appointed by his predecessor, and proceeded to check, so far as he could consistently with the previous commitments of Harrison, the removal of the supporters of Van Buren's administration. In the canvass of 1840 no decision had been made relative to a fiscal agent for the receipt and disbursement of the public moneys. The issue of a bank was repeatedly pressed as a desideratum by prominent Whigs and the newspaper organs of their party. President Tyler, in his first message, while reserving to himself in express terms the power to veto any measure which would contravene the Constitution, recommended the repeal of the sub-treasury law, and the substitution of a new fiscal agent. He had always denied the power in Congress of national incorporation operating *per se* over the Union. In private conversations with Clay and other prominent Whigs, before the meeting of Congress, he had urged a scheme which would not involve his Constitutional objections. This they rejected, and Mr. Clay again proposed, essentially, instead, the re-establishment of the old United States Bank. The President vetoed the bill, as he did another, in alleged accordance with his suggestion for a fiscal agent, which was offered for his approval. The sub-treasury law in the meantime had been repealed; great excitement prevailed, and all of Mr. Tyler's Cabinet, with the exception of Daniel Webster, resigned, and a simultaneous assault was made upon him by the press and orators of the Whig party throughout the country. He, however, remained firm, and immediately filled his Cabinet with eminent State's rights Whigs and Conservatives.

The most important acts of the long session (two hundred and sixty-nine days) of 1841–1842 were a new tariff law with incidental protection, an act establishing a uniform bankrupt law, and an apportionment of representatives according to the census of 1840. The momentous treaty with Great Britain, settling the northeastern boundary of the United States, was ratified at Washington on the 28th of August, 1842. The provision in its eighth article concerning the African squadron for the protection of American commerce, and the prevention of the slave trade on the coast of Africa, was the suggestion of Mr. Tyler. In May, 1843, the President appointed Caleb Cushing, of Massachusetts, a commissioner to the Chinese government. On the 12th of April, 1844, a treaty was concluded at Washington, providing for the annexation of Texas to the United States, but on the 8th of June it was rejected by the Senate. On the 25th of January, 1845, a joint resolution for annexing Texas was adopted in the House of Representatives by a vote of 120 to 98; and the same was adopted in the Senate, on the 1st of March, by a vote of 27 to 25, and the same day it was approved by the President. Thus, two days before the expiration of his term of office, Mr. Tyler had the satisfaction of witnessing the consummation of an act which he had long earnestly desired and persistently striven for.

The terms proposed were ratified on the 4th of July following by a Constitutional Convention assembled at Austin, Texas, and that State became one of our great Union. Upon the expiration of his Presidential term Mr. Tyler returned to private life, upon his farm in Virginia.

In the Democratic Convention which assembled at Baltimore, Maryland, on the 13th of May, 1844, to nominate candidates for President and Vice-President, Mr. Tyler was the first choice of a large following for the Presidency, and it was thought that his friends held the balance of power in several States. Mr. Van Buren, also a candidate, was so objectionable to many of the Democratic party that it was urged that, between him and the candidate of the Whig party, they would prefer Mr. Clay. The friends of Mr. Tyler, to secure the defeat of Mr. Van Buren, and the nomination of a candidate in sympathy with the policy and measures of the administration of Mr. Tyler, notably the annexation of Texas, resolved upon the two-thirds rule, and under its application, Mr. Van Buren was discarded, and Mr. Tyler withdrawing, James K. Polk was nominated, and subsequently elected as the successor of Mr. Tyler.

During the long period of relief from the strife and anxieties of political life, which was now enjoyed by Mr. Tyler in the blessings of a competence and of domestic bliss, there was an episode not the least creditable in his honorable career, and highly characteristic in its marked exemplification of his sense of duty as a citizen. In 1847 he was designated by the justices of Charles City County for an essential but humbly named duty, and to which, in common with other citizens, he was liable. It was at the instance, it was said, of those who wished to inflict a mortification by conferring, in derision, upon an ex-President of the United States the humble position of an overseer of the public road. Mr. Tyler promptly accepted the appointment, and was no less decided in the execution of the trust—the emphatic meed, without dissenting voice, accorded, being that "he was the best overseer of the roads that Charles City ever had."

Mr. Tyler was twice most happily married; first, March 29, 1813, to Letitia, the third daughter of Robert Christian, of "Cedar Grove," New Kent County, long a member of the Virginia Assembly, and a member of a family* which has for quite two hundred years been

---

* The late curiously erudite Dr. J. R. Christian, of Holly Springs, Miss., traced the origin of the Christian family to Scotland, where, prior to the 16th century, the name was rendered MacChristian. They were established in Wigtonshire, Scotland, until the year 1422, after which they figure in Man, only a few miles distant. The name is historic. John Christian, of Undrigg Castle, married Isabella, daughter of Henry Lord Percy, the famous Earl of Northumberland. William MacChristian, of Albdale and Milntown, parish of St. Frisity, was

GEORGE SANDYS,
Treasurer of the Colony of Virginia in 1621.

Contemporaneously the author of the first book written in what is now the United States of America, "Ovid's Metamorphosis," printed at Oxford in 1632.

honorably and usefully represented in the judiciary, and in varied local trusts in Virginia. She died at Washington, September 10, 1842. Her virtues are gracefully recorded by Miss Holloway, in *The Ladies of the White House.* The second marriage of Mr. Tyler is invested with touching interest, and was the romantic sequel of a tragic occurrence which profoundly moved the sympathies of the American nation. The powerful armament of the United States steamship "Princeton" claimed the attention of the Secretary of the Navy, and by the invitation of her builder and commander, Captain Stockton, on the 28th of February, 1844, a large party of distinguished persons, accompanied with ladies, were present on board during an excursion on the Potomac to witness the trial of her powers. The day was charmingly bright and pleasant, and the occasion one of rare social gratification, when, with the closing scene and the setting sun, a terrible accident spread disaster around. One of the largest guns, on being fired for the third time, whilst the frigate was opposite Mount Vernon, burst, and the explosion killed instantly the Secretary of the Navy, Thomas W. Gilmer; the Secretary of State, Abel P. Upshur; Commodore Beverley Kennon, chief of one of the Naval Bureaus; Virgil Maxcy, recently *Chargé d'Affaires* to The Hague; Hon. David Gardiner, of New York (who was accompanied by his lovely and accomplished daughter), and three domestics, besides wounding twelve of the crew. The tender and soothing attentions of the President (who was present) to Miss Gardiner in her terrible bereavement sensibly touched her heart. A sympathetic bond was established, and the happy sequence was the marital union of John Tyler and Julia Gardiner† on the 26th of June following. The

Master of the House of Keys for Ireland in 1422. Evan Christian, born in 1579, was appointed Deempster or Judge of the Isle of Man at the age of twenty-six, and held the office for forty-eight years. Gilbert Christian married in 1720, and removed from Scotland to Ireland. Several of the name emigrated to America and founded families in Pennsylvania, the Valley of Virginia and Tennessee. But the family was much earlier seated in Eastern Virginia. Thomas Christian patented lands in James City County in 1667, and, October 26, 1687, was granted 1,080 acres in Charles City County.

† The father of Mrs. Tyler, Hon. David Gardiner, born May 2, 1784, a graduate of Yale College, for a time New York State Senator, was a descendant in the ninth generation from Lion Gardiner, a native of England, a soldier and engineer by profession, who joined the camp of the Prince of Orange, in the Netherlands, as master of works of fortifications, and who was stationed at Fort Orange, near the city of Woerden. Accompanied by his wife, Mary Williamson (born at Woerden, and died in 1665), he came as engineer with the colonists who embarked from London, July 10, 1635, and who settling on the banks of the Connecticut River, under the patent granted in 1631, by Charles II. to William, Viscount, Say and Seal, Lord Brook and others, formed the germ of the colony of Connecticut. Lion Gardiner acted as Lieutenant or Deputy of the patentees, and commanded from 1635 to 1639 the fort built at Say-Brook, named in honor of Lords Say and Brook, and which was of great benefit in defending the colony from the attacks of the savages. Securing the friendship of Wyandanch, sachem

issue of President Tyler, by his first marriage, was seven children, four daughters and three sons: i. *Mary*, married Henry L. Jones; ii. *Robert*, Signer of Patents, Prothonotary of the Superior Court of Pennsylvania, President of the Repeal Association, of which William H. Seward was Vice-President, Register of the Treasury of the Confederate States, the able editor of the Montgomery (Ala.) *Advertiser*, and a Centennial Commissioner in 1876; married Priscilla, daughter of the distinguished tragedian, Thomas A. Cooper. Their accomplished daughter, Mrs. Priscilla Goodwyn, inherits the histrionic genius of her maternal grandfather; iii. *John*, private secretary of his father, Major in the Confederate States Army, and a brilliant and vigorous writer; iv. *Letitia*, married James Semple, of the United States Navy, and Chief of Parole of the Confederate States Army; v. *Elizabeth*, married William Waller, and had issue, among others, John Tyler, a gallant but rash young officer, successively of the Confederate Navy and Army, who sealed his devotion to the South with his life; and William Griffin, assistant editor of the Savannah (Ga.) *News*, married, first, Jeannie Howell, the sister of the second wife of Jefferson Davis, and, secondly, Bessie Austin; vi. *Alice*, married Rev. Mr. Dennison. Their daughter Bessie is an artist of ability, which is meritoriously instanced in the portrait of her ancestor, Governor Tyler, in the State Library at Richmond; vii. *Tazewell*, Surgeon Confederate States Army, lately deceased in California, married Anne Bridges, of New Kent County, Virginia.

of the Montauketts, through intelligence received from him he was the instrument of saving the infant colony of Connecticut from threatened massacre, which had been plotted by the Pequot, the Narragansett and other tribes. Lion Gardiner also obtained by purchase from the chieftain Wyandanch various extensive tracts of valuable land, among others that in New York, known as Gardiner's Island, comprising 2,400 acres of arable land, besides 900 acres of ponds and sand beaches. It was conveyed March 10, 1649, and is in possession of the descendants of Lion Gardiner to the present day. He died in 1663. John Gardiner, the grandson of Lion Gardiner, received from Governor Dongan the last patent of Governor's Island, erecting it into a lordship and manor, and was proprietor when Robert Kidd, the famous pirate, buried his treasures upon it. He was killed by a fall from his horse while on a visit to Croton, Conn., June 25, 1738, aged seventy-eight. The mother of Mrs. Tyler was Juliana (born February 8, 1799), daughter of Michael McLachlan, of the Highland clan of McLachlan, in Scotland. His father fell in the rebellion of 1745, when the son emigrated to the Island of Jamaica, and thence to the city of New York. The Gardiner family, in its intermarriages includes, among other well-known names, those of Conkling, Howell, Coit, Gray, Green, Chandler, Lathrop, Mulford, Avery, Buel, Griswold, Thompson, Huntington, Dering, Dayton, Van Wyck, Lee, Davis, L'Hommedieu, and Bancroft. Hannah, great-granddaughter of Lion Gardiner, and the wife of John Chandler, of Worcester, Mass., being the grandmother of George Bancroft, the historian. Mrs. Tyler, with her younger children, at present resides in Richmond, Virginia.

The issue of the second marriage of President Tyler was also seven children, five sons and two daughters (making a total by the two marriages of fourteen children): viii. *David Gardiner*, a lawyer, residing at the paternal seat, "Sherwood Forest," Charles City County; ix. *John Alexander*, civil engineer, a gallant soldier in the Prussian Army in the Franco-Prussian War, and in the Confederate Army. For merit in the first service he was invested by the hands of Kaiser William himself with a medal and ribbon; died September 2, 1883, at Sante Fe, New Mexico; x. *Julia*, married William H. Spencer, of New York, and died in 1871; xi. *Lachlan*, an accomplished and successful physician in Washington, D. C.; xii. *Lyon Gardiner*, a talented lawyer of the Richmond bar, late a Professor in William and Mary College, and an accomplished writer, married Anne Baker, daughter of the gallant Colonel St. George Tucker, of the Confederate States Cavalry, poet, and author of the historical novel, *Hansford: A Tale of Bacon's Rebellion*, the son of Hon. Henry St. George Tucker, and grandson of Hon. St. George Tucker (jurisconsult), and his wife Frances, daughter of Richard Bland, and who was the widow of John Randolph, and the mother of the brilliant and erratic John Randolph "of Roanoke." The maternal grandfather of Mrs. Tyler was Hon. Thomas Walker Gilmer; xiii. *Fitz Walter*; xiv. *Pearl*. President Tyler, surrounded by his interesting family, enjoyed the peaceful quiet of private life for a long series of years, broken alone by generous and inspiring services as an orator on special occasions, and to which his powers of eloquence subjected him, until the stirring events of 1861 appealed to his patriotism, and again enlisted his willing energies in the cause of his beloved State. He was a member of and presided with great dignity over the earnest and momentous deliberations of the Peace Conference which was proposed by the Virginia Assembly at his suggestion, and which met in Willard's Hall, at Washington, D. C., February 4, 1861. He was also a member of the first Confederate States Congress, and while in attendance on that body died at Richmond, Virginia, January 17, 1862, and was buried in the adjacent beautiful and picturesque Hollywood Cemetery. Glowing eulogiums upon his worth were delivered in both houses of the Confederate Congress by Honorables R. M. T. Hunter, William C. Rives, Louis T. Wigfall, William H. Macfarland, A. M. Venable and others. In person President Tyler was tall and slender, with a fair complexion, blue eyes, brown hair, an aquiline nose, and impressive and engaging countenance. An excellent portrait of him is exhibited in the State Library at Richmond, Virginia. His literary efforts evince mental endowments of a high order, as well as the devotion and enthusiasm of the scholar. "To purity of taste, elegance of diction, and strength of reasoning he superadds the ornaments of a lively fancy and a copious command of impressive and striking images." His "Life" (published in 8vo, New York, 1843) presents the principal events of his life and literary and political efforts to that period. His quite numerous addresses thereafter, exist chiefly in the columns of the contemporary press and in fugitive publications. The most important have been collected by his grandson, Lyon Gardiner Tyler, in the *Letters and Times of the Tylers*, now in press. The great secret of the popularity of Mr. Tyler was doubtless in the earnestness of purpose, the innate generosity and simplicity of nature, the winning sympathy, and the inspiring cordiality which was manifest in his entire presence. His ready adaptation to circumstances, and assimilation with the tastes of every circle or auditory, united in a persuasive sway which we are wont to term personal magnetism.

WILLIAM BRANCH GILES.

The ancestors of William Branch Giles were early seated in the colony of Virginia. Christopher Branch, "ancient planter," appears as a patentee of lands in 1624, and George Giles in 1630, both located in Henrico County. William Giles conveyed lands in the same county to Colonel William Byrd in 1681. Another of the name is mentioned, in an humorous connection, by Colonel William Fontaine, an eye-witness of the memorable surrender of York, October 19, 1781, who, in a letter of graphic detail, dated October 26, 1781, and which is preserved in the autographic collection of the Virginia Historical Society, narrates the incidental embarrassing personal experience of the erst truculent and redoubtable British trooper, Colonel Banastre Tarleton: "The hero was prancing through the streets of York on a very fine, elegant horse, and was met by a spirited young fellow of the country, who stopped him, challenged the horse, and ordered him instantly to dismount. Tarleton halted and paused awhile through confusion; then told the lad if it was his horse, he supposed he must be given up, but insisted to ride him some distance out of town to dine with a French officer. This was more, however, than Mr. Giles was disposed to indulge him in; having been forced, when he and his horse were taken, to travel a good part of a night on foot at the point of a bayonet, he therefore refused to trust him out of sight, and made him dismount in the midst of the street crowded with spectators."

William Branch Giles was born in Amelia County, Virginia, August 12, 1762. After a preliminary course of instruction at the venerable William and Mary College, he matriculated at Princeton College, New Jersey, from whence he graduated with distinction in 1781. Adopting the profession of the law, he was admitted to the bar, and in the courts of Petersburg, Virginia, soon attained a lucrative practice. In August, 1790, he entered the arena of politics, first as a Federalist, and was elected a delegate from Virginia to the United States House of Representatives. In December of the same year, however, he separated himself from the Federalists upon the question of establishing a United States Bank, and entered the ranks of the Republican, or Democratic, party, and was thereafter a bitter antagonist of his former party associates. January 23, 1793, he charged Alexander Hamilton, the Secretary of the Treasury, with corruption and peculation in office. In 1796 he opposed the creation of a National Navy, and the ratification of Jay's treaty, and the proposed war with France in 1798. In that year he declined a seat in Congress that he might aid James Madison in the Virginia Assembly (to which body he was elected from Amelia County) in passing the celebrated resolutions of 1798. In 1800 he was again elected to Congress, and was one of the most zealous supporters of President Jefferson, who is said to have conferred with him almost nightly during the sessions of Congress, to assure himself that no untoward conviviality of Mr. Giles might deprive him of efficient support on the following day. In 1803 Mr. Giles declined a re-election to Congress, and was succeeded in that body by John W. Eppes, the son-in-law of Mr. Jefferson. In August, 1804, Mr. Giles was elected by the Executive Council of Virginia to the United States Senate, to fill the vacancy occasioned by the resignation of Wilson Cary Nicholas, for whose unexpired term he was first elected by the State Assembly early in December following, and on the 4th of the month by the same body, for the ensuing Senatorial term, commencing March 4, 1805, and ending March 4, 1811. Mr. Giles was re-elected for another term by the Assembly, January 2, 1811, but resigned his seat November 23, 1815, before the completion of his term, which did not expire until March 4, 1817. He zealously and with conspicuous ability supported the administration during the war with Great Britain, 1812–1815. He re-entered public life in 1816 as the delegate from Amelia County, in the Virginia Assembly, but ill-health demanded his retirement to his farm in Amelia County. Some political essays from Mr. Giles which were published in the Richmond *Enquirer* in 1824, attracting the attention of Henry Clay, he sent to Mr. Giles, in the month of April of that year, a speech on the Tariff which he had recently delivered in Congress, accompanying the speech with an ironical epistle, in which after adroitly complimenting Mr. Giles on his ability and statesmanship, of the exercise of which the government had been so long and unfortunately deprived because of his ill-health, he amusingly congratulates Mr. Giles upon his finding time to withdraw himself from the disputes with his miller and overseer, in which he had been contentedly engaged, and to again give the public the benefit of his fine talents in such brilliant contributions to the press. Mr. Giles, singularly enough, failed to discern the biting humor of this effusion, and made a cordial response to Mr. Clay, who made merry with his friends over the matter. This being reported to Mr. Giles, he, in an irate mood, addressed, February 19, 1826, a communication to Mr. Clay which was tantamount to a challenge to a deadly encounter. The son of Mr. Giles, Thomas T. Giles, was the bearer of the communication, which he tendered Mr. Clay in the presence of Hon. William S. Archer. Mr. Clay declined to receive it upon the ground that he could not "recognize Mr. Thomas T. Giles as an organ free from objection." The whole correspondence was subsequently published by Mr. Giles. In 1826 Mr. Giles again entered the Virginia Assembly as a delegate from Amelia County, and in the spring of the following year presented in that body certain resolutions calling for an inquiry into the relative rights of the general and State governments. In the same year he was elected by the Assembly Governor of Virginia, which office he held by annual re-election until 1830. He was a member also of that brilliant constellation of genius, the State Constitutional Convention of 1829-30, and engaged prominently in the important debates in that body. He died December 4, 1830, at his seat, "The Wigwam," in Amelia County, in the sixty-ninth year of his age. In an obituary, which appeared in the Richmond *Enquirer*, he is recorded as having been: "In his public life he was distinguished as a zealous patriot, an honest politician and an able statesman, adoring liberty and hating despotism—devoted to his country, but unprejudiced in his devotions—loving the Constitution and jealous of its violation—attached to the Federal Government, but despising its usurpations—he executed to the last the best energies of his mind in endeavoring to maintain the rights of the State and the liberties of the people. * * * The most spotless integrity and liberality was conspicuous in all his intercourse with his fellow-man, an unreserved candor in his communications which disdained everything like concealment. A charm of conversation and a courtesy of manner which passes all description, won for him the love and admiration of all who could feel and estimate such qualities. Having spent a life of usefulness and distinction, after sixteen years of disease he gradually sunk into the arms of death with the serenity and calmness of philosophy and the peace and quiet of an easy conscience."

The success in public life of Mr. Giles, it is generally conceded, was due scarce less to his proficiency in parliamentary tactics than to his ability in debate. It is true that he was a man of chivalric impulse, and his championship, in 1815, of the unfortunate cousin of John Randolph of Roanoke (Miss Ann Cary Randolph, then Mrs. Gouverneur Morris), in the inhuman assault of Randolph upon her, made John Randolph his bitter enemy. Mr. Giles published a "Speech on the Embargo," in 1808; "A Political Letter to the People of Virginia," in 1813; a series of letters, signed "A Constituent," in the Richmond *Enquirer*, in January, 1818, against the plan for a general education; letters of invective against James Monroe and Henry Clay, arraigning them for their "hobbies," the South American cause, the Greek cause, internal improvements and the

Tariff. He addressed a letter to Chief Justice John Marshall disdaining the expressions, not the general sentiments, in regard to Washington, ascribed to him in the Life of Washington. He also appeared before the public as a correspondent of John Quincy Adams. His writings were collected and published in 1827, under the general title of *Miscellanies*. Giles County, Virginia, formed in 1806 from the counties of Monroe and Tazewell, was named in his honor. He married, March 3, 1810, Miss Frances Anne Gwynn. Of the issue of this happy marriage, a son, Thomas T. Giles, a member of the Richmond bar, and long the zealous chairman of the Executive Committee of the Virginia Historical Society, died January 18, 1883, in the eightieth year of his age. Two daughters married respectively the late A. D. Townes, and the late Gustavus A. Myers, a distinguished lawyer. The son of the last, the late Major William Branch Myers, was an artist of merit, and several portraits executed by him are preserved in the collections of the Virginia Historical Society, where also is an excellent full length portrait of Governor Giles. He is represented seated before a table with writing materials, and with a crutch, rendered necessary from rheumatic affliction, resting against his chair. His countenance bears a shrewd expression. His dress is that of his day—the striking ruffled shirt, blue coat with brass buttons, etc. The *tout ensemble* impresses one as that of a quondam fox-hunting English squire, who enjoyed the good things of this world with keen zest.

JOHN FLOYD.

The received tradition in the distinguished Floyd family of Virginia is that its progenitor, a native of Wales, was a very early settler in that portion of the Colony known as the Eastern Shore. The name is indeed of early record. Walter Floyd appears, with associates, as a patentee of four hundred acres of land in "Martin's Hundred," on "Skiffe Creek," April 24, 1632. Nathaniel Floyd patented eight hundred and fifty acres in Isle of Wight County November 20, 1637; and John Floyd, Thomas Hunt, Edward Bibby, and George Clarke were the grantees, September 28, 1681, of Hog Island, containing twenty-two hundred acres, upon the Atlantic coast, opposite the counties of Northampton and Accomac. Walter Floyd was in all probability the father or grandfather of the John Floyd last named, and the lineal progenitor of the subject of the present sketch, but the connecting links have not been preserved. The family account commences with three brothers (whom it is fair to presume were the sons of John Floyd, as above): William, John ("who went North"), and Charles Floyd, who migrated to Georgia, and was the ancestor of General John Floyd, of Darien, in that State. William Floyd removed to the county of Amherst, then a wild region, and married there Abidiah, the fifth child of Robert and —— (Hughes)

Best beloved of the Royal Governors of Virginia.

Davis.* Their eldest son, John Floyd, was born in 1751. He married, in 1769, a Miss Barfoot, who died within a year, leaving an infant daughter, who was taken charge of by the mother of Mrs. Floyd. Soon afterwards John Floyd removed to the county of Botetourt, where he engaged in teaching school, and writing in the office of the county surveyor, Colonel William Preston, in whose family he lived. His duties were unremitting; when his services were not demanded in the surveyor's office, he was in the saddle as the deputy of the county sheriff, Colonel William Christian. In 1774 he went to Kentucky, where he located and surveyed for himself and others many rich tracts of land on Elkhorn Creek, and within the present counties of Clarke, Woodford, Shelby, and Jefferson. The service was attended with many hardships and much danger from savage hostility. Colonel Floyd returned to Virginia in 1776, soon after the Declaration of Independence, and took command of a schooner—the "Phœnix"—which had been fitted as a privateer by Dr. Thomas Walker, Edmund Pendleton, Colonel William Preston, and one or two others. Sailing to the West Indies, he took a valuable prize; but on his return, when nearly in sight of the capes of Virginia, he was overtaken by a British vessel of war, captured, and taken to England, where he remained in irons, a prisoner, for nearly a year. He obtained his liberty through the sympathy of the jailer's daughter, who stealthily left his cell unlocked. He begged his way to Dover, where he was first concealed and then secured a passage to France by a clergyman who was thus in the habit of assisting American fugitives. Making his way to Paris, he was there furnished by Benjamin Franklin with means to return to America. In November, 1778, he married his second wife, Jane, daughter of Colonel John and Margaret (daughter of Colonel James Patton) Buchanan. Colonel Floyd remained in Virginia until October, 1779, when he removed to his fine estate in Kentucky,† on Bear Grass Creek, six miles from Louisville, where he built a stockade fort, which was known as Floyd's Station. In 1783 he was a member of the first court of Kentucky, which held its first session at Harrodsburg, and, in addressing the body, ardently said that he felt that he had set his foot on the threshold of an empire. He was a conspicuous actor in the stirring

---

* Robert Davis, the father of him of the same name of the text, a native of Wales, removed from Eastern Virginia and settled in Amherst County about 1720. He became wealthy by traffic with the Catawba Indians, and took up extensive tracts of rich and valuable lands. The tradition in the Floyd family is that he married a half-breed Indian girl. This, if true, would account in some measure for the striking physique of the Colonels John Floyd, father and son. The descendants of Robert Davis are numerous, and their connections embrace the best esteemed of the Virginia families.

† He was accompanied to Kentucky by his brothers Isham, Robert, and Charles Floyd, and his brothers-in-law LeMaster, Sturgis, and Pryor, husbands of his sisters. Three other sisters married respectively Alexander, Powell, and Tuley.

VIRGINIA AND VIRGINIANS.

scenes of the period. Alternately a surveyor, a legislator, and a soldier, his services were essentially important to the infant settlement. He was the principal surveyor of the Transylvania Company, and was chosen a delegate, from the town of St. Asaph, to the Assembly that met at Boonesborough on the 24th of May, 1775, to make laws for the colony. Honorably acquitting himself in all stations to which he was called, he finally met a violent death at the hands of the savages, on the 13th of April, 1783. The county of Floyd, Kentucky, commemorates his name. His third son,‡ John, the subject of this sketch, was born in Jefferson County, on the 24th of April, eleven days after the death of his father. Mrs. Floyd, after the death of her husband, married, secondly, Captain Alexander Breckinridge, his successor as surveyor of Jefferson County.‖ In 1796 young John Floyd entered Dickinson College, Carlisle, Pennsylvania, as a student, but through the failure of his guardian to meet his expenses he had to return home. He was fortunately enabled to resume his studies in 1801. Returning home in his twenty-first year, he married, May 13, 1804, in Franklin County, Kentucky, his second cousin, Lætitia (born September 29, 1799), the tenth child of Colonel William and Susannah (Smith) Preston. In October following he entered the University of Pennsylvania as a student of medicine, and graduated thence M. D. in April, 1806, and settled in Montgomery County, Virginia. He was appointed a justice of the peace in June, 1807; commissioned as major of militia in 1808; served as surgeon in the Virginia Line, in 1812, in the second war with Great Britain, and in the same year was elected a member of the House of Delegates of Virginia. In 1817 he was elected to the United States House of Representatives, and served ably in that body until 1829. "He was," it has been claimed, "the efficient head of the Virginia delegation. Others harangued more lengthily and learnedly, but his opinions were most deferred to, and his moral influence the greatest. 'We laugh,' said a facetious partisan member, 'at your Barbour's [P. P.] hair-splitting, but we indulge in no such merriment when we feel the glance of Floyd's savage eye.'" Mr. Floyd's influence in Congress was not the result of his superior eloquence or learning, for in both he was surpasssed; it was a concession to a sound and practical judgment united with a high and haughty courage, and, above all, an honesty that never entertained the first thought of barter or compromise. Mr. Floyd was elected Governor of Virginia by the Assembly, to succeed William B. Giles, in 1830; and in 1831 was unanimously re-elected by the same

---

‡ The elder sons were William Preston, born in 1780, and George Rogers Clark Floyd, born in 1782. The last distinguished himself in the war of 1812, in which he attained the rank of Lieutenant-Colonel.

‖ The issue of this marriage was six sons. Captain Breckinridge died in February, 1801, and Mrs. Breckinridge on the 13th of May, 1812.

body, under the amended constitution of the State. The second year of his administration is memorable as that of the tragic occurrence known as the "Southampton Insurrection." On Saturday night the 20th of August, 1831, a body of sixty or seventy slaves arose upon the white inhabitants of Southampton County and massacred fifty-five unsuspecting men, women, and children in their beds. The leader of this inhuman massacre was a negro slave named Nat Turner, about thirty-one years of age, born the slave of Benjamin Turner, of Southampton County. From childhood Nat was the victim of superstition and fanaticism. He stimulated his fellow-slaves to join him in the massacre by declaring to them that he had been commissioned by Jesus Christ, and that he was acting under inspired direction in atrocious designs. In the confession which he voluntarily made while in prison, he said: "That in his childhood a circumstance occurred which made an indelible impression on his mind and laid the groundwork of the enthusiasm which was so fatal in its termination. Being at play with other children, when three or four years old, I told them something, which my mother overhearing, said it happened before I was born. I stuck to my story, however, and related some things which went, in her opinion, to confirm it. Others being called upon, were greatly astonished, knowing these things had happened, and caused them to say, in my hearing, I surely would be a prophet, as the Lord had showed me things which happened before my birth." His parents strengthened him in this belief, and said in his presence that he was intended for some great purpose, which they had always thought from certain marks on his head and breast. Nat, as he grew up, was fully persuaded he was destined for some grand accomplishment. His powers of mind being much superior to his fellow-slaves, they looked up to him as one guided by divine inspiration. This belief he was assiduous to impress by exercises of apparently religious devotion and by the austerity of his life and manners. After a variety of alleged revelations from the spiritual world, Nat claimed that on the 12th of May, 1828:— "I heard a loud noise in the heavens, and the spirit instantly appeared to me and said that the serpent was loosened, and Christ had laid down the yoke he had borne for the sins of man, and that I should take it on and fight the serpent, for the time was fast approaching when the first should be last and the last should be first; and by signs in the heavens that it would make known to me when I should commence the great work; and, until the first sign appeared, I should conceal it from the knowledge of men. And on the appearance of the sign (the eclipse of the sun in February, 1831) I should arise and prepare myself, and slay my enemies with their own weapons. And immediately upon the sign appearing in the heavens the seal was removed from my lips, and I communicated the great work laid out for me to do to four in whom I had the greatest confidence." The massacre was laid for the 4th of July, but Nat fell sick, and the design was postponed until the "sign appeared again." Nat commenced the massacre by the murder of his master and family—Mr. Joseph Travis—with whom he had been living since the commencement of 1830; who was, Nat said, "a kind master, and placed the greatest confidence in me." Their first victims they slaughtered in their beds with axes. The wretches procured here "four guns that would shoot and several old muskets, with a pound or two of powder." Nat then paraded his force at the barn, "formed them in line as soldiers, and, after carrying them through all the manœuvres he was capable of, marched them" on to further diabolism.

They proceeded from house to house, murdering all the whites they could find, their force augmenting as they proceeded, till they numbered between fifty and sixty men, all mounted, and armed with guns, axes, swords, and clubs. They then started to Jerusalem, the county seat, and proceeded a few miles, when they were met by a party of the white inhabitants, who fired upon them and forced them to retreat. Their force of forty strong stopped for the night, putting out sentinels, but, being suddenly attacked by the whites, were thrown into great confusion. Nat, however, escaped with a portion of his adherents; but they were all hunted down save Nat, who supplied himself with provisions, and, scratching a hole under a pile of fence rails in a field, concealed himself for six weeks, leaving his hiding-place only for a few minutes at a time, in the dead of night, to obtain water, which was near. Finally he grew bolder, and ventured to the houses in the neighborhood to gather intelligence by eavesdropping. He was at last discovered by an accident. A dog, passing his cave one night when he was out, was attracted by some meat in the cave, crawled in, and was just emerging with it when Nat returned. A few nights after, two negroes were hunting with the dog, and passed the cave just as Nat came out of it. The dog, seeing him, barked, when Nat (thinking himself discovered) spoke to the negroes and begged them not to betray him; but, on making himself known, they fled from him. Knowing that he would be betrayed, Nat left his hiding-place, and was pursued incessantly until he was taken, about two weeks afterwards. Nat was executed at Jerusalem, November 11, 1831.

Governor Floyd served most acceptably in that office until March 31, 1834, when he was succeeded by Governor Littleton Waller Tazewell. He subsequently served for some time as Brigadier-General of the 17th Brigade of Virginia Militia. Governor Floyd had been in feeble health previous to his gubernatorial term, and his disease finally exhibited itself in paralysis. But he rallied after the first attack, and hopes were entertained that he would live for many years; but excitement, produced by the unexpected arrival, on a visit, of his son, Dr. William Preston

Floyd, caused a return of the paralysis on the 15th of August, 1837, which terminated his life, at the Sweet Springs, Montgomery County, Virginia, the following morning. The gifted John Hampden Pleasants, in an obituary which appeared in the Richmond *Whig*, August 24, 1837, glowingly eulogizes the worth and services of Governor Floyd, whom he characterizes as "a man gifted with the noblest qualities of our nature; * * * scrupulously just, and even obstinately honest; one of the very few public men of our country who died the same man he started in the beginning of his career, and who ran his course without the imputation or suspicion of tergiversation which springs from the fear of consequences, moral or personal cowardice. He entered life a States-rights man of the strict school of '98, and he battled for the cause to the end, and died in the faith. An ardent supporter of General Jackson, he renounced him the instant he conceived him to have deviated from those principles to which he was not merely affectionately, but passionately attached. His courage and honesty led him to scorn to palter with his own principles and understanding; and thus, when Nullification came on the stage, he adopted it as the doctrine of '98, which Mr. Jefferson, with the concurrence of the old Republicans, had pronounced the 'rightful remedy,' and which they had actually carried into practice at that era. He knew the unpopularity of the doctrine, but his honesty was made of sterner stuff than to barter his opinions for convenience or profit; and to his courage it was a matter of indifference what were the odds he encountered.* None who knew Governor Floyd well, could have failed to receive the impression that nature had endued him with the qualities of the hero, and that the stage and the opportunity only were wanting to have enabled him to shine among those who dazzled mankind with deeds of chivalry and prowess. The day has not long passed when some deemed the dark form of civil conflict not remote; and it is within our knowledge that many who then thought and feared had turned their eyes to him as the man worthy of leading the rebels against Federal tyranny and usurpation to the field. This brave and noble spirit is no more, and he deserves to be mourned in sincerity by every good man and patriot—himself inflexibly upright and a devoted patriot."

Governor Floyd was of a singularly handsome and commanding physique. "In height and erectness of person, gait, color and straightness of hair, swarthy skin, and, above all, his keen and dark rolling eye, he was the personification of an Indian chief—characteristics accounted for,

---

* It is noteworthy that the symbolic seal adopted by Governor Floyd was eminently characteristic. It was the well-known vignette on the title-page of Sanderson's *Signers of the Declaration of Independence:* A coiled serpent, ready to strike, on the summit of an isolated rock. This, engraved as a book-plate, garnished every book in his library, and was so used also by his distinguished son, Governor John Buchanan Floyd.

perhaps superstitiously, in a popular legend which ascribes them to the fact of his mother, before his birth, having been alarmed by a threatened savage attack upon her residence." It will be recollected that he was born a few days after his father had been slain by the Indians. Mrs. Floyd survived her husband several years, dying at "Cavan," her home, in Burke's Garden, Tazewell County, December 12, 1852. She was a mate worthy of so chivalric a husband, and possessed mental traits of a high order. They had issue twelve children, as follows:

i. *Susannah Smith*, born March 4, 1805; died August 29, 1806.
ii. *John Buchanan*, born June 1, 1806; died August 26, 1863; married his cousin, Sarah B., daughter of General Francis Preston; no issue; Governor of Virginia; Secretary of War of the United States under Buchanan; Major-General C. S. A., etc.
iii. *George Rogers Clarke*, born November 25, 1807; died August 15, 1808.
iv. *William Preston*, M. D., born January 16, 1809.
v. *George Rogers Clarke*, born September 13, 1810.
vi. *Benjamin Rush*, lawyer, born December 10, 1811; married Nancy Matthews, of Wytheville, Va. (issue: i. Malvina, married Major Peter Otey, C. S. A.; ii. John; iii. Benjamin Rush).
vii. *Lætitia Preston*, born March 13, 1814; married her cousin, Colonel William L. Lewis, of Sweet Springs, Va. (issue: i. Susan M., married Alfred Frederick, of South Carolina; ii. Lætitia, married Thomas L. P. Cocke; iii. William J., married Miss Dooley, of Richmond, Va.; iv. John Floyd; v. Charles).
viii. *Eliza Lavalette Madison*, born December 16, 1816; married Prof. George F. Holmes, LL.D., University of Virginia (issue: Mary Ann, Lætitia P., Henry H., Isabella, and Frederick L.).
ix. *Neickettie*, born June 6, 1819; married Hon. John W. Johnston, United States Senator (issue: i. Lætitia F.; ii. Louisa B.; iii. Sarah B., married Henry Carter Lee; iv. Lavalette; v. William F.; vi. George Ben., a popular physician of Richmond, Va.; vii. Miriam; viii. Joseph; ix. Coralie).
x. *Coralie Patton*, born June 26, 1822; died July 14, 1833.
xi. *Thomas Lewis Preston*, born August 16, 1824; died Sept. 4, 1824.
xii. *Mary Lewis Mourning*, born March 10, 1827; died July 26, 1833.

There is an excellent portrait of Governor Floyd in the State Library at Richmond, Virginia. Floyd County, formed in 1831 from Montgomery County, was named in his honor.

At the organization of the Virginia Historical Society, December 29, 1831, Chief Justice John Marshall was elected President and Governor John Floyd First Vice-President. The last presided at several meetings of the Society, and took the deepest interest in its foundation and mission.

LITTLETON WALLER TAZEWELL.

The ancestor of the Tazewell * family, in Virginia, was William Tazewell, a lawyer by profession, who settled in Accomac County in 1715. He was the son of James Tazewell, of Somersetshire, England, was born at Lymington, in that county, July 17, 1690, and was therefore twenty-five years old at the time of his arrival in the colony. He speedily found employment in his profession, and, as the records of Accomac County attest, attained an extensive and lucrative practice. Soon after settling in Virginia he married Sophia, daughter of Henry and Gertrude (daughter of Colonel Southey Littleton) Harmanson. The issue of this marriage was: i. *John*, Clerk of the Virginia Convention of June, 1776, and an eminent lawyer; died in 1781; ii. *Littleton*, brought up in the office of the Secretary of the Colony, Thomas Nelson, and married Mary, daughter of Colonel Joseph Gray, of Southampton County, who was a member of the House of Burgesses; iii. *Anne*, and iv. *Gertrude*. With the view of being near the relations of his wife, Littleton Tazewell sold his estate in Accomac County (which long afterwards became the property of his distinguished grandson, the subject of this sketch) and purchased land in Brunswick, became the clerk of the court of that county, and died at the early age of thirty-three years. He left issue, a son, Henry Tazewell, who was born in 1753; was a student at William and Mary College, and of law, in the office of his uncle, John Tazewell, and was soon admitted to the bar. In 1775, in the twenty-second year of his age, he was returned by his native county of Brunswick a member of the House of Burgesses, which was convoked to receive the conciliatory propositions of Lord North; and with an alacrity that was most honorable, he prepared an answer in detail, which was read and approved by Robert Carter Nicholas and Edmund Pendleton, but which, from accident, he was prevented from presenting, and it was anticipated by the answer of Thomas Jefferson, which was ultimately adopted. In the Convention of June, 1776, he was placed on the committee which re-

---

* The family was assumed by the late Hugh Blair Grigsby, LL.D., to be of Norman origin, and to deduce from one Tankersville, a knight under William the Conqueror, whose name is inscribed on the roll of Battle Abbey. He traces the changes in orthography as Tan'sville, Tanswell, and Tazewell. Indeed, the name is at this day variously rendered Tanswell, Tarswell, Tassell, Taswell, and Tazewell. In the *Miscellanea Genealogica et Heraldica* (Vol. I, p. 254) the family is traced to the year 1588, and the arms given as: Vair, purpure and erm. on a chief gu. a lion passant or. Crest—A demi-lion purpure, in the paws a chaplet of roses gu., which, however, differ from those used by John Tazewell and by Governor Littleton Waller Tazewell in book-plate and seal-ring respectively. By the former, from example in the possession of the writer, they were: Ar. or a fesse sa. three crescents between three eagles displayed. Crest—An eagle's head bearing in its beak a branch, head to the left. Motto—Vi quid Nimis. By the latter, from an impression of the seal-ring furnished by Robert Page Waller, Esq., of Norfolk, Va.; the same, with the difference of two instead of three crescents, which may have been a mistake of the engraver.

Curious Old Valentine of cut paper of 1753,
From the original in possession of R. A. Brock,
Secretary Virginia Historical Society.

ported the Declaration of Rights, and the Constitution. He was continuously returned a member of the House of Delegates, under the new Constitution, until his elevation to the bench, serving with conspicuous ability and wielding much influence in the councils of that body. He was the zealous friend of religious freedom, and advocated the abolition of primogeniture and entails, and the separation of the Church from the State. In 1785 he was made a judge of the General Court of the State, and as such was a member of its first Court of Appeals. In 1793, when the Court of Appeals was established, he was appointed one of its five judges. In 1794 he was elected over James Madison to succeed John Taylor "of Caroline," in the United States Senate, over which he presided in 1795, and bore in that body a distinguished part in the discussions on the British Treaty, sustaining with unqualified applause the leadership of the Republican party. In person he was singularly handsome, with a graceful and dignified mien. He died at Philadelphia, January 24, 1799, and his remains rest in that city near those of the eloquent James Innes. The county of Tazewell, formed in 1799 from Russell and Wythe, was named in his honor. The wife of Henry Tazewell was Dorothea Elizabeth, daughter of Judge Benjamin Waller,† at whose residence in Williamsburg, Virginia, a long low wooden building, the subject of this sketch, Littleton Waller Tazewell, was born December 17, 1774. His mother, who died three years after his birth, was a lovely woman, and her name, which, from the distasteful abbreviation of Dolly, has gone out of vogue, was a popular one in the last century. It was borne by

†The progenitor of the family in England, according to its records, was Alured de Waller, who came from Normandy with William the Conqueror, settled in the county of Kent, and died A. D. 1183. Richard Waller of this family distinguished himself at the battle of Agincourt, where he took prisoner the Duke of Orleans, commander-in-chief of the French army, and received from Henry V. of England, in honor of his heroic services, a crest of *the arms of France hanging by a label from an oak*, with the motto: *Hæc functus virtutis*. The ancient arms of the family were, and are: *A shield sable, three walnut leaves, or, between two bendlets or*. The crest granted as above being: *A walnut tree proper, on the sinister side an escutcheon pendent, charged with the arms of France (three fleurs-de-lis) with a label of three points, white*. Of this family was the famous poet laureate Benjamin Waller. The immediate ancestor of the Wallers of Virginia was Edmund Waller, who came from England near the close of the seventeenth century and settled in the county of Spotsylvania. He was its first clerk, and a member of the House of Burgesses. He had three sons, William, John, and Benjamin, the last, of the text (born 1716), who settled in Williamsburg, and was for a series of years, an assistant of Thomas Nelson, Secretary of the Council of Virginia, and finally a judge of the Court of Admiralty. He was a member of the House of Burgesses and of the patriot conventions of 1775 and 1776. He married Martha Hall, of North Carolina, and had issue ten children—his descendants being represented in the names of Tazewell, Taylor, Corbin, Bush, Travis, Byrd, Aylett, Cabell, Claiborne, Speed, Young, Mercer, Tucker, Langhorne, Garland, Massie, Duval, Robertson, Brockenbrough, and others equally worthy.

a daughter of Governor Alexander Spotswood, and by the wives of Patrick Henry and James Madison also. It has been oft honored in verse and prose, and symbolizes what a true woman is—the gift of God. Until 1786, young Tazewell lived with his grandfather, Benjamin Waller, who taught him the rudiments of English and Latin, and superintended his studies until his death in 1786, Judge Waller having committed him on his death-bed to the care of his life-long friend George Wythe. Young Tazewell lived with the latter until he removed to Richmond, when he became an inmate of the family of Bishop James Madison, President of William and Mary College. His first regular tutor was Walker Murray, with whom he prosecuted the study of Latin, and in whose school he was a classmate of John Randolph—cementing a friendship which continued without abatement until the death of that brilliant orator and eccentric being. Young Tazewell at an early age entered William and Mary College, and took the degree of Bachelor of Arts July 31, 1792. Having finished his college course he commenced the study of law in Richmond in the office of the eminent John Wickham, (whose wife was the half-sister of his father,) and lived with him as a member of his family. While engaged in the study he regularly attended the courts of Richmond, in which Judge Wythe presided as sole Chancellor and Edmund Pendleton as the President of the Court of Appeals. The bar of the State metropolis at this period comprised many men of eminence and vied in distinguished ability with that of any court in the United States. It was a potent school for the young lawyer. Tazewell received his license to practice law on the 14th of May, 1796. It was signed by Judges Peter Lyons, Edmund Winston, and Joseph Jones. The ability of Tazewell was at once discovered by John Marshall, who pronounced him an extraordinary young man. Tazewell surely made his way at the bar in the courts of James City and its neighboring counties. In the spring of 1796, when he had attained his twenty-first year, he was returned to the House of Delegates from the county of James City, and continued a member of that body until the close of the century—including the memorable sessions of 1798–99, and of 1799–1800. To the important papers from the pen of James Madison, the famous resolutions offered by John Taylor of Caroline, and the "Virginia Report," Tazewell gave a cordial support. John Marshall, having vacated his seat in the House of Representatives to accept the appointment of Secretary of State in the Cabinet of President John Adams, Tazewell, in his twenty-sixth year, was elected to succeed him, and took his seat on the 26th of November, 1800. At the close of his Congressional term in 1801, Mr. Tazewell returned home and withdrew from public life. On the 26th of June he qualified as an attorney in the Hustings Court of Norfolk, and, in the following year, made that city his residence. Its bar, at this period, was an able one, comprising such members as the venerable James Nimmo, General Thomas Matthews, Colonel John

Nivison, Robert Barraud Taylor, Alexander Campbell, and William Wirt; yet, amidst such an array of learning, the ability of Tazewell was at once recognized, and his practice speedily became extensive and lucrative. The flagrant outrage upon the American flag in 1807, which has been alluded to in preceding sketches as one of the prime instigations to the second war with Great Britain, was a humiliation which touched the local sensibilities of Norfolk to the quick. On the 22d of June, the frigate "Chesapeake," built by its native mechanics, launched in the waters of the Elizabeth River, in view of the city, put out to sea from Hampton Roads, under command of Captain James Barron. On the following day, unsuspecting of danger, she was attacked by the British frigate "Leopard," and became her prize after three men had been killed, and sixteen wounded. The British commander, after taking from the "Chesapeake" certain seamen, whom he alleged were deserters from the British flag, declined to take possession of the captured frigate, which returned to the Roads. The wounded men were taken to the Marine Hospital, in Norfolk, where one of them died. Intense indignation prevailed in the city. It was believed that the outrage was deliberately designed, and the cry for vengeance burst from the whole people. In full assembly, with the venerable General Matthews presiding, they appointed, as in the days of '76, a Committee of Safety. A preamble, duly setting forth the outrage on the "Chesapeake," was adopted, and it was resolved that there should be no intercourse with the British frigates in the Norfolk waters, or with their agents, until the decision of the United States Government was known, under the penalty of being deemed infamous; and the Committee of Safety— Thomas Matthews, Thomas Newton, Jr., Luke Wheeler, Theodric Armistead, Richard E. Lee, Moses Myers, William Pennock, William Newsum, Thomas Blanchard, Daniel Bedinger, Seth Foster, J. W. Murdaugh, Richard Blow, and Francis S. Taylor—were authorized to take such measures as the emergency demanded. As soon as the British commander—Commodore Douglas—read the resolves, he addressed, on the 3d of July, an insolent letter to the Mayor of the Borough, in which he declared if the resolutions were not *instantly annulled*, he would prohibit every vessel bound in or out of Norfolk from proceeding to her place of destination. He closed his communication by saying that he had proceeded with his squadron of four fifty-gun frigates to Hampton Roads to await the answer of the Mayor, which he hoped would be forwarded without delay. It is thought that Mr. Tazewell had regulated the popular proceedings from their initiation. In the delicate dilemma, which was ominous of vengeful deeds and of so much menace to the commercial interests of Norfolk, he came to the assistance of the Mayor and dictated a reply to the audacious Briton which elicited the admiration of the whole American Nation. The letter, written on the 4th of

July, thus began: "Sir, I have received your menacing letter of yesterday. The day on which this answer is written ought of itself to prove to the subjects of your sovereign that the American people are not to be imtimidated by menace; or induced to adopt any measures except by a sense of their perfect propriety. Seduced by the false show of security, they may be sometimes surprised and slaughtered while unprepared to resist a supposed friend. That delusive security is now passed forever. The late occurrence has taught us to confide our safety no longer to any thing than to our own force. We do not seek hostility, nor shall we avoid it. We are prepared for the worst you may attempt, and will do whatever shall be judged proper to repel force whensoever your efforts shall render any acts of ours necessary. Thus much for the threats in your letter." The letter was delivered by Mr. Tazewell (who was accompanied by Tazewell Taylor), to Commodore Douglas, in presence of the Captains of the Fleet (among whom was Sir Thomas Hardy, whom Lord Nelson so affectionately addressed in his dying moments). It had a due effect. The threats were all recanted, and a letter of the 5th of July breathed nothing but amity and peace—an amusing somersault, like unto which is scarcely to be recalled in the annals of diplomacy.

In 1816, during an absence from home, and without his knowledge, Mr. Tazewell was elected by the people of Norfolk to the House of Delegates. His speech in that body against the Convention bill, and in reply to General Alexander Smyth, is memorable for its ability and eloquence. The bill passed in the House but was lost in the Senate. In 1820 Mr. Tazewell was one of the Commissioners under the Florida treaty. In 1824 he was elected to the United States Senate. He was elected to fill a vacancy caused by the resignation of John Taylor of Caroline. It is a coincidence that his father, thirty years before, was chosen to fill the vacancy in the Senate caused by the resignation of the same individual. L. W. Tazewell took his seat in January, 1825. His first efforts in the debates was on the bankrupt bill of that session—a searching examination of its details, which annihilated the hopes of its friends. His speech, on the 21st of January, in behalf of his motion to strike out the third section of the bill for the suppression of piracy in the West India seas, which had been reported from the Committee of Foreign Affairs, and had been introduced by its chairman, James Barbour, was lauded throughout the country. The section proposed to be stricken out authorized the President of the United States in time of profound peace to declare, on the representations of a naval officer, any of the ports of Spain in the West Indies in a state of blockade. It was stricken out by the decisive vote of 37 to 10. Had it remained in the bill, a war with Spain in all probability would have resulted in less than ninety days. On the election of John Quincy Adams to the Presidency, Mr. Tazewell became hostile to his administration and opposed its prominent measures. His speech on the exclusive constitutional competency of the executive to originate foreign missions without the advice and consent of the Senate, as a constitutional thesis, it is claimed, "stands pre-eminent in our political literature as a model of profound research, of thorough argumentation, and of overwhelming strength." Mr. Tazewell was re-elected to the Senate on the 1st day of January, 1829. Whilst in attendance on that body he was elected by the Norfolk district a member of the Convention which assembled in Richmond, October 5th, 1829, to revise the first Constitution of Virginia. In that illustrious body Mr. Tazewell made the opening speech in support of a resolution which he offered, and which marked out the course of the campaign which he believed to be best adapted to attain the general end in view. He engaged with conspicuous ability in the important discussions of the convention. His speech on the tenure of the judicial office is claimed to have been one of the most able efforts in that body of intellectual giants. Mr. Tazewell was also, in 1829, tendered the mission to Great Britain, but declined the honor. He continued in the Senate until 1833, serving as Chairman of the Committee on Foreign Relations, and as President *pro tem.* of the body during a portion of the twenty-second Congress. In January, 1834, he was elected Governor of Virginia to succeed John Floyd, and entered upon the duties of his office March 31st. He resigned March 31, 1836, before the expiration of the term, upon a disagreement with the State Legislature. That body had passed resolutions instructing the Senators from Virginia to vote for the resolutions to expunge from the journal of the Senate the resolutions censuring General Jackson. These instructions Governor Tazewell declined to approve. He was succeeded in the office of Governor by Lieutenant-Governor Wyndham Robertson. Mr. Tazewell was never afterwards in public service. Though so effective with juries as an advocate, his style of address is said to have been singularly simple and free from artifice. His arguments were conversational and his gestures not more striking than those of animated converse. His postures were negligent. His voice was pleasant and of ample compass. He was never vociferous. His logic was consummate, and in putting his arguments before a jury he exhibited great adroitness. He acquainted himself with the calling or prejudices of every juryman—and was thus guided in his appeals to them.

When the passions were to be assailed he indulged in a style of fervid appeal, which was the more effective as it was rare. Of the person of Mr. Tazewell, his friend and eulogist, Hugh Blair Grigsby, LL.D., says: "As soon as the visitor fixed his eyes on Mr. Tazewell, all else was forgotten. He was, without exception, in middle life, the most imposing, and in old age, the most venerable person I ever beheld. His height exceeded six feet. * * * His head and chest were on a large scale, and his vast blue eye, which always seemed to gaze afar, was aptly termed by Wirt an 'eye of ocean.' In early youth he was uncommonly handsome. In middle life he was very thin, though lithe and strong," but in his latter days he was large of stature, with massive features, and hair of silvery whiteness, which fell in ringlets about his neck. He died at Norfolk, May 6, 1860. He was the author of a "Review of the Negotiations between the United States and Great Britain respecting the Commerce between the Two Countries," etc. London, 8vo, 1829, and which first appeared under the signature "Sinex," in the Norfolk *Herald,*" in 1827. A portrait of Governor Tazewell is in the State Library at Richmond, Virginia. He married, in 1802, Anne Stratton, daughter of Colonel John Nivison, of Norfolk, Virginia.

WYNDHAM ROBERTSON.

The clan Donnachie, or Duncan, or Robertson, trace descent from Duncan, King of Scotland, eldest son of Malcolm III., their immediate ancestor being a son of the "ancient and last Celtic Earl of Atole" who, in the reign of Alexander II., received the lands of Strowan. A great grandson of this founder was named Andrew, and was styled of Athole or "de Atholia," which was the uniform designation of the family; and from Duncan, a son of Andrew, they derive their distinctive appellation of the clan Donnachie, or "children of Duncan." This Duncan was twice married, and acquired by both marriages considerable territory in the district of Rannoch. By his first wife he had a son Robert "de Atholia," who also had a grandson named Robert; and from him the clan Duncan or Donnachie derive the name of Robertson from their lowland neighbors. This Robert is famous in history, and known as the chief who arrested and delivered to the vengeance of the government Robert Graham and the master of Athole, two of the murderers of James I., for which he was rewarded with a crown charter, dated 1451. He was mortally wounded in a conflict with Robert Forrester, of Solwood, with whom he had a dispute regarding the lands of Little Dunkeld. Binding his head in a white cloth, he rode to Perth and obtained from the king a new grant of the lands of Strowan. Returning home he died of his wounds. His eldest son was twice married; his son, again, becoming progenitor of various families of Robertsons. Towards the close of the century an heiress of the clan married "Thomas of Loudoun," while another married "David of Hastings," and an heiress of the Leeds branch married a Stewart of Invermeath. The clan were valiant and powerful supporters of the House of Stewart, and devoted to the cause of Charles I. It furnished, during the past two centuries, many warriors and learned men, famous in Scottish annals. Alexander Robertson, the celebrated Jacobite chief and poet, was born about 1670. After a warlike and eventful life he died, in the eighty-first year of his age, in his own house. Carr of Rannoch's poems were published after his death, with a history of the Robertsons of Strowan. He was Sir Walter Scott's prototype of the Baron "Bradwardine," in *Waverley*. The ancestor of the Robertsons of Virginia was William Robertson, son of the Bailie of Edinburgh, Scotland, and a relative of Alexander Robertson, of Strowan, Baron Bradwardine, who emigrated to the colony in the early part of the eighteenth century, and settled in Bristol parish, near the location of Petersburg. His son, William Robertson, born in the year 1750, was a vestryman, warden, and deputy of Bristol parish from 1779 to 1789, a member of the council of Virginia, and for a series of years its secretary. He married Elizabeth, daughter of Thomas and Elizabeth (Gay) Bolling, of "Cobbs" (fourth in descent from John Rolfe and the Indian Princess Pocahontas), and had issue twelve children, those who survived being as follows: i. *Archibald*, born 1776; died 1861; married Elizabeth M. Bolling; ii. *Thomas Bolling*, born February 27, 1778; married, April, 1821, Lelia, daughter of Fulwar Skipwith; studied law with the distinguished John Thompson; member of the House of Delegates from Dinwiddie County 1805-6; appointed, in the summer of 1807, by President Jefferson, Secretary of the then territory of Orleans; continued in this station until Louisiana was erected into a State; member of Congress 1812-18, when he resigned, resuming the practice of law; appointed, in 1819, Attorney-General of Louisiana; elected Governor of the State in 1820; appointed, in 1825, United States Judge for the district of Louisiana. During the recess of Congress, 1815, he visited England and France, and being in Paris at the time of the return of Bonaparte from the campaign which ended in his overthrow at Waterloo, he wrote a concise and animated account of the interesting scenes which were passing before him, in letters to his friends in Virginia, which were published in the Richmond *Enquirer*, and in book form. He died October 5, 1828, at the White Sulphur Springs, Greenbrier County, Virginia, where a monument marks his remains; iii. *William*, born 1786; member of the Virginia Assembly; married Christiana, daughter of Frederick Williams, and had issue; iv. *John*, born 1788; died 1873; Attorney-General of Virginia; member of State Assembly, and Chancellor of Virginia; member of Congress, representing Richmond for more than half a century; a quaint, vigorous, and accomplished writer, publishing many *brochures*; married, in 1814, Anne Trent, and left issue; v. *Anne*, born 1790; died 1842; married Henry Skipwith, M. D., and left issue; vi. *Jane Gay*, born 1796; died 1840; married, 1818, John H. Bernard, of "Gaymont," Caroline County, Virginia, member of the State Senate; left issue; vii. *Wyndham*, the subject of this sketch, born January 26, 1803. He first attended the private schools in his native city—Richmond—and completed his education at William and Mary College under the presidency of the brilliant John Augustine Smith, graduating

REV. JOHN BUCHANAN D.D.
Rector of St. Johns Church Richmond Va. from 1785 to his death in 1820.

thence in 1821. Entering upon the study of law, he was admitted to the bar in 1824. In 1827 he went to Europe for recreation, visiting the cities of London and Paris. Returning home he resumed the practice of his profession. The French Revolution of 1830 enkindled the patriotism of the citizens of Richmond to highly enthusiastic demonstrations in civic procession, with flags and banners flying, the parade of the military with salute of musketry and cannon, and a mass meeting. Mr. Robertson was the chosen orator on the occasion, to voice the public sentiment, an office which he discharged so eloquently and acceptably that the common sympathy then established carried with it a regard and confidence which was enduring and found expression in many positions of honorable trust conferred on him. In 1833 Mr. Robertson was elected a member of the Council of State. In 1834, at the first meeting of the James River and Kanawha Company, the successors to the franchises of the old James River Company, Mr. Robertson proposed, in lieu of the projected canal, a measure that looked to a railroad connection with Lynchburg, to progress alternately westward, on the one hand, to the Mississippi, and on the other to the Kanawha. Although his proposition was defeated, it had the favor of sagacious and able minds, Dr. John Brockenbrough, Judge Philip Norborne Nicholas, Moncure Robinson, and Hon. John Robertson being among its supporters. After nearly half a century the wisdom of the measure proposed has been vindicated in the displacing of the canal by the Richmond & Alleghany Railroad erected on its banks, and which we may hope, may yet grasp the consummations so long ago ardently outlined by Mr. Robertson. On the 31st of March, 1836, Mr. Robertson became senior member of the Council, and as such, Lieutenant-Governor, and on the same day, by the resignation of Governor Tazewell, succeeded him for the remaining year of his term as Governor of Virginia. The period is somewhat memorable. Then began the initiatory movements of the undisguised and fateful crusade by the Northern section of our Union against slavery. We can now calmly survey its turbulent course in thankful acceptation of an issue which is destined to progressively redound in blessings to the South. A different sentiment then prevailed in Virginia. In his first message to the Legislature, Governor Robertson called attention to the abolition movement, designating it as "a mad fanaticism, the march of which, if unchecked, could well be over violated faith, the rights of the slave-holding States, chartered liberty, and the cause of humanity itself," and recommended that measures should be taken for a convention of all the States to take measures to avert such dire consequences. The Democracy being largely in the majority in the Legislature of 1836-7, one of that party—David Campbell—was chosen to succeed Governor Robertson on the expiration of his term, March 31, 1837, and he retired to private life. In 1841, his health being impaired, he removed to the country and engaged in agricultural pursuits. In 1858 he returned to Richmond, and in 1860 acquiesced in the wishes of his old constituents to serve them in the House of Delegates. A friend to peace and the Union, Mr. Robertson actively opposed secession, and the overtures of South Carolina for a Southern Convention as endangering both, and hastening the loss of what they were designed to save. After South Carolina and other Southern States had seceded, he still urged a refusal on the part of Virginia to follow them, and brought, as the organ of a committee, into the House of Delegates, January 7, 1861, the resolution known as the Anti-Coercion Resolution, denying the existence of present cause for secession, but declaring her purpose, if a war of coercion was undertaken by the Federal Government on the seceded States, to fight with the South. The resolution was adopted. The State now addressed itself to measures of reconciliation, some of which were proposed, and all were advocated by Mr. Robertson. They were, however, all futile, and the proclamation of President Lincoln calling for troops from Virginia, speedily determined her lot with her Southern sisters, peopled by her own offspring, and Mr. Robertson, ever a dutiful son, was henceforth zealously active in all measures of sustenance and defense, in the lamentable fraticidal strife which ensued. The painful struggle over, he removed to the native place of his wife (Mary T., daughter of Francis Smith, Esq.), Abingdon, Virginia, where he has since resided. Mr. Robertson has been an ardent student of history for many years, naturally with as pecial regard for that of his native State. He has frequently contributed the results of his research to periodicals, and at the annual meeting of the Virginia Historical Society, December 15, 1859, he read an exhaustive paper on the "Marriage of Pocahontas with John Rolfe," which was published by the Society. He has had in preparation for a number of years past, a genealogical account of his kindred, "The Descendants of Pocahontas," which, it is believed, is now ready for publication. There is an excellent portrait of Governor Robertson in the State Library at Richmond, Virginia.

DAVID CAMPBELL.

Of all the family names of Scotland, there is hardly another so invested with lustre in the varied manifestations of human greatness, so renowned for valorous deeds, or so proudly enshrined in the national affection, as that of Campbell: and the race transplanted in America has flourished alike, and in its distinguished representatives, by numerously attested examples, has lost naught of that which constitutes true nobility; for in every department of learning and of useful service, and in heroism by sea and land, has the name lent honor to our national annals.

It is believed that a majority of those in this country, of the name, who claim Scottish origin, are descended from Duncan Campbell, of the noble branch of Breadalbane.* Duncan Campbell, born in Inverary, Scotland, accompanied, it is thought, the English army sent by Queen Elizabeth, in March, 1579, under the Earl of Essex (who was succeeded by Mountjoy), to suppress the rebellion in Ireland, headed by Hugh O'Neale, Earl of Tyrone. After the forfeiture of lands in Ulster was declared in the reign of James I., in 1612, Duncan Campbell, who had married Mary McCoy, bought a lease from one of the English officers, and remained there. His son Patrick bought the lease and the estate in remainder, thus acquiring the estate in fee simple. Another son, John Campbell, born in 1621; married, in 1655, Grace, daughter of Peter Hay,† and had issue:

i. *Dugald*, whose descendants settled in Rockbridge County, Virginia.

ii. *Robert*, born in 1665; married in 1696. His descendants settled in Orange (now Augusta) County, Virginia, in 1740.

iii. *John*, born in 1666; died in 1734; emigrated to America in 1726, and settled in Donegal, Lancaster County, Pennsylvania, but soon removed with several of his family to that part of Orange County, Virginia, which in 1738 was formed into Augusta County. Had issue:
i. *Patrick*, born in 1690; "a strong churchman;" removed to Virginia in 1738, and was the father of General William Campbell, the hero of King's Mountain (after whom the county of Campbell, formed in 1784 from Bedford, was named), born in 1745, and was killed in September, 1781; married Elizabeth, the sister of the orator Patrick Henry, and she married, secondly, General William Russell, of the Revolution, born in Culpeper County, Virginia, in 1758, and died in Fayette County, Kentucky, July 3, 1825. ii. *John*, born in 1692; a minister of the Protestant Episcopal Church at York, Pennsylvania; died in 1764; married, and had issue: James, born in 1731; removed to Vir-

---

* The Breadalbane branch are of the same lineage as the House of Argyll and Lorne. The arms of Duncan Campbell, as preserved in the hands of his descendants, are identical in their quarterings with the Marquis of Breadalbane, as follows: Quarterly, first and fourth, gyronny of eight or. and sa. for Campbell; second or. a fesse chequey ar. and az. for Stewart; third, ar. a lymphad, her sails and oars in action, all sa. for Lorne. The Breadalbane arms agree with those of Argyll save in the addition of those of Stewart. The crest of the Marquis of Breadalbane is a boar's head, erased ppr., and his motto is, *Follow Me*. The crest of the Duke of Argyll is a boar's head couped or., and over the crest the motto, *Ne Obliviscaris*.

† The name of Hay is a most worthy one. A Dr. Peter Hay died at Williamsburg, Virginia, in 1767, and his library was advertised that year for sale at auction. The Rev. Robert Rose, of fragrant memories for piety, worth, and usefulness, and whose remains lie in the church-yard of the venerable St. John's, at Richmond, Virginia, was of this connection.

ginia in 1760; Ellen Frances, and John, born in 1740; died in 1797; one of the most eminent lawyers of Pennsylvania; married Ellen Parker, and their descendants in the names of Lyon, Chambers, and others, are quite numerous. The late Parker Campbell, banker of Richmond, Virginia, was a son. iii. *Robert*, migrated to Virginia; had issue five children, of whom four daughters survived. iv. *William*, died in youth. v. *James*, died in England. vi. *David*, married, in 1735, Mary Hamilton (who came to America in the same ship with him), and, about the year 1772, settled at the "Royal Oak," in the Valley of the Holstein (now rendered Holston), about one mile west of Marion, the county seat of Smyth County. He left issue seven sons: i. *John*, born April 20, 1741. ii. *Colonel Arthur*, born in 1742; hero of Indian wars; married a sister of General William Campbell; removed in 1804 to Yellow Creek, Knox County, Kentucky, where he died in 1815. He had two sons, who died in the war of 1812—Colonel James Campbell, at Mobile, and Colonel John B. Campbell, who fell at Chippewa, where he commanded the right wing of the army under General Winfield Scott. iii. *James*; iv. *William*; v. *David*, first clerk of Washington County, which office he held until March 17, 1779, when he was succeeded by his brother John. Removing to Tennessee, he became distinguished in its annals. vi. *Robert*, Colonel, and Indian fighter, born in 1755; displayed great bravery in many conflicts with the Cherokees, and subsequently at the battle of King's Mountain; nearly forty years a magistrate of Washington County, and in 1825 removed to Tennessee; died near Knoxville in February, 1832. vii. *Patrick*.

Of the above sons of David Campbell, the eldest-born, John, was one of the justices (commissioned by Governor Patrick Henry) who, after the county of Washington (embracing portions of Wythe, Tazewell and Grayson, and all of Smyth, Russell, Buchanan, Dickinson, Wise, Scott and Lee, and its own present limits) had been formed in 1776, met at Abingdon and organized and held the first county court, January 28, 1777. He succeeded, March 17, 1779, his brother David Campbell as clerk of the county, and continued to hold the office by successive re-election until 1814. In 1778 he married Elizabeth, daughter of Edward and Mary (Robinson) McDonald, ‡ of the section of what is now Botetourt County, Virginia, and, it is said, built the first dwelling in Abingdon (a log-house), on the lot on which the Arlington Hotel now stands. In 1788 he purchased of Thomas Madison, attorney of James Buchanan, a farm of eleven hundred acres in the south-western portion of Washington County, to which he gave the name of "Hall's Bottom," and shortly

‡ His grandfather, Bryan McDonald, the son of a Highland chief of Glencoe, Scotland, migrated to America near the close of the 17th or the beginning of the 18th century and settled in Newcastle, now in the State of Delaware, whence Edward McDonald removed to Virginia.

after removed to and continued to reside there until his death, on the 20th of April, 1825. David Campbell, his eldest son, and the subject of this sketch, was born August 2d, 1779, at "Royal Oak," and was about eight years of age when his father removed to "Hall's Bottom." There he grew up, receiving such education as the frontier settlements could provide. In the way of books it was necessarily limited, but this great disadvantage was largely compensated for by the character of the people among whom he was reared; by their recitals of the scenes and deeds of the Revolution, in which they bore so conspicuous and important a part, and which were then but as the acts of yesterday; and by the lessons of self-reliance which were taught by all his surroundings. In 1794, being then in his fifteenth year, David Campbell was appointed an Ensign in "old" Captain John Davis' company of militia in the 2d Battalion of the 70th Regiment, which position he held until he removed to Abingdon as an assistant in the clerk's office there. In the spring of 1799 the 70th Regiment was divided and the 105th Regiment formed. In the 2d Battalion of this regiment David Campbell was commissioned as Captain of a company of Light Infantry assigned to it, and which he raised and organized. In the fall of the same year Captain Campbell married his cousin Mary Hamilton, by whom he had no issue. He now studied law, and obtained a license, but never practiced his profession. He was fond of reading (history and the English classics being his special favorites), and thus enriched his mind and acquired his style of written composition. In 1802 he was appointed deputy clerk of the county court of Washington County, and chiefly discharged the duties of the office to the year 1812, on the 6th of July of which he was commissioned a Major in the 12th Infantry, United States Army. He assisted Colonel Parker in collecting recruits, organizing and drilling them at Winchester, and marched with his command for the Lakes of Canada on the 29th of August, and efficiently served there under the command successively of Generals Smyth and Van Rensellaer. On the 12th of March, 1813, he was promoted to the rank of Lieutenant-Colonel of the 20th United States Regiment and participated in the arduous campaigns of that regiment on the St. Lawrence and towards Lake Champlain. The troops on the Northern frontier were greatly exposed during the campaigns of 1812 and 1813, and the constitution of Colonel Campbell, naturally delicate, gave way under the hardships to which he was exposed. He was so severely attacked with rheumatism as to incapacitate him for duty, and in consequence applied to the Secretary of War for a transfer to the Southern Division of the Army. His application was recommended by his superior officers, Colonel Randolph and General Parker, but from some cause was disapproved by the Secretary of War, and Colonel Campbell was necessitated to resign his commission January 28th, 1814. Upon returning home, he in a short time entered the service of Virginia as Aide-de-Camp to Governor Barbour, and gave valuable assistance in organizing the large militia force called into service in the neighborhood of Richmond and below it and about Petersburg in the summer of 1814. These services Colonel Campbell performed without pay. In the session of the Assembly of 1814–15 a law was passed for raising 10,000 troops and under it Colonel Campbell was elected General of the 3d Brigade. On the 25th of January he was appointed Colonel of the 3d Virginia Cavalry, and by the formation of the 5th Division of militia was afterwards transferred to the 5th Regiment of cavalry. Upon his return to Abingdon, Virginia, he re-entered the clerk's office, where he continued until 1820, when he was elected to the Senate of Virginia for four years. He actively participated in public affairs both before and after his election to the Senate. He was remarkable for his ready and correct judgment of men, and this, coupled with the opportunity which his position gave him, enabled him to exercise a wide-spread influence in his resident section of the State. In 1824 he was elected clerk of the county court of Washington, and continued to hold the office until he was elected Governor of Virginia, in 1836, and entered upon the office March 31, 1837.

Virginia at this period was preponderantly Democratic in politics; so decided was the sentiment of Washington County, in the Presidential election of 1828, that only thirteen votes against General Andrew Jackson were cast. David Campbell was a Jackson Democrat, as was also each of his four brothers. In his first message to the General Assembly, among other matters of public utility he proposed the establishment of the common school system, of which he was one of the earliest advocates. This was, no doubt, greatly stimulated by the fact that his own section of the State was, by its remoteness from the institutions of learning of high grade, deprived of their advantages, and was due, also, largely to his attachment to Republican institutions; and his decided conviction was potential, if not essential, in their preservation. Whilst Governor, and during the administration of President Van Buren, the Sub-Treasury scheme and the Standing Army bill, as they were commonly called, were made party measures; being opposed to them, he warmly supported General Harrison in the canvass of 1840, and ever after acted with the Whig party. He was alike opposed to centralization on the hand, and nullification and secession on the other. Governor Campbell was succeeded in the office, March 31, 1840, by Thomas Walker Gilmer, and retired to his home in Abingdon. Soon afterwards the office of Justice of the Peace being tendered him, he accepted it, and was diligent in the discharge of its entire duties to the year 1852, when he retired to private life after having spent nearly a half century in the public service. In person Governor Campbell was about five feet eleven inches in height, spare, and erect in carriage, with dark hair and eyes, an intellectual countenance, and pleasing manners. He was not gifted as a public speaker. As a writer, his style was simple, terse, and vigorous.

He was not a member of any religious denomination, but, profoundly convinced of the truth of the Bible, he believed that the highest and best manifestation of religion was a life in accordance with its teachings.

For the last two years of his life he was confined by declining health to his chamber, but gave no evidence of that mental decay which sometimes attends old age, and his interest in public affairs seemed unabated. He died, calmly and peacefully, March 19, 1859, in the eightieth year of his age. A portrait of Governor Campbell is exhibited in the State Library at Richmond. A nephew, Hon. John A. Campbell, of Abingdon, Virginia, a distinguished jurist, late Colonel Confederate States Army, gallantly commanded during our late war the 48th Virginia Regiment, which he raised and organized. It was incorporated in the 2d Brigade of the Division of General "Stonewall" Jackson, which was composed of the 21st, 42d, and 48th Virginia Regiments, the Irish Battalion, and the Battery of Lawrence S. Marge, afterwards Colonel Marge. The Brigade was for a time commanded by Colonel William Gilham of the 21st Virginia, then by Colonel Jesse S. Burks of the 42d Virginia, who, receiving a disabling wound at the battle of Kernstown in March, 1862, was succeeded by Colonel Campbell, who remained in command until the month of May, when he also was severely wounded in front of Winchester, Virginia. Before recovering sufficiently to return to the army Colonel Campbell was elected Judge of the Sixteenth Judicial Circuit of Virginia, and at the request of his constituents resigned his commission in the army. The Campbell family of the common ancestry of Governor Campbell has been numerously and distinguishedly represented in Ohio, Pennsylvania, Maryland, Virginia, Kentucky, Tennessee, and other States.

THOMAS WALKER GILMER.

The ancestry of Thomas Walker Gilmer was highly worthy. His paternal great-grandfather, Dr. George Gilmer, a native of Scotland,* and a graduate of the University of Edinburgh, migrated to Virginia early in the eighteenth century, and settled in Williamsburg, where he

---

* He was of the same lineage, it is said, as the Gilmours of Craig-Millar Castle, seated two and a half miles south of Edinburgh. The arms of the Gilmer family of Virginia are: Az. a chevron between two fleurs-de-lis in chief d'or; and in base, a writing-pen, full feathered ar. Crest—A garland of laurel proper. Motto: *Preseveranti dabiter.*

Exterior View, before alteration, of
ST. JOHN'S CHURCH, RICHMOND, VIRGINIA,
Built in 1740.

Interior View, before alteration, of
ST. JOHN'S CHURCH, RICHMOND, VIRGINIA,
Built in 1740.

successfully combined the vocations of physician, surgeon, and druggist for quite fifty years, dying January 15, 1757, widely loved and esteemed in the colony. He was three times married: first, to a daughter of Dr. Ridgway (a medical partner in early life), by whom he had no issue; secondly, May 13, 1732, to Mary Peachy (died October 1, 1745), daughter of Thomas and Susan (Peachy) Walker, of King and Queen County, Virginia, and sister of Dr. Thomas Walker, the patriot and early explorer of Kentucky; thirdly, December 11, 1745, to Harrison (died November 1, 1755), daughter of Dr. Archibald Blair, of Williamsburg, Virginia, a sister of Hon. John Blair, President of Virginia Council and Acting Governor of Virginia, and a niece of Commissary James Blair, President of William and Mary College. By his second marriage, Dr. George Gilmer had issue four sons: i. *Peachy Ridgway*, born March 6, 1737-8, married Mary Meriwether, settled at "Lethe," Rockingham County (and had issue: i. Thomas Meriwether, married Elizabeth Lewis, and removed to Georgia, settling on Broad River. He was the father of a large family, among them Hon. George Rockingham Gilmer, member of Congress, Governor of Georgia, and author of "The Georgians;" ii. George; iii. Mary Peachy; iv. Elizabeth Thornton, married Major Robert Grattan; v. Lucy; vi. Frances Walker, married Richard Taliaferro); ii. *George*, born January 19, 1742-3, studied medicine with his uncle, Dr. Thomas Walker, and graduated at Edinburgh, Scotland. The issue of Dr. George Gilmer by his third marriage was: iii. *John*, born April 26, 1748; an officer under Lafayette in the Revolution; married Mildred Meriwether, and died, in 1790, at his seat on Broad River, in the State of Georgia; iv. *William*, born May 22, 1753, died May 30, 1753.

Dr. George Gilmer, the second of the name, returning to Virginia after graduating, succeeded to the practice of his father in Williamsburg, but after a time removed to Albemarle County, where he married his first cousin Lucy (born May 5, 1751), daughter of Dr. Thomas Walker by his first marriage with Mildred (*nee* Thornton), widow of Nicholas Meriwether. He settled at " Pen Park," and soon attained a lucrative practice in his profession. The friend and intimate associate of Thomas Jefferson, he was an ardent patriot from the beginning to the end of the struggle for Independence. He served Albemarle in the House of Burgesses, and, as early as 1774, offered a resolution in that body on the subject of the Crown Lands, which was seconded by William Henry. He was gifted as an orator, and, when Lord Dunmore seized the powder of the colony, Dr. Gilmer harangued the citizens of Albemarle with such eloquence, that a company was immediately formed to march to Williamsburg to demand redress. Of this company Charles Lewis was chosen captain, and Dr. George Gilmer lieutenant. The company marched to Williamsburg, but their patriotic mission was anticipated by Patrick Henry. In the Convention of 1775, which met at Williamsburg, Dr. Gilmer was returned by Albemarle County as the alternate of Thomas Jefferson. His wife was a worthy mate to such a patriot. During the early days of the struggle for Independence, the patriots in different sections of the country found great difficulty in corresponding with each other, and it became necessary to establish a secret means of intercommunication by private letter-carriers. Mr. Jefferson, during a visit to his friend Dr. Gilmer at this period, in conversation with him, deplored the want of funds to defray the expense of such correspondence. Mrs. Gilmer, who was present, immediately left the room, and speedily returning with her personal jewels, of much value, handed them to Mr. Jefferson, and, with tearful eyes, asked him to use them in the cause of her country. Nor was she less a heroine than a patriot. When the British troops, under the command of Tarleton, entered Charlottesville in pursuit of the Assembly, as has been detailed in a preceding sketch, Mr. A., a friend of Dr. Gilmer, was a guest of Mrs. Gilmer, her husband being absent professionally. Mr. A., mounting his horse, attempted to escape, but was shot down, and carried off by the enemy. Mrs. Gilmer, learning that he was still alive, determined to succor him; and, accompanied by a maiden sister only, made her way perilously through the village, filled with drunken and disorderly troopers, to the presence of Tarleton himself, on her errand of mercy. He was so filled with admiration at the courage displayed by Mrs. Gilmer, that he not only delivered to her the helpless and insensible form of her friend, but sent his own surgeon to attend him until Dr. Gilmer returned. Mr. A. happily recovered, to gallantly serve his country, and to bequeath to his descendants a debt of gratitude to the worthy couple of "Pen Park."

The issue of Dr. George and Lucy (Walker) Gilmer was: i. Francis Walker, an accomplished scholar and writer, the first professor of law of the University of Virginia, and who selected in Europe the remaining six professors with which that institution* was organized in 1825; ii. Peachy R.; iii. Mildred, the first wife of the eminent William Wirt; iv. George, married Eliza, daughter of Captain Christopher Hudson, a gallant patriot of the Revolution. Of their issue, Thomas Walker, the subject of this sketch, was born at "Gilmerton," his father's seat, in Albemarle County, April 6, 1802. He early exhibited studious habits, and, at the age of fourteen, was sent to live with his uncle, Mr. Peter Minor, at "Ridgway," for private tuition in his family. The tutor, a meek and quiet young man, was but a few years older than young Walker Gilmer, and occupied the same room with him and a cousin of the same age, William Gilmer. The mischievous boys often made the mild teacher the victim of their pranks, one of which was to

---

* Sketches, Essays, and Translations by Francis W. Gilmer. Published, Baltimore, 1828, 12mo. He also reported "Cases decided in the Court of Appeals of Virginia, 1820 to 1821." Richmond, 1821, 8vo.

crawl under his bed after he was asleep and to slowly raise themselves under him until he would roll out upon the floor. Before he would recover from his surprise, they would be snoring in their pallet.

The beset pedagogue was at a loss to what to ascribe his nocturnal visitations, and quite believed himself haunted by evil spirits. He reported his troubles to Mr. Minor, who immediately suspected the true offenders, and soon detected them. The following morning the lads were aroused from their slumbers by an unusual tread upon the stairway, and soon had reason to tremble at the stern presence of their uncle Peter, accompanied by a negro man, "Pudding," bearing a plentiful supply of birchen rods. The order was given to "horse Walker," and, in a twinkle, he was hoisted upon "Pudding's" back, and the birch uplifted over him. Walker begged a parley, and forthwith commenced an extemporaneous plea of apologies, entreaties, and promises of amendment, which arrested the impending rod, and finally prevailed upon his uncle to pardon him. To William, too, who stood by in quaking suspense, mercy was also extended; and long after, in mature years, when the reputation of his fellow delinquent was established as an orator, he would often jocularly recall this early occasion of peril, and say to Gov. Gilmer that he had heard all his great speeches, but never one so powerful and impressive as the pathetic effort from the back of "Pudding."

From "Ridgway," young Walker Gilmer was sent to school to Dr. Frank Carr, an excellent classical scholar, and a gentleman of extensive learning and much literary taste. The friend and companion of William Wirt, he is reported to have assisted him in the preparation of "The Old Bachelor." Here young Gilmer's talents were fitly nurtured. He was thoroughly grounded in classic lore, and acquired a thirst for letters which was invaluable to him in his subsequent career. He remained two years under the care of Dr. Carr, and then continued his scholastic course under Mr. John Robertson, a Scotchman, of whom it is said that he "taught more clever men than any other single teacher ever did in Virginia, and whose classical knowledge was such that he would often hear a recitation in Homer without reference to the book." From the school of Mr. Robertson, young Gilmer was sent to that of a Mr. Stack, in Charlottesville. Whilst here, as a member of a Thespian Society, he exhibited fine histrionic talents. Young Gilmer completed his studies in Staunton, the pecuniary embarrassment of his father bringing them to an abrupt termination. He now entered the office of his uncle, Peachy R. Gilmer, at Liberty, Bedford County, Virginia, as a student of law. This gentleman was an eminent lawyer, a fine classical scholar, and possessed extraordinary conversational powers. Some of his letters were pronounced, by his friend and brother-in-law, William Wirt, as "inimitable specimens of epistolary style." Whilst at Liberty, and, indeed, for some years previously, young Walker Gilmer was much aided and stimulated in his studies by correspondence with his uncle, Francis W. Gilmer, then a member of the bar of Winchester, Virginia. He was a close and assiduous student, and in less than a year applied for and obtained a license to practice law, and located himself in Scottsville, Albemarle County, within a few miles of "Mt. Air," the residence of Captain Hudson, his maternal grandfather; but, tempted by the wide field offered in the new western country, he removed in a short time to St. Louis, Missouri. Very flattering prospects of success dawned upon him in that thriving city, but he was induced to abandon them and return to Virginia from a desire to aid his father in the management of his affairs and in the care of a large family. A striking instance of his magnanimity and generosity at this period is given. Always a favorite with his grandfather, Mr. Hudson, the latter had made a will constituting him his sole heir. When Walker Gilmer heard this, he insisted successfully that Mr. Hudson should alter the provisions of the will, and divide the estate equally among his brothers and sisters, after having first secured a competent provision for his father. In his new field of practice in Charlottesville, and the bar of Albemarle and the adjacent counties, Mr. Gilmer met with formidable competition in a host of legal and forensic talent, headed by Philip Pendleton Barbour, subsequently a Judge of the Supreme Court of the United States; but competition only inspired greater exertion, and six years of unflagging devotion to his profession placed him in the front rank of the Albemarle bar. "As a lawyer, he was distinguished for acuteness of mind, adroitness in debate, clear perception of the true issue, skill in the examination of testimony, a fine grasp of the strong points of his cause, and intuitive detection of the weak ones of his opponents." He was rather an able and skillful advocate than a profound jurist; and wielded more power over the sympathies and instincts of the jury than over the learning of the judge. In the year 1825, the disposition to amend the Constitution of Virginia began to manifest itself among the friends of reform in notable signs of a desire for concerted action. Notices were published for holding a Convention in Staunton, on the 25th of July, of that year, to consider the best means of effecting the common object, and meetings were held in many counties to appoint delegates to this Convention. A meeting of the citizens of Albemarle in favor of a Convention assembled in Charlottesville, in response to a call in the *Central Gazette*. Thomas Jefferson Randolph, the grandson of Thomas Jefferson, presided; and Thomas W. Gilmer offered a series of resolutions asserting the right of the people to change the existing defective Constitution, and recommending the appointment of delegates from the county to the Convention to be held in Staunton. The resolutions were adopted, and Thomas Mann Randolph, Valentine Wood Southall, and Thomas Walker Gilmer appointed delegates. The Convention met as appointed, and Mr. Gilmer attended. Thirty-eight counties were represented. Among the delegates were some of the most prominent men of Virginia, among whom were Charles Fenton Mercer, Judge John Scott, John R. Cooke, Callohill Minns, Daniel Sheffey, Lucas P. Thompson, Philip Doddridge, and others of like reputation and influence. The Convention remained in session for several days, and finally recommended, by a very large majority: 1. The white basis of representation; 2. The extension of the right of suffrage; 3. The abolition of the Council of State—a lingering relic of the earliest form of government of Virginia as a colony; 4. The adoption of some practical provision for future amendments; and, 5. The adoption of a memorial to the Legislature to submit the question of a Convention to the vote of the people. Mr. Gilmer took an active part in the debates, and offered an important amendment to the resolution of the committee on the extension of suffrage, which was adopted. The speeches in the body were characterized by the Richmond *Enquirer* as being able and eloquent. It is noteworthy that the third and fourth measures of reform recommended were both rejected by the State Convention of 1829–30. Benjamin Watkins Leigh, by an effective speech, killed the former; and, when the Convention were about to adopt the latter, John Randolph of Roanoke gave it a summary quietus with a senseless sneer and a demonstration with his skinny forefinger. While in attendance upon the Staunton Convention, Mr. Gilmer met with Miss Ann E. Baker, the daughter of Hon. John Baker, a member of Congress from Virginia. She became his wife in the month of May following. During the political canvass which resulted in the election of General Andrew Jackson to his first term as President, Mr. Gilmer became one of the editors of the *Virginia Advocate*, a newspaper published in Charlottesville, and devoted to the success of the party of General Jackson. He had for several years been a constant contributor to the *Central Gazette*, also published in Charlottesville, by C. P. McKennie, and had acquired some reputation as a writer. His co-editor of the *Advocate* was John A. G. Davis, professor of law in the University of Virginia, a man of rare modesty, brilliant talents, and profound learning. The *Advocate* was ably edited, and did good campaign service. During the editorial career of Mr. Gilmer a controversy arose between the *Virginia Advocate* and the *Lynchburg Virginian* about the opinion of James Madison on the Bank question, which was carried on for some time with acrimony, and ended in a personal difficulty between Mr. Gilmer and Richard H. Toler, the editor of the *Virginian*. Mr. Gilmer went to Lynchburg and demanded an apology from Mr. Toler for some offensive language he had used towards him, and, not feeling satisfied with the result of the interview, assaulted Mr. Toler. The parties afterwards became friends, and frequently met in the State Legislature on the most amicable terms. In the spring of 1829, Mr.

Gilmer was returned by the county of Albemarle to the State House of Delegates. This period, which witnessed the birth of the great Whig and Democratic parties, was one of convulsive throe to the Nation; the political cauldron seethed with mad passions of party spirit. Mr. Gilmer was placed on the important committee of Courts of Justice, and, at the end of two weeks, he is recorded as moving to add to the standing committees one on Revolutionary Claims. It was formed with himself as chairman. He studied the subject fully, and by active research established, in his exhaustive report, unsatisfied claims of Virginia on the Federal Government which had been overlooked or neglected in former settlements. He moved resolutions of instruction to the Virginia Senators in Congress in relation to the bounty lands for the Virginia State and Continental Lines, which drew attention to the matter, and resulted in an advantageous change of the former provisions in favor of the officers and men of the Virginia State Line. During the Legislative session an effort was made to renew the charters of the State banks, though it would be three years before they expired. This measure was ably and successfully opposed by Mr. Gilmer. At the spring election of 1830, Mr. Gilmer received the verdict of approval of his course in a re-election to the House of Delegates with an increased majority; and when, after the adoption of the amended constitution, new elections were held, his popularity was further vindicated by a vote nearly double of that of any other candidate for local suffrage of his county. When the General Assembly met in December, 1830, Mr. Gilmer was nominated for Speaker of the House of Delegates by William M. Rives, of Campbell County, who said in his nominating speech: "Mr. Gilmer has left the traces of his genius upon the memory of the members of the last session, and the proofs of his ability on the journal." The former Speaker, Linn Banks, was, however, elected. This session of the Legislature was one of the most important ever convened in Richmond. Upon it devolved the task of remodeling the Statute Laws in accordance with the amended constitution. The ablest men in the State had been summoned to this duty in the House of Delegates. Among them may be named: Benjamin Watkins Leigh, James Barbour, Richard Morris, Archibald Bryce, Vincent Witcher, Thomas S. Gholson, William H. Brodnax, George W. Summers, George C. Dromgoole, and John Thompson Brown. The debates were marked by great ability, learning, and eloquence. Mr. Gilmer took an active part in all of the leading questions of the session, and won laurels from the ablest champions in this brilliant arena. In the winter of 1830-1, Mr. Gilmer was induced, by the solicitations of his friends, to undertake the editorial conduction of a political newspaper to be published at Richmond. He accordingly published a prospectus in the *Enquirer* of April 12, 1831, proposing to issue, on the 1st of July, a newspaper to be called the *Times*, but the scheme was abandoned in consequence of his being appointed, by Governor John Floyd, Commissioner of the State to prosecute the Revolutionary Claims of Virginia on the United States. Governor Floyd, in his annual message, in speaking of this appointment, says of Mr. Gilmer: "If zeal, talent, and assiduity furnish any augury of success, we may confidently indulge the most pleasing anticipations of it." Mr. Gilmer spent the greater part of the summer, autumn, and winter of the year 1831 in Washington City, collecting the materials and preparing the evidence for asserting the claims of Virginia before Congress, and thus escaped the excitement, during the legislative session of 1831-2, on the slavery question. In the spring of 1832 he was again elected a member of the House of Delegates. Mr. Gilmer was also a delegate from Albemarle County to the Convention held in Charlottesville, June 12, 1832, to nominate a candidate for Vice-President on the ticket with General Jackson, and of which James Barbour was the choice; but the previous nomination, by the Baltimore Convention, of Martin Van Buren, negatived their action.

In 1832, Littleton Waller Tazewell having resigned his seat in the United States Senate, William Cabell Rives, who had just returned from his mission to France, was nominated by Mr. Gilmer, in the Virginia Legislature, to fill the vacancy, and was elected without opposition. Though Mr. Gilmer, by his absence as Commissioner at Washington, had fortunately escaped the excitement of the discussion of the slavery question, he had now to bear his part in the fury of the storm which rose about nullification and appalled the hearts of the stoutest patriots with the menacing thunders of civil war. On the 10th of December, 1832, General Jackson issued his proclamation, which, together with the ordinance of nullification and the other proceedings of the Convention of South Carolina, was made the subject of a special message to the General Assembly by Governor Floyd. It was referred to a special committee, of which Mr. Gilmer was a member. General W. H. Brodnax, the chairman of the committee, reported a series of resolutions disapproving the ordinance of nullification as passed by South Carolina, and requesting that State to suspend it until after the adjournment of Congress; but also condemning in strong terms the heresies of the proclamation of General Jackson, and reiterating the *right of secession* as the proper remedy when all peaceful opposition to unconstitutional legislation by the Federal Government had failed. An interesting debate occurred on this report, in which Mr. Gilmer participated in a speech of great ability. He announced the essence of State Rights to be the right of a State to judge for itself of infractions of the Constitution, and of the modes and measures of redress. The crisis was a fearful one, and Virginia met it nobly. She stood upon the troubled waters and lulled them into peace—sternly rebuking, on the one hand, the evil and mad spirit of arbitrary power which produced the proclamation,

REV. MILES SELDEN,
Last Colonial Rector of St. John's Church, in 1773.
From a miniature in the possession of the family.

and, on the other, calming and soothing the excited feelings of her too intemperate sister. Mr. Leigh was sent to bear a message of counsel and peace to South Carolina. Henry Clay, on the 12th of February, offered in the United States Senate his Compromise Bill, which was adopted; and when the Convention of South Carolina reassembled in March the ordinance of nullification was repealed.

In the spring of 1833 Mr. Gilmer was again re-elected to the House of Delegates. When the Assembly met in December the subject of the removal of the public deposits from the Bank of the United States was warmly discussed, and resolutions were adopted in the House of Delegates condemning the course of General Jackson as an arbitrary assumption of power, and instructing the Virginia Senators to vote for restoring the deposits to the United States Bank. Senator William C. Rives resigned his seat rather than obey the instructions, and Benjamin Watkins Leigh was elected in his place. In the spring of 1835 Mr. Gilmer was again elected to the House of Delegates. The session of 1835–6 was perhaps the stormiest ever held in the State. The recently amalgamated political parties of heterogeneous and diverse elements were in an embryo state, and every man distrustful of his next neighbor in politics. The discussions on the recently developed designs of the abolition party, which was rearing its hydra head, were fierce in the extreme. The question of the Presidential succession, with all the issues of the preceding administration involved, was a prolific factor of ferment. A fire-brand was thrown into the House by the Expunging Resolutions introduced by Colonel Joseph S. Watkins, of Goochland County. This measure of party servility was adopted, and Senator John Tyler, as has been narrated in a preceding sketch, refused to obey the instructions, and resigned his seat, which was filled by the election of William C. Rives.

In the Presidential election of 1836 Mr. Gilmer voted for Hugh Lawson White, of Tennessee, in opposition to Mr. Van Buren. Both Judge White and General Harrison were voted for by the Whigs of Virginia. The shattered condition of the health of Mr. Gilmer induced him to spend the latter part of the winter of 1837–8 in the South, and at the solicitation of capitalists in Virginia he extended his journey as far as Texas, as agent for them in the selection of lands. This trip made Mr. Gilmer cognizant of the resources of the infant republic of Texas, and enabled him to form a just estimate of its value to the United States, and he was henceforth an ardent and fast friend of its annexation to our Union. Whilst in Texas he was appointed by the government as joint commissioner with Mr. A. G. Burnley, to negotiate a loan of ten millions of dollars for the State. On receiving the appointment he hastened by home, on his way to the Northern cities, to effect the loan; but his negotiations were broken off by the unfavorable turn of the money affairs of the country, which soon resulted in the suspension of specie payments by the banks. He was compensated, however, by the government of Texas, with $5000 in the bonds of the republic, for his services. Mr. Gilmer was again elected to the House of Delegates of Virginia in 1838. Whilst engaged in legislative service Mr. Gilmer was a frequent contributor to the newspaper press, and in 1834 he published in the Richmond *Whig* a series of articles on the "Right of Instruction" and other subjects; and whilst in the North, endeavoring to effect a loan for Texas, he contributed to the *Pennsylvanian* some very interesting articles on the history of the Texan Revolution, which were extensively copied by the press. In the summer of 1835 he wrote letters weekly from the watering-places of Virginia to the *Whig*, in which he graphically described the scenery of the country and portrayed the characters and manners of those with whom he was thrown. February 22, 1837, he delivered an address before the Virginia Historical Society, at its annual meeting, which was published in the current number of the *Southern Literary Messenger*.

When the Legislature met in 1838, Mr. Gilmer was elected Speaker of the House of Delegates by acclaim, his being the only nomination. He was re-elected Speaker when the House of Delegates met again, in December, 1839. February 14, 1840, he was elected Governor of Virginia, to succeed David Campbell on the expiration of his term on the 31st of March. He entered zealously upon his duties. He was *ex officio* President of the Board of Public Works, and, not being satisfied with the means of information at the command of the Board, he made a careful personal examination of nearly all the important public works of the State. This tour, in the summer of 1840, was at his own private expense. The information thus obtained enabled him to prepare a very able and valuable message to the Assembly, lucidly presenting the public and material interests of the State. He also reopened with Governor Seward, of New York, a controversy for the surrender of Peter Johnson, Edward Smith, and Isaac Gransey, charged with slave-stealing in Virginia, and who were fugitives from justice. Their rendition was ably demanded. Seward, after a delay of six months, replied, refusing to surrender the fugitives. The exasperated Assemby of Virginia, on the 13th of March, 1841, enacted in retaliation a law which subjected all vessels trading from any port in New York to Virginia to a search for stolen slaves. It was, however, made prospective, to allow New York another opportunity to redress the grievance complained of; and the Governor was authorized to suspend the operation of the law when the demand of the State should be complied with, and the law of New York extending the right of trial by jury should be repealed. On the 16th of March, three days after the passage of the retaliatory law, a demand was made by Governor Seward on the Executive of Virginia for the surrender of R. F. Emry, charged with felony in New

York, and arrested in Virginia. Governor Gilmer refused to comply with the demand until the demand of Virginia for the surrender of the slave stealers, as above, should have been complied with. Thus was the issue joined between North and South, but the Legislature of Virginia receded from its bold position, and failed to sustain Governor Gilmer. Debate ensued, and modified resolutions were passed and communicated to the Governor on the 18th instant. On the same day he sent to the Assembly a message in which he ably vindicated his course, and resigned his office. The resignation of Governor Gilmer was a complete surprise to the Legislature. Much heated discussion ensued, and party spirit ran high. The passions of his opponents led them to extreme measures. It was proposed to supply his place by a new election, and the commencement of the gubernatorial term was changed by enactment to the 1st of January; but the Legislature were unable to agree to elect a successor, and adjourned, leaving the office of Governor to be filled successively by the senior Councillor of State for the yearly term of such precedence, as provided by law. He was thus succeeded until the 31st of March following by John Mercer Patton.

As soon as the resignation of Governor Gilmer became known he was solicited to declare himself a candidate for Congress from the Albemarle district. He accordingly did so, and was elected by a handsome majority, and took his seat, on the 31st of May, in the Congress which had been convened by the proclamation of President Harrison, dated the 17th of March.

In the meanwhile, the death of President Harrison, which occurred on the 4th of April, just one month after his inauguration, had devolved the Executive office on John Tyler, the Vice-President. There was a Whig majority in both branches of Congress. John White, of Kentucky, was elected Speaker of the House of Representatives. Mr. Gilmer entered actively on the work of reform in Congress. He proposed the entire separation of the political press from the patronage of the Government, and that the Executive should be required to report to the Senate his reasons for all removals from office. These were capital reforms, but failed. Mr. Gilmer labored, too, through the medium of a special committee, of which he was chairman, for retrenchment. He served also as a member of the important Standing Committee of Ways and Means. On the 17th of June he offered a resolution for the appointment of a committee to examine into the number of the officers or agents of the Government, modes of transacting business, and expenditures, to report at the next session if any reduction in the expenses of the civil list, or in the number of persons employed, might be effected. The resolution was adopted, and Mr. Gilmer placed at the head of the committee.

President Harrison, in removing to Washington to assume his office, had incurred much expense, which had considerably embarrassed his estate. A proposition to give to his family $25,000, the Presidential salary for one year, so enlisted the feelings and sympathies of all, that few men could be found of the opposite party, much less of those who had voted for him, bold enough to oppose it. Every impulse of Mr. Gilmer led him to vote for the bill, but they were controlled by his sense of duty as a Representative. In a brief speech he insisted that Congress ought not to vote it in their representative capacity out of the public funds, but privately from their own personal resources. They had no right to be generous with the money of the people. He also ably opposed the distribution among the States of the proceeds of the sales of the public lands. He voted against the United States Bank in every form in which it was presented. The extra session of Congress adjourned on the 13th of September, after a session of about one hundred days. At the regular session, which began on the first Monday of December, 1841, Mr. Gilmer was transferred from the Committee of Ways and Means to that of Foreign Relations, of which John Quincy Adams was chairman. The action of Mr. Adams in presenting, January 24, 1842, a petition from Haverhill, Massachusetts, for an immediate dissolution of the Union, the debate which resulted from a resolution to censure him therefor, and the singular conduct of Mr. Adams in the committee, so disgusted Mr. Gilmer and four other members of it that they refused to serve any longer on it with Mr. Adams, and they were excused by the House. In the debate on the general appropriation bill, Mr. Gilmer, in a speech of great ability, advocated striking out all the contingent expenses. He zealously supported President Tyler in the independent course which the latter pursued. Mr. Gilmer was re-elected to Congress, in 1843, over William L. Goggin, after a warm canvass. When Congress assembled December 2, 1843, the majority in the House of Representatives was changed, and was now largely Democratic. John Winston Jones, of Virginia, was elected Speaker. The Cabinet of President Tyler having resigned, as detailed in the preceding sketch of his career, on the 15th of February, 1844, he nominated Mr. Gilmer to the Senate to be Secretary of the Navy. The nomination was at once unanimously confirmed. Mr. Gilmer immediately entered upon the discharge of the duties of his post with the avowed determination to carry into execution the reforms which he had advocated in Congress, but an All-wise Providence intervened, and by a most afflicting dispensation removed him from his sphere of human usefulness. He was, as has been narrated, one of the victims of the awful catastrophe on the steamer "Princeton" on the 28th of February, 1844. Thus died Thomas Walker Gilmer, in the forty-second year of his age, stricken down on the very harvest-field of his faithful labors, and with the sheaves of gathered honors standing thick around him. He left issue four sons and two daughters: i. John, died unmarried; ii. Elizabeth, married Colonel St. George Tucker, Confederate States Cavalry, soldier, poet, and novelist; iii. Rev. George Hudson, a minister of the Presbyterian Church; iv. Rev. Thomas Walker, of the faith of his brother, married Miss Minor; v. James B., a member of the bar of Texas, married Mrs. Elizabeth Ford; vi. Juliet. An excellent portrait of Governor Gilmer is in the State Library at Richmond. A marble slab marks his remains at "Mt. Air," Albemarle County, Virginia.

JOHN MERCER PATTON.

John Mercer Patton was worthily descended. His father, Robert Patton, a native of Scotland, emigrated thence to America* some time before the Revolution, landing at Charleston, South Carolina, where he lived for awhile, but soon removed to Fredericksburg, Virginia, where he established himself as a merchant. He was very successful, and acquired a competent fortune. He was a high-spirited man, and in full sympathy with the struggle of his adopted countrymen for freedom, as a well-authenticated incident, which has been transmitted, emphatically evidenced:

Being a non-combatant, he was on terms of social intercourse with the invading Britons. On one occasion, whilst dining with some officers of Tarleton's legion, one of them took upon himself to denounce in unmeasured terms the people he had come to subdue. He was very free in the use of the terms "rebels," "rebellion," etc., which he finally coupled with abusive terms with the names of certain officers of the patriot army. This, Robert Patton (who had been an indignant listener, but had curbed his feelings) could not allow to go unrebuked. He calmly but decidedly told the officer that he felt it to be right to inform him that some of those whom he had just named were his friends. This warning being disregarded by the officer, Patton threw a glass of wine in his face. This produced a storm of fury from the insulted officer, when Patton said the affair must be then and there settled; and going to the door, locked it and put the key in his pocket. They fought with pistols across the table, and the officer was killed.

Robert Patton married, October 16, 1792, Ann Gordon, daughter of the gallant General Hugh Mercer, who fell, mortally wounded, at the battle of Princeton, January 3, 1777, and who died nine days afterwards, and is buried in Christ Church, Philadelphia. Robert Patton died November 3, 1828, and his wife May 12, 1832. They had issue:

i. *Hugh Mercer*, born November 22, 1793; died in the autumn of 1844.
ii. *Robert*, born September 11, 1795; member of the House of Delegates, 1821; died September 13, 1830.
iii. *John Mercer*, born August 10, 1797; died October 28, 1858; mar-

---

* He was accompanied by a brother, who also settled in Virginia, and whose descendants in Fairfax County have intermarried with the Mason and other prominent Virginia families.

ried, January 8, 1824, Peggy French (born 1804; died September 14, 1873), daughter of John Williams,† of Culpeper County, Virginia.

iv. *Isabella Gordon*, born October 21, 1799; died November 3, 1804.

v. *William Fairlie*, M. D., Surgeon United States and Confederate States Navies, born June 15, 1802; resides with his son-in-law, General John R. Cooke, ‡ late Confederate States Army, at Richmond, Virginia.

vi. *George Weedon*, born March 8, 1804; died October 29, 1804.

vii. *Eleanor Ann*, born September 13, 1805; married John Chew, of Fredericksburg, Virginia, and has issue.

viii. *Margaretta Patton*, born November 1, 1807; died July 2, 1852; married Hon. John M. Herndon, sometime Secretary of the Commonwealth of Virginia, son of Dabney and Elizabeth Herndon, and a brother of the gallant Lieutenant William Lewis Herndon, United States Navy, who went down with the ill-fated "Central America" off the South Atlantic coast; of the late Hon. Charles Herndon; of Dr. Dabney Herndon, who died a few years ago at his post of duty, during the yellow fever visitation of Mobile, Alabama; of Dr. Brodie Herndon, of Savannah, Georgia; of the widow of the late Commodore Matthew Fontaine Maury; and of Miss Mary Herndon, of Fredericksburg, Virginia.

John Mercer Patton, the third son of Robert and Anna Gordon (Mercer) Patton, as above, was liberally educated, and, adopting the profession of the law, commenced practice in his native city, Fredericksburg. He soon attained honorable distinction at the bar, and, embarking in politics, he was elected to Congress in 1830, and continued to serve in that body with conspicuous ability until 1838, when he removed to Richmond, and was elected a member of the Council of State; and as the senior Councillor, on the resignation, March 18, 1841, of Governor Thomas Walker Gilmer, succeeded him as Acting Governor of Virginia, serving as such until the expiration of his yearly term as senior Councillor, on the 31st of March, when he was succeeded by senior Councillor John Rutherfoord. In learning and ability the rank of

---

† Three brothers of the family of Peere Williams, sergeant-at-law, London, and famous reporter—John, William, and Otho Williams—migrated to America early in the eighteenth century. John settled in South Carolina, William in Virginia, and Otho in Maryland. From the last was descended General Otho II. Williams of the Revolution. William Williams had issue two sons, John and William, who owned large tracts of land near Culpeper Court House, Virginia. The last was the father of John Williams of the text.

‡ His sister Flora married the late Major-General J. E. B. Stuart, Confederate States Army.

Mr. Patton was acknowledged as second to none practicing in the higher courts of Virginia in his day, and which included an array of legal talent which has been scarcely surpassed at any period or in any section of the United States. In 1849 he was associated with the late eminent jurisconsult Conway Robinson in a revision of the Code of Virginia. Mr. Patton died at Richmond, October 28, 1858, and is buried in Shockoe Hill Cemetery there. A handsome fluted column of white marble, emblematically capped with several volumes, marks his resting-place. The tomb of his wife is near by. They had issue:
i. *Robert W.*, who died in 1877; Hugh, Philip, Lucy Ann, all died in infancy; ii. *John Mercer*, a distinguished practitioner of law; Captain of the Richmond Light Infantry Blues (organized in 1793— the oldest company in the State), 1852-55 and in 1859-60; Reporter, with Roscoe B. Heath, of " Cases decided in a Special Court of Appeals," and General Index to Gratton's Reports (volumes 2 to 11 inclusive; published at Richmond in two volumes, 8vo, 1856, '57); Colonel, 1861-2, of the 21st Regiment Virginia Volunteers, and for a time in command of the 2d Brigade (composed of the 21st, 42d and 48th Virginia Infantry, and the Irish Battalion), Stonewall Jackson's division; author of several theological works, among them *The Death of Deaths;* married Sarah, daughter of Alexander and Mildred C. (Lindsay) Taylor,* and has issue; now resides at Ashland, Virginia; iii. *Isaac W.*, married Miss Merritt; Colonel of Louisiana Infantry, severely wounded and made prisoner at the fall of Vicksburg, and afterwards commanded one of the forts in Mobile Bay to the end of the late war; iv. *George S.*, married Susan S., daughter of Andrew and Susan (Thornton) Glassell; † Colonel of 22d Virginia Infantry; wounded twice in previous battles; and then at 2d Manassas; killed by a shell while commanding a brigade at the battle of Winchester, in 1864; v. *W. Tazewell*, Colonel of 7th Virginia Infantry; killed whilst leading his regiment in the memorable charge of Pickett's division on the heights of Gettysburg, in 1863; vi. *Hugh Mercer*, Lieutenant Confederate States Army; wounded at the second battle of Manassas; married Miss Bull, of Orange County, Virginia; vii. *James F.*, Lieutenant Confederate States Army; wounded at the battle of Cold Harbor; made Judge of Court of Appeals of West Virginia; married a daughter of Hon. Allen T. Caperton, United States Senator; died in March, 1882; viii. *William M.*, married Miss Jordan, of Rockbridge County, Virginia; ix. *Eliza W.*, married John Gilmer, of Pittsylvania County, Virginia.

---

* Alexander Taylor was descended in the fourth generation from James Taylor, from Carlisle in England, who settled on the Chesapeake Bay, and died in 1698. President Zachary Taylor was also of his lineage, and other descendants have intermarried with the Pendleton, Penn, Hopkins, Lewis, Lee, Chew, Gibson, Morton, Glassell, Taliaferro, Conway, Ashby, Battaile, and other well known families of Virginia.

† The Glassells of Virginia are connections of the Duke of Argyll; and his

RICHARD CHANNING MOORE,
Beloved Protestant Episcopal Bishop of Virginia.
Silhouette cut by Brown of Philadelphia, in 1830.

JOHN RUTHERFOORD.

The frequent representation of those of Scottish blood among the honored Executives of Virginia is worthy of remark. Another instance now passes in review. Possibly no other city in the United States has been more honored in a class of citizens so representative of material prosperity and influence as has that of Richmond in her merchants, whose probity, system, and promptness have been widely proverbial quite from the period of its accession to such titular dignity in 1782. Prominent among these useful and excellent men was the justly esteemed father of the subject of this sketch.

Thomas Rutherfoord, son of Thomas and Janet (Meldrum) Rutherfoord, who were both natives of Kircaldy, Scotland, was born in Glasgow, where his parents then resided, January 9, 1766. Having received the educational advantages of the grammar schools, and finally of two sessions in the College of Glasgow, he entered, in July, 1780, the employment of Hawkesley & Rutherfoord, of Dublin, Ireland—a mercantile firm, of which his elder brother, John Rutherfoord, was the junior partner. They were exporters as well as importers, and conducted a large trade with the ports of Europe and America. It was customary in the last century for youths designed for a mercantile life to fit themselves for the calling by a regular term of indentured apprenticeship, which was entered upon by the payment of a fee. This had been the training of the employers of Thomas Rutherfoord, they having served as fellow-apprentices, in the province of Maryland, in the house of Spiers & Company, merchants and factors. Their pleasurable reminiscences of American life, as narrated to young Thomas, inspired in him a desire for a like residence abroad. This, together with his exemplified prudence, sagacity, and business habits, induced Messrs. Hawkesley & Rutherfoord to intrust him, at the early age of eighteen, with a cargo of goods valued at £10,000 for disposition in Virginia. He set sail from Dublin, October 10, 1784, furnished with a letter of recommendation to General Washington from Sir Edward Neversham, member of Parliament from the county of Dublin. The vessel, the "Jane and Diana," anchored in Hampton Roads, Virginia, December 21st following, and soon thereafter the youthful merchant located in Richmond, Virginia. He met with deserved success, was admitted a partner with his employers, and soon succeeded to the entire business, and extensively engaged as merchant, miller, and importer and exporter. He became in time one of the largest real estate owners in Richmond. He was a man of strong individuality of character and excellent judgment, and a clear and vigorous writer. He contributed at different periods of his life excellent papers to the press, on the commercial requirements of the nation and the destructive influence of political agitation. During the discussion of the tariff question in Congress, in 1839–1840, the papers from his pen were among the ablest submitted to that body. His life, as a zealous member of the Presbyterian Church, was one of marked and uniform piety. He died January 31, 1852, affectionately reverenced for his worth and manifold usefulness by the entire community which he had seen grow up around him, and to the prosperity and progress of which he had so greatly contributed. His remains rest beneath a handsome marble tomb in Shockoe Hill Cemetery, the predecessor of Hollywood Cemetery, and where lie also the remains of Chief Justice Marshall, Bishop Richard Channing Moore, John Hampden Pleasants, Judge Robert Stanard, Benjamin Watkins Leigh, John Wickham, Major James Gibbon, and many other distinguished contemporaries of Mr. Rutherfoord, whose memories are cherished in Virginia. Mr. Rutherfoord was married, August 21, 1790, by the good Parson John D. Blair (so lovingly remembered), to Sarah, daughter of Geddes and Mary (Jordan*) Winston. Mrs. Rutherfoord died March 2, 1839. It is of interest to note that her sisters married as follows: *Mary*, the Rev. John D. Blair; *Martha*, Henry S. Shore; *Margaret*, Dr. John Adams, iong the Mayor of Richmond; and *Rebecca*, William Radford.† The issue of Thomas and Sarah (Winston) Rutherfoord was as follows: ‡

i. *Maria*, born August 9, 1791; died April 14, 1793.
ii. *John*, the subject of this sketch.
iii. *Jane*, born March 13, 1795; married, January 11, 1815, S. H. B. Meade, of Amelia County. She died October 2, 1839; he died January 21, 1842.
iv. *Sarah*, born February 23, 1797; married, November 18, 1815, William Beverley Randolph, of "Chatsworth," Henrico County, Virginia. She died April 18, 1819; he died May 3, 1874.
v. *Thomas*, born June 24, 1799; died August 13, 1803.
vi. *Mary*, born April 10, 1801; married, in 1826, Richard E. Hardaway, who died in 1830.
vii. *William*, born May 18, 1802; married, April 20, 1843, Sarah Radford Sherrard. She died September 15, 1873, in her fifty-first year; he died November 5, 1873. His son William married,

---

* Her two sisters married, respectively. Robert Rives (the father of the late Hon. William Cabell Rives) and Colonel William Cabell, Sr., of "Union Hill."

† The descendants of Geddes Winston, who was of the same family as that of the mother of the orator Patrick Henry, in the names of Rutherfoord, Radford, Munford, Blair, Shore, Minge, Sheppard, Adams, Heron, Pickett (Gen. George E. Pickett, C. S. Army), Moseley, Carrington, Harrison, and others equally worthy, are among the most estimable of the people of Virginia.

‡ Of the grandchildren of Thomas Rutherfoord, which are quite numerous in the several issues, many have married, and he is now represented in some of the most respected family names in the State.

October 28, 1874, Leslie, daughter of Dr. John F. Carter. He died November 12, 1876, and she married secondly, October 4, 1877, Edward S. Rose, real estate agent of Richmond.

viii. *Martha* (Patsey), born August 13, 1803; died May 4, 1873; married, November, 1842, Thomas Garland Tinsley, of Hanover County. Both dead. Their son, James Garland Tinsley, is interested largely in manufacturing enterprises in and near Richmond.

ix. *Thomas*, born March 20, 1805; married first, 1840, Isabella Syme; secondly, Sarah, daughter of Spotswood Wingfield, of Hanover County.

x. *Samuel Jordan*, born May 1, 1806; married, November 20, 1834, Frances C. Watson; died December 26, 1880. His son Thomas M. Rutherfoord, who married, April 16, 1872, Laura W., daughter of the late James Thomas, Jr., is a prominent tobacco manufacturer of Richmond. A daughter, Mary Elizabeth, married, April 22, 1836, Charles A. Rose, a lawyer of Richmond. Both dead, leaving issue.

xi. *Alexander Hawkesley*, born August 30, 1807; married April 10, 1838, Keziah K. Clarke. Of his issue: James Clarke, returning from a European tour in 1861, was appointed a Captain on the staff of Brigadier-General James Dearing, Confederate States Cavalry, and gallantly fell in action. Another son, Alexander Hawkesley Rutherfoord, Jr., married, October 16, 1878, Rosa, daughter of the late Hon. James A. Seddon, member of Congress, Secretary of War of the Confederate States, etc. A daughter, Annie C. Rutherfoord, married, April 24, 1878, Gideon A., son of Isaac Davenport, Jr., a prominent banker of Richmond.

xii. *Elvira Rebecca*, born February 4, 1809; died July 20, 1810.

xiii. *Augustus Smith*, born December 5, 1811; died August 10, 1875.

John Rutherfoord, the subject of this sketch, and the eldest son of Thomas and Sarah (Winston) Rutherfoord, as above, was born in Richmond, Virginia, December 6, 1792. After preliminary preparation in the schools of his native city, he completed his collegiate course at Princeton, New Jersey. Having studied law, he was admitted to the bar of Richmond, and entered upon a successful practice. Taking a deep interest in politics, he early rendered effective service to the Democratic party, to which he was attached. In 1826 he was elected to the House of Delegates from the city of Richmond (then entitled to only one Delegate) and served, with some intervals, in that body until 1839, when he was appointed one of the Councillors of State, as provided by the amended constitution of 1830. As Senior Councillor, Mr. Rutherfoord, on the 31st of March, 1841, succeeded John Mercer Patton as Acting

Governor of Virginia, and continued so to serve until March 31, 1842, when he was succeeded by John Munford Gregory. Governor Rutherfoord continued to serve as a member of the State Council until the year 1846. In 1836 he was elected President, or Principal Agent, as the office is termed, of the Mutual Assurance Society of Virginia, the oldest institution of fire insurance in the State, and which was established by William Frederick Ast, a native of Prussia, in 1794. In this position Governor Rutherfoord efficiently served for the long period of thirty years. His predecessor was James Rawlings, a highly esteemed citizen of Richmond, who resigned the position to accept that of President of the Farmers' Bank of Virginia, vacated by Philip Norborne Nicholas to accept the Judgeship of the Sixth Judicial Circuit. Governor Rutherfoord in early life took a great interest in the volunteer military, in which he attained the rank of Colonel, by which title he was familiarly known. He was the originator and first Captain of the Richmond Fayette Artillery, organized June 20, 1821, as the Richmond Light Artillery, by the former membership of two companies of artillery commanded respectively by William West and Andrew Stevenson, and which had served in the war of 1812. The name of the company was changed in honor of the generous friend of America, Lafayette, on the occasion of his second visit to this country in 1824. The company rendered gallant service in the cause of the South in our late war, its first commander in that period being Captain (subsequently Colonel) Henry Coalter Cabell.

Governor Rutherfoord married, April 24, 1816, Emily Anne (died August 26, 1871), daughter of John and Rebecca (Tucker) Coles,* of "Enniscorthy," Albemarle County, Virginia. They had issue: i. *John Coles* (born November 14, 1825; died August 14, 1866), of "Rock Castle," Virginia, represented Goochland County in the House of Delegates for a number of years; married Ann Roy. Their daughter, Ann Seddon, married, June 25, 1880, Bradley S. Johnson, son of General Bradley T. Johnson, late Confederate States Army, now of Baltimore, Maryland. ii. *Emily Anne*, died November 16, 1880; married January 24, 1853, Patrick Henry Aylett† (born May 9, 1826), son of Philip Aylett, of King William County, Virginia, and grandson of the orator Patrick Henry; editor of the Richmond *Enquirer* and of the *Times*; Confederate States District Attorney for Eastern Virginia;

---

* John Coles was the son of Major John Coles, a native of Ireland, and his wife Mary, daughter of Isaac Winston. Another daughter of John Coles was the wife of Hon. Andrew Stevenson, Speaker of Congress and United States Minister to England; and yet another the wife of John Singleton, of South Carolina. Edward Coles, the first Governor of Illinois, was his son.

† Patrick Henry Aylett was a descendant in the seventh generation of John Aylett, who emigrated from Essex County, England, in 1656, and settled in Virginia.

killed at the calamity at the State Capitol by the falling through of the floor of the Court of Appeals room, April 27, 1870. Left issue three daughters: Emily, married, December 20, 1876, John Enders, Jr.; Sarah, married Thomas Bolling, Jr., a descendant of the Indian princess Pocahontas; and Page.

Governor Rutherfoord died at Richmond, August 3, 1866, and is buried in Shockoe Hill Cemetery. Governor Rutherfoord was endowed with a strong and well-balanced intellect. Unassuming and winning in manner, gentle and modest, yet firm in his convictions and steadfast in purpose, he was alike faithful in his public and private relations, and maintained a character admirable for its virtue and purity, its integrity, gentleness, serenity, and generosity. There is an excellent portrait of him in the State Library at Richmond.

JOHN MUNFORD GREGORY.

The ancestors of John Munford‡ Gregory were early seated in the Colony of Virginia. The family of Munford is interlinked with many others of prominence, and that of Gregory has always been held in esteem. Joseph Gregory received a patent of five hundred acres of land on Ware Creek (probably in James City County), December 6, 1652 (Virginia Land Records, Book No. 3, p. 136). Early grants are also of record to Thomas, Roger, and Richard Gregory, severally. The two last Christian names are favored ones in the family to the present day. The present deduction, however, commences definitely with John Gregory, a resident of Charles City County. He was the father of two gallant patriots of the Revolution, whose names are recorded on the pension list of Virginia.|| They were John Gregory, Jr., a man of family, and William Gregory, Jr., who, in 1776, were commissioned severally First and Second Lieutenant of a volunteer company raised in their native county, and which was assigned to the Sixth Virginia Infantry on Continental establishment. The brothers served gallantly in the campaigns in the North, both being promoted to the rank of Captain—William in the staff department, to which he was transferred, and John as the commandant of his company, at the head of which "he was killed in action on the Jersey line at a place called Quibbletown." He left an infant son, John Munford Gregory, who, at maturity, mar-

---

‡ By tradition the name of Munford was originally De Montford, and the blood that of the family of the Earl of Leicester—the Virginia representative having been proscribed for political offences, and forced to flee from England. To the support of this tradition there is a grant of land of record to Robert Mountfort, dated 1695. Under that and the name Munford he received extensive patents. There are early grants also of record to Edward, James, and Joseph Munford, severally.

|| The names of Obadiah, John, William, and Speltby Gregory also appear as pensioners.

ried Letitia Power, daughter of Ralph Graves, a veteran of the Revolution, who served in the cavalry corps of Major William Nelson. Their son, the subject of this sketch, John Munford Gregory, was born in Charles City County, July 8, 1804. He attended the "old field" schools until he attained the age of sixteen, after which he alternately taught school himself and was employed in farm labor. Removing to James City County, he for a time taught there; and having commenced the study of law, entered William and Mary College, from which he was graduated with the degree of Bachelor of Law in 1830. He was, in the same year, elected the delegate from James City County in the State Assembly, to which body he was continuously returned until 1841, when he was elected a member of the Council of State, and, as Senior Councillor by rotation, succeeded John Rutherfoord as Acting Governor of Virginia, March 31, 1842. He continued the State Executive until January 1, 1843, when he was succeeded by Governor James McDowell. In 1853 Governor Gregory was appointed United States Attorney for the Eastern District of Virginia, which position he held until the year 1860, when he was elected Judge of the Sixth Judicial Circuit of Virginia, and continued to serve in this capacity until displaced by the Federal authorities in 1866. He then resumed the practice of his profession, but was soon elected Commonwealth's Attorney for Charles City County, in which position he served until the year 1880, when feeble health compelled his retirement. In 1881 Governor Gregory removed to Williamsburg, Virginia, where he at present resides, supported, in his declining years, by the soothing ministrations of an affectionate daughter. Steadfast in purpose and of sterling integrity, the dignities enjoyed by Governor Gregory have been the just meed of unostentatious worth. He instanced his simplicity of character by refusing to occupy the gubernatorial mansion whilst the Executive of the State upon the ground of temporary tenure of office. Governor Gregory married Miss Amanda Wallace, of Petersburg, Virginia. Their issue was: i. *William Thomas*, M. D., a popular physician, married Miss Apperson, of New Kent County; ii. *Mary Elizabeth*, widow of the lamented and lately deceased James P. Purcell, a highly esteemed citizen of Richmond, and a member of the well-known firm of Purcell, Ladd & Co., of that city, wholesale druggists; iii. *John Munford*, Judge of the Supreme Court of the State of California, married a daughter of Rear Admiral Craven, United States Navy; iv. *Letitia Alice*, resides with her father in Williamsburg, Virginia; v. *Margaret Carroll*, married Richard E. Waddill, a member of an estimable family of Charles City County; vi. *Amanda Wallace*, married Colonel Robert A. Caskie, lately a gallant officer of Confederate States Cavalry, son of the late John Caskie, Esq., of Richmond, and now residing in Missouri; vii. *Martha Hill*, married Robert Galbraith, of South Carolina.

JAMES McDOWELL.

The honored names of McDowell and Preston, so closely interlinked, were both represented in the memorable siege of Londonderry, in 1688. The founder of the distinguished McDowell family of Virginia and Kentucky. Ephraim McDowell, there battled for the Protestant cause, with an elder brother, who sealed his devotion with his life. Ephraim McDowell, who was, it is said, a relative and near neighbor of John Lewis, the founder of the famous Lewis family of Virginia, emigrated from Ireland and settled in the province of Pennsylvania some time prior to the year 1735; but, after a brief residence there, migrated to Virginia, to the home of his relative John Lewis. His son John McDowell and wife, who was Magdalene Woods, and whom he married in Pennsylvania, accompanied him. Father and son settled on the noted grant of Benjamin Burden, John McDowell becoming the surveyor of Burden, and securing from him a tract of one thousand acres of land in what is now Rockbridge County, and upon which he settled, calling his home "Cherry Grove." He was killed by the Indians, with eight companions, near Balcony Falls, December 25, 1742. He left issue:

i. *Samuel;* Judge; father of the celebrated surgeon Ephraim McDowell, M. D., born in Rockbridge County, Virginia, November 11, 1771; completed his medical studies at Edinburgh, Scotland, settled in practice at Danville, Kentucky, in 1795, and for years was the leading practitioner in the West; married, in 1802, a daughter of General Evan Shelby; successfully performed, in 1809, the operation for the extirpation of the ovary—the first on record—and acquired a world-wide celebrity; died at Danville, June 25, 1830. He was recently honored with a statue at Frankfort, Kentucky. The descendants of Samuel McDowell are represented in the worthy names of Reid, Moore, and others.

ii. *James,* married Elizabeth McClung, and, dying in 1770, a posthumous son was born the same year—James, Colonel and the commandant of a brigade in the war of 1812; married Sarah, daughter of William Preston (and granddaughter of the founder of the Preston family, John Preston). Their issue was: i. Susan S., married William Taylor, of Alexandria, lawyer, and member of Congress, and had issue; ii. Elizabeth, married Hon. Thomas H. Benton, of Missouri, and had, with other issue, Jessie, married General John C. Fremont; iii. James, the subject of this sketch.

iii. *Sarah,* married Colonel George Moffett, of Augusta County, distinguished in Indian warfare, and in the Revolution, in which he fought from the beginning to the close. Their descendants are represented in the names of McDowell, Bell, McCue, Hedges, Carson, Cochran, Crawford, Kirk, Miller, and others equally estimable.

SCENE IN VIRGINIA.

James McDowell, the subject of this sketch, was born at the family seat, "Cherry Grove," Rockbridge County, October 11, 1795. He received elementary tuition successively from the Rev. Wm. McPheeters, D. D., and Rev. Samuel Brown. The wife of the latter, who was Mary Moore, was the heroine of a thrilling story of Indian captivity, which is presented in a little book entitled *The Captives of Abb's Valley*. James McDowell later entered Washington College, then attended Yale College for a year, and completed his education at Princeton College, New Jersey, from which he was graduated Master of Arts in 1816. He spoke the Latin salutatory oration on the occasion of his graduation. Of the class of 1816, Mrs. Miller, the daughter of Governor McDowell, narrates that the Rev. John Maclean, D. D., so long the able and honored President of the College, thus pleasantly collocated some of its members: "There were three Macs in that class, and I tell you, madam, they were not the meanest fellows in it either. They were McIlvaine [the Protestant Episcopal Bishop of Ohio], McDowell, and [with a significant smile] Johnny Maclean."

So pleased was Colonel McDowell with the success of his son James at college that upon his return home he presented him with a valuable tract of land, some 2,500 acres, in Bourbon County, Kentucky. Young McDowell now commenced the study of law in the office of the eminent Chapman Johnson, at Staunton, Virginia, but after having so perfected his knowledge therein as to be awarded a license to practice, suddenly relinquished the profession through peculiar conscientious scruples, which he thus enunciated: "Others may be, but I don't know how I can be an honest man and a lawyer." In September, 1818, he married his cousin Susan, daughter of General Francis and Sarah B. (daughter of General William Campbell, the hero of King's Mountain, who married the sister of Patrick Henry the orator) Preston. James McDowell now removed to his plantation in Kentucky, but, after a residence there of a year or two, returned to Virginia to overlook the interests of his father, who had been stricken with paralysis, and near whom he took a farm, in the neighborhood of Lexington. This he made his permanent home, and here he raised his large family of children. He first entered public life in 1831, as a member of the House of Delegates from Rockbridge County.

The summer of that year is memorable in the annals of Virginia as the period of the negro insurrection in Southampton County, which has been circumstantially detailed in the preceding sketch of Governor John Floyd. This tragic outbreak created a panic which pervaded the State even to its borders. The utmost terror prevailed, and so supplanted reason that people stood in dread suspense, awaiting supernatural visitations and terrible calamities. They watched the sun, and from the spots upon it drew portents of evil; and when night came the darkness was full of spectres. Labor was interrupted and all occupation disordered by the measures for safety adopted, which called men from every occupation by day and night for weeks as patrols. The wide-spread consternation gradually settled into a belief in the necessity of legislation regarding the slave population of the State. This subject largely occupied the deliberations of the session of the Legislature of 1832-3, and engaged the ablest minds in the body. Mr. McDowell, who had been again returned to the House of Delegates from Rockbridge County, took a deep interest in the prolonged discussion, and, in common with a number of leading Virginians, advocated progressive emancipation. From this time onward Mr. McDowell was continuously in public life, in the service of his State and in the National Council. An exalted patriotism governed all of his actions, for though decided and conscientious in his party sentiments and adherences, he had no sympathy with the popular catch-word "Our party, right or wrong." Our country, not our party, was the paramount consideration with him. He belonged to the Democratic school of politics—an affiliation which, it appears, some of his compatriots of the period could not appreciate. One of them, the late Henry A. Wise, then an uncompromising Whig, expressed his "wonder that such a *gentleman* as Mr. McDowell should be a *Democrat*." Yet Mr. Wise soon solved the paradox satisfactorily to himself, it may be inferred, since his asseverations as a Democrat, a few years later, were as enthusiastic as they had been as a Whig.

In 1838 Mr. McDowell delivered before the Alumni Association of Princeton College an earnest and eloquent address which for years was spoken of in the strongest terms of admiration. So enduring was the impression made by this address that the committee of trustees of the College having in charge the arrangements for the one hundredth anniversary of the foundation of the College—celebrated in June, 1847—selected James McDowell for the orator on that occasion. But his engagements, public and private, debarred his acceptance of the invitation.

In December, 1842, Mr. McDowell was elected, by the Legislature, Governor of Virginia, and on the 1st of January following entered upon the duties of the office, succeeding Acting Governor John Munford Gregory. Governor McDowell was an earnest Christian and a consistent member of the Presbyterian Church. He was also a steadfast advocate of the cause of temperance, and, in accordance with his convictions of duty, excluded both wine and dancing from his private and official entertainments. Old School Presbyterianism and total abstinence held sway at the gubernatorial mansion during his term. An expressive *bon-mot* of the late and lamented Colonel Thomas P. August, a prominent lawyer of Richmond, of infinite wit, who attended one of the entertainments of Governor McDowell, has been treasured by his friends. Taking a glass of lemonade, Colonel August, with a significant application of his hand to his chest, offered as a toast: "Governor McDowell's two

Aids—*lemon-ade* and *promen-ade.*" Before the close of his term of three years as the Executive of Virginia, Governor McDowell was elected to a seat in the United States House of Representatives, made vacant by the death of his brother-in-law, William Taylor. He served in Congress with conspicuous ability until 1851, and would doubtless have been returned again but that death intervened before the day of election. He died at Lexington, August 24, 1851, in the fifty-sixth year of his age. His wife had preceded him to the grave. They left issue nine children—two sons and seven daughters—as follows:

i. *James*, a physician, married Miss Elizabeth Brant, of St. Louis, Missouri, and has issue.
ii. *Sally C. P.*, married, first, Hon. Francis Thomas, Governor of Maryland, and secondly, Rev. John Miller, now of Princeton, New Jersey. She has issue by the second marriage.
iii. *Mary B.*, married Rev. Mr. Ross, of Bladensburg, Maryland.
iv. *Frances Elizabeth*, died unmarried.
v. *Sophonisba*, married Professor James W. Massie, of the Virginia Military Institute, late Colonel Confederate States Army (now deceased), and has issue.
vi. *Susan P.*, married Major Charles S. Carrington, a prominent lawyer of Richmond, Virginia.
vii. *Margaret Canty*, married Professor Charles S. Venable, LL.D.. of Virginia, and late Colonel Confederate States Army, on the staff of General R. E. Lee. Has issue.
viii. *Thomas L.*, married Miss Constance Warwick, of Powhatan County, Virginia. He died in the Confederate States Army service, leaving issue one child.
ix. *Eliza*, married Bernard L. Wolfe, Major Confederate States Army, and has issue.

As a speaker, Governor McDowell was eloquent and effective. In Congress he acquired influence and reputation by the gravity of his demeanor and the moderation of his course, and particularly by his wise and cordial support of all measures tending to strengthen the bonds of National Union. His most memorable effort in Congress was his speech on the admission of California as one of the United States, which is said to have produced an impression equal to any other ever delivered in that body.

WILLIAM SMITH.

To the distinguished representation of the name of Smith in the annals of Virginia some reference has been made in a preceding sketch in this serial. Doubtless the paternal ancestor of the subject of this biography was seated in the colony early in the seventeenth century, but it is proposed to deduce first his descent maternally, which is more definitely preserved. Alexander Doniphan,* a native of Spain, whose name was thus Anglicized, a Protestant, migrated to England for religious freedom, and thence to Virginia, where he married, some time before the year 1662, an heiress, Margaret, daughter of George Mott, a native of Scotland, and thus came into possession of a large landed estate, of nearly 18,000 acres, located in the Northern Neck. He settled in that part which was subsequently erected into King George County, and died in 1716, leaving issue three sons and three daughters, as follows: Alexander (the ancestor of the distinguished and venerable General A. W. Doniphan, United States Army), Mott, Margaret, Elizabeth, Anne, and Robert. The second son, Alexander Doniphan, married twice—first, Mary Waugh, and, secondly, Catharine Dobbins. Of his issue by the first marriage was a daughter, Elizabeth, born April 12, 1744; died January 15, 1809; married, in 1773, William Smith, son of Joseph and Kitty (Anderson) Smith,† born February 5, 1741; died January 22, 1803. Of their issue of four daughters and three sons, the eldest, Mary Waugh, born January 1, 1775; died September 15, 1811; married, December 18, 1794, Caleb, (son of Thomas) Smith, born in 1761, and died in November, 1814. They had issue:

i. *Eliza*, born September 25, 1795; died August 14, 1797.
ii. *William*, the subject of this sketch, born September 6, 1797.
iii. *Thomas*, born November 15, 1799; married Ann Maria Goodwin, of Caroline County; died April 4, 1847. He studied law with his brother William, and practiced for a time, but later entered the ministry of the Protestant Episcopal Church. By his unwearying exertions he caused the erection of the handsome Gothic church in Parkersburg, West Virginia. Had issue six sons and four daughters. Of the former, Thomas G., who is married, resides with his family in Parkersburg. Another son, Caleb, was reading law when the war with Mexico broke out. He enlisted, served with distinction, and was made a Lieutenant of the United States Artillery. In 1861 he joined the 49th Virginia Regiment, was made Major, and wounded and permanently disabled in the first battle of Manassas; died December 22, 1874.
iv. *Mary Frances*, born January 9, 1802; married, December 14, 1820, Professor Alexander Keech, President of Potomac Academy, Virginia, who was offered by Mr. Jefferson a professorship in the University of Virginia.

---
* The tradition held by Alexander Doniphan's descendants is that he was of noble Castilian blood, and had been knighted for gallantry on the field of battle. The parchment patent of his rank, it is said, was carried to Kentucky by his great-grandson, Dr. Anderson Doniphan, in 1792, and is believed to be in the possession of his present representatives.
† The descent of William Smith, as preserved by his descendants, was as follows: "During the reign of George I., Sir Walter Anderson, a native of Wales

v. *Catharine Elizabeth*, born April 10, 1804; married, December 7, 1826, John A. Blackford, and died December 4, 1844.
vi. *Martha*, born July 24, 1806; married William Bell (died July 1, 1879), brother of the wife of Governor Smith.
vii. *James Madison*, born March 15, 1808; married, first, Mary Bell; secondly, May 22, 1845, his cousin, Martha Smith Boutwell; died December 15, 1853, at Donna Anna, New Mexico, on his way to take charge of an Indian Agency, to which he had been appointed by President Pierce.
viii. *Anna Maria*, born December 3, 1809; married, January 17, 1833, Rev. Richard Johnson of South Carolina, of the Episcopal Church, who was attached to Hampton's Legion during the late civil war, and gained by his gallantry the sobriquet of "The Fighting Parson." He died February 7, 1872. Two sons only, living respectively in South Carolina and Georgia, survive of their issue.

William Smith, the subject of this sketch, entered, at the age of seven years, the old field schools of his native county, King George, and some years later received tuition in Fredericksburg, Virginia, where he resided in the family of Judge John Williams Green. In 1811 he was sent to Plainfield, Connecticut, to continue his studies at the academy of Jabez W. Huntington, subsequently United States Senator. Here he made considerable progress in the study of Latin and Greek; but the war with Great Britain breaking out in June, 1812, young William caught the patriotic fire of the period, and wished to enter the naval service. Having written his father to procure him a midshipman's appointment, the latter deemed it prudent to recall his ardent son home. He now for a time enjoyed private tuition; but, upon the death of his father in November, 1814, he was sent to the classical school of Rev. Thomas Nelson, at "Wingfield," Hanover County. Mr. Nelson was a highly successful teacher for a long series of years, and many of his pupils distinguished themselves in science and in legislation. Young Smith continued with Mr. Nelson until the age of eighteen, when he entered upon the study of law, first with Green and Williams at Fredericksburg, then with T. L. Moore in Warrenton, and finally for a brief period in the office of General William H. Winder, in Baltimore, Maryland. Hav-

and an officer in the British Navy, and Sir Sydney Smith, a native of England, settled in Richmond County, Virginia; and Joseph Smith, a son of the last, married Kitty, daughter of Sir Walter Anderson." Another daughter, Anne Anderson, married Mott Doniphan, son of the emigrant settler, Alexander Doniphan. Walter Anderson received from Lord Fairfax a grant of 818 acres of land on Carter's Run, west side of the Rappahannock River, and another of 395 acres in June, 1728.

ing passed an examination by Judges Hugh Holmes, Robert White, and John W. Green, he was licensed to practice law, and qualified in the Court of Culpeper County, in August, 1819. His talents, energy, and fidelity speedily gained him success in his profession. An ardent Democrat in politics, the ability of Mr. Smith was soon extendedly in request by his party. He responded cheerfully to its calls, though at personal sacrifice, and persistently declined all political preferment for a long period. In 1836, when in his thirty-ninth year, he consented to become a candidate for the State Senate, to which he was elected, and served through the term of four years. He was re-elected to this body, but resigned after serving one session. In the Presidential campaign of 1840 Mr. Smith effectively canvassed the State in the interest of his party, and greatly enhanced his reputation as a public speaker.

Early in the career of Mr. Smith as a lawyer he had been impressed with the illy-provided mail service of Culpeper County, and determined to improve such facilities. In 1827 he obtained a contract for carrying the mails twice a week from Fairfax Court House to Warrenton, and thence to Culpeper Court House. He renewed this contract in 1831. With this small beginning he in four years built up a daily four-horse post-coach line from Washington City to Milledgeville, Georgia. In 1834 a violent attack was made upon the administration of the Post-office Department, W. T. Barry being then Postmaster-General. In the rapid development of the postal facilities of the Southern country the expenditures of the Department were largely increased. In the Blue Book, or official register of the United States Government, the salaries or compensation of its officers or contractors appear in connection with the names; and, in the case of the contractors, compensation for instances of additional service ordered to be performed is indicated by an asterisk. Every extra allowance beyond the stipulations of the original contract was thus designated. As the route of Mr. Smith was one of rapid development his entries of service were abundantly thus marked. The circumstance was noted in debate by Senator Benjamin Watkins Leigh, from Virginia, who, without calling the name of Mr. Smith, yet affixed upon him the life-long sobriquet of "Extra Billy." Mr. Smith obtained, January 1, 1835, the mail contract by steamboat and coach-line between Washington and Richmond. The previous contractors, Messrs. Edmond, Davenport & Co., of the latter place, started a passenger line in opposition, and for a few months there was a lively competition, which is transmitted in traditions of free passage, and finally of the additional gratuitous inducement of a bottle of wine. It was ended by the transfer, for a consideration, of the contract to the former contractors. During this contest, in the month of March, Mr. Smith was seized, in Fredericksburg, Virginia, with a violent attack of inflammatory rheumatism, which confined him to his bed, incapable of movement without assistance. Early in March, whilst still prostrated, and at a time when the ground was covered with snow, intelligence was brought him that three of his coaches had been overturned in Potomac Run, which was very much swollen in volume. Under the stimulant of strong excitement he demanded that he should be taken from bed, dressed, and placed upon his riding horse, and would take no denial. This was, with difficulty and much pain to himself, accomplished. Urging his horse to full speed he speedily reached the run, plunged into the foaming flood, and ordered the drivers to his assistance. Reaching the coaches, singularly enough, he found that the excitement had freed him from the rheumatism. Dismounting into the water, his active example soon righted the trouble, and the coaches resumed their route. The rheumatism was dispelled, not to return again. The resolution of Mr. Smith was strikingly exhibited on another occasion. Being deprived unexpectedly of the services of the captain and pilot of a steamboat which he ran between Baltimore and Norfolk, he undauntedly took command of the boat and charge of the wheel himself, and successfully made the hazardous trip. Such energetic purpose merited the fullest pecuniary success, but it was unfortunately otherwise. The attention of Mr. Smith being divided between politics, his profession, and his contracts, subjected him to the peculation of his agents, and financial disaster was the result. In 1841 Mr. Smith was elected to Congress over the Hon. Linn Banks, and served in that body until 1843. In December, 1845, he was elected Governor of Virginia for the term of three years, succeeding James McDowell, January 1, 1846. During his term he was an unsuccessful candidate for the United States Senate. In 1850 Governor Smith determined to go to California, where two of his sons were residing. He arrived in San Francisco in May, and engaged in the practice of his profession with much success. His first considerable fee was $3,000 for the examination into the celebrated Suter title. California was admitted into the Union September 9, 1850.

Governor Smith was returned by San Francisco as its delegate to the Constitutional Convention which met at Benicia in the autumn of 1850, and was unanimously elected the permanent President of the body. In the State Assembly, which convened soon after, Governor Smith was nominated for United States Senator, but was not elected. When, on the 1st of December, 1852, Governor Smith determined to return to Virginia, such had been his success from his practice that he left in San Francisco property acquired therefrom which yielded him an annual rental of $18,000. Upon reaching Virginia, Governor Smith found the people of the State much agitated about a redivision into Congressional Districts, rendered necessary by the Census of 1850. Upon the Legislature, then in session, devolved this duty. Under the new apportionment Governor Smith was elected to Congress in May, 1853, and served in this body by successive re-election until March 4, 1861. Returning home, he was prostrated by sickness, and confined to his room for two

BLANDFORD CHURCH.

months. In the meanwhile the initial movement of our recent lamentable civil war had been instituted. Governor Smith, feeling that the struggle on the part of the South "would need the employment of every element of its strength" in the contest, was impelled by a sense of duty to enter the army, though in the sixty-fourth year of his age, and "wholly ignorant of drill and tactics." He therefore offered his services to Governor Letcher, and was promptly commissioned as Colonel and assigned to the command of the 49th Regiment of Virginia Infantry, then being organized, and containing only three companies, with which it inaugurated its subsequent long and brilliant career by a gallant participation in the first battle of Manassas. Its first commander thus warmly testifies to its valorous worth: "I will say that, in the numerous bloody fights in which it was engaged, it never broke in battle or gave me the slightest uneasiness or concern as to its conduct." During the summer and autumn it remained in camp at Manassas, completing its organization and being perfected in drill. During this period Colonel Smith, at the solicitations of his friends, announced himself as a candidate for the Confederate States Congress, and was elected. He attended this body when it convened at Richmond in February, 1862, leaving his regiment in the command of the Lieutenant-Colonel. Upon the adjournment of Congress, on April 16th, he rejoined his command. At the reorganization of the regiment, May 1st, he was elected its Colonel, upon which he resigned his seat in Congress. He participated with his command in the operations on the Peninsula, about Yorktown, and in those later near Richmond. In the battle of the Seven Pines the loss of the regiment was fifty-five per cent. of its number. Of its service here Colonel Smith narrates: "Anderson's brigade, of which my regiment was a part, was ordered to keep on the left of the Williamsburg road, and 'To the front, forward march' was the only order I received during the fight of some hours. In obeying this order we had to encounter a formidable abattis, consisting of heavy felled timber, in which was also a row of rifle pits, and also, on the Williamsburg road, a formidable earth-work—the whole occupied by an enemy whom we could not see until we came into the closest proximity. It was on this occasion, upon the complaint of my men that they could not see the foe, that I gave the order to 'flush the game,' which excited so much humorous newspaper comment." Colonel Smith effectively participated in the battle of Sharpsburg, Maryland, on the 17th of September, 1862, the 49th Virginia constituting the right of the line in that memorable engagement. Colonel Smith was here severely wounded. One of his wounds, through the shoulder, it was feared would prove fatal. Before his wounds were healed he returned to the field, in April, 1863, having been promoted to the rank of Brigadier-General, and took command of the 4th Brigade, then lying at Hamilton's Crossing, near Fredericksburg, Va.

He now announced himself as a candidate for Governor of Virginia, and was elected to this office by a large majority in May. Early in August, 1863, he was promoted to the rank of Major-General. He entered upon his duties as Governor, January 1, 1864. He found that local defence was greatly needed, from the frequent raids with which the capital was menaced by the enemy. He accordingly organized two regiments for this purpose from those who by reason of disability, as foreigners or contractors, or by age or non-age, were exempt from duty in the regular service. To each of these regiments was attached a company of cavalry. When called to the defence of the city lines, Governor Smith always assumed command of them, and the service thus rendered was in several exigencies highly important. Another great want in the State was supplies of every description—food for man and beast. Towards this provision Governor Smith assumed the authority to employ as a purchasing fund the sum of $110,000, which he drew in part from the State contingent fund, and borrowed the remainder from the State banks. He commissioned agents, some of whom were supplied with cotton with which to secure through the blockade such supplies as could only be obtained from abroad; others procured from the South corn, rice, and other needful supplies. The measure was signally successful, and profitable to the State, as an advance of ten per cent. upon the cost was charged to cover transportation and contingent expenses, whilst the public was protected from speculative extortion. It greatly assisted the Confederate Commissariat in times of need, and upon the conclusion of the war the Confederacy was indebted to the State in the sum of $300,000 for such supplies.

Upon the evacuation of Richmond, April 3, 1865, Governor Smith determined to remove the seat of government to Lynchburg. General Lee surrendering to General Grant three days after his arrival in that city, he determined to remove the State Government to Danville, Virginia; but here, again, rapidly maturing events frustrated his hopes. Returning home, he surrendered himself to the dominant Federal authorities, and received his parole. In the meantime, however, a reward of $25,000 had been offered for his apprehension, and it is a gratifying commentary upon the Virginia people that no one had thought of securing it by discovering him.

Governor Smith, since the war, has resided in Warrenton, Virginia, devoted to agricultural pursuits. He married, in 1811, Miss Bell, with whom he blissfully lived for the long period of fifty-eight years, being bereaved of his excellent companion January 7, 1879. They had issue:

i. *William Henry*, born 1822; entered the United States Navy as a midshipman; obtaining leave of absence, in 1850, entered into a private maritime enterprise, and was lost at sea in that year somewhere off the Sandwich Islands.

ii. *James Caleb*, was licensed a lawyer, and, removing to California, was appointed a Judge of the Superior Court of San Francisco; member of the California Assembly; became a member of a great land company in Central America, was elected its president, and died at New Grenada of fever.
iii. *Mary Amelia*, born in 1827; unmarried, and resides with her father.
iv. *Austin E.*, born 1829; in February, 1853, removed to San Francisco, California; appointed by President Buchanan naval officer of that port; resigned in 1861, and, going to Washington to settle his accounts, was held as a prisoner of war; finally exchanged, he entered the Confederate States Army as an Aid on the staff of General Whiting; died from the effects of a wound received at the battle of Gaines' Mill.
v. *Ellen*, vi. *Catherine*, and vii. *John*, all died in infancy.
viii. *Thomas*, born 1838; graduated A. M. from William and Mary College; after attending a law course of two years at the University of Virginia, settled in Charlestown, West Virginia; served as a volunteer in the suppression of the John Brown raid; appointed, in 1861, Major of the 36th Virginia Regiment; commanded it at Fort Donelson; captured a battery of the enemy under special orders, armed his regiment with superior arms from the field, and successfully retreated; promoted to the rank of Colonel, and gallantly commanded his brigade to the close of the war. Since has served as Judge of Fauquier County, and at present efficiently represents it in the State House of Delegates.
ix. *P. Bell*, born 1839; graduated A. M., William and Mary College, and A. B., University of Virginia. In 1859 commenced the practice of law at Warrenton, Virginia. Having lost an arm by accident in youth, he was disabled from service in the Confederate Army; served in 1864 as Governor's Aid to his father. Accidentally killed himself October 13, 1865.
x. *Littleton Moore*, born 1840; died March 10, 1849.
xi. *Frederick Waugh*, born 1843; volunteer in the 49th Virginia Regiment; wounded at the battle of Fredericksburg; appointed Sergeant-Major; later served on the staff of his father, and subsequently joined the command of Colonel John S. Mosby, in which he continued to the close of the late war. Is married, and now living in Arizona Territory.

Governor Smith retains in a remarkable degree his entire faculties, mental and physical. His erect and alert carriage misleads one as to his age. He is still a most effective speaker, as his present earnest advocacy in public of the cause of temperance fully evidences. There is a fine portrait of him in the State Library at Richmond.

JOHN BUCHANAN FLOYD.

The worthy descent of the subject of the present sketch has been quite fully presented in preceding biographies in this serial. John Buchanan Floyd, the eldest son of Governor John and Lætitia (Preston) Floyd, was born at Smithfield, Montgomery (now Pulaski) County, June 1, 1806. After a course of private tuition, he entered the College of South Carolina, from which he was graduated in 1826. Having studied law, he was admitted to the bar in 1828, and commenced practice in his native county. In 1836 he removed to Helena, Arkansas, where he continued to reside for three years in the successful practice of his profession. In 1839 he returned to Virginia, settling in Washington County. He had from the outset of his career taken a deep interest in politics, and rendered efficient service to the party of which he was an enthusiastic follower—the Democratic—as a public speaker. In 1847 he was returned by Washington County to the State House of Delegates, and, whilst still a member of the Assembly, was elected by it Governor of Virginia, succeeding Governor William Smith, January 1, 1849. It is of interest to note that the noble work of art, the Washington Monument, which graces the public square at Richmond, was authorized and commenced during the term of Governor Floyd. It was erected in accordance with the act of Assembly passed February 22, 1849. A premium of $500, offered for the best design, was awarded Thomas Crawford, of Rome, for the model submitted by him, and which was selected. The ceremony of laying the corner-stone took place on the 22d of February, 1850, in the presence of a large concourse of people. Zachary Taylor, President of the United States, and many prominent dignitaries were in attendance by the invitation of the General Assembly. On the 27th of June articles of agreement were entered into with Crawford, stipulating that the equestrian group (in bronze) should be fifteen English feet from the upper surface of the platform to the top of the chapeau, and that the surrounding six statues should be ten feet in height. On the 10th of October, 1857, Crawford died in London, after completing models of all the statuary, except Lewis and Mason, and the "trophies." A contract was then made with Randolph Rogers, of New York, for the completion of the work, and the statues were cast at the Royal Foundry at Munich. The equestrian statue arrived in Richmond in November, 1857, and was drawn through the streets of the city, from the river landing to the square, by the citizens themselves on the 24th of the month. It was erected with the statues of Henry and Jefferson, and unveiled on the 22d of February, 1858, with appropriate ceremonies, General Winfield Scott and others of distinction being present. The statue of Mason was received and erected early in 1860, and, the civil war coming on soon after, the monument remained in *statu quo* until 1867, when the statues of Marshall, Lewis, and Nelson were received. The allegorical figures were all received in 1868, and with their erection the monument was completed. The following indicates the disposition of the statuary and the inscriptions on the shields of the allegorical figures:

Finance, opposite Thomas Nelson, Jr., ... { Yorktown, Saratoga.
Colonial Times, opposite Andrew Lewis, ... { Point Pleasant, Valley Forge.
Justice, opposite John Marshall, ... { Great Bridge, Stony Point.
Revolution, opposite Patrick Henry, ... { Eutaw Springs, Trenton.
Independence, opposite Thomas Jefferson, .. { King's Mountain, Princeton.
Bill of Rights, opposite George Mason, ... { Guilford C. H., Bunker Hill.

The total cost of the monument was $259,913.26, of which, from donations and the interest thereon, was realized $47,212.67. A faithful representation of the monument and its interesting surroundings, from a special photograph, is presented in this work.

Upon the expiration of the term of Governor Floyd he was succeeded, January 1, 1853, by Governor Joseph Johnson. In 1855 Governor Floyd was again returned to the House of Delegates by Washington County. In 1856 he served as Presidential Elector, and voted for James Buchanan, for whose nomination he had warmly exerted himself in the Democratic National Convention, and in whose favor, during the Presidential canvass, he had made many effective speeches in different parts of the country. In March, 1857, Governor Floyd was appointed by President Buchanan Secretary of War. His administration of the War Department was energetic, and it is claimed by his friends that his measures were actuated by a desire for its greater efficiency. The hostility of the Indian tribes in the West requiring the presence of troops, they were ordered thither by Governor Floyd. This measure and the distribution of arms among the fortifications of the Southern ports, subjected him to sectional animadversion when the great civil war was unhappily inaugurated. When Major Robert Anderson moved his garrison from Fort Moultrie to Fort Sumter, December 20, 1860, and President Buchanan refused to withdraw the United States troops from Charleston harbor, Floyd resigned, and retired from Washington to Virginia, and was an earnest advocate for secession by the Southern States. He was appointed, May 23, 1861, a Brigadier-General in the Confederate States Army, and commanded with Generals Henningsen and Wise in Western Virginia. The operations of General Floyd for a time were marked with considerable success, but on the 10th of September, from an unfortunate want of concert between himself and General Wise, the forces under their respective commands were divided by the Gauley River, a deep and rapid stream. The force of General Floyd lay near Carnifax Ferry. Here General Rosecrans, by a rapid march of sixteen miles, threw a largely superior force upon Floyd, attacking him vigorously. Night put an end to the struggle, when Floyd withdrew in the darkness. The Federal loss was 225, whilst the casualty of the Confederates was only twenty men wounded. New differences developing themselves between Generals Wise and Floyd, disturbed their unity of action and rendered their commands ineffective. Floyd lingered for awhile in the mountains, had some desultory engagements with the enemy, subsequently retired to Southwestern Virginia, and from there was transferred by the Confederate Government to the department of Tennessee and Kentucky. He was in chief command of Fort Donelson when it was besieged by General Grant. The Confederate authorities being dilatory in measures of sustenance recommended by General Floyd, and further defence of the post being impossible, Generals Floyd and Pillow, declining to surrender themselves as prisoners, turned the command over to General Buckner, and with about 3,000 men of the garrison retreated on the night of the 15th of February into Tennessee. The fort was surrendered by General Buckner the next day, February 16, 1862. Its fall was a serious blow to the Confederacy, and the retreat of General Floyd was severely criticised. He never again held a command in the Southern army, but the Legislature of Virginia, indignant at the treatment he had received, conferred on him the commission of Major-General, and directed him to recruit and organize a division of troops from among the classes not embraced in the Conscription of the Southern Confederacy. These classes were so restricted that the task was not easily performed. By the autumn of 1862, however, General Floyd had succeeded in raising a force of nearly 2000 men, with which he moved into the country embracing the headwaters of the Big Sandy River, where he several times surprised the troops of the enemy in that section, and captured and destroyed their depots of supplies. The exposure to which he was subjected in this incessantly active service seriously affected his health, and he was ultimately obliged to return home, to be prostrated upon what was destined to be his deathbed. His disease finally assumed the form of cancer, or, more definitely, schirrhus of the stomach,—which, it will be recollected, caused the death of Napoleon I. He died August 26, 1863, at Abingdon, Virginia.

General Floyd married in early life his cousin Sarah Buchanan, daughter of General Francis Preston, but had no issue. He was of commanding physique, and possessed oratorical powers of a high order. There is an excellent portrait of Governor Floyd in the State Library at Richmond.

JOSEPH JOHNSON.

The honored career of Joseph Johnson was the just result of intrinsic merit and resolution of character. No factitious advantages of birth or education attended him. He was born December 19, 1785, in Orange County, New York, and was the second son of Joseph and Abigail (Wright) Johnson. His parents were poor, but their virtues commanded esteem. His father had been a soldier in the war for Independence. Joseph was but five years of age when his father died, leaving a widow with five children. The family moved to Sussex County, New Jersey, in 1791, Joseph then being six years old. They resided there until 1801, when the mother, with a married daughter and son-in-law, and her two little sons, moved to Harrison County, Virginia. Joseph was then fifteen years of age, and was the chief stay and protection of his mother and younger brother. He, of his own volition, soon formed an engagement to live with a respectable farmer in the neighborhood named Smith, and whose health was delicate. This proved to be an auspicious business contract. Joseph soon won the regard of Mr. Smith, became his chief manager, and lived with him until his death. He subsequently, before attaining his majority, married the daughter of his late friend and employer. This was a mutually fortunate and happy union. Mrs. Johnson was noted for her gentle and amiable character. She lived and died an earnest Christian, without an enemy, and beloved by all who knew her. Four years after his marriage Joseph Johnson purchased the interests of the remaining heirs in the farm of his wife's father, and it continued his home through life. It adjoins the village of Bridgeport, a depot on the Parkersburg branch of the Baltimore and Ohio Railroad. Harrison County is now in the new State of West Virginia, carved from the old mother. At the time of Mr. Johnson's marriage, that portion of Virginia was almost covered with primeval forest, educational facilities were limited, and, as the time of Joseph Johnson by day was fully occupied, the simple rudimental knowledge which he acquired was the result of study by night, and later in odd moments. His application was continuous, extending into manhood, and he was thus truly, so far as his knowledge extended, a self-educated man. The demand upon his time as a farmer continued exacting. As a means of improvement he originated a debating society, which met at night in the village near him, and subsequently became famed for the ability of its members, many of whom were honored with public station. Here the talents of young Johnson attracted attention. His analytical and logical powers of mind, and skill as an orator were rapidly developed and acknowledged. In the discussions pending the last war with England, Johnson at once took position with the Republican party, as the advocates of war were then called. As the Captain of a rifle company of militia he was first brought into public view. When the Atlantic sea-board was threatened, in 1814, he called them together, and by a stirring speech influenced

ARMORIAL BOOK-PLATE
Of the eccentric "John Randolph of Roanoke."

them to a unanimous tender of their services to the General Government. They were promptly accepted, and the company marched to Norfolk. There, in the front, Captain Johnson continued in the service until peace was announced in the following year, when with a small remnant of his company he returned home.

Now commenced the long and useful political career for which his talents, decision of character, and unsullied integrity so eminently fitted him. In 1818 he was elected to the House of Delegates, defeating the noted old public servant, John Prunty. In 1822 Mr. Johnson was again elected to the House of Delegates, but declined a re-election on the expiration of his term. In 1823 the Hon. Edward B. Jackson, of Harrison County, declined a re-election to Congress, and persuaded Mr. Johnson to offer himself as a candidate for that body. He did so. The opposing candidates were Edwin S. Duncan, afterwards a Judge of the General Court of Virginia, Colonel Thomas S. Haymond, and the celebrated Philip Doddridge. After a meeting of the candidates in the city of Wheeling, the first two withdrew from the canvass, leaving as competitors Doddridge and Johnson. Doddridge was the senior of Johnson, an eminent lawyer, a forcible and eloquent speaker, and in ability compared favorably with any public man of the period. Yet, after a heated and exciting contest, Johnson triumphed. He took his seat in the eighteenth Congress in December, 1823. Henry Clay was made Speaker of the House, and there was then convened in the two branches of Congress the most imposing array of intellect that has ever graced the National halls. It was during this session that the election of President of the United States devolved on Congress. In this memorable contest Mr. Johnson voted alone for Andrew Jackson from first to last. In 1825 he was re-elected to Congress over Philip Doddridge in a spirited contest. In the spring of 1827 Mr. Johnson returned to private pursuits, and was succeeded in Congress by Isaac Lefler, and he in turn, after a single term, by Philip Doddridge, who served until his death, November 19, 1832, when Mr. Johnson was elected to fill the vacancy, and served during the last session of the twenty-second Congress. He declined re-election in the spring of 1833, and recommended and supported John J. Allen, subsequently a distinguished Judge, who was elected. In 1835 Mr. Johnson again offered himself for Congress, was elected over Mr. Allen, and served continuously until 1841, when he declined re-election, and supported Samuel L. Hays, who, however, was defeated by the Whig candidate, George W. Summers. In 1845 Mr. Johnson was again elected to Congress, over Colonel G. D. Camden. This was the seventh time he had been elected to Congress. At the close of the twenty-ninth Congress, in 1847, Mr. Johnson issued an address to his constituents, thanking them for their past confidence, declining re-election, and expressing his wish and purpose to retire permanently from public life; but his constituents demanded his service in the House of Delegates, in which he served in the session of 1847–48. In 1850 he was elected a member of the State Constitutional Convention, and served in that body as chairman of the committee on suffrage. Whilst a member of the Convention he was elected Governor of the State by the Legislature, under the provisions of the then existing constitution. In the autumn of 1851 the constitution which he had helped to frame was adopted, and under its provisions Mr. Johnson, who had been nominated by the Democratic party, was elected Governor over George W. Summers, by the popular vote, for the term of four years from January 1, 1852. This was the first election of a Governor of Virginia by the votes of the people, and Johnson was the first and only State Executive from the section now comprised in West Virginia. In his first message to the General Assembly, in 1851, Governor Johnson recommended the completion of the James River and Kanawha Canal to Clifton Forge as its western terminus for the time, and the extension of the Central Railroad (now Chesapeake and Ohio) from Staunton, by Clifton Forge, westward to the Ohio River, at or near Guyandotte; together with a general system of railroads for the residue of the State. His recommendations were adopted by the Legislature, and the work on the different lines began and rapidly pushed forward until the breaking out of the civil war in 1861. In the same message he called attention to the importance and critical tenure of the relations of the State with the Union, and foreshadowed the culmination which was so unhappily realized.

In addition to the stations enumerated, Governor Johnson had several times served as Presidential Elector; and now, upon the expiration of his term, December 31, 1855, having attained the allotted age of the Psalmist, three-score and ten years, he finally retired to private life. His mental and physical powers were happily but little impaired. In his home of more than fifty years, surrounded by life-long friends, he dispensed a generous and joyous hospitality. In all the relations of private life he was a model of excellence. Proverbially punctual, his morals were pure and lofty.

In person he was below the medium height, but with robust physique. He was dark in complexion, with brilliant black eyes that were singularly expressive in debate. He was permitted to remain in peaceful quietude for but a few years. In 1860 he discerned the pending fratricidal conflict, and was sorely grieved. A strict constructionist of the Federal Constitution, regarding it as a written compact between the States composing the Union, he held that the Union was the creature of the States. He was never a secessionist *per se*. He loved the *Union of our fathers*, and always advised moderation and patience. He earnestly hoped for a peaceful solution of the sectional differences until President Lincoln called upon Virginia and other States for troops to subjugate those of their own blood. At this critical period he was called upon by his old constituents to address them publicly at their court house on their duty in the trying exigency. Though in the seventy-sixth year of his age, he promptly acceded to their request, and urged them to side with their near kindred and to protect their friends. During the war the section in which Governor Johnson lived was overrun by the Federal troops, and for personal safety he was forced to leave his home in the charge of a daughter and retire across the mountains with the Confederate army. Soon after the close of the war Governor Johnson returned to his home, where he lived peacefully until his death, February 27, 1877, in the ninety-second year of his age. The next day a public meeting of the citizens of Clarksburg was held to give expression to their sense of loss and appreciation of his worth. An excellent portrait of Governor Johnson is in the State Library at Richmond. Of the surviving children of Governor Johnson, a daughter, Mrs. John A. English, resides in Baltimore, Maryland; another daughter, Mrs. C. S. Minor, resides in Bridgeport; Henry G. Johnson is a farmer in Harrison County, J. S. Johnson a successful lawyer in Grafton, West Virginia, and Dr. G. W. Johnson is a practicing physician in Missouri. A granddaughter, the daughter of Mrs. John A. English, is the wife of Dr. George H. Eyster, New York City.

HENRY ALEXANDER WISE.

The ancient family of Wise deduces definitely from William Gwiss, or Wise de Gaston, who located in County Devon, England, about A. D. 1100.* From Sir William Wise, of this lineage, knighted by Henry VIII., sprang *John Wise*, who migrated to Virginia about the year 1650. He was granted, March 24, 1655, 200 acres of land in Northampton County, on " Nondrice's Creek," in consideration of the transportation of four persons, one of whom was Hannah Wise, presumably his wife. (State Land Records, Book No. 4, p. 52.) He also received, September 24, 1668, a grant of 1,060 acres in Accomac County (formed from Northampton), "between Skiskanessok and Annancock Creeks." (No. 6, p. 176.) The tradition is that he also secured an Indian title and the friendship of his aboriginal neighbors by the payment of "six Dutch blankets," and from this circumstance his extensive plantation was known as the "Dutch Blanket Tract." He was a Justice of the Peace

---

* There are branches of the family also in Warwickshire and Staffordshire, England, and County Waterford, Ireland. Of the last is Lieutenant Lucien Napoleon Bonaparte Wyse, of the French Navy, son of Sir Thomas Wyse, K. C. B. (Minister to Athens), and his wife Lætitia, daughter of Lucien Bonaparte, Prince of Cassino. Admiral Charles Wise, of the British Navy, represents the ancient branch. The arms of the Wise family are: *Sa., three chevronels, ermine*. The ancient crest was a mermaid ppr.; but that now used, granted in 1400, is *a demi-lion rampant (gu., guttée, ar.), holding in his paws a royal mace.* Motto: *Aude, Sapere*.

and a man of consideration and influence in the colony. He died in 1695, leaving issue three sons and two daughters: John, William, Richard, Barbara (married Robins), and Hannah (married Scarburgh). The eldest son, *John Wise*, married Matilda, daughter of Colonel Edmund Scarburgh, a member of the Council. He died in 1717, leaving issue three sons and three daughters: John, Thomas, Samuel, Mary Cave, Eliza, and Hannah, of whom *John Wise*, the eldest son, married Scarburgh, daughter of Colonel Tully Robinson, of Welsh descent; was a Justice of the Peace, and died in 1767, leaving issue: John, Tully Robinson, Cassey, and Mary, of whom *John Wise*, the eldest son, Colonel and County Lieutenant of Accomac and Justice of the Peace (died 1770), married Margaret, daughter of Colonel George Douglas, lawyer—a native of Scotland, and of the family of ("Black Douglas") the Earl of Angus—and had issue: John, Tully,† Cassey, Elizabeth, and Mary, of whom *Major John Wise*, the eldest, educated a lawyer, Clerk of Accomac County, served two terms in Virginia Senate as Speaker (died 1812), married twice—first, Mary (died August 9, 1796), daughter of Judge James Henry, and, secondly, Sarah Corbin (died 1813), daughter of Colonel John Cropper,‡ of "Bowman's Folly," a gallant officer of the Revolution, and President of the Virginia branch of the Order of Cincinnati. Had issue by the first marriage five children, and by the second five: Margaret Douglas Pettit, married her cousin Tully Robinson Wise; || James Henry; Henry Alexander; John Cropper; Tully Robinson Scarburgh, of whom *Henry Alexander Wise*, the subject of this sketch, was born at Drummondtown, Accomac County, December 3, 1806. Left an orphan at the age of seven years, he was educated by his father's relatives, and, in 1822, was sent to Washington College, Pennsylvania, where he was distinguished as a debater, and whence he graduated in 1825. Attended the law school of Hon. Henry St. George Tucker, at Winchester, from the autumn of 1825 to that of 1828, when he returned home, and cast his first vote for Andrew Jackson as President. He was married the same year, on the 8th of October,

† Tully Wise married another daughter (Tabitha) of Col. Geo. Douglas, and from them are descended: Geo. D. Wise; Capt. Henry A. Wise, U. S. Navy (author, married a daughter of Edward Everett); Gen. Geo. D. Wise, U. S. Army; and Hon. Tully R. Wise, 4th Auditor in the administration of President Tyler.

‡ He was a grandson of Sir William Bowman, who built "Bowman's Folly."

|| Of their issue is Tully Robinson, distinguished lawyer in California; George Douglas, member of Congress from the Richmond district; James Madison, married Ann Dent, daughter of the late James and Ann Dent (daughter of Hon. Alexander McRae, and granddaughter of William Black, of the Falls Plantation, James River, and his wife Anne Dent, of Maryland) Dunlop; Gen. Peyton, married Laura Mason, daughter of Gen. R. H. Chilton, C. S. Army, Adjutant-General of R. E. Lee; Franklin Morgan, married Ellen, daughter of Col. Christopher Q. Tompkins, U. S. Army; and Lewis Warrington Wise.

to Ann Eliza, daughter of Rev. Obadiah Jennings, D. D., of Washington College, who was subsequently pastor of a Presbyterian Church in Nashville, Tennessee. Mr. Wise moved to Nashville, soon after his marriage, to reside, and formed a law copartnership with Thomas Duncan, Esq. In 1831 he returned to Accomac County. In 1832 he was a Delegate to the Democratic National Convention at Baltimore, Maryland, where he advocated the nomination of Jackson as President, but refused to acquiesce in the nomination of Van Buren as Vice-President. During the Nullification excitement he published an address to the electors of York district, in which he declared himself opposed, on the one hand, to the measures adopted by South Carolina, and, on the other, to the Force bill and the President's proclamation maintaining the doctrines of the Virginia Resolutions of 1798, " that each State for itself is the judge of the infraction of the Constitution and of the mode and manner of redress." In 1833 he was nominated by the Jackson party of the Eastern Shore of Virginia for Congress, in opposition to the Nullification candidate, and was elected by 400 majority. His opponent, Richard Coke, of Williamsburg, challenged him after the election, and, in the duel resulting, the right arm of Mr. Coke was fractured. On the removal of the Government deposits from the Bank of the United States by President Jackson in 1833, Mr. Wise, together with sixteen other Democrats in the House of Representatives, went over to the opposition. He was re-elected to Congress in 1835, and again in 1837, as a supporter of the principles of Hugh Lawson White and John Tyler, who, in 1836, had been candidates for President and Vice-President, in opposition to the regular Democratic candidates— Van Buren and Johnson. He was at this time opposed to the President's pet bank scheme to the Sub-Treasury, to the reference of abolition petitions to any committee, and to a protective tariff; and he was a zealous advocate for the admission of Texas to the American Union. His wife dying in 1837, he married secondly, in November, 1840, Sarah, daughter of Hon. John Sergeant, of Philadelphia. In 1837 he acted as the second of Wm. J. Graves, of Kentucky, in a duel with Jonathan Cilley, of Maine—both members of Congress—in which the latter was killed: an occurrence that created a deep feeling in the country, and led to much denunciation of Mr. Wise, on whom for a time the chief opprobrium of the affair rested. The nomination of John Tyler in 1840, by the Whigs, as a candidate for Vice-President, in conjunction with General Harrison as President, was largely due to the management of Mr. Wise; and on the accession of Mr. Tyler to the Presidency, after the death of General Harrison, his influence on the policy of the administration was very great, especially with reference to the Bank question and the annexation of Texas. In 1842 Mr. Tyler appointed him Minister to France, but the nomination was rejected by the Senate. He was subsequently appointed Minister to Brazil, and in that capacity resided at Rio Janeiro from

May, 1844, till October, 1847. In the Presidential canvass of 1848 he supported the Democratic candidate, General Lewis Cass, and was chosen an Elector. He was a member of the Convention of 1850, which revised the Constitution of Virginia, and in 1852 was again chosen a Presidential Elector, and cast his vote for Franklin Pierce. In December, 1854, he was nominated by the Democrats as their candidate for Governor, and immediately entered into a most animated canvass against the "Know-Nothing" party, which had just been organized in Virginia. Mr. Wise conducted the contest untiringly, and was brilliantly successful. From January to May he traversed the State in all directions, travelling more than 3000 miles, and making fifty speeches, and such was the enthusiasm he created that persons would travel fifty miles to hear him. He was elected Governor by upwards of 10,000 majority. In 1850 his second wife died, and in November, 1853, he was married (a third time) to Mary Elizabeth, daughter of Dr. James Lyons, a sister of the late Hon. James Lyons, and a granddaughter of Hon. Peter Lyons, a native of Ireland, the opponent of Patrick Henry in the famous "Parson's Cause," and a Judge of the Court of Appeals of Virginia. During the administration of Governor Wise the Lecompton controversy of 1857-8 occurred, and though personally attached to President Buchanan, whose election he had advocated in 1856, he warmly joined with Senator Douglas in opposing that "schedule of legerdemain," as he termed the Lecompton Constitution. In 1859, Governor Wise published an elaborate historical and constitutional treatise on Territorial Government, and the admission of new States into the Union, in which he upheld the doctrine of Congressional protection of slavery in all the Territories.

Near the close of Governor Wise's term occurred the seizure of Harper's Ferry by John Brown and his followers, and the execution of Brown at Charlestown, December 2, 1859, was one of the last acts of his administration. Governor Wise was a member of the State Convention which met at Richmond, February 13, 1861, to consider the relations of Virginia to the Federal Government, and was one of the Committee on Federal Relations, to whom the principal business of the Convention was referred. The Committee made three reports March 10th. The majority report affirmed the doctrine of States Rights, demanded a fair partition of the Territories and equal rights therein, expressed the hope of a restoration of the Union, recommended amendments to the Constitution, recognized the right of secession, and advised a conference of the border States. Mr. Wise presented another report, giving the list of demands, requiring both the General Government and the seceded States to abstain from hostilities in the hope of a peaceable adjustment of difficulties, and insisting that the President should only maintain a sufficient number of men in the forts, arsenals, etc., to preserve the public property therein. A third report advised the immediate secession of the State. Upon the passage of the Ordinance of Secession, he entered heartily into the war. He was appointed a Brigadier-General in the Confederate Army, June 5th, 1861, and ordered to Western Virginia. There he served in conjunction with General John B. Floyd until September, when he was ordered to report at Richmond. Thence he was sent to Roanoke Island, North Carolina, with instructions to defend it. At the time of the attack upon the island by General Burnside and Commodore Goldsborough, February 7th, 1862, he was sick at Nag's Head, but the greater part of his brigade (known as Wise's Legion) took part in the action, and his son, Captain O. Jennings Wise, commanding the Richmond Light Infantry Blues, was killed. During the remainder of the winter, General Wise remained in Richmond, being in feeble health. Upon his restoration, he was placed with his brigade in 1863 in command of the district between the Mattaponi and James rivers. His brigade consisted of the 24th, 34th, and 46th Virginia Regiments of infantry, one battalion of artillery, and a few companies of cavalry, with head-quarters at Chaffins Farm. During the period of his command over this district there were some gallant attacks upon the enemy, including a highly successful reconnoissance behind Williamsburg, where the enemy were in force, and the final recapture of that city from the Federals under the command of General Dix. He was relieved at Chaffins Farm by General Eppa Hunton, and sent with his brigade to Charleston, South Carolina, under the command of General Beauregard. While in Carolina his command drove the enemy from John's Island, in the rear of Charleston, and served gallantly and efficiently in Florida in two severely contested battles.

From Carolina General Wise returned to Virginia, and was put in command of the defences of Petersburg. He participated in the battle of Drewry's Bluff, his brigade driving the enemy before them, and pursuing them until withdrawn by his superior commander, General Whiting, who feared to uncover Petersburg. At this point too, on the 15th of June, his brigade alone kept at bay for a whole day the corps of General A. J. Smith, until Lee had crossed with his army to the south side of the James. From that time onward its history was that of General Lee's army at Petersburg, with its horrible monotony of rags, starvation and blood, ended at last by the surrender at Appomattox. After the war, General Wise made Richmond his residence, engaging in the practice of law, his son John S. Wise being associated with him. He published in 1860 several disquisitions on slavery, and in 1873 the "Seven Decades of Union," which is still a highly popular work. He served also as one of the State Commissioners on the Boundary Line between Virginia and Maryland, the final report on which was submitted to the General Assembly and published in 1874. General Wise died at

VIEW IN WEST VIRGINIA.

Richmond, September 14th, 1876, and is interred in Hollywood Cemetery. He had issue by his first marriage:
  i. *Mary Elizabeth*, married Dr. A. Y. P. Garnett, a highly successful physician of Washington, D. C., and lately a surgeon in the Confederate States Army.
  ii. *Obadiah Jennings*, lawyer and editor of the Richmond *Enquirer*; Captain Richmond Light Infantry Blues; died February 8th, 1862, from effects of wounds received at Roanoke Island.
  iii. *Henry Alexander*, Clergyman Protestant Episcopal Church; died August, 1868; married Harriet, daughter of Richard Barton Haxall, merchant miller of Richmond, and has issue: Barton.
  iv. *Ann Jennings*, married Frederick Plumer Hobson (now deceased), and has issue: John Cannon, Henry Wise.

Issue by the second marriage:
  v. *Richard Alsop*, M. D., Professor of Chemistry, William and Mary College; married a daughter of William F. Peachy; now Superintendent of the Eastern Lunatic Asylum at Williamsburg, Va.
  vi. *Margaret Ellen*, married Wm. C. Mayo, of Richmond, son of Edward C., and grandson of Col. John Mayo, who built Mayo's bridge across James River, connecting the cities of Richmond and Manchester.
  vii. *John Sergeant*, born at Rio de Janeiro, Brazil, December 25th, 1845; was educated at the Virginia Military Institute and the University of Virginia; lawyer; Lieutenant of Infantry of Confederate States Army; Captain Richmond Light Infantry Blues; late United States District Attorney for the Eastern District of Virginia, from May, 1882, to March, 1883, and now Congressman at large from Virginia; married Eva Douglas, of Nashville.
  viii. *Spencer Sergeant*, died in infancy.

General Wise had no issue by his third marriage.

A county of Virginia was named in honor of Governor Wise. There is a portrait of him in the State Library at Richmond.

JOHN LETCHER.

"Honest John Letcher," whose crest was his immaculate integrity, and whose talisman, duty, shamed in his honored and useful career mere heraldic boast. As nearly as man may of himself alone be the arbiter of his life's own destiny, was he the exemplification of the hackneyed term "self-made." His success is an enduring beacon to aspiring youth, and an assurance of what integrity, industry, and lofty purpose may accomplish in the race of life. His life-springs yield to no personal disparagement in comparison with any class, however favored, and in him they united, it is believed, the several races of justly termed Great Britain. His father, William Letcher, was a scion of a hardy Welshman early seated in the colony. His mother was of that staunch and sterling Scotch-Irish yeoman stock of the Valley of Virginia, which has supplied the armies and filled the councils of our nation and extended its Western empire. She was a Houston, and a near relative of the unflinching hero of San Jacinto. John Letcher was born in Lexington, Rockbridge County, Virginia, March 29th, 1813. His parents possessed scarce more of this world's goods than the "cotter's content" as sung by their national poet. Young Letcher commenced life with the necessity of toil staring him in the face, but with a resistless craving of the intellect. His home was within the shadow of one of our most beneficent seats of learning—now the hallowed Washington and Lee University—and his earliest associations were with students. Yet that which circumstance gave them could only be his by incessant toil. But the lofty goal of education was ever before him, and with a strong heart and unflagging purpose he grappled with and overcame all obstacles. At the age of fifteen we find him working at the trade of a tailor—whence, it must not be forgotten, also issued a recent Executive of our nation—but devoting every leisure moment to study. Unceasing labor brought him limited means, and soon after his majority he entered Washington College, now Washington and Lee University, where he acquired the foundation of a classical education. He subsequently attended Randolph Macon College. His penchant was, however, for law, and upon leaving college in 1836, he commenced its study in the office of the late Hon. William Taylor. Here he remained for three years, and in 1839 was licensed to practice. Whilst diligent in acquiring professional lore, he had not been neglectful of other branches of learning, but had applied himself also to classic and general attainment as well, always keeping in view the aphorism, "Knowledge is power." He commenced his professional career in his native town, and was for years intimately associated with his late legal instructor, Mr. Taylor, and with Governor James McDowell, whose encouragement, sympathy and friendship in his early years of struggle he ever gratefully cherished. The ability and fidelity of the young practitioner immediately insured him success even amid competition with eminent talents, among whom may be named Briscoe G. Baldwin, Thomas J. Michie, John W. Brockenbrough, A. H. H. Stuart, and others whose names are household words in Virginia. Whilst pursuing his legal studies, he was a frequent contributor to the old Richmond *Enquirer*, the Fincastle *Democrat*, and other newspapers the exponents of the Democratic party, with which he affiliated. In 1839 Mr. Letcher established at Lexington the *Valley Star*, and edited it with ability until 1840, in the advocacy of Democratic principles and the cause of education. At the bar he rose rapidly; a retentive memory, clear mental powers of analysis, and a habit of observation enabling him to comprehensively grasp the relations of his profession to real life as well as the issues of the day. It is easily to be apprehended that he soon became prominent in the political area as a public debater and canvasser. In the contest of 1840 he was present in the most heated encounters, traversing the entire Valley of Virginia, meeting the strongest intellects of the period, and meriting and receiving the warmest recognition alike from friend or foe. It was during this tour, whilst speaking in New Market, Augusta County, that an attractive face in a coquettish blue bonnet, among his auditors, so held him captive that a few years later witnessed the consummation of a life union of unalloyed marital content with its fair possessor—Miss Susan Holt. Plain, practical and frank of speech on the stump, as in private life, John Letcher seldom failed to carry conviction to his auditors, and he always commanded the respect even of his political opponents. In 1844 he resumed editorial control of the *Valley Star*, and was conspicuous for his zeal in the advocacy of the interests of Virginia and of the South, with voice as well as with pen. Among the measures which he earnestly pressed was the annexation of Texas, of which Republic his cousin, General Samuel Houston, was the President. In 1848 Mr. Letcher served as Presidential elector on the Democratic ticket, and when the Convention of 1850 was called to remodel the State Constitution, he was returned to that body by a majority of over 1,200, although his district was strongly Whig. His labors in the Convention were alike satisfactory to his constituents of both political parties, and strengthened his reputation for integrity and ability. In 1851 he was elected, without opposition, to Congress, and continued to serve in that body for four successive terms. Here he made a National reputation—one than which no more enviable could public servant possess.

Though others may have been accorded the origination of great measures, his was a moral influence of which few politicians may boast. His political creed was "Strict construction, frugality in public expenditure, honesty in the public servant;" and in very truth he was a jealous guardian of the Constitution—the citadel of American liberty—and an uncompromising sentinel, challenging every infraction of the invested rights of the nation. By his rigid adherence to sterling principles and his unswerving fidelity to the interest of the people, he justly earned the proud sobriquet, "*Honest John Letcher—the watch-dog of the Treasury*," which distinction he righteously maintained throughout life. In 1859, after a spirited contest, John Letcher was elected Governor of Virginia over William L. Goggin, and took his seat January 1st, 1860, at one of the most trying periods in the history of the Commonwealth. Soon the fires of secession were lighted throughout the length and breadth of the Southern land, and popular clamor within and without her borders demanded that Virginia should be hurled into the vortex of disunion. Governor Letcher was inherently attached to the Union. Calmly, sorrowfully, amid the tempestuous waves of passion and under bitter vituperation, he surveyed the situation, looking into the future with almost prophetic ken, and counselled moderation, forbearance, and conciliation. He loved the Union sincerely and absorbingly. An incident attendant upon the deliberations of the Convention is characteristically noteworthy. Many hot-blooded politicians, followers of the school of Calhoun, were untiring in their efforts to influence the action of the Convention and control that of Governor Letcher, who by them was regarded with great suspicion. Some of the most intemperate and daring among them threatened to haul down the American flag, which, with that of Virginia, floated over the State Capitol. Against this the will of Letcher interposed, and not until Virginia had severed her bonds with the Union by solemn act of Convention would he suffer the Stars and Stripes to be removed. Then, the issue having come between honor and dishonor; after Virginia had sued for peace and compromise almost on bended knee; when she had thrown herself into the breach and had been insultingly rebuffed— then it was that the lamb became a lion's whelp, and John Letcher raised the rallying cry that echoed and re-echoed throughout the Sunny South. Then it was that his executive ability was pre-eminent and became all-sustaining to the people. During nearly three years of the conflict, Governor Letcher controlled the war policy of the State, and was a tower of strength to the Southern Confederacy. His every energy, physical and mental, was devoted to the cause. Never despairing, ever fruitful of resource, quick to determine and equally quick to act. When he spoke, the highest in authority gave respectful ear. His foresight anticipated many an issue that might otherwise have proved disastrous. It was his habit to meet difficulty on the threshold and overcome it there and then, and this served him and the Confederacy in many a critical moment. During the bread riot in Richmond, when the fate of the city trembled in the balance and the Confederate authorities were powerless, it was his decision that averted the impending catastrophe. The threats and entreaties of President Davis and the Secretary of War were whistled down the wind by the overwrought mob, but when the War Governor came to the front, watch in hand, and surrounded by the faithful Public Guard * of the State, commanded by the late Captain Edward S. Gay, and gave the rioters three minutes in which to disperse, they knew that his resolve was fixed and brooked no disobedience. It was

---

* This company, organized in 1801, had its quarters in the old State Armory near the Tredegar Iron Works, and a portion of which, spared by the conflagration of April 3d, 1865, is still standing, a memorial of the past. The Guard, which patrolled the public buildings and grounds at Richmond, used to be jocosely termed the "Standing Army of Virginia," as it was for years the only military body upon State establishment in the Union. It was disbanded by Federal authority in 1867.

Governor Letcher who hurried troops to the front as soon as the State seceded, and saw that they were drilled by the State Cadets of the Virginia Military Institute; and it was he who virtually placed Lee in command of the Virginia troops, and who first recognized the military genius of Jackson, and whose influence later retained in the service that chieftain when, upon a conflict of authority between himself and General Loring, and his complaints were disregarded by the Confederate War Department, he tendered his resignation through his personal friend, Governor Letcher. But the record of Governor Letcher is historical, and naught of detail may now add to its lustre. He knew no policy inconsistent with his duty to his State, and while his relations to the Confederacy challenge a breath of suspicion, his motto was Virginia, first, last, and always. He passed from the gubernatorial chair with the affection and enduring gratitude of the entire people of his beloved State. Immediately after the war he was arrested by the United States authorities, without specific charge, and for some months was confined in the Old Capitol prison at Washington. During the war his home was burned by the vandal raider, General Hunter, at the time of the destruction of the Virginia Military Institute, in June, 1864, and upon Governor Letcher's release from prison he returned to Lexington and applied himself to building up his shattered fortunes in the practice of his profession. He remained in private life until 1875, when he was elected to the House of Delegates, and there originated the well-known "dog law" for the protection of sheep husbandry. In 1876, whilst in attendance upon the Assembly, he was suddenly and without premonition, after a busy day of legislative service, stricken with paralysis. Whilst thus prostrate the State Senate, to show their appreciation of his public services, passed a joint resolution providing for the payment of all expenses incident upon his illness, but with lofty patriotism he gratefully but firmly declined the provision. He said, "The precedent is an unsafe one at all times, and especially so now in the distressed condition of our people, whose lot I claim to be my lot." Governor Letcher peacefully passed to the final reward of a well-spent life, at Lexington, in the midst of his family, January 26th, 1884. A joint resolution of respect to his memory was passed by the General Assembly then in session, and eloquent and touching eulogies to his worth were delivered in both of its branches. In the preamble to the resolutions the eminent services of Governor Letcher are thus recited: "Through a life-time covering the most eventful period in the history of Virginia, the great powers of his mind and the warm affections of his heart were devoted with constant faithfulness and energy to the service of his State and country. As a representative of Virginia in the Congress of the United States, as her Governor in the most trying epoch of her history, he won the love and admiration of her people, and a place in that history, where his name will live as long as unswerving honesty in the administration of public trust and great ability, wisdom and patriotism in the discharge of official duty shall be honored among men." His venerable wife and seven children survive Governor Letcher: *Samuel Houston*, a prominent lawyer of Lexington, who gallantly served as the Colonel of the 58th Virginia Infantry during the late war; *John Davidson*, a civil engineer; *Greenlee Davidson*, now a cadet at the Virginia Military Institute; *Elizabeth Stuart; Margaret Kinney*, married, February 26th, 1884, Robert J. Showell, of Maryland; *Virginia Lee*, and *Fannie W. Letcher*. There is an excellent portrait of Governor Letcher in the State Library at Richmond, Virginia.

FRANCIS H. PIERPONT.

Another example is now presented of an honorable and successful career attendant upon probity and persistent purpose.

Francis H. Pierpont, third son of Francis and Catharine (Weaver) Pierpont, was born January 25th, 1814, in Monongalia County, Virginia, four miles east of Morgantown, on the farm settled by his grandfather, John Pierpont, a native of New York, in 1770, then in West Augusta County, who erected a dwelling and a block-house, also, for protection against the Indians. In the last was opened the first land office in that section of the State. John Pierpont married a daughter of Colonel Z. Morgan, the proprietor of Morgantown, and who migrated thither from Eastern Virginia. Joseph Weaver, the maternal grandfather of the subject of this sketch, a native of Central Pennsylvania, settled on a farm near Morgantown about 1785. In 1814 Francis Pierpont moved from the homestead to land purchased by him in Harrison County, about two miles from the present Fairmont, Marion County, West Virginia. In 1827 he made his residence in Fairmont and conducted a tannery in connection with his farm. His son, young Francis, assisted his father in his several occupations until manhood. His educational opportunities were in the meanwhile limited. In June, 1835, he entered Allegheny College, at Meadville, Pa., from whence he was graduated with the degree of Bachelor of Arts in September, 1839. He now taught school until 1841, when he removed to the State of Mississippi, where he continued teaching, but the following year he was recalled to Virginia by the failing health of his father. Having studied law in the leisure intervals of his career as a teacher, he was now admitted to the bar. From 1848 for a period of eight years, he served as the local counsel of the Baltimore and Ohio Railroad Company for the counties of Marion and Taylor. In 1853 he engaged in mining and shipping coal by rail, and a little later in the manufacture of fire bricks. In December, 1854, he married Julia A., daughter of Rev. Samuel Robinson, a Presbyterian minister of New York. In religious faith Mr. Pierpont was himself a member of the Methodist Episcopal Church, with which he connected himself at the age of seventeen. Reared in a section in which there were but few slaves, and deeply impressed in his youth by several instances of emancipation of which he was cognizant, his prejudices against the institution of slavery strengthened with his years. His observation of the plantation system in Mississippi confirmed him as an uncompromising opponent of slavery. He early took an interest in politics, and though not an aspirant for office, he actively participated in the campaigns of the Whig party, with which he affiliated from 1844 to 1860. In 1848 he was a Presidential elector on the Taylor ticket. In the momentous Presidential campaign of 1860, Mr. Pierpont charged the Democratic party with a predetermined design to dismember the Union, and asserted that the split in the party at Baltimore was with the expectancy that it would secure the election of a Republican President and precipitate secession. Whilst the Ordinance of Secession, passed April 17th, 1861, by the State Convention at Richmond, was ratified by the people of Eastern Virginia, the vote in Western Virginia was largely against it. In this dilemma, Mr. Pierpont conceived the idea of a "restored government," and at his instigation a Convention *en masse* was held at Wheeling on the 11th of May, 1861, which was attended by the leading men of Northwestern Virginia. After a session of two days spent in fruitless discussion, Mr. Pierpont proposed a Convention to be held at Wheeling on the 11th of June following, to be composed of delegates favorable to the Union, from among those who might be elected on the 23d of May to the General Assembly, and of twice the number of citizen delegates from each county as it was entitled to as representatives in the General Assembly. He also proposed the appointment of a "Committee of Safety," to consist of nine members, whose duty it would be to supervise the election of delegates and to call the Convention. The resolutions were adopted, and Mr. Pierpont was appointed on the "Committee of Safety," which met the next day after the adjournment of the Convention. To the committee Mr. Pierpont stated his views regarding the relation of the seceded State to the Union, and held that "its officers being in rebellion had abdicated the government of the State," and that "the loyal citizens of the State were entitled to the government of the State during such insurrection." He suggested the passage by the ensuing Convention of an ordinance embodying this enunciation, and that the body should make provision for the establishment of a State government, fill its offices with "loyal" men, and secure the occupancy of the Monongahela Valley by Federal troops. He further suggested that upon the recognition of the State by the Federal Government, it might be erected into a separate State. The plan was favorably received and became the basis of future action. In

SOUTH VIEW OF THE CAPITOL, RICHMOND, VIRGINIA,
Where the Confederate Congress held its sessions.

the Convention held at Wheeling on the 11th of June, forty counties of the mountain region were represented. It met in the Custom House; and each delegate, as his credentials were read, took an oath to the National Constitution and its Government. The Convention was organized by the appointment of Arthur I. Boreman, of Wood County, as permanent President, and G. L. Cranmer, Secretary.

The Convention went earnestly to work. A committee was appointed to draw up a Bill of Rights, and on the following day it reported through its chairman, John S. Carlile. All allegiance to the Southern Confederacy was denied in that report, and it recommended a declaration that the functions of all officers in the State of Virginia who adhered to it were suspended, and the offices vacated. Resolutions were adopted declaring the intention of the "people of Virginia" never to submit to the Ordinance of Secession, but to maintain the rights of the Commonwealth in the Union. On the third day of the session, June 13th, an ordinance was reported for vacating all the offices in the State held by State officers acting in hostility to the General Government, and also providing for a Provisional Government by the election of officers for a period of six months. A Declaration of Independence of the old government was adopted on the 17th, which was signed by all the members present, fifty-six in number, and on the 19th the ordinance for the establishment of a Provisional Government was adopted. On the 20th there was a unanimous vote in favor of the ultimate separation of Western Virginia from Eastern Virginia. On that day the new or "restored Government" was organized. Francis H. Pierpont, of Marion County, was chosen Provisional Governor, with Daniel Polsley, of Mason County, as Lieutenant-Governor, and an Executive Council of five members. Governor Pierpont was prompt and energetic. His first official act, the next day after his accession, was to notify the President of the United States that the existing insurrection in Virginia was too formidable to be suppressed by any means at the Governor's command, and to ask the aid of the General Government. It was promised, and thus the action of the Convention was sanctioned by the Government. Governor Pierpont was authorized to raise volunteer regiments and officer them for the United States service. He speedily organized twelve regiments of militia. He procured a greater and lesser seal of State.

Money was needed. There was no treasury, and Governor Pierpont borrowed on the pledge of his own private means $10,000 for the public service. He also secured by military seizure $28,000 which had been transmitted from Richmond to Weston, Lewis County, to pay for work on the lunatic asylum there; and collected from the United States Government $50,000, the share of the State of Virginia in the proceeds of the sale of public lands appropriated by Congress in 1836. A legislature was elected, met on the 1st of July and immediately elected John S. Carlile and Waitman T. Willie to represent the "restored Government" in the Senate of the United States as successors of Messrs. Hunter and Mason, from Virginia, who had resigned. Representatives were also elected by the people, and both were admitted to seats in Congress, which met in extra session on the 4th of July. The Convention re-assembled on the 20th of August and passed an ordinance for the erection of a new State, in which slavery was prohibited, to be called Kanawha. This ordinance was ratified by the people on the 24th of October following. At a subsequent session of the Convention, on the 27th of November, the name was changed to West Virginia, and a State Constitution framed, which was ratified by the people on the 3d of May, 1862, when, also, Governor Pierpont was elected Governor to fill the remaining portion of the term of Governor Letcher. The Legislature, at a called session, also approved of the division of the State and the establishment of a new Commonwealth. Governor Pierpont was tireless in his official duties. His daily office duties for several of the earlier months of his administration, it is stated, occupied from thirteen to sixteen hours. The State Auditor refusing at this period to issue warrants for an appropriation of $50,000 made by the Legislature for the public service, Governor Pierpont, by an arrangement with the bank, disbursed this sum in recruiting by personal check. West Virginia was admitted as a State into the Union on the 20th of June, 1863, by an Act of Congress, approved by the President, on the 31st of December, 1862. Governor Pierpont, who had been elected in the month of May Governor for the term of three years, commencing January 1, 1864, now removed the seat of Government to Alexandria, Virginia. Upon the issuing by President Lincoln of his proclamation emancipating the slaves, Governor Pierpont apprehending a conflict between State and Federal authority regarding the freedmen, recommended to the Legislature, which assembled in December, to call a Convention to pass an ordinance of general emancipation, and accordingly, on the 22d of February, 1864, an ordinance was passed in Convention abolishing slavery in the State forever. Another ordinance also made it the duty of the Governor to nominate all the judges of the State for confirmation by the Legislature. Governor Pierpont about this time conducted quite a spicy correspondence with General B. F. Butler, (sometimes designated as "Beast,") whose lawless acts he complained of to President Lincoln, and urged his removal. The President is said to have expressed himself as being satisfied of the truth of the complaints, and said to Governor Pierpont that he would remove Butler if the Governor would tell him how to silence the press, which Butler seemed to control, and through its medium appeared to the Northern populace as the embodiment of all that was potent in subduing the "rebellion." On the 25th of May, 1865, Governor Pierpont removed his seat of Government to Richmond, the capital of the late Confederate Government. He was immediately waited upon by citizens from all portions of the State, and generally took counsel with them in their misfortune.

In response to his inquiries he learned that but few in any county, and in some none, could vote or hold office because of the disqualification imposed by the Alexandria constitution for participancy in the rebellion. He at once sent his Adjutant-General personally to all the counties that had elected delegates to the Alexandria Legislature, summoning the members to Richmond whose legal term expired on the 1st of July. They attended in June and met in the gubernatorial reception room. The Governor explained to them that without the removal of the disfranchisement he could not reconstruct the State, as there was nobody to vote; that they had the power to remove the disability, and that if they would agree to do so, he would call them in extra session at once. They assented. The extra session was called, the disability to vote was removed, and a resolution was passed giving the next legislature conventional authority to remove the disqualification to hold office. He also found, upon his arrival in Richmond, the United States Marshals busy libelling the property of the late Confederates for confiscation. A few days afterward President Johnson issued a proclamation confiscating the estates of certain classes unless pardoned. It was stipulated that all petitions should be recommended by the Governor. He soon perceived that the President was temporizing, and was led to apprehend that the "pardon mill" was a farce at least, if no worse. He accordingly determined to recommend all petitions offered him. He next protested to the Attorney-General against the further iniquity of libelling property which it was never designed to confiscate, and which only entailed grievous expense on the owners. His protest was effective. He next interposed for the suppression of the class of pardon-broker harpies, who obstructed the due course of the Executive clemency as provided. He refused to recommend any petition which would pass into the hands of a broker, and thus disarmed these rapacious thieves. He next interposed for the relief of citizens who were under civil indictment for offences which were within the province of military authority, and recommended leniency and conciliation to the courts. With a contingent fund supplied by the Alexandria Legislature, he rehabilitated the Western Lunatic Asylum and the Institution for the Deaf, Dumb and Blind, at Staunton, which was destitute of suplies and necessary equipments. He also appointed, upon the recommendation of those duly interested, efficient regents for the University of Virginia and the Virginia Military Institute, without reference to party affiliation. Governor Pierpont continued in office beyond the period of his term, which expired January 1, 1868, and held until April 16, 1868, when he was succeeded by General Henry H. Wells, appointed Provisional Governor by General John M. Schofield, commanding the Military Department of Virginia. Governor Pierpont then retired to private life. He was subsequently elected Clerk of Marion County Court, and now resides in Fairmont.

HENRY H. WELLS.

Henry H. Wells was born in Rochester, New York, September 17, 1823. He was educated at the Romeo Academy in Michigan, and, studying law, was admitted to the bar in Detroit, where he successfully practiced his profession from 1846 to 1861. He served as a member of the Michigan Legislature from 1854 to 1856. Upon the breaking out of the late civil war, he entered the volunteer service of the Union army, in which he served with distinction, attaining the brevet rank of Brigadier-General. Having resigned from the army, he located in 1865 in Richmond, Virginia, and resumed the practice of law. He was appointed April 16, 1868, by General John M. Schofield, United States Army, commanding the First Military District of Virginia, Provisional Governor of Virginia, superseding Governor Francis H. Pierpont. He held this station until April 21, 1869, when he resigned, and Gilbert Carleton Walker, Governor-elect of the State by popular vote, was appointed in his stead by General E. R. S. Canby, United States Army, then commanding the First Military District of Virginia. General Wells was soon after appointed United States Attorney for the Eastern District of Virginia, which position he held until 1872, when he resigned, and resumed the practice of law. In 1875 he removed to Washington City, and in September of that year was appointed and entered upon the duties of United States Attorney for the District of Columbia. His son, H. H. Wells, Jr., received the appointment of Assistant Attorney for the District. They held office until 1879, when they were succeeded respectively by George B. Corkhill and R. Ross Perry. General Wells now resides in Washington, engaged in the practice of his profession.

GILBERT CARLETON WALKER.

Gilbert Carleton Walker was born in Binghamton, New York, August 1, 1832. After a preliminary course of tuition in Binghamton Academy, he entered Williams College, Massachusetts, and subsequently Hamilton College, New York, graduating from the latter institution in July, 1854. Having studied law, he was admitted to the bar in September, 1855, and commenced practice in Oswego, New York. Entering politics, in 1858 he served as a member of the State Democratic Convention. In 1859 he removed to Chicago, Illinois, continuing the practice of his profession there and participating in politics. In 1864 he located in Norfolk, Virginia, and soon became the President of a bank, the Exchange National, and also held other positions of honor and trust. He subsequently settled in the city of Richmond, and in January, 1869, was elected, on the Liberal Republican ticket, Governor of Virginia over Henry H. Wells by a majority of over 18,000 votes. On the 21st of April following he was appointed, by General Canby, Provisional Governor, to succeed General Henry H. Wells, the State then not having been readmitted to the Union. He thus acted until January 1, 1870, when he entered upon the regular gubernatorial term, under the State Constitution of 1869, of four years, to which he had been elected. He was succeeded, January 1, 1874, by General James Lawson Kemper as Governor. In 1875 he was elected to the Forty-fourth Congress from the Third District of Virginia, as a Conservative, over Rush Burgess, Republican, and served as Chairman of the Committee on Education and Labor. In 1877 Governor Walker was reelected to the Forty-fifth Congress, as a Democrat, over Dr. Charles S. Mills, Republican, and served on the Committee on the Revision of the Laws of the United States. He was, in 1876, an aspirant for the Democratic nomination of Vice-President of the United States, and it was thought at one time that he had enlisted much support in the South. He was for several years associated in the practice of law in Richmond with General George J. Hundley, and was also the President of the Granite Insurance Company, which he organized. In 1881, Governor Walker removed to his native place, Binghamton, New York, and for a time practiced his profession there. He is now located in New York City, and enjoys there an extensive and lucrative law practice. In person Governor Walker is highly prepossessing. His imposing stature, graceful mien, finely chiselled features, and silvered head, render him marked in a multitude. He is a pleasing speaker, and his personal advantages enhance his powers over an audience. As a public speaker he is effective and never fails to enchain attention and command applause. He has also frequently proven himself an acceptable lecturer on literary and scientific topics before educational institutions and other bodies. There is a strikingly faithful portrait of Gov. Walker in the State Library at Richmond.

JAMES LAWSON KEMPER.

The Kemper family of Virginia is of German extraction. Its founder, John Kemper, was a member of one of the twelve families from Oldensburg which, accompanied by a Government agent of Great Britain, arrived in Virginia in April, 1714, and constituted the Palatinate Colony, seated by Governor Alexander Spotswood upon his lands at Germanna, which, according to Colonel William Byrd in the "Westover MSS.," was "located in a horse-shoe peninsula formed by the Rapidan River, containing about 400 acres." There is a locality corresponding to this in Madison County, upon which the ruins of a settlement are said to have been identified. The settlers soon becoming restless and dissatisfied under the management of Governor Spotswood, determined to secure lands of their own, and succeeded in obtaining a grant on the Licking River, some twenty miles distant, to which they removed in 1719. They called the new settlement Germantown, which is eight miles from the Warrenton of the present day. They erected a church and applied themselves earnestly to industrial pursuits. Their religious worship and all business was transacted in their native tongue, which was long the only language spoken. Their religion, for the free exercise of which they left home and crossed the ocean for the American wilderness, was the "Reformed Calvinistic Church." This colony, augmented in number by another band of emigrants, were the progenitors of many of the most worthy of the present families of Madison and other counties contiguous thereto. John Kemper married, in 1717, Alice Utterback, and their son, John Peter Kemper, married, in 1738, Elizabeth, daughter of John and Agnes (daughter of Dr. Haeger, the pastor of the settlement) Fishback. From this worthy pair was descended in the fourth generation James Lawson Kemper, the subject of this sketch, born in Madison County in 1824. After a preliminary tuition in the schools of his native county, he entered Washington College (now Washington and Lee University), and was graduated thence with the degree of Master of Arts. He then studied law in the office of Hon. George W. Summers, in Charleston, Kanawha County.

In 1847 he was commissioned a Captain in the volunteer service of the United States by President James K. Polk, and joined General Zachary Taylor's army of occupation in Mexico, just after the battle of Buena Vista, and thus failed of the desired honor of active service in the Mexican war. Returning home and entering political life, Captain Kemper was soon honored with the suffrage of his native county, and for ten years represented it in the House of Delegates, of which body he served two years as Speaker, and was for a number of years Chairman of the Committee on Military Affairs. He served also as President of the Board of Visitors of the Virginia Military Institute. On the 2d of May, 1861, he was commissioned by the Virginia Convention, on the nomination of Governor Letcher, Colonel of Virginia volunteers, and assigned to the command of the 7th Regiment of infantry, which command he assumed at Manassas. Colonel Kemper was first engaged with his regiment in the battle of Bull Run, July 18, 1861, and thereafter at the first battle of Manassas, July 21, 1861, where his regiment was temporarily incorporated in a brigade commanded by Colonel Jubal A. Early, and aided in striking the final blow on the extreme left of the Federal line, which immediately preceded the retreat and final rout of that army. Three days after the battle of Manassas his regiment was assigned to a brigade commanded by General

Longstreet. This brigade was subsequently commanded by General A. P. Hill, and under him Colonel Kemper with his 7th Regiment was in the hottest of the fight at the battle of Williamsburg, May 5, 1862, and engaged with the enemy for nine successive hours, capturing several pieces of artillery and four hundred prisoners. Immediately after the battle Colonel Kemper was promoted to the command of the old brigade, which had been successively commanded by Generals Longstreet, Ewell, and A. P. Hill, and at its head participated in the first day's fight at Seven Pines, May 31, 1862, and in the seven days' sanguinary encounters around Richmond, commencing June 26th following.

In the second battle of Manassas, Brigadier-General Kemper commanded temporarily a division composed of several of the brigades afterwards composing Pickett's division. Here, with these same "Pickett's Men," subsequently so celebrated for valor, he was posted to oppose the extreme left of the enemy; but acting upon the momentary dictation of his own judgment, he changed front so as to strike the right flank of the enemy, and soon after this accomplishment received orders from General Lee to make the same movement which he had already so successfully effected with the infliction of a terrible loss on the enemy. General Kemper commanded his own brigade in the battles of South Mountain and Sharpsburg. Soon after the return of the invading army from the Maryland campaign, Kemper's brigade was incorporated in Pickett's division. At the battle of Fredericksburg, in December, 1862, General Kemper with his brigade was temporarily detached from the division, and joined the troops on Maryes Heights on the afternoon of that day under a hot fire. He was again detached from the division early in 1863, and sent with his brigade to North Carolina, where he commanded the forces at Kingston opposed to the Federal force under General Foster, who then held Newbern. He rejoined Pickett's division in front of Suffolk, Virginia, participated in the operations at that place, and marched with the division into Pennsylvania, his troops participating in the ever memorable charge at Gettysburg, and meeting their full share of its terrible massacre. General Kemper was desperately (it was supposed mortally) wounded whilst gallantly leading his brigade, and was being carried in a bloody blanket to the rear when he was met by General Lee, and the following colloquy ensued: Said General Kemper—"General Lee, they say I am dying, and you see the last of me. Before I go, I have one thing to demand: I have seen in the fight what you have not seen—I have seen the splendid heroism of my boys; when you make up your reports do them justice and cover them with glory; they have won it." General Lee replied with deep emotion: "I will. I will do all you ask, but I trust God will spare your life and yet restore you. I hope you will live, General Kemper, for Virginia to honor and reward you, as she will." Upon the examina-

IVY-GROWN GRANITE LODGE.
Entrance to Hollywood Cemetery, the beautiful "City of the Dead," at Richmond.

tion of his wound, it was thought that it would be impossible for him to live. This fact was reported to the officers and men of his brigade, and they waited in a drenching rain near the hospital for several hours, expecting to hear momentarily of his death. In fact, a coffin was obtained and placed in an ambulance, so that as soon as breath had fled, they might take his body and retreat with it. He was held a prisoner in the hospital for three months, but upon the written certificates of several United States surgeons that he must soon die, he was finally exchanged. After his exchange and return to Virginia, General Kemper was for a long time too much disabled to perform any duty in the field. He attempted to return to the command of his brigade, but was totally unable to do so. To this day he carries a ball near the base of his spine, the effects of which have finally caused partial paralysis. Although unable to perform field duty, he was assigned to the important command of the local forces in and around Richmond, the frequently beleaguered capital of the Southern Confederacy. March 1, 1864, he was commissioned a Major-General. General Kemper continued in command of the forces protecting Richmond until its evacuation. At all times his position was delicate and peculiarly embarrassing, yet his duties were performed with such manifest fidelity and regard for the feelings of all with whom he held relation, that he won alike the affections of the people and the commendation of his superior officers. After the close of the war, General Kemper retired to his home in Madison county, and resumed the practice of law. His voice was highly effective in the Walker gubernatorial campaign, which triumphantly redeemed Virginia from military bondage; and in the Presidential canvass of 1872, as one of the Greeley and Brown electors for the State at large, he stumped every section of the State, and, by his earnest and potent appeals, was most influential in reconciling the people of Virginia to that ticket. In 1873 he was elected Governor of Virginia, and took his seat January 1, 1874, as the successor of Governor Walker. His administration was highly satisfactory.*

---

* The first year of his incumbency, 1870, was marked by several calamitous visitations, and is memorable in the annals of Virginia as the year of disasters. On the 27th of April occurred the "Capitol disaster." In the room of the Court of Appeals, on the third floor of the State Capitol, on the morning of that day a large concourse of persons, including many distinguished men, had assembled to hear the decision of the Court as to the constitutionality of the "Enabling Act," under which Hon. Henry K. Ellyson (now one of the proprietors of the Richmond *Dispatch*) had been elected Mayor of Richmond. His seat was contested by George Chahoon, who had been the military appointee of the Federal Government. Suddenly and without warning, by the falling through of the floor, the audience were precipitated to the hall of the House of Delegates below. The awful scene was heartrending in the extreme. In confused mass were piled and lay struggling, amid the *debris* of the floor and galleries, the dead and dying. Piteous moans and screams of anguish rent the air and

Upon the expiration of his term January 1, 1878, he was succeeded by Governor F. W. M. Holliday. and retiring to his home in Madison county, has not since re-entered public life. Governor Kemper married Miss Cave, of Orange county, descended in the fourth generation from Benjamin Cave, the joint patentee with Abraham Bledsoe, on the 28th of September, 1728, of 1,000 acres of land on the Rapidan river, and a member of the House of Burgesses. She died some years ago, leaving issue several children, of whom the eldest, Meade C. Kemper,

smote the ears of the crowd which pressed to the rescue of the victims. Sixty-five persons were killed and two hundred maimed and wounded. The whole city and State were thrown into mourning, of which the only parallel was the preceding horror, the burning of the Richmond Theater, December 26, 1811. The second memorable visitation was on October 1st, when James river was flooded at Richmond to a little more than twenty-four feet above high tide, water invading the streets of the city so as to admit the propelling with poles of a fishing smack along Seventeenth to Franklin street. The height that the water attained is indicated by a memorial stone of granite with brass tablet bearing appropriate inscription, erected by order of the city council on the north side of Main street, near Fifteenth street, in front of the St. Charles Hotel. For convenience of reference it is deemed that mention of other noteworthy floods in James river will not be unacceptable here. As remarkable as the flood of 1870 had seemed to those who witnessed it, it was eclipsed by another, which reached the maximum height of twenty-five feet six inches on the night of Sunday, November 25, 1877. They were both instanced by great loss of life and destruction of property ; the angry waters being laden with almost every kind of portable property, houses, furniture, provinder, produce, etc., etc. Accounts of two similar preceding visitations have been preserved in the annals of Virginia. Colonel William Byrd, writing June 5, 1685, from his seat near the present site of Richmond, says : "About five weeks since there happened here such a deluge that the like hath not been heard of in the memory of man ; the water overflowing all my plantation came into my dwelling-house. It swept away all our fences, * * carried away a new mill, stones, house and all. The water hath ruined my crops, and most of my neighbors'." There was another like disaster in 1771, lasting from May 27th to June 8th, when, according to the inscription on an obelisk erected on Turkey Island, then the seat of William Randolph (the founder of the famous Virginia family of the name) to commemorate it—" all the great rivers of the country were swept by inundations never before experienced, which changed the face of nature and left traces of their violence that will remain for ages." The water came within Shockoe Warehouse, in Richmond, which then stood where the Exchange Hotel is now located. The third memorable catastrophe of 1870 was the burning of the Spotswood Hotel (so famed during the days of the Confederacy, and which was located on the southeast corner of Main and Seventh streets, where the Pace Block now stands) between two and three o'clock A. M. on Christmas Day. Six persons perished in the flames, among them Captain Samuel C. Hines, who sacrificed his life on the altar of friendship in endeavoring to save E. W. Ross, a fellow-member of the fraternity of the Knights of Pythias. His sublime offering has been justly commemorated by the order in the institution of Hines Lodge, one of the most flourishing in the city. The morning of the fire was so intensely cold that the water cast on the burning building congealed in mammoth icicles from portions of the edifice yet unreached, and on the buildings contiguous thereto.

M. D., is a practicing physician in West Virginia. An excellent portrait of Governor Kemper is in the State Library at Richmond.

FREDERICK WILLIAM MACKEY HOLLIDAY.

William Holliday, the paternal grandfather of the subject of this sketch, of staunch Scotch-Irish lineage, was born in the north of Ireland, and accompanied his parents to America, a youth of fourteen years. They settled in Pennsylvania, and he subsequently located permanently in Winchester, Virginia, having married, in Baltimore, Maryland, Mrs. Blair, *nee* Duncan, who had previously resided in Philadelphia. William Holliday became a successful and prominent merchant. His son, Richard J. McKim Holliday, M. D., a skilled and prominent physician of Winchester, uniformly beloved for his noble and generous traits, married Mary C. Taylor. Her father, Samuel Taylor,* M. D., born near Dover, Delaware, after a preliminary reading under Dr. James Craik, the personal friend and family physician of General Washington, completed his medical studies in Philadelphia, and located in Berryville, then in Frederick, but now Clarke county, Virginia, where he married a daughter of Dr. Robert Mackey, who efficiently served as a surgeon in the Revolution, and at its close settled in Winchester, where his professional ability and social worth were warmly and justly esteemed. Several prominent families in that city and in other portions of the State are descended from him. Dr. Samuel Taylor also rendered the nation service as a surgeon in the war of 1812.

Frederick William Mackey Holliday, the son of Dr. Richard J. McKim and Mary C. (Taylor) Holliday, was born in Winchester, February 22, 1828. After preparatory tuition in the academy of his native place, he entered the junior class at Yale College, from which he was graduated with distinguished honors in 1847. On his return to Winchester, he read law for a year with Barton and Williams, eminent practitioners there, and then entering the University of Virginia, in one session he graduated in Law, Political Economy, and Moral and Mental Philosophy, and was selected as the " Final Orator " of the Jefferson Society of that Institution. Returning to his home, he entered diligently upon the practice of his profession, devoting his leisure moments to literary pursuits. His fidelity and ability speedily secured him reputation in his profession, whilst his scholarship entailed frequent service by request as a lecturer. These early efforts exhibit a remarkable maturity and depth of thought and

---

*The progenitor of this family in America was Robert Taylor, an English emigrant, who settled in Delaware County, Pennsylvania, in 1685. His son, Isaac Taylor, was a member of the Pennsylvania Assembly from Chester County, in 1711 and 1712, and in 1726, and whose son Benjamin was the father of Joseph (born in 1732), who was the father of Dr. Samuel Taylor, who was thus fourth in descent from the emigrant ancestor.

accuracy of expression for one so youthful, and the prognostications which they make with regard to the working of our institutions have been most curiously verified in both our State and National Government. He found time withal to serve his party efficiently as a canvasser in several Presidential campaigns, though he persistently declined all political office. Within a year after coming to the bar he was elected Commonwealth's Attorney for all the courts of the city of Winchester and county of Frederick, and continued to hold this position by successive re-election until the breaking out of our late civil war, when at the first sound of conflict he abandoned all else and went with the first troops to Harpers Ferry, and was appointed aide to General Carson, who was then in command there. Returning to Winchester for a short time to arrange his official business, he was tendered the command of a choice company of infantry, of which organization, or its desire, he had no knowledge until they marched in a body to his door. He promptly accepted the proffered command, and assiduously devoted himself to its thorough discipline and drill. It for a time was employed in detached service, during which period Captain Holliday was offered a position upon the staff of General "Stonewall" Jackson, but declined to surrender his company, which was soon assigned to the 33d Virginia Infantry, Colonel A. C. Cummings, "Stonewall" Brigade, and he by successive promotion attained the command of the regiment. As a field officer, Colonel Holliday exhibited fine military perception and judgment, and was conspicuous for his gallantry, participating in all the encounters in which his command was engaged, including the sanguinary battles of Kernstown, McDowells, Winchester, Port Republic, and those around Richmond, without being absent from duty for a single day until August 9, 1862, when at the battle of Cedar Run, or Slaughters Mountain, he lost his right arm. This injury entailed prolonged suffering and unfitted him for service in the field. He was then elected to the Confederate Congress, of which body he continued a member until the close of the war. Returning to his home, he resumed the practice of his profession, taking position in the front rank of a bar long and justly celebrated for its learning and ability. Upon the death of General Robert E. Lee, Colonel Holliday, at the request of the authorities and citizens of Winchester, delivered an address on his life and character, which was a chaste and eloquent utterance replete with noble conceptions. In 1875, by invitation he delivered an address before the Alumni of the University of Virginia on "Higher Education," which from the bold presentment and searching analysis of the subject, the breadth of its range and the beauty and purity of its diction, enlisted the attention and excited the admiration of his audience, and, in published form, widely of scholars and statesmen.

Colonel Holliday was the Commissioner for Virginia at the United

States Centennial Exposition held in Philadelphia, and was appointed elector at large for the State in the Presidential canvass of 1876. From the conclusion of the war until then he had taken but little active part in politics, though ever a close and critical observer of the drift of public affairs, and he had been repeatedly urged to enter public life. The judicious and effective manner in which he conducted that canvass directed attention to his varied gifts and abilities as a statesman and speaker. Though, in harmony with his tastes his preference was for private life, in deference to his duty as a citizen he accepted the nomination for Governor of the State the following year, was elected for the term of four years without opposition, and entered upon the duties of the office January 1, 1878. His public acts during his term were chiefly expressed through his inaugural and annual messages, and vetoes, which, in the discussion of the relations of the State debt, and their cogent arguments for maintenance of the public credit, are regarded as State papers of the highest order. By invitation of the authorities, also during his term of office, he attended the commencements of nearly all the colleges and institutions of learning in the State, and delivered addresses to the students, as he did at different times to conventions of the teachers of the Public Schools, and to National organizations the guests of the city of Richmond or the commonwealth, which were published in the papers of the day. His "Address of Welcome," at Yorktown in 1881, is an able and glowing conception. Governor Holliday has not resumed the practice of his profession since his retirement from office, devoting his time mainly to study and the cultivation of his farm near Winchester. He has spent much of his time in travel in both hemispheres, having visited Mexico, the West Indies, the Sandwich Islands, the western slope of the Pacific and the interior States and Territories in the Western, and Great Britain and Ireland, and a large portion of the north of the continent of Europe in the Eastern—most of it on foot In these tours he keenly enjoyed the study afforded by critical observation of the grandeur and beauty of nature and of art, the material development and the social life of the countries through which he wandered. He was everywhere the recipient of marked attention, private and official. Governor Holliday has been twice married, first in 1868 to Hannah Taylor, daughter of Thomas McCormick of Clarke county, Virginia. She lived but a short time. In 1871 he married secondly, Caroline Calvert, daughter of Dr. Richard H. Stuart, of King George county, who also died within a year. No issue survives by either marriage.

The following are among the published addresses of Gov. Holliday:
"Oration before the Library Company and Citizens of Winchester, Virginia, July 4, 1850."
"Principle and Practice, an Address before the Winchester Library Company, April 14, 1851."

"Oration before the United Fire Department and Citizens of Winchester, July 4, 1851."
"In Memoriam—General Robert E. Lee—Ceremonies at Winchester, January 19, 1871."
"The Higher Education, the Hope of American Republicanism, an Address before the Society of the Alumni of the University of Virginia, June 29, 1876."
"Welcome Address, Yorktown, Virginia, October 19, 1881, by appointment of the Commission of the Congress of the United States for the Centennial Celebration."

In person Governor Holliday is of commanding stature, being fully six feet in height and finely proportioned. Markedly intellectual in feature, genial and prepossessing in manner, his presence inspires confidence and respect. Himself the synonym of honor, jealous of the slightest infraction of that of Virginia, a pure executive and a faithful citizen, his administration reflects enduring lustre upon himself and those whom he represented. Time will yet vindicate the justness of his actions and of his recent affirmation : "As Governor in a prominent light before the people of my own State and before the world, I rejoice in all my efforts then to keep alive in the hearts of Virginia the honor and glory of a famous commonwealth, and, from subsequent events, am only the more confirmed in the correctness of my course. I would not for my life blot one word I then spoke or wrote."

WILLIAM EWAN CAMERON.

The descent of William Ewan Cameron, representative as it has been of valor, genius and worth, may justly excite regard. According to family tradition, he was paternally descended from the Scotish chieftain of the clan Cameron, Sir Ewan Lochiel, who during the civil wars adhered to the Stuarts until their cause was hopeless, and whose prowess is celebrated in song as well as preserved in history. *Rev. John Cameron* was educated at King's College, Aberdeen, and being ordained by the Bishop of Chester in 1770, came to America. His first charge was St. James' Church in Mecklenburg county, Virginia. In 1784 he removed to Petersburg, Virginia. In 1793 he served as rec'or of Bristol parish. He was an excellent scholar, and for a time conducted a classical school. His learning was recognized in the degree of Doctor of Divinity, conferred by William and Mary College. Of the issue of Dr. Cameron, a daughter became the wife of Rev. Andrew Syme, of Petersburg, Virginia; another the wife of Walker Anderson, whose son was Judge Walker Anderson, of Florida. Judge Duncan Cameron, of the Supreme Court of North Carolina, was his son. Another son, *William Cameron*, married Anna, daughter of Daniel Call, an eminent lawyer, Reporter of the Virginia Court of Appeals, and brother-in-law of Chief Justice John Marshall, and of his issue was *Walker Anderson Cameron*, who married in 1841, Elizabeth Harrison Walker, a granddaughter of Benjamin Harrison, of "Berkeley," and a great-granddaughter of William Byrd, of "Westover," James River, Virginia. Of their issue was the subject of this sketch, who was born in Petersburg, Virginia, November 29, 1842. His advantages of education were limited, and he was early thrown upon his own resources by the death of his parents. At the age of sixteen he went to the West in pursuit of fortune. Upon the breaking out of our late civil war in 1861, he was in St. Louis, Missouri. He promptly returned to his native State and enlisted as a private in Company A, 12th Regiment Virginia Volunteers. His soldierly merit speedily secured his promotion successively through the non-commissioned grades to the rank of Lieutenant of his company, and subsequently to the posts of Regimental Adjutant and Brigade Inspector. He served with uniform gallantry throughout the war, was several times severely wounded, and surrendered finally at Appomattox Court House with the rank of Captain. Upon the conclusion of the war he was led by Hon. Anthony M. Keiley, who was then conducting the *Daily News* of Petersburg, to employ his pen in journalism, and first contributed to the *News* a serial of sketches of the war. The *News* soon fell under the ban of Federal authority, and was suppressed, but was renewed by its proprietors as the *Index*, which is still conducted as the *Index and Appeal*. William Ewan Cameron was first employed on the *Index* as local editor, but in a few months was sent to Norfolk, Virginia, to edit the *Norfolk Virginian*, in the publication of which the proprietors of the *Index* were interested. From Norfolk he was recalled to Petersburg to take editorial charge of the *Index*, which he conducted until 1870, when he became the editor of the Richmond *Whig*. In 1868, Captain Cameron fought a duel, growing out of political differences, with Robert W. Hughes (now United States Judge for the Eastern District of Virginia), and was severely wounded. In 1872 he assumed control of the Richmond *Enquirer*, which he conducted until October, 1873. Returning to Petersburg, he for a time served on the editorial staff of the *Index*. In 1876 he was elected the Mayor of Petersburg, and thus served by four successive elections until nominated as Governor of Virginia. In 1877 Captain Cameron resumed editorial control of the *Whig*, and continued that connection with some interruption until December, 1879. In 1881 Captain Cameron was elected Governor of Virginia over the Conservative candidate, Major John Warwick Daniel, and entered upon the duties of the office January 1, 1882, for the term of four years. Governor Cameron exhibited much talent as a journalist. He is a vigorous writer and an effective speaker. He is of medium stature and prepossessing in person. He is married and has issue.*

---

*Sketch of Governor Fitzhugh Lee in volume II., VIRGINIA AND VIRGINIANS.

AMBROSE POWELL HILL,
LIEUTENANT-GENERAL CONFEDERATE STATES ARMY.

The name Hill is of early prominence in the annals of Virginia. The primary ancestor of the subject of this sketch in Virginia it is believed was Edward Hill, who received a grant of 450 acres of land in Charles City county, July 25, 1638.* (Virginia Land Registry, book No. 1, p. 579.) In 1644 he appeared with the rank of Captain as Speaker of the House of Burgesses. In March, 1645, he was sent with Captain Thomas Willoughby as commissioners to Maryland " to demand the return of persons who had left the colony." He served as a member of the House of Burgesses from Charles City county from 1645 to 1654, the last year as Speaker of the body. In 1656, as commandant with the rank of Colonel of the Colonial Rangers and the friendly Indians under Totopotomoi, the Pamunkey Chief, he was disastrously defeated in an encounter with the Richahecrian Indians from mountains at a point in the present eastern limits of Richmond, known as Bloody run, which has its source in a bold spring. The slain were so numerous (Totopotomoi being among them) that the tradition is that the streamlet ran with blood, and hence its designation. Such was the indignation against Hill that he was disfranchised by the Assembly. His son, Edward Hill, Jr., however, became a man of station in the colony, serving as County Lieutenant of Charles City county with the rank of Colonel, and as a member of the council, but he, too, fell under the ban of the General Assembly, and in May, 1676, was " disabled from holding office for participating in the patriotic uprising known as ' Bacon's Rebellion.' " Ambrose Powell Hill, a lineal descendant of Captain Ambrose Powell,† a vestryman of Bromfield parish in 1752, and the son of Major Thomas Hill,‡ was born in Culpeper county November 9, 1825. He entered West Point Academy July 1, 1842, and graduated thence July 1, 1847, the fifteenth in merit in a class of

---

* There were previous grants to John Hill and Nicholas Hill in Elizabeth City county in 1635 and 1637, respectively, and to Richard Hill in James City county, May 4, 1633, and subsequent grants to John Hill and Thomas Hill, the latter receiving 3,600 acres in James City county, the last grant being in James City county December 1, 1643. Col. Edward Hill, the elder, is said to have been of the family of the Marquis of Downshire, and the arms of his tombstone are said to establish the claim. John Carter, the son of Robert ("King") Carter and grandson of John Carter, the founder of the Carter family in Virginia, married in 1723, Elizabeth Hill, a daughter of Colonel Edward Hill, the younger.

† It has been suggested that Captain Ambrose Powell was of the lineage of Captain Nathaniel Powell, some time acting Governor of Virginia, and who was slain in the memorable Indian massacre of March 22, 1622.

‡ A brother of Major Thomas Hill was a prominent politician and represented Culpeper county in the Virginia Assembly for twenty years or more.

thirty-six, among whom were Generals John S. Mason, O. B. Wilcox, H. G. Gibson, A. E. Burnside, John Gibbon, R. B. Ayers, Charles Griffin, Thomas H. Neill, W. W. Barnes, E. L. Viele and L. C. Hunt, of the United States Army, and General Harry Heth, of the Confederate Army. Entering the First Artillery as Brevet Second Lieutenant, Hill became First Lieutenant September 4, 1851. He was engaged during the Mexican war at Huamantla the 9th of October, and at Atlixas the 12th of October, 1847, and in Florida against the Seminole Indians in 1849-50, and from 1852 to 1855. He was an assistant on the coast survey from November, 1855, until March 1, 1861, when he resigned his commission. Upon the breaking out of hostilities between the North and South, he was chosen Colonel of the Thirteenth Virginia Regiment, which, at the first battle of Manassas, with the remainder of the command of General Joseph E. Johnston, arrived on the field just in time to secure and complete the victory of that memorable day. Colonel Hill was promoted February 26, 1862, to the rank of Brigadier-General, and by his signal gallantry at the battle of Williamsburg, in May, drew the eyes of the public upon him. He greatly distinguished himself in the sanguinary seven days battles around Richmond, commencing on the 26th of June, in command of one of the largest divisions of the Army of Richmond, and which was composed of the brigades of Anderson, Branch, Pender, Gregg, Field and Archer. At Meadow Bridge, with only a portion of his command, he made the first attack upon McClellan, and in a terrible conflict encouraged his troops by a fearless intrepidity which constantly exposed him to the fiercest fire of the enemy. Successful at this point, General Hill was placed first in the line of advance and bore the brunt of the action at Fraziers Farm, where, with his own division and one brigade of that of Longstreet, he fought and overcame a largely superior force which broke the spirit of the enemy and achieved final victory.

In this series of battles the division of Hill lost 3870 men killed and wounded. Immediately after this battle General Hill was promoted, July 14, 1862, to the rank of Major-General. In the campaign of Northern Virginia the division of A. P. Hill was sent to reinforce Stonewall Jackson, who had been despatched to check the advance of Pope. At the battle of Cedar Run, Hill gallantly sustained the prestige he had won. He also bore a conspicuous part in subsequent operations, marching with Jackson in his flank movement towards the Rappahannock and Manassas. At the second battle of Manassas he repeated a similar exhibition of valor to that of Fraziers Farm, and with dauntless abandon met and repulsed at the point of the bayonet six distinct and separate assaults of the enemy, a majority of the men a portion of the time being without cartridges. The next day (August 30, 1862), his division was again engaged, and late in the evening drove the enemy before them, capturing two batteries, many prisoners, and resting at night on Bull Run. At Sharpsburg the accomplishment of A. P. Hill was in brilliancy not surpassed by any other recorded during the war. With three brigades, numbering scarce 2,000 men, he drove back Burnside's Corps, 15,000 strong.

After the battle of Sharpsburg, when General Lee determined to withdraw from Maryland, Hill was directed with his division to cover the retreat of the army, and in the performance of this duty at Botlers Ford, on the 20th of September, 1862, was enacted one of the most terrible episodes of the war. Lee's army was well across the Potomac when it was found that some brigades of the enemy had ventured to cross during the preceding night and were making preparations to hold their position. General Jackson at once ordered A. P. Hill to drive the enemy back. After some preliminary movements, a simultaneous charge was made by Hill, and the enemy forced in a confused mass into the river. "Then," writes General Hill, describing the action with graphic horror, "commenced the most terrible slaughter this war has yet witnessed. The broad surface of the Potomac *was blue with the floating corpses of our foe.* But few escaped to tell the tale. By their own account they lost 3,000 men killed and drowned from one brigade alone." In this battle Hill did not use a piece of artillery; but relying upon the musket and bayonet, he punished the enemy beyond precedent. At the battle of Fredericksburg, Hill's Division formed the right of Jackson's force, at Chancellorsville the center, and participated in the flank movement that crushed Hooker. The death of the illustrious Jackson devolved the command upon Hill, and he was soon after wounded. Upon the reorganization of Lee's army he was made, May 24, 1863, a Lieutenant-General, and placed in command of the third of the three corps into which it was divided. His was the first corps in action at Gettysburg. In Lee's flank movement of the same to get between Meade and Washington City, A. P. Hill sustained the only reverse of his career. Having fallen upon a superior force of the enemy at Bristoe Station, concealed by a railroad embankment, in a vain effort to dislodge it he lost several hundred in killed and wounded, and five pieces of artillery. In the momentous campaign of 1864 General Hill was again conspicuous, his corps, with that of Ewell, opening the action in the Wilderness. A few days thereafter his feeble health so gave way that he was unable to remain on duty, when General Jubal A. Early was assigned to the command of his corps. After the scenes of Spotsylvania Court House, General Hill reported for duty, resumed command of his corps, and fought with it to the last day in front of Petersburg. August 25, 1864, at Reames Station, he attacked the enemy in his intrenchments and carried his entire lines, capturing seven stand of colors, 2,000 prisoners and nine pieces of artillery.

At the final attack on the Southside Railroad and the defense of Petersburg, he was restlessly active in his exertions to repel the Federal attack. On the morning of April 2, 1865, desiring to obtain a nearer view of a portion of the line of the enemy, he left his staff behind him in a place of safety, rode forward accompanied by a single orderly, and soon came upon a squad of Federals who had advanced along a ravine far beyond their lines. He immediately ordered them to surrender, which they were on the point of doing, under the supposition that a column of troops was just behind him. But soon discovering that he was so slightly attended, they fired upon him, and he fell, pierced through the heart by a rifle ball. The following night his body was hastily buried in the cemetery at Petersburg, but was subsequently reinterred in Hollywood Cemetery, Richmond, where his remains are marked by the words, "Lt.-Gen. A. P. Hill," cut into the granite curbing in front of the grave. The trust reposed in A. P. Hill by the illustrious chieftains Lee and Jackson found solemnly impressive exemplification in the dying ejaculation of each, which, too, are remarkable for their semblance. "Tell A. P. Hill to prepare for action," were amongst the words of Stonewall Jackson. "Tell Hill he must come up," were the last words of the peerless Lee. What more honorable tribute?

ROBERT EDWARD LEE,
GENERAL-IN-CHIEF OF THE CONFEDERATE STATES ARMY.

"With faith untouched, spotless and clear his fame,
So pure that envy could not wrong the same."

The record of all time with its mighty roll of heroes and patriots presents no more lustrous name than that of the immortal subject of this sketch. His lineage, which has been already traced in this serial, was illustrative of the excellencies which marked his own resplendent career. Robert Edward Lee, the third son of "Light-Horse Harry" and Anne Hill (Carter) Lee, was born at "Stratford," Westmoreland county, Virginia, January 19, 1807. Entering the United States Military Academy July 1, 1825, he was graduated thence second in grade of a class of forty-six, July 1, 1829, and commissioned Brevet Second Lieutenant, Corps of Engineers. Among his classmates were Generals Joseph Eggleston Johnston, Albert G. Blanchard and Theophilus H. Holmes, of the Confederate States Army, and Generals B. W. Brice, T. A. Davies, A. Cady, T. Swords, Seth Eastman, W. Hoffman, Sidney Burbank, O. M. Mitchell, C. P. Buckingham and James Barnes, of the United States Army. Lieutenant Lee served as Assistant Engineer in the construction of Forts Monroe and Calhoun for the defense of Hampton Roads, Virginia, 1829–'34; as Assistant to the Chief Engineer at Washington, D. C.,

GENERAL ROBERT E. LEE,
In Confederate uniform, from life during the war,
never before engraved.

1834–'37; as Assistant Astronomer for establishing the boundary between the States of Ohio and Michigan, 1835; as Superintending Engineer of the improvement of St. Louis harbor, Missouri, and of the Missouri and Upper Mississippi rivers, 1837–'41, having general charge of the improvement of the Lower Mississippi and of the Ohio river below Louisville, Kentucky, 1840–'41. He was promoted to First Lieutenant September 21, 1836, and to Captain of the Corps of Engineers July 7, 1838. Had charge of the construction and repairs of the defenses at the Narrows entrance to the New York harbor, 1841–'44, 1844–'46; was Member of the Board of Visitors to the Military Academy, 1844; Assistant to the Chief Engineer at Washington, D. C., 1844; Member of the Board of Engineers for Atlantic Coast defenses from September 8, 1845, to March 13, 1848; served in the war with Mexico, 1846–'48, being engaged on the march as Chief Engineer of the column commanded by Brigadier-General John E. Wool, and earned the brevets of Major, Lieutenant-Colonel and Colonel for gallant and meritorious conduct in the battles of Cerro Gordo, Contreras, and Churubusco, and at Chapultepec, where he was wounded. His services as an engineer at Vera Cruz and the subsequent operations in Mexico were highly eulogized by General Winfield Scott. Colonel Lee was on special duty in the Engineer Bureau at Washington, D. C., in 1848; Superintending Engineer of the construction of Fort Carroll, Patapsco river, Maryland, 1848–'52; member of the Board of Engineers for Atlantic Coast defenses from July 21, 1848, to April 11, 1853; Superintendent of the United States Military Academy from September 1, 1852, to March 31, 1855; in command at Jefferson Barracks, Missouri, 1855; appointed Lieutenant-Colonel Second Cavalry March 3, 1855; on frontier duty at Camp Cooper, Texas, 1856; with expedition against the Comanche Indians, 1856; at Camp Cooper, Texas, 1856–'57; at San Antonio, Texas (commanding the Second Regiment), 1857; on leave of absence, 1857–'59; in command of the forces at Harpers Ferry for suppressing the John Brown raid, October 17–25, 1859; in command of the Department of Texas from February 6 to December 12, 1860, and on leave of absence, 1860–'61; promoted Colonel of the First Cavalry March 16, 1861. Ordered to Washington from his regiment in Texas, Colonel Lee arrived at the Federal capital April 1, 1861, three days before the inauguration of President Lincoln. The political horizon was even then overcast with the portents of the mighty civil war which was soon to convulse the nation. South Carolina, Mississippi, Florida, Alabama, Georgia and Louisiana had already seceded from the Union, and the Provincial Government of the Confederate States had been formed at Montgomery. The Virginia Convention, loth to assent to the dissolution of the Union, was still in solemn deliberation. But all counsels and peaceful overtures failed, and the proclamation of President Lincoln calling for 75,000 men to subdue the seceded States forced Virginia with her sisters of the South. The ordinance of secession, which she passed on the 17th of April, determined Colonel Lee. To the Hon. F. P. Blair, who brought him the tender of the supreme command of the United States Army, he replied: "I look upon secession as anarchy. If I owned the four millions of slaves in the South, I would sacrifice them all for the Union. But how can I draw my sword against Virginia?" On the 20th he resigned his commission and repaired to Richmond. Governor Letcher immediately appointed him to the Command-in-Chief of the Virginia force, and the convention unanimously confirmed the nomination. Upon the appearance of General Lee before that body, on the 25th of April, its venerable President John Janney glowingly addressed him, thus concluding:

"Sir, we have by this unanimous vote expressed our conviction that you are at this day among the living citizens of Virginia, 'first in war.' We pray to God most fervently, that you may so conduct the operations committed to your charge that it will soon be said of you, that you are first in peace,' and when that time comes you will have earned the still prouder distinction of being 'first in the hearts of your countrymen.'"

General Lee thus replied: "Mr. President and Gentlemen of the Convention: Profoundly impressed with the solemnity of the occasion, for which, I must say, I was not prepared, I accept the position assigned me by your partiality. I would have much preferred your choice had fallen upon an abler man. Trusting in Almighty God, an approving conscience and the aid of my fellow-citizens, I devote myself to the service of my native State, in whose behalf alone will I ever again draw my sword." Transferred from the State service to that of the Confederacy, with the rank of General, his first service was in the mountains of Northwest Virginia, where with inadequate forces he held the invading column of the enemy in check and restored the confidence which had been shaken by reverses in that department. In the fall of 1861 he was transferred to the command of the South Atlantic States. In March, 1862, he was recalled to Virginia and charged "with the conduct of military operations in the armies of the Confederacy." In the battles before Richmond, General Joseph E. Johnston being disabled by a wound on the 31st of May at the battle of Seven Pines, on the 3d of June, 1862, General Lee was assigned to command in person the Army of Northern Virginia, and thenceforward, as has been recorded in preceding pages, to the memorable 9th day of April, 1865, when it finally laid down its arms at Appomattox Court House, he remained at its head. Then, when all was lost save honor, he unmurmuringly took his place as a modest citizen of his scarred and harrowed State, to "abide her fortunes and share her fate." Refusing numerously proffered gratuities and sinecure stations which were pressed upon him by loving admirers, he found his meet field of beneficence in the Presidency of a time-honored seat of learning, Washington College, which had its origin in "The Augusta Academy," the first classical school in the valley of Virginia, founded in 1749 by Robert Alexander, a Scotch-Irish immigrant, and a Master of Arts of Trinity College, Dublin. Under his successor, Rev. John Brown, the Academy was first removed to "Old Providence," and again to "New Providence Church," and just before the Revolution, for the third time, to Mount Pleasant, near Fairfield, in the now county of Rockbridge. In 1776 Rev. William Graham (whose remains rest in the church-yard of the venerable St. John's at Richmond) baptized it as "Liberty Hall Academy." It was now removed, in 1777, to near the old Timber Ridge Church; and finally, in 1785, to Lexington. In 1796 it was endowed by General Washington with one hundred shares of the Old James River Company, which had been donated him by the Virginia Assembly, and the trustees of the academy, in honor of the illustrious benefactor, rechristened it Washington Academy. The Assembly soon after gave the institution, which it had already incorporated, the name of "The College of Washington in Virginia." "The Cincinnati Society," of Virginia, on dissolving in 1813, donated their fund, amounting to nearly $25,000, to the college, and, thus endowed, its career onward for quite seventy years was one of usefulness and honor. The civil war, however, brought grievous disaster. The college was dismantled, its scientific apparatus destroyed, its library sacked, its every apartment pillaged, and with the close of the weary struggle, four professors, a handful of students and the bare buildings, were all that remained.

Accepting the Presidency of the College October 2, 1865, he zealously entered upon its duties, winning the meed of being "the best College President this country has ever produced," and magnifying the college into a university among the first in honor and influence in the nation. In the fulness of his noble mission, General Lee was stricken with a fatal malady, and sank to rest October 12, 1870. General Lee married June 30, 1831, Mary Anne Randolph, born October 1, 1808, died November 5, 1873, daughter of George Washington Parke and Mary Lee (Fitzhugh) Custis,* of "Arlington," Virginia. The issue of this blissful union was three sons and four daughters:

* George Washington Parke Custis, son of John Parke and Eleanor (Calvert) Custis, grandson by her first marriage with Daniel Parke Custis of Martha Dundridge, and the adopted son of General George Washington, whom she married secondly. Daniel Parke Custis was the son of Colonel John and Frances (Parke) Custis. His mother was the eldest of the two daughters of Daniel Parke, Aide to the Duke of Marlborough, Governor of the Leeward Islands, etc. The younger daughter, Lucy, married Colonel William Byrd, of "Westover."

VIRGINIA AND VIRGINIANS. 261

i. *George Washington Custis*, Major-General Confederate States Army, succeeded his father in the Presidency of Washington-Lee University.
ii. *William Henry Fitzhugh*, Major-General Confederate States Army; has been twice married, first to Charlotte, daughter of William Fanning Wickham; secondly, November 28, 1867, to Mary Tabb, daughter of George W. Bolling, of Petersburg, Virginia. Issue by both marriages.
iii. *Robert Edward*, Captain Confederate States Army; married Charlotte (died September 22, 1872), daughter of R. Barton Haxall.
iv. *Mary*, v. *Anna* (died 1870), vi. *Mildred*, and vii. *Eleanor Agnes*—died October 15, 1873.

The remains of General and Mrs. Lee, and of their youngest daughter, rest in a mausoleum annex to the Memorial Chapel erected in the College grounds by the Lee Memorial Association. In a chamber directly over the crypt is the sarcophagus and famed recumbent statue of the great chieftain, executed by the sculptor Valentine.

HERE LEE RESTS.

"He loved not war, but could not well renounce
    That fealty to his native land first due —
O, countrymen, there was a soldier once
    From instinct brave, but brave from duty, too!
A great self-mastered spirit, who outvied
The empty pageants which his age supplied!
* * * * * * *
Lie still in glory, hero of our hearts,
    Sleep sweetly in thy vaulted chapel grave!
The splendor of the far excelling star departs—
    Not so the lustre of the god-like brave!
Thy glory shall not vanish, but increase,
Thou boldest son of war and mildest child of peace!

Lie still in glory! patient, prudent, deep!
    O, central form in our immortal strife,
With an eternal weight of glory, sleep
    Within her breast, who gave thee name and life!
Lie very still! no more contend with odds!
Transcendent among men—resplendent with the gods!"

THOMAS JONATHAN JACKSON,
LIEUTENANT-GENERAL CONFEDERATE STATES ARMY.

"A frame of adamant, a soul of fire."

Thomas Jonathan (known during the recent great civil war by the *sobriquet* of "Stonewall") Jackson was born January 21, 1824, in Clarksburg, Harrison county, Virginia. His great-grandfather, a native of England, was an early settler of the western wilds of Virginia, and Edward Jackson, his grandfather, was surveyor of Lewis county, and for some years represented it in the State Assembly. The son of the last, Jonathan Jackson, removed to Clarksburg, where he studied and commenced the practice of law with his cousin, John G. Jackson, and acquired considerable reputation. He married Julia, daughter of Thomas Neal, of Wood county, and these were the parents of the subject of the present sketch. Jonathan became pecuniarily embarrassed, and dying in 1827, left his family penniless. His children were four in number—two sons and two daughters—Thomas, the youngest, being only three years old. The widow remarried in 1830, but died the following year of a pulmonary affection. Thomas was thus doubly orphaned at the early age of seven. After living for a time with some of his relatives in the vicinity of his birth, becoming dissatisfied, he determined to seek the residence of an uncle, Cummins Jackson, the half-brother of his father, distant eighteen miles, which he journeyed alone and afoot. He was kindly received by his uncle and two maiden aunts who lived with him. His elder brother Warren was also an inmate of the family. Cummins Jackson was a man of vigorous mind, resolute and of vehement passions. He was a farmer, lumber-getter and miller, and slave owner. He gave his orphaned nephews the advantages of schooling whilst with him, but the eldest, Warren, who was of a restless disposition, persuaded Thomas to accompany him to the home of a relative on Blennerhasset Island. The two lads proceeded down the Ohio river to its mouth and finally located on a lonely island of the Mississippi near the southwestern corner of Kentucky. Here they spent the summer alone in a cabin, earning their living by cutting fire-wood for the river steamers. Our future hero, thus early, at the age of nine years, learned the life lesson of self-reliance. But the malaria of their field of action overcame the adventurous lads, and becoming enfeebled with the ague, they had fain to return home by the charity of a steamboat captain. Thomas again made his residence with his uncle Cummins Jackson, and by his kindness received a plain English education. In arithmetic he surpassed his schoolmates, but in other branches he made his way slowly, and only by dint of persistent application. When not at school he assisted his uncle in the several occupations of the last, a frequent task being the transportation, with an oxen team, of logs from the forest to the saw-mill. While thus early and arduously engaged, his constitution gave signs of weakness, and a year or two later he suffered a slight attack of paralysis, the effects of which gradually wore away, but he was troubled through life with weak digestive organs.

At the age of sixteen he was elected constable of the extensive county of Lewis. The duties of this office gave him opportunity for the study of men and cultivated his will power and self-possession.

He became a daring and skillful rider (though he continued through life an exceedingly ungraceful one) and became very fond of horse racing, a sport to which his uncle was addicted. Thomas was his favorite jockey, and it was proverbial among the people of the section that if a horse had any winning qualities in him Tom Jackson was the rider to bring them out. Thomas, indeed, is traditionally transmitted as being at this period an ardent frequenter of races, house-raisings, and country dances. Nevertheless, he was truthful, laborious, modest and self-reliant, scorning everything base. Moreover he was ambitious of preferment and insatiably thirsted for knowledge. In 1842, hearing of a vacancy in the United States Military Academy at West Point, Thomas Jackson, with his accustomed decision and energy, made application for the appointment, and being cordially supported by his friends, waited upon the Secretary of War, dressed in a suit of homespun, his remaining wardrobe being contained in a pair of saddle-bags. The Secretary of War, Hon. John C. Spencer, was so much pleased with Jackson's resolute bearing that although hardly prepared to enter the Academy a warrant for his appointment was ordered to be immediately made out. Young Jackson's zeal and purpose found striking exhibition on this occasion. Being pressed by a friend to remain in Washington for a few days to see the objects of chief interest in that city, he declined, urging that as the studies of the Military Academy were in progress, it was best that he should repair there forthwith. He accordingly contented himself with a hasty panoramic view of the city from the top of the dome of the capitol. He entered the Military Academy July 1, 1842. In his studies Cadet Jackson made steady progress. In drawing he never became an adept; his greatest success being in natural philosophy and ethics. He was graduated with the usual rank of brevet Second Lieutenant, July 1, 1846, the seventeenth in grade in a class of fifty-nine members. Among his classmates were Generals George B. McClellan, John G. Foster, Jesse L. Reno, D. N. Couch, Truman Seymour, M. D L. Simpson, S. D. Sturgis, George Stoneman, Innis N. Palmer, Alfred Gibbs, George H. Gordon, Frederick Myers, Joseph N. G. Whistler, and Nelson H. Davis of the United States Army, and Generals John A. Brown, John Adams, Dabney H. Maury, D. R. Jones, Cadmus M. Wilcox, Samuel B. Maxey and George E. Pickett of the Confederate States Army, besides others distinguished in civil life and the walks of literature. The war with Mexico being then in progress, Lieutenant Jackson had an opportunity for immediate service, and was ordered to report himself to the First Regiment of the Artillery, then at New Orleans. Proceeding thither, he soon moved with the troops for Mexico, serving under General Zachary Taylor, until General Winfield Scott took the field, when he was transferred to the command of the latter. His military career was distinguished and his promotion rapid. He was engaged in the siege of Vera Cruz, March 9–29, 1847; the battle of Cerro Gordo, April 17–18; skirmish of La Hoya, June 20; skirmish of Oka Laka, August 16, 1847. Shortly after the battle of Cerro Gordo, Jackson was assigned to the light field battery of Captain John B. Magruder. He participated in the battle of Contreras, August 19–20, 1847 and was promoted to the rank of First Lieutenant, and brevetted Captain August 20 for " gallant and meritorious conduct in the battles of Contreras and Churubusco." In the last named engagement Magruder's First Lieutenant, Johnstone, was killed and Jackson thus became second in command, and took charge of a section of the battery. He was engaged in the battle of Molino del Rey, September 7; the storming of Chapultepec, September 13, 1847, where for his conspicuous gallantry he was brevetted Major, a promotion, it is said, then unprecedently rapid. In the battle of Chapultepec Jackson with his section found himself placed unexpectedly in the presence of a strong Mexican battery, at so short a range that in a few moments a majority of his horses were killed and his pieces nearly unmanned by the terrific storm of grape-shot to which they were subjected, whilst seventy men out of two regiments of infantry with difficulty maintained their position in his rear. General Worth perceiving the desperate position of Jackson's guns, sent him word to retire. He replied that it was more dangerous to withdraw his pieces than to hold his position. Magruder, who moved rapidly to the support, having his horse killed under him as he did so, found that Jackson had lifted by hand a single gun across a deep ditch to a position from which it could be effective, and this gun he was rapidly loading and firing with the assistance of a Sergeant alone, the remainder of his command being either killed, wounded or crouching in the ditch. Another gun was now quickly put in position, and in a few moments the Mexicans were driven from their battery, which was turned upon the flying enemy. Years afterwards, whilst a quiet professor, with the *sobriquet* of " Old Jack," accorded because of his grave and serious demeanor — when asked by his pupils why he did not run when his command was so disabled, he placidly replied : " I was not ordered to do so," and to the query if he was not alarmed when he saw so many of his men falling around him, answered, "No; " that his only fear was lest the danger would not be great enough for him to distinguish himself as he desired. Major Jackson participated in the closing scene of the war, the assault and capture of the City of Mexico, September 13–14, 1847. He served in garrison at Fort Columbus, New York, in 1848, in Fort Hamilton, New York, 1849–51, and in the Florida hostilities against the Seminole Indians in 1851. The arduous service he had undergone impaired his naturally delicate constitution, and in consequence he resigned his commission in the

"STONEWALL" JACKSON.
From a portrait said by his widow to be the best likeness of him in existence.

army February 29, 1852, and returning to Virginia, was elected Professor of Natural and Experimental Philosophy and Instructor of Artillery Tactics in the Virginia Military Institute at Lexington, which position he usefully filled until the breaking out of our late unhappy civil war. Immediately after the secession of Virginia, April 17, 1861, the Corps of Cadets was ordered to Richmond by Governor Letcher. They were marched thither under the command of Major Jackson, and stationed for some time at the State Agricultural Fair Grounds (converted into a camp of instruction, and called "Camp Lee"), as drill masters to the troops arriving there. Jackson was now commissioned by Governor Letcher, Colonel, and on the 3d of May, 1861, took command of the small "Army of Observation" stationed near Harpers Ferry. The prescribed limits of this sketch prevent a detailed account of the glorious career of Colonel Jackson, and a brief recapitulation must suffice here. Promoted to the rank of Brigadier-General June 17, he encountered the advance of the Federals under General Patterson at Falling Waters July 2, checked him and brought off without loss forty-five prisoners. He bore a distinguished part in the battle of Bull Run August 21, where in the language of the gallant and lamented General Barnard E. Bee he "stood like a stone-wall." October 7th following he was promoted to the rank of Major-General and assigned to the command of the forces in and around Winchester. In January, 1862, he conducted an expedition against Bath and Romney, which in the suffering and exposure to cold which it entailed surpassed the privations of Valley Forge of the Revolution. It resulted in the capture of a large quantity of supplies. March 23, 1862, the battle at Kernstown, with the Federals under Shields, was fought, which was so far successful as to recall to Winchester large bodies of Federal troops which had been sent from thence.

Early in May, 1862, Jackson again assumed the offensive, and by a rapid march cut off a detached body at Front Royal and compelled the Federals under Banks to retreat hastily to the Potomac. From the quantity of stores massed at Winchester by Banks and captured by General Jackson, the former has been derisively termed "Jackson's Commissary General." Fremont and McDowell attempted to cut Jackson off, but he succeeded in eluding them by a display of energy, decision, and fertility of resource, which gained for him the distinction of one of the great commanders in the world's history. Hastening his forces to Richmond, his timely arrival at Gaines Mill gave the victory to the Confederate arms; on the 29th he engaged McClellan's rear guard at Fraziers Farm; and July 1st was engaged at Malvern Hill. He next moved his corps against General Pope, and on the 9th of August fought the sanguinary battle of Cedar Run with the force of General Banks. General Lee having joined Jackson, the latter was dispatched, August 24th, to gain the rear of General

Pope, which he did, capturing at Manassas prisoners, cannon and stores. Lee came to his support, and on the 30th was fought the second battle of Manassas. Jackson took part in the invasion of Maryland. September 15th, captured Harpers Ferry with 11,000 prisoners, and rejoined Lee at Antietam in time to do the severest fighting at that battle. October 11, 1862, Jackson was promoted to the rank of Lieutenant-General, and December 13th following witnessed the important battle of Fredericksburg. By Jackson's flank movement at Chancellorsville, May 2, 1863, the Eleventh Corps of Hooker's army was routed and compelled to fall back, but in the darkness as he returned with his staff to the rear he was fired upon by his own men and received wounds from which he died on Sunday, May 10, 1863. He died as became a Christian and a soldier. Shortly before he expired, on being told of his hastening dissolution, he responded feebly but firmly: "Very good; it is all right." A few moments before he died he cried out in his delirium: "Order A. P. Hill to prepare for action! pass the infantry to the front rapidly! tell Major Hawks—" then stopped, leaving the sentence unfinished. Presently a smile of ineffable sweetness spread itself over his pale face, and he said quietly and with an expression as if of relief: "Let us cross over the river and rest under the shade of the trees;" and then, without pain or the least struggle, his spirit passed from earth to the God who gave it.

The remains of "Stonewall" Jackson lie in an unpretentious grave at Lexington, Virginia. It may be of interest to note that the favorite war steed of General Jackson, "Old Sorrel," lived many years and was affectionately cared for, an honored pensioner of the Virginia Military Institute. General Jackson was twice married, first to a daughter of Rev. George Junkin, D. D., and secondly to a daughter of Rev. Dr. Morrison, of North Carolina. A sister of Mrs. Jackson is the wife of General Daniel H. Hill, late Confederate States Army. Only one child of General Jackson, by his second marriage, survives — Miss Julia Jackson — who, with her mother, has been the object of the most respectful attentions throughout this country. The graciousness of their reception during a visit to Massachusetts is noteworthy, as a generous expression of the people of that State, and it is held in connection therewith as a somewhat curious exemplification that the most marked attentions were at the hands of the then Chief Magistrate of the State, General Benjamin Franklin Butler.

A bronze statue of General Jackson, executed by J. H. Foley, R. A., and presented to the State of Virginia by English admirers of the great soldier, stands in the Capitol grounds at Richmond, Virginia. It is shown in Vol. II. from a special photograph taken for this work. It was unveiled with appropriate ceremonies, October 26, 1875, Gov. Kemper and Rev. M. D. Hoge, D. D., delivering addresses.

MATTHEW FONTAINE MAURY—PHILOSOPHER OF THE SEAS.

In the lineage of Matthew Fontaine Maury there was commingled a double strain of the conscientious Huguenot blood with meritorious Virginia springs. He was seventh in descent from John de la Fontaine, born about 1500 in the province of Maine, near the borders of Normandy; commissioned in the household of Francis I., of France; served continuously during the reigns of Henry II., Francis II., and until the second year of Charles IX., when he resigned; martyred as a Protestant in 1563. His grandson, Rev. James Fontaine, pastor of the United Churches of Vaux and Royan; born in 1658; married A. E. Boursiquot; fled to Great Britain from religious persecution. His daughter, Mary Anne, born in Taunton, England, 1690, married in Dublin, Ireland, in 1716, Matthew Maury, a Huguenot refugee (died in 1752), and they emigrated to Virginia in 1718. Their son, Rev. James Maury, born 1717, died 1767, a learned and beloved minister of the Protestant Episcopal Church, married Elizabeth Walker, of estimable Virginia lineage. Their son, Richard Maury, married Diana Minor, of worthy descent. They had issue nine children, of whom the seventh, and the third son, was the subject of this sketch, Matthew Fontaine, born 16th of January, 1806, in Spotsylvania County, Virginia. His father removed to Tennessee in young Matthew's fourth year, and established himself near Nashville. In his sixteenth year young Maury entered Harpeth Academy. In 1825 he was appointed Midshipman in the United States Navy, making his first cruise in the frigate Brandywine, on the coast of Europe and in the Mediterranean. The voyage across the Atlantic was rendered memorable by tempestuous weather and the presence of General Lafayette, a return passenger to France. In 1826 Maury was transferred to the sloop of war Vincennes, for a cruise around the world. Having passed with credit the usual examination, he was appointed, in 1831, Master of the sloop of war Falmouth, then fitting out for the Pacific, but was soon transferred to the schooner Dolphin, serving as acting First Lieutenant, until again transferred to the frigate Potomac, in which he returned to the United States in 1834. He then published his first work, *Maury's Navigation*, which was adopted as a text-book in the navy. He was now selected as astronomer, and offered the appointment of hydrographer to the exploring expedition to the South Seas, under the command of Lieutenant Wilkes, but declined these positions. In 1837 he was promoted to the grade of Lieutenant, and not long afterwards met with the painful accident by which he was lamed for life. For several years, unable to perform the active duties of his profession, he devoted his time to mental culture, to the improvement of the navy, and to other matters of national concern. His views, forcibly stated, were published first and mainly in the *Southern Literary Messenger*, over the *nom de plume* of Harry Bluff, and under the general caption of "*Scraps from the Lucky Bag.*" To the influence of these essays has been justly ascribed the great reforms then made in the navy, as well as the establishment of a naval academy. He also advocated the establishment of a navy yard at Memphis, Tennessee; which was done by act of Congress. Under his directions were made, at that point, by Lieutenant Marr, the first series of observations upon the flow of the Mississippi. He proposed a system of observations which would enable the observers to give information, by telegraph, as to the state of the river and its tributaries. He advocated the enlargement of the Illinois and Michigan Canal, that vessels of war might pass between the gulf and the lakes. He suggested to Congress efficacious plans for the disposition of the drowned government lands along the Mississippi. In the interest of commerce, he brought forward and successfully advocated the "warehousing system."

In 1842 he was appointed Superintendent of the Depot of Charts and Instruments, at Washington. Up to this time the field in which Maury labored was limited to his own country. Placed in a position which afforded the means necessary to the full employment of his powers, he speedily developed the plans which he had previously cherished and so earnestly advocated. The simple Depot for Charts and Instruments was transformed into an Observatory. Surrounded by such men as Fergusson, Walker, Hubbard, Coffin, Keith, and other faithful workers, whom he inspired with his own enthusiasm, he made the Naval Observatory national in its importance and relations to the astronomical world. This accomplished, he added to those labors of the astronomer, fruitful of results for future years, the task of unraveling the winds and currents of the ocean, and collected from the log-books of ships of war long stored in the government offices, and from all other accessible sources, the material suited to his purpose. By numerous assistants, it was tabulated, and by him discussed, thus yielding for the guidance of the mariner on a single route, the combined experience of thousands. Yet Maury's first chart to navigators, with his new route, which he was wont to afterwards delightedly call his "*Fair Way to Rio*," was as first doubted and declined as being opposite to all previous tending, but its accuracy being triumphantly demonstrated by Captain Jackson, commanding the W. H. D. C. Wright, of Baltimore, the maratime world hastened to acknowledge the beneficence conferred, and to contribute aid to the speedy and complete application of Maury's system to all seas.

Maury also instituted the system of deep-sea sounding, rendering easy of accomplishment all operations of that character since undertaken, and leading directly to the establishment of telegraphic communication between the continents by cable, on the bed of the ocean. In these labors he was effectively assisted by Colonel John M. Brooke (now a professor in the Virginia Military Institute), then on duty in the Naval Observatory, and whose deep-sea sounding apparatus first brought up specimens, whilst it fathomed the depths of the ocean.

But to these immediately practical and beneficial results there was something to be added. The investigations, of which they were the first fruits, presented materials for a work to make clear to landsmen as well as mariners, the wonderful mechanism of the sea, with its currents and its atmosphere, "*The Physical Geography of the Sea,*" which, translated into various languages, is an enduring monument to the genius and usefulness of its author. By Humboldt, Maury was declared to be the founder of a new and important science. The principal powers of Europe recognized the value of his services to mankind. France, Austria, Russia, Prussia, Denmark, Belgium, Portugal, Sweden, Sardinia, Holland, Bremen, and the Papal States, bestowed orders of knighthood and other honors. The Academies of Science of Paris, Berlin, Brussels, St. Petersburg and Mexico conferred the honor of membership.

When Virginia, seceding from the Union, called upon her sons, he promptly resigned from the Federal Navy to take part in the defense of his native State, declining, from a sense of duty, highly honorable positions, which he was invited to fill in Russia and France severally. He was selected as one of the Council of Three appointed by the Governor of Virginia in the important crisis, and so served until its army and navy were incorporated with those of the Confederacy, when he was sent abroad by the Southern Government, invested with suitable powers of provision for its material naval wants. This trust he duly filled until the close of the war.

Then, in anticipation of a large emigration from the Southern States to Mexico, with the view of aiding his countrymen there, he went thither. He was cordially received by the Emperor Maximilian, who appointed him to a place in his Cabinet. Thence he was sent on a special mission to Europe. The revolution terminating his relations with Mexico, he was left in straitened circumstances, when he resumed, as a means of support, his scientific and literary labors. He made experimental researches in new application of electricity, in which he was eminently successful, and prepared his Manual of Geography, subsequently published in America. During this period the University of Cambridge conferred on him the degree of LL.D.; and the Emperor of the French invited him to the superintendency of the Imperial Observatory at Paris. He patriotically preferred to accept the chair of Physics in the *Virginia Military Institute*. Whilst serving here, he prepared his latest work, the *Physical Survey of Virginia*.

Stricken with a gastric complaint in October, 1872, he died at Lexington, Virginia, February 1, 1873. His remains rest beneath a monument of native James river granite in Hollywood Cemetery, near Richmond. Commodore Maury married in early life, Anne, daughter of Dabney and Elizabeth Herndon, of Fredericksburg, Virginia (the sister of a devotedly heroic brotherhood). Their issue was five daughters and three sons.

HISTORY OF VIRGINIA.

INTRODUCTORY.

In the study of the history of a commonwealth, be it empire, state or kingdom, it is necessary that we understand something of the causes which have acted in producing and advancing, or destroying and retarding, the various institutions—civil and otherwise—of that particular commonwealth. Then, in order that the history of Virginia be properly understood, it is essential that we examine the causes which led to its settlement and organization as a State.

In the year 1492 Christopher Columbus lifted the veil which hung over the stormy waters of the Atlantic, and exposed the American continent to the view of Western Europe. This was the first practical discovery of America. That the continent was seen by white men as early as the tenth century, there can no longer remain a doubt. The examination of Icelandic records and documents preserved in the archives of the Antiquarian Society of Copenhagen, by recent historians, put at rest the long-doubted claim that the Northmen were the first discoverers of America. Even so great an authority as Humboldt says, after having examined the records, "*The discovery of the northern part of America by the Northmen can not be disputed.*"

A Norse navigator, in the year 986 A. D., while sailing in the Greenland sea, was caught in a storm and carried westward to the coast of Labrador. Several times the shore was sighted, but no landing attempted. The shore was so different from the well-known coast of Greenland that it was certain that an unknown land was in sight. Upon reaching Greenland Herjulfson, the commander, and his companions told strange stories of the new land seen in the west.

In the year 1001 the actual discovery of the continent was made by Lief Ericson, who sailed west from Greenland, and landed on the coast of America in $41\frac{1}{4}°$ north latitude. It was the spring of the year, and from the luxuriant vegetation that everywhere adorned the coast the Northmen named it Vineland (the land of vines). These adventurers of the deep continued to visit these shores during the eleventh, twelfth and thirteenth centuries; it was as late as A. D. 1347, that the last voyage of the Northmen to America was made. Says Ridpath: "An event is to be weighed by its consequences. From the discovery of the western world by the Norsemen nothing whatever resulted. The Icelanders themselves forgot the place and the very name of Vineland." Europe never heard of such a land or such a discovery. The curtain was again stretched from sky to sea, and the New World lay hidden in its shadows.

He that was to announce to Europe the existence of the American continent was to come from the classic land of Italy, and the sunny land of Spain,—the country under whose patronage the discovery was to be made. Christopher Columbus was the name of him whose discoveries, considered in all their bearings upon human history, are the grandest recorded in the annals of the world. A name around which, as time rolls away, will gather the wreaths of imperishable fame.

No sooner had the existence of a trans-Atlantic continent been made known than all nations from Scandinavia to the Strait of Gibraltar became frenzied with excitement. A new world, as it were, was to be added to the old. Monarchs, discoverers and adventurers at once rushed forward in quest of the "Eldorado" to be found somewhere beyond the western seas.

Spain at once prepared for the conquest of her newly acquired possessions, and with a series of splendid triumphs in the south, the civilization of the Incas and Montezumas perished from the earth. France was not slow to profit by the discoveries of Columbus. Far away, hundreds of miles toward the Arctic Circle, she took possession of the country lying along the St. Lawrence and around Lake Champlain, and hastened to plant colonies in the same. Between the Spanish possessions on the south and those of France on the north, lay a territory extending from the thirty-fourth to sixty-eighth parallels of north latitude, and from the Atlantic on the east to the Pacific on the west. England laid claim to all this region, and based that claim upon the discoveries of John and Sebastian Cabot, who were the first to explore the eastern coast of America, they having sailed from Salvador to the Capes of Virginia as early as the year 1498. Nearly an hundred years had passed away, and no permanent settlement had been made in all this vast domain. From the everglades of Florida to the pine-clad hills of Nova Scotia, no white man had ever landed on these shores. It was in the year 1583 that a young nobleman, whose life and tragic death were to become familiar to every student of English history, first appeared at the English court—it was none other than Sir Walter Raleigh, an English gallant, who had taken part in the French Protestant wars, and who now appeared at the British court to make application for assistance in fitting out an expedition for the purpose of planting a colony in North America. He hoped thus to prevent the Spanish monarchy and the equally intolerant French court from gaining possession of the entire continent to the exclusion of England and her interests. Queen Elizabeth was then upon the British throne. Raleigh

POCAHONTAS,
From the DePass picture in Capt. John
Smith's "General Historie."

was young, rich, handsome and fascinating in his address. He soon became a great favorite of the maiden queen, and she gave him a commission making him lord of all the continent of North America lying between Florida and Canada.

The whole of that part of the continent claimed by Great Britain without any well defined boundaries, was called Virginia, in honor of the virgin queen. Two ships were sent out to make discoveries. They were commanded by experienced officers, and sailed from London in April, 1584, and in July reached the coast of North Carolina, on which a landing was effected. Here they remained until September, when they returned to England, and gave such a glowing description of the country which they had visited, that seven ships were immediately fitted out, conveying one hundred and eighty men, who sailed as colonists to the New World. As the ships neared the Carolina coast, they came within sight of the beautiful island of Roanoke. Charmed with the climate, with the friendliness of the natives, and with the majestic growth of the forest trees, far surpassing anything they had seen in the Old World, they decided to locate on this island. Most of the colonists were men unaccustomed to work, and who expected that in some unknown way, in the New World, wealth would flow in upon them like a flood. Not realizing their fond hope, they became disheartened, and when the supply ships arrived bringing abundant supplies, they crowded on board and returned to England. Fifteen, however, consented to remain and await the arrival of fresh colonists from the mother country.

In the year 1587 Raleigh sent out another fleet, carrying a number of families destined to augment the Roanoke colony, but when they arrived, no trace of the fifteen men who remained on the island could be found, they having been murdered by the Indians, and it was only by the promise of the commander to hasten back to England and return with reinforcements that they could be prevailed upon to remain upon the island. Shortly after the fleet sailed on the homeward voyage an event occurred which is worthy of note in a history of this country. This was no less than the birth of the first white child in North America. The child was the daughter of Ananias and Eleanor Dare. She was christened "Virginia," in honor of their adopted country. She was born August 18th, 1587. Her fate is involved in the mystery which enshrouds the fate of the entire colony. Scarcely had the ships returned to Europe when a war broke out between England and Spain, and the "Island Empire" brought every available force to bear upon her powerful rival, both on land and sea. The invincible Armada had to be overcome and the safety of England secured, before Raleigh could send aid to his colony on Roanoke. It was 1590 when the vessels were dispatched, and when they arrived at the island the commander was alarmed to find that the colony had forever disappeared. What their fate was must ever remain a profound mystery.

That they all fell victims to savage ferocity is most probable. Some writers have indulged the idea that they were merged into the tribe of Tuscarora Indians; but while humanity may dictate such a hope, "credulity must entertain a doubt of the hypothesis." This was the last attempt of the noble Raleigh to colonize America. Thus he saw the cherished hope of his life a signal failure. Soon after, an ignominious death upon the scaffold put an end to all his ambitions.

THE ABORIGINES OF AMERICA.

With the discovery of America were discovered the Indians inhabiting the continent—nations having an unwritten history. Who the first inhabitants were we do not know; for all the ages through which the New World passed, prior to its discovery by Columbus, are destitute of history and chronology. But that a race, far superior to the Indians, once existed on this continent, there can not be the least doubt. From the Atlantic on the east to the Pacific on the west, from the Great Lakes to the Gulf, in every portion of the continent, we trace them by their vast monumental ruins, rivaling in magnitude those of the eastern continent. Here they built cities which may have flourished while the Pyramids were being built, or they may have been in ruins when Cleopatra's needle was being fashioned. But who were they? What their origin and what their fate? Alas! we shall never know. Contemporary history furnishes no aid, for they were isolated from all the world beside. They have disappeared from the earth with not a vestige of history left behind them.

> "*Antiquity* appears to have begun,
> Long after their primeval race was run."   *Campbell.*

Whether they were the ancestors of the Indians is a question; it is not probable that they were. Perhaps no problem has ever attracted so much attention from historians and scientists as that of the origin of the American Indians.

Hundreds of thousands of individuals existing in all the various stages of society, from the lowest stage of barbarism to that of the half-civilized state, were found roaming over the vast domain of both the Americas. They were altogether ignorant of the country from which their ancestors had come, and of the period at which they had been transplanted to the New World; and although there were traditions among them seeming to cast some light upon those subjects, yet when thoroughly investigated they tended rather to bewilder than to lead to any satisfactory conclusions; and the origin of these nations has ever been a subject of curious speculation among the learned. Conjecture has succeeded conjecture, hypothesis has yielded to hypothesis, as wave recedes before wave; still it remains involved in a labyrinth of inexplicable difficulties, from which the most ingenious minds will perhaps never be able to free it. Of the many theories which have been advanced, we select the following:

Gregoria Gracia, one of the first missionaries in Mexico, after long association with them, has formed the opinion that they are the descendants of many nations, and therefore thinks it absurd to attempt to trace their origin to any one nation.

John De Laet, a celebrated Flemish writer, maintains that America received its first inhabitants from Scythia. "The resemblance" of the North American Indians, in features, complexion, customs, and mode of life is more nearly like those of the ancient Scythians than any other nation.

Moreaz, in his history of Brazil, says that the continent was certainly peopled by the ancient Carthagenians.

George Huron, like Laet, supposes that the primitive American colonies were Scythian, but is of opinion that the Phœnicians and Carthagenians subsequently reached the continent, and still later that the Chinese and other eastern peoples reached these shores, either voluntarily or have been driven on the coast by tempests. He thus accounts for the difference existing among the numerous tribes.

Charlevoix is clearly of the opinion that they are of Tartar extraction, and Adair says he has been forced to believe that they have descended directly from the Israelites.

Major Carver, who was an officer in the Provincial army, supports the theory that they have descended from the Tartars and Chinese. He is the first writer, with whose writings the author is acquainted, to maintain the theory that they reached America by way of Behrings Straits, a theory since advocated by Mr. Jefferson and many others.

Dr. Robertson, the able philologist, traces their origin to the Tartars, by a similarity of language. He says that many of the names of American chieftains are of Tartar origin, for instance: Tartarax, who formerly reigned in Quiavira, means the Tartar; Manew, the founder of the Peruvian empire, most probably came from the *Manchew* Tartars; *Montezuma*, the title of the Mexican emperors, is of Scythian origin, for according to some authors, it was the appellation of the Scythian chieftains. But the most recent of all is that of Mr. Wallace, who claims that they are the remains of the inhabitants of a great Pacific continent now submerged, and that they escaped to America at the time of the subsidence of their native continent. In opposition to this theory Rev. Wyatt Gill, for many years a missionary to the Hervey Islands, Polynesia, declares that there is not the least resemblance in feature, complexion, mode of life or language existing between the South Sea Islanders and the Indians of North America.

Then, among this maze of theories are we nearer a solution of the vexed problem than we were before a solution had been attempted?

That they came from Europe is altogether improbable; that they are
descended from the Israelites has little or nothing to support it, whilst
it is highly probable that they are descended from some of the tribes of
Southern Asia.

That they are the descendants of the ancient Scythians, seems to the
author to be the most probable. The following facts appear to be almost
conclusive:

First. Both the Scythians and Indians belong to the *Ganowanian*, or
bow-and-arrow family of men. It will be remembered by those who claim
them to be the descendants of the tribes of North-eastern Asia, that those
tribes are spearmen.

Second. The Scythians wandered over a wide extent of country, but
not tilling it, they claimed no property in land; the Indians did the
same, and both held in abhorrence and scorn the confinement of a fixed
habitation.

Third. The entire absence of anything like a fixed system of law, except that the strictest honesty characterized both.

Fourth. The dress of both was similar, being made from the skins of
the animals belonging to the fauna of their respective countries.

Fifth. War was the delight of both, and mercy and humanity were
alien to their warfare.

Sixth. Mounds, or tumuli, which constitute the remains of the earliest
inhabitants of America, are found nowhere in Asia except in ancient
Scythia, beyond the Indus. Herodotus, "the father of history," says
the Scythians threw earth upon the tombs of their deceased relatives
until they resembled a high mound or artificial mountain.

Seventh. The same author informs us that the Scythians were the only
people of antiquity who practiced the barbarous custom of scalping
their enemies, a custom universally practiced by the Indians of North
America.

Eighth. The Scythians were divided into tribes, just as the Indians
were.

Ninth. The similarity that (according to Dr. Robertson) exists between
many words in use by both.

Tenth. The fact that they were thoroughly acquainted with the architecture of Southern and Western Asia is fully attested by the ruined
structures of Mexico and Central America.

From the foregoing it would seem that the evidence is largely in
favor of the claim that the Indians of North America are the descendants of the ancient Scythians. What the labors of archæological societies and the researches of antiquarian societies may develop upon the
subject, remains yet to be seen. It is doubtful, however, whether a
satisfactory solution of the mysterious problem will ever be reached.

Such were the inhabitants of the New World, who for two hundred
years disputed the possession of this country with the Anglo-Saxon, but

who have been driven before the march of civilization to the western confines of the continent, where their final extinction as a race is only a question of time.

SETTLEMENT AT JAMESTOWN.

We have not space, in a work of this character, to notice in detail that interesting portion of history known as the Period of Voyage and Discovery. The world was ready for great events. With the fifteenth century came the revival of learning in Europe ; Copernicus had systematized the universe ; Vasco de Gama had doubled the Cape of Good Hope, and Portuguese navigators were steering their ships over Indian seas. The Turks had entered Europe and made Constantinople the capital of the Mohammedan world ; Amerigo Vespucci's first account of the Western World had been published and eagerly read all over Europe ; Grecian scholars had "crossed the Alps" and laid the foundation for that intellectual development which was to dispel the darkness and gloom that had enshrouded Europe during the long centuries of the Dark Ages. The printing press came just in time to supply the demand which the thirst for knowledge had created, and now the next great event in the world's history was to be the founding of a permanent English settlement in the New World.

One hundred and fifteen years had passed away since the discovery, and it was now the year 1606. In that year James I., who had succeeded his cousin Elizabeth on the English throne, granted to a company of wealthy London merchants a patent for all that part of the American continent lying between the thirty-fifth and fortieth degrees of north latitude. The London Company, as the corporation was styled, had, as the effect of its creation, the founding of a colony on the Atlantic coast of Virginia. An expedition was at once fitted out, and one hundred and five colonists bade adieu to the shores of the Old World to find a home on the shores of the New. On the 26th day of April, 1607, they reached the entrance to Chesapeake Bay, and to the points on either side they gave the names of Charles and Henry, in honor of the sons of King James. Further within the bay, on another point, they bestowed the name of Point Comfort, because of the comfortable anchorage they found there. Captain Christopher Newport, an experienced navigator, steered them up a beautiful river which, in honor of the king, they called James river. The voyage was continued up the river about fifty miles, when they landed, May 13th, began the erection of houses, and Jamestown was founded. A distinguished historian has said, "This is the most important event recorded in profane history." Here was planted the germ from which was to spring the grandest republic the world has seen. Here on the banks of the James had landed the men who were destined to light a lamp of liberty which all the tyranny of after ages could not extinguish.

THE BEGINNING.

Of the one hundred and five colonists who came to Virginia, more than half are classed as "gentlemen," and the remainder as laborers, tradesmen and mechanics. Many of them probably had been unaccustomed to labor, strangers to toil, and improvident. Such were the founders of the first American States. From that beginning came the Virginias of after times.

The London Company had prepared a form of government for the colony before the departure from England. This code of laws was put in a box, sealed and hidden until the arrival in Virginia, when it was to be opened and the government established according to its provisions. By it all power was vested in a body of seven councilors, whose names were as follows: Bartholomew Gosnold, the navigator John Smith, Edward Wingfield, Christopher Newport, John Ratcliffe, John Martin and George Kendall. At their first meeting Edward Wingfield was chosen president; in other words, the first governor of Virginia. This was the beginning of civil government in America.

While most of the colonists engaged in felling the forest, building cabins and erecting a fort for protection against the savages, Captains Newport and Smith decided to explore the country, and accordingly sailed up the James river as far as the falls of that river, when they paid a visit to Powhatan, king of the Indians in these parts. Here, just below the falls, near the present site of the city of Richmond, was the capital of him whose word was absolute law to the savage nations over which no civil code could ever have exerted the least influence. This monarch of the forest received the foreigners with courtesy, and manifested no uneasiness at their intrusion. After a short stay the party returned to Jamestown, and Newport sailed for England. Shortly after his departure the colonists began to realize their true condition. They were three thousand miles from home and friends, upon an unknown shore, surrounded by wild beasts and wilder men, subject to pestilential diseases over which their physicians had no control, and added to this were civil dissensions. These resulted in the displacement of Wingfield in the office of president, and the deposing, imprisonment, and finally the execution of Kendall. Newport was in England, and Ratcliffe, Martin and Smith were the only remaining members of the council. Ratcliffe was chosen president, but being a man of neither courage nor ability, he voluntarily resigned an office which he was incompetent to fill. Smith and Martin alone were left. The latter elected the former president, and for the first time not the least opposition was manifested toward the new administration.

CAPTAIN JOHN SMITH,

Who, by his efficient management of the affairs of the colony, won the title of "The Father of Virginia," was a soldier, a traveler, and a statesman. His life is one filled with adventure and daring exploit. He was born in Lincolnshire, England, in 1579, and was early apprenticed to a merchant; but at the age of fifteen he left his master and went to Holland, served awhile in the Dutch army, then found his way to Austria, where he enlisted under the flag of that country and engaged in a war with the Turks. He was, at length, wounded, taken prisoner, and after his recovery he was carried to Constantinople, where he was sold as a slave and taken to the Crimea, in Russia, and subjected to the severest treatment and his life rendered a burden. From such abject slavery he determined to escape. An opportunity soon presented itself. He was engaged in threshing wheat about three miles from home, where his master visited him once a day. Smith watched his opportunity and dispatched him with a flail; hid his body in the straw, mounted his horse and fled into the woods. After many days' wandering he found his way into Poland, thence he traveled through Germany, France and Spain to Morocco, in Northern Africa, where he remained some time, then set out for England, where he arrived just as the expedition was fitting out to colonize the new continent of America. He immediately attached himself to the expedition and sailed for Virginia, where he afterward displayed those high qualities of statesmanship which secured the permanency of the colony.

At the time that Smith began his administration the colony was on the verge of ruin. Already disease had carried off one-half of the settlers, among whom was Gosnold, a member of the council and one of the best men in it, and had not the early frosts of winter put a stop to the ravages of the pestilence, not one would have survived to tell the fate of the colony. With the disappearance of disease and the better administration of Smith, everything began to show signs of improvement. One of the first acts of the new management was to begin the erection of better buildings; the fortification was strengthened, a store-house devised, and other preparations made for the winter. The great object now was to secure a stock of provisions for the ensuing winter. The Indians had grown a plentiful harvest, but to secure a portion of it was no easy task. Smith, however, determined to undertake it, and in company with five companions he descended the James river as far as Hampton Roads, where he landed, and went boldly among the natives, offering to exchange hatchets and coin for corn; but the savages only laughed at the proposal, and mocked the strangers by offering a piece of bread for Smith's sword and musket. Smith, ever determined to succeed in every undertaking, abandoned the idea of barter and resolved to fight. He ordered his men to fire among the savages, who ran howling into the woods, leav

CAPT. JOHN SMITH,
After the original in his "General Historie," edition of 1629.

ing their wigwams, filled with corn, to the mercy of the English, not a grain of which was touched until the Indians returned. In a short time sixty or seventy painted warriors, at the head of whom marched a priest bearing an idol, appeared and made a furious attack. The English a second time opened fire, made a rush, drove the savages back, and captured their idol. The Indians, when they saw their deity in the possession of the English, sent the priest to humbly beg for its return, but Smith stood firm, with his musket across the prostrate image, and dictated the only terms upon which he would surrender it, viz : that six unarmed Indians should come forth and load his boat with corn. The terms were acceded to, the idol given up, and Smith and his party returned to Jamestown with a boat-load of supplies.

Smith could not remain long inactive. No sooner had he seen the colony in tolerable condition for this, its first winter in the New World, than he, in company with six Englishmen and two Indians, embarked in the pinnace and sailed up the Chickahominy river. The opinion prevailed at Jamestown, and also with the London Company, that by proceeding up this stream it was possible to reach the Pacific Ocean, then called the South Sea. Smith knew the utter absurdity of such an opinion, but humored it for the purpose of gratifying his desire for making explorations. He ascended the river as far as possible in the pinnace, then leaving it, as he thought, in a safe place, he left it in the care of four Englishmen, and with the remainder of the party the journey was continued in a canoe, and when they could proceed no further in it, Smith traveled on foot with only an Indian guide. The men left with the pinnace disobeyed orders, went on shore, and one of them fell into the hands of the Indians, who learned from him the direction in which the captain had gone. Pursuit was made at once, but when they came up with him they found that he was no easy prey. He defended himself so bravely that they dared not approach him until he fell into a swamp, where he was at length forced to surrender. His captors carried him before their chief, who received him with all the pomp and ceremony known at a savage court. A long consultation was held to determine the fate of the distinguished prisoner, and it seemed that the death angel which had hovered around him all along his journey of life was about to claim the victory. The consultation terminated unfavorably; the executioners rushed forward and dragged their prisoner to a large stone upon which it had been decided his head should be crushed. The awful moment was come; the club was raised that was to dash out his brains, and thus end his toils and difficulties, and with them the hope of Virginia. But an advocate appeared as unexpectedly as would have been an angel just descended from heaven, to ask his release. It was none other than Pocahontas, the chieftain's own favorite daughter, who stepped forth and begged that the prisoner might be spared, and when she found her entreaties unavailing, she seized his head and placed it beneath her own to protect it from the fatal blow. Powhatan could not resist the pleadings of his favorite child, and yielded to her wishes. Smith was released and allowed to live. In a few days he concluded a bargain with the old chief by which he was to receive a large tract of country in exchange for two cannon and a grindstone, which he was to send back from Jamestown by the Indians who accompanied him home. When they arrived at Jamestown, Smith, under pretext of instructing the Indians in the use of the cannon, discharged them into the trees, at which the savages were so frightened that they would have nothing to do with them. The grindstone was so heavy that they could not carry it, so they returned with a quantity of trinkets instead.

RETURN OF NEWPORT.

During the winter and spring the little colony had not been forgotten by the company in England. Newport, soon after his arrival in London, was again dispatched to America in company with another vessel commanded by Francis Nelson, both vessels freighted with everything which could be necessary for either the colony or the crew. Newport arrived in safety, but Nelson, when nearing the capes, was caught in a storm and driven so far out to sea, that he was forced to put into the West Indies, where he made the necessary repairs, and then reached his destination. Smith and Newport decided to again visit Powhatan, who received them in the same dignified manner as on the previous occasion; and during the conference the chieftain exhibited so much diplomatic skill that he was on the eve of closing a bargain with Newport which would have been very disadvantageous to the colony; but Smith prevented the transaction by passing some blue beads before the eyes of the monarch; and by placing great value upon them, and impressing him with the fact that they were only worn by the greatest personages, succeeded in exchanging a pound or two of them for about seven hundred bushels of corn. But no sooner had they returned to Jamestown with this new supply to their former stock, than, as is generally the case with ill-gotten gains, a fire broke out and consumed the greater part of it, together with a number of their cabins and some arms and bedding.

But this was not all; Newport, instead of returning to England immediately, remained fourteen weeks at Jamestown, consuming the provisions that he should have left for the defenseless and helpless colony after his departure. His delay was occasioned by the fact that he had brought over with him several refiners of gold who had discovered some glittering earth near Jamestown, which they pronounced gold. All the available force was engaged in loading the ship with this worthless clay. The idea prevailed to such an extent that Smith says there was no talk, no hope, no work, but dig gold, wash gold, refine gold, load gold. The cargo was at last completed, and Newport sailed for London. When the Phœnix, the vessel of Captain Nelson, was to be loaded, Smith, instead of permitting it to be freighted with "fools' gold," fitted her out with a cargo of cedar timber. This was the first valuable shipment made from Virginia to England.

Smith accompanied the Phœnix as far as the capes, taking fourteen men with him and two open boats, which were to be used in carrying out his long cherished design of exploring the Chesapeake. In this work nearly three months were consumed, and three thousand miles of coast and river were explored and accurately mapped. The map of the Chesapeake Bay made by Smith at this time is still preserved, and is a marvel of exactness. It is the original upon which all subsequent descriptions have been based.

VIRGINIA UNDER THE SECOND CHARTER.

It was on the 23d day of May, 1609, that King James revoked the first charter of the London Company, and at the same time granted a new one by which the government was completely changed. The new patent included all the country lying between the mouth of the Cape Fear river on the south and that of the Hudson on the north, the Atlantic on the east and an undefined boundary on the west. The company was permitted to choose its own councilors, and they in turn were to select the governor. Lord Delaware was chosen to this high position for life. The British government now began to dream of a flourishing empire in the west, which should be tributary to the parent one then rapidly rising to the first place among the nations of Europe, and accordingly surrounded Delaware with stately officers whose high-sounding titles would indicate that they were the dignitaries of an opulent kingdom, instead of a half-starved colony on the distant shores of Virginia. Sir Thomas Gates was commissioned lieutenant-general; Sir George Somers, admiral; Christopher Newport, vice-admiral; Sir Thomas Dale, high marshal; Sir Fernando Wainman, master of cavalry, and a long list of others constituted the royal establishment. But the long array of titled nobility was not without its effect upon the future of Virginia. Five hundred emigrants were speedily collected, and in June a fleet of nine vessels sailed for Jamestown. The gentlemen composing the new government sailed in the Sea Vulture, the largest vessel in the fleet. When nearing the capes of Virginia a fearful storm was encountered. One small vessel was lost, and the Sea Vulture was driven far to sea, and finally stranded upon the rocks of the Bahamas, and did not reach Jamestown till April of the next year. The other vessels outrode the storm and reached their destination. When the news of the appearance of so large a fleet in the bay was received, it was thought to be a part of the Spanish navy, the object of which was the conquest of the colony. Everything was put in a state of defense against the supposed enemy. Smith had, in the meantime, by his kindness, won the good will of the Indians, and hundreds of them now responded to his call, and joined in defense against the supposed invasion. Fear was, however, soon changed to rejoicing; the supposed enemy proved to be friends. The emigrants having landed, elected Captain Francis West (the brother of Lord Delaware), temporary president, the council being all dead save Smith; but he obtaining the sympathy of the sailors, refused to surrender the government of the colony. For the sake of health, to avoid dissension between the old and newly arrived colonists, and for trading with the Indians, Smith decided to establish two new settlements, and accordingly selected a company of the best men, placed them under command of Francis West, and sent them to the falls of the James, there to erect cabins and establish a permanent settlement. He then placed another company under Martin and dispatched them to a place called Nansemond, with the same object in view. Martin exhibited his imbecility by making an attack upon the natives in his immediate vicinity, and then by his cowardice and carelessness permitted them to return, attack his position and kill and wound a number of his men. He then sent to Jamestown for reinforcements, and when they arrived, set a limit to his own management by leaving his men to their fate and going to Jamestown, where he remained cowering under Smith's denunciations of his perfidy and cowardice. The president not hearing of his colony at the falls, determined to pay it a visit; and upon his arrival found that West had selected, as the site of the projected town, a location subject to inundation and many other disadvantages. He offered to purchase from Powhatan the site upon which the city of Richmond now stands, but the restless adventurers, dreaming of rich gold fields further up the river, refused the offer, despising alike the president's kindness and authority. But Smith was born to rule. With five of his own men he rushed boldly into the midst of the mutineers, and arrested the ringleaders of the opposition, but a hundred infuriated men gathered around him and compelled him to release the prisoners. He escaped to the supply-ship which lay at the foot of the falls, and being supported by the sailors, he here spent nine days in making every effort to conciliate the turbulent spirits who were in a frenzy of excitement over the "guilded hopes of the South Sea mines," but all in vain. Discouraged and well-nigh exhausted, Smith set out on his return to Jamestown, but no sooner had he departed than the Indians attacked those left behind. Those of the terrified wretches who escaped fled to Smith, whose boat had grounded on an island above Jamestown. Here the disturbers were again arrested. The president returned to the falls, satisfied the demands of the savages, and left all again under the care of West, who listened to the deceitful statements of the prisoners and released them. Thus Smith again saw his authority set at defiance, and for the last time left the falls of the James. His work was nearly completed. On the journey down the river his powder flask exploded while he was sleeping and tore the flesh from his body in a frightful manner. Crazed with pain, he threw himself into the river to cool the burning sensation, and was nearly drowned before his companions could rescue him. Nearly one hundred miles lay between him and the only surgeon, Dr. Russell, in Virginia, and to him he must go before his wounds could be dressed. In this pitiable condition he arrived at Jamestown, where Ratcliffe and Archer were then on trial on a charge of treason, and, fearing his evidence, they hired an assassin to murder him; but when the fiend saw the pitiable condition of his intended victim, his heart failed him and he was unable to fire the fatal shot. The term of Smith having expired, Captain George Percy, a younger brother of the Earl of Northumberland, was elected president, and Smith, in September, 1609, sailed for England, never to return again to the scenes of his toils and sufferings. An eventful life was rapidly drawing to its close. "The Father of Virginia," the benefactor of his country and his race, he who had faithfully discharged every duty imposed upon him, was yet to feel the sting of base ingratitude. Those whose interests he had best served were the first to condemn his actions. Like Columbus, Boone, Robert Harris, and a host of others whose lives were to be known, their labors appreciated, and names honored by succeeding generations, his name has become the most celebrated that appears in the early history of America. Truly has it been said that great men are never known by the generation in which they live.

THE STARVING TIME.

At the time Smith left Jamestown, there were four hundred and ninety-three persons in the colony, all well sheltered and supplied; but the master spirit was gone, and soon anarchy ruled supreme. Such was the inactivity, profligacy, recklessness and insubordination, that by the approach of early winter they were confronted with starvation. In addition, the Indians determined upon the utter extinction of the colony, and hung upon the outskirts of the settlements, burning houses and murdering all who were so unfortunate as to fall into their hands. Then a pestilence broke out, and the fatality was so great that by the return of the spring of 1610, there remained but sixty persons alive in

ROBERT BOLLING,
The husband of Jane Rolfe, the grand-daughter of Pocahontas.

From the original in the possession of the Bolling family.

the colony, and they must have perished had not assistance reached them. But just as the last ray of hope was yielding to despair, Sir Thomas Gates and his crew, who had been wrecked in the West Indies, arrived at Jamestown; but what must have been their feelings, when, instead of finding the colony in a happy and prosperous condition, they met only a few famished wretches begging for bread! Gates supplied their wants from his store-ship and assumed the government.

JAMESTOWN ABANDONED.

The few survivors had, however, resolved to abandon Jamestown at the first opportunity, and thus forever bid adieu to a place which promised nothing but death. In vain did the governor remonstrate. Four pinnaces lay at anchor in the river. It was the intention to sail for Newfoundland, and there the remnant of the Virginia colony should remain among the fishermen until some vessel would carry them to England. Thus, the efforts of the London Company, as had those of Raleigh and Gosnold before, ended in failure. The colonists crowded on board the pinnaces, and on the 8th of June dropped down the river. But Lord Delaware was already within the bay, and ere the disheartened colonists had reached the mouth of the James, his ships hove in sight, bearing new emigrants, plentiful supplies, and a governor who gave a promise of better things. The hitherto discouraged but now rejoicing colonists were taken on board and all returned to the deserted village, where, before nightfall, all was happiness and contentment.

Lord Delaware's administration was characterized by justice and mildness; he endeared himself to the colonists and inspired them with hope, but he did not long remain; in the early autumn his health failed, and he delegated his authority to Percy—the same who had relieved Smith and sailed for England.

Sir Thomas Dale was already under sail to Virginia bearing a governor's commission, and upon his arrival he assumed the government and made martial law the basis of his administration. He was a soldier by profession, and had served with distinction in the Danish wars. Jamestown needed a strong government, and there was, therefore, very little complaint against his military rule. During his administration the population was augmented by the arrival of three hundred emigrants from England.

The last act of Governor Dale marks an era in the history of Virginia. This was nothing less than a division of property. Ever since the founding of the colony, all property had been held in common, after the manner of the primitive eastern nations; the colonists had worked together and the products of the harvest had been deposited in one common store-house, where all was under the control of the council. Governor Dale changed all this, and caused the lands to be laid out into lots of three acres each, one of which was to be given to each of the colonists—to hold forever—upon which he might plant orchards and cultivate grain with the understanding that no one had the right to gather but himself. Thus the right of property in land was, for the first time, recognized in the New World. The colonists saw the advantage of individual labor, and the good results were soon apparent in the general improvement of the colony.

Dale now surrendered the government to Sir Thomas Gates, and by his (Gates') permission selected three hundred men and began a settlement on a narrow neck of land, nearly surrounded by water, which he called Henrico in honor of Prince Henry. Other settlements were made on both sides of the river at considerable distances from the parent town, and the foundation of the first American State was thus securely laid.

VIRGINIA UNDER THE THIRD CHARTER.

It was now the year 1612, and King James, who made "change" the rule of his reign, granted a third charter to the company, under which many important changes were made. By it the privileges and immunities were greatly increased; their jurisdiction was extended over all the territory within a radius of three hundred miles from Jamestown; they were permitted to elect their own officers, to decide all questions of law and right—in fact, to govern the colony on their own responsibility. This was the germ from which sprang democratic government in America.

MARRIAGE OF ROLFE AND POCAHONTAS.

In the year 1613, Captain Samuel Argall, then cruising in the Chesapeake, made a voyage up the Potomac, when he learned of the presence of Pocahontas, whom he succeeded in enticing on his boat and then carried her to Jamestown. The authorities detained her with expectation that her father, Powhatan, would pay a ransom for her, but the old chief became highly enraged and at once prepared for war; but before hostilities began a Mr. John Rolfe, a highly respected young planter, struck by her beauty and fascinated by her manners, wooed and won her affections and the promise of her hand.

Powhatan gave his consent to the union, and sent her uncle and two brothers to witness the ceremony, which was celebrated with great pomp, according to the rites of the English Church. In 1616 she accompanied her husband to England, but was very unhappy. Captain Smith, who was then in London, called to see her, but appeared to be somewhat reserved in his manner. This added to her burden of grief, and she wept like a child. Smith inquired the cause of her grief. "Did I not save thy life in America?" said she. "Didst thou not promise that if I went into thy country thou wouldst be my father, and I shouldst be thy daughter? Thou hast deceived me; behold her now a stranger and an orphan." Pocahontas was warmly received. Lady Delaware introduced her to Queen Anne, and many families of distinction paid every attention to the modest daughter of this western wilderness; but nothing could be done to dispel the gloom which surrounded her, and in a short time she fell a victim to the dread disease, the small-pox, and died just as she was about to re-embark for America.

One son, the issue of this union, became a man of prominence in the affairs of the colony, and to him many of the first families of Virginia, among whom were the Randolphs and the Bollings, trace their ancestry.

Early in the year 1616, Gates and Dale both sailed for England, and left the government in the hands of Sir Thomas Yeardley, whose administration was similar to those of his predecessors—Dale and Gates. The colony increased in numbers, the social condition improved; obedience on the part of the colonists and respect on the part of the savages brought about a feeling of security and confidence hitherto unknown in the history of the colony.

In 1617, Yeardley was succeeded by Captain Argall, who proved himself to be the most tyrannical governor that had yet swayed the scepter over Virginia. He was a sailor by profession, and accustomed to the rigid discipline of the seas, where he had long held despotic sway over the decks of his own vessel. Naturally tyrannical, cruel and covetous, he was entirely unfit to administer the government as it then existed in Virginia, and, as might have been expected, his administration became a synonym for fraud, corruption and violence. When the news of his high-handed oppression reached England, the London Company requested Delaware to return to Virginia and again assume the government. He yielded to their importunities and sailed for Virginia, but died on the way. Argall continued his oppressive sway until 1619, when he was superseded by Sir George Yeardley, who, through the influence of Sir Edwyn Sandys, treasurer of the London Company, was appointed to fill his place.

THE ESTABLISHMENT OF REPRESENTATIVE GOVERNMENT.

With Sir George Yeardley governor, and important changes in the London Company, the colonists expected a period of prosperity, and their expectations were fully realized. Martial law was abolished; the

RUINS OF JAMESTOWN, VIRGINIA,

The first town founded in America, and first capital of Virginia—destroyed by its own inhabitants in 1676, during "Bacon's Rebellion," to prevent Lord Berkeley's taking shelter there—never rebuilt.

governor, in accordance with instructions from the company, divided the plantations along the James river into eleven districts, called boroughs, and issued a proclamation commanding the citizens to ELECT TWO REPRESENTATIVES from each borough to take part in the government: the election was held in the latter part of June, and the first House of Representatives in the New World convened at Jamestown on the 30th of July, 1619.

This body was called the House of Burgesses, and by it were "debated all matters thought expedient for the good of the colony." A number of acts were passed which were pronounced by the company to be "well and judiciously carried," but unfortunately we have no record of them.

In this eventful year, Sir Edwyn Sandys recognized the fact that the stability of the colony could only be secured by the establishment of family ties. Up to this time very few of the colonists had come to Virginia with the intention of finding a permanent home; by far the greater number were adventurers who left England with the determination to sometime return—either after they had accumulated a fortune, or gratified a desire for adventure. The endearments of home and friends are the ties that bind men to a settled habitation, and now, if these could be found on this side of the Atlantic, then would these adventurers relinquish the fond hope of returning to seek them in the mother country, and the permanency of the colony would be assured. To achieve this end was the determination of Sir Edwyn, and during this year he sent over twelve hundred and sixty emigrants, among whom were *ninety* "agreeable young women, poor but respectable and incorrupt," who were designed as wives for the colonists. Shortly after, another consignment was made of "sixty young maids of virtuous education, young, handsome, and well recommended." Such is the compliment paid by the historian to the first mothers of Virginia. It has been said that they were *sold* to the planters at prices ranging from one hundred to one hundred and fifty pounds of tobacco. Such was not the case. They were transported at the expense of the company, and when they were chosen as wives by the planters the fare for transportation was charged and paid by the husbands. Thus domestic relations were established; then came habits of thrift, an increase of comforts, and consequent happiness. Within the next two years fifty patents for land were granted and 3,500 emigrants found homes in Virginia.

INTRODUCTION OF AFRICAN SLAVERY.

It was the policy of King James to increase the population of the colony as rapidly as possible, and with that end in view, despite the protests of the London Company, he sent over one hundred "idle and dissolute" persons who were in custody for various misdemeanors, and were only transported to escape a worse fate at home. They were sold out as servants to the planters, who endured their presence only because of the profits derived from their labor, and the increased assistance thus secured in carrying into effect the various industrial enterprises then projected by the colonists.

This beginning created a desire on the part of the planters to employ other labor than their own, and unfortunately the opportunity to gratify that desire came only too soon. It was in the month of August, 1619, that an event occurred which was destined to stamp its impress upon the pages of American history; an event so far-reaching in its effects that no prophetic eye could foretell what they were to be. No one thought that an institution was then taking root which in the distant future would involve the American States in civil war and almost wreck society itself. This event was none other than the introduction of African slavery. A Dutch vessel sailed up the James river and sold twenty Africans as slaves to the colonists. The world knows the result.

A LIBERAL CONSTITUTION.

Another change was now to take place. A new constitution was prepared for Virginia, and Sir Francis Wyatt was appointed to supersede Yeardley in the government. The new code was modeled after the English constitution, and was a long step toward representative government. It acknowledged the right of petition, and of trial by jury; but the most remarkable provision was that which bestowed the power upon the House of Burgesses to veto any objectionable acts of the company.

THE INDIANS ATTEMPT THE DESTRUCTION OF THE COLONY.

Three years of prosperity had spread the settlements far and wide; they extended for a hundred and forty miles along the banks of the James and far into the interior; several had also been made on the Potomac, so that by the year 1622, there were no less than eighty families dotting the country around the Chesapeake. The only cause for anxiety was the fear of Indian hostilities, and well indeed might this anxiety exist, for there was now a plot being laid which if it had been carried out in detail would not have left an Englishman alive in Virginia. The friends of the colonists were gone. Pocahontas had died in a foreign land, and Powhatan had also passed away—beloved and honored by all who knew him. His brother, the cunning, treacherous and revengeful Opechancanough, had succeeded him. He had long looked with a jealous eye upon the encroachment of the English, and saw in their occupation of the country the fate of his own race; and, now that he was vested with the power which his honored brother had withheld from him, he determined to annihilate the colony at one fell blow. To meet the colonists in the open field only insured his own defeat, owing to the disparity in arms; and the fact that the number of fighting men were now nearly equal would have resulted in just what he wished to avoid—the destruction of his own people. His only hope of success lay in some great stroke which should destroy the power of the colony at once; his cruelty and revenge dictated a general massacre. In order to avoid suspicion he renewed the treaty of peace with Governor Wyatt, and only two days before the blow was to be struck he declared that the sky would fall before he should violate the terms of the treaty. The friendly relations were continued up to the fatal day, even to the very hour. They borrowed boats from the English, brought in venison and other provisions for sale, and even sat down to breakfast with their unsuspecting victims. The fatal hour arrived. It was twelve o'clock, noon, on the 22d day of March, 1622, when every hamlet in Virginia was attacked by a band of yelling savages, who spared neither age, sex nor condition. The bloody work went on until three hundred and forty-seven men, women and children had fallen victims at the bloody and barbarous hands of that perfidious and inhuman people. Had not a converted Indian, who lived with a Mr. Pace, revealed the plot, and thus put the people of Jamestown and immediate settlements on their guard, and therefore in a state of defense, every settlement would have been laid in ruins and the inhabitants put to the tomahawk. But the plot failed. There were yet sixteen hundred fighting men in the colony, and the Indians were made to pay dearly for their perfidy. The English pushed into the wilderness, burning wigwams, killing every Indian that fell into their hands and destroying crops, until every tribe was driven far into the interior. Confidence was once more restored, and a feeling of security brought a return of prosperity; emigration again revived, and at the end of the year the population numbered 2,500.

DISSOLUTION OF THE LONDON COMPANY.

Differences between the king and Parliament had produced two powerful political parties in England—the Royalists, supporting the king, and Patriots, defending Parliament. To the latter belonged the greater number of the London Company, and, as a political measure, the king determined to dissolve the company by declaring its charter null and void. It was true that the operations of the company, in a financial point of view, had been a failure. In eighteen years they had expended a half million dollars, and had sent 9,000 emigrants to Virginia, only

2,500 of whom were now in the colony. The annual exports did not exceed 20,000 pounds.

We have not space to follow in detail the proceedings, legal and otherwise, of the crafty James. He sent John Harvey, John Pory, Abraham Piersey, Samuel Mathews and John Jefferson, commissioners to "make more diligent inquiry touching divers matters, which concerned the State of Virginia." The commission arrived in Virginia early in the year 1624, and after remaining a short time returned and reported the company in a state of bankruptcy, and the government of the colony in a very bad state, with no prospect of an improvement under the present management. James caused a *quo warranto* to be issued against the company, and the cause was tried at the Trinity term of King's Bench, for the year 1624. The judges were dependent upon the king for their places, and it was not difficult to determine the result of a trial in the result of which James had such a deep interest. Chief Justice Ley rendered the decision against the corporation, and the London Company ceased to exist. But their mission was filled; the foundation of the Old Dominion was securely laid, and it only remained for others to rear the structure.

VIRGINIA UNDER THE ROYAL GOVERNMENT.

There was but little change made in the government of the colony. This was not the object of the king when he canceled the charter of the company; his action was directed against the corporation, and not against the State, and ere the few proposed changes could be made King James died—March 27,.1625—and was succeeded by his son, who came to the throne under the title of Charles I. He paid very little attention to his American subjects. Governor Wyatt was continued in office until 1626, when he went to England to attend to the private affairs of his father, who had recently died, and Sir George Yeardley was appointed to fill the vacancy. His previous liberal administration was remembered by the colonists, and Charles could not have performed an act that would have met with greater approbation on their part. Yeardley's career was closed by death, November 14, 1627, and in obedience to instructions to the council, they elected Francis West, governor, the day after the burial of Yeardley. He continued in office until March, 1628, when John Pott was chosen in his stead, who in turn was, in a few days, relieved by John Harvey, who arrived from England and assumed the government early in the year 1630.

VIRGINIA AND CHARLES I.

Four years had now passed away since Charles began his reign, and during all that time he had been engaged in the domestic affairs of his kingdom; but he now turned his attention to Virginia as a fruitful field from which to reward his courtiers. This he did by granting them patents for large tracts of land, regardless of location, improvements, or anything else, and finally, in utter disregard of the protestations of the colonists, set a limit to his recklessness by granting to Sir Robert Heath a patent for *one-half* the territory of Virginia, extending from the 36° north to Florida. But as all that part, including the present Carolinas, was not settled until long after, and the charter finally became void because of Heath's failure to comply with its conditions, the colonists could not consider themselves so badly damaged after all, though the act was an evidence of the way in which they might at any time be divested of their rights.

THE MARYLAND CHARTER—GOVERNOR HARVEY.

Cecil Calvert, Lord Baltimore, in 1632, obtained a patent for all that part of Virginia embraced within the present limits of Maryland, and at once proceeded to colonize it, notwithstanding the fact that there were already several settlements of Virginians within the territory, to whose remonstrances he gave no heed. William Claibourne, who had been a member of the council and also colonial secretary of state, had obtained a license from the king "to traffic in all American ports where there was no license," and these permits had been approved by Governor Harvey. Claibourne settled upon Kent Island, in Chesapeake Bay, not far from the present city of Annapolis, and when ordered to abandon it by the Maryland authorities he defended it by force. He was finally arrested, tried, found guilty of murder, piracy and sedition. He escaped to Virginia, and when demanded by the authorities of Maryland, Harvey refused to give him up, but sent him to England for trial. The Virginians were highly incensed at Harvey for not protecting Claibourne and keeping him in the colony, for they regarded the Marylanders as nothing more than an infringement upon their rights. Harvey was tried on a charge of malfeasance in office. Of the trial we know but little. The first entry upon the records relating to the subject is as follows: "An assembly to be called to receive complaints against Sir John Harvey, on the petition of many inhabitants, to meet 7th of May, 1635;" and the next one is: "On the 28th day of April, 1635, Sir John Harvey thrust out of his government, and Captain John West acts as governor until the king's pleasure is known." When Charles I. heard of the action of the colonists, he regarded it as unwarrantable insolence—little short of treason. He reinstated Harvey in the government, and we hear of no more dissatisfaction during the remainder of his administra-

SEAL OF THE COUNCIL CHAMBER
Of the Colony of Virginia, with the arms of the
Virginia Company of London.

tion, which came to an end in 1639, when Sir Francis Wyatt again assumed the government.

ORGANIZATION OF THE FIRST COUNTIES.

Virginia was the first State in the world, composed of separate political divisions, based upon the principle of universal suffrage. It was in the year 1634 that the territory of Virginia was divided into *eight* shires, or counties, similar to those of England, and named as follows: James City, Henrico, Charles City, Elizabeth, Warwick River, Warosenoyoke, Charles River and Acomac. Lieutenants were appointed for each district, whose business it was to supervise the military affairs. Sheriffs, sergeants and bailiffs were to be elected as in England, and commissioners were appointed to hold county courts in the different shires. This was the origin of the county court system in Virginia.

FIRST PUBLICATION OF THE ACTS OF THE LEGISLATURE.

Wyatt continued in office for nearly two years, and was then succeeded by Sir William Berkeley—a name destined to become notorious in the history of Virginia—who arrived and assumed the government in February, 1642. The assembly convened in March, and its first act was to pass a solemn protest against a petition which Sir George Sandys was having numerously signed, to be presented to Parliament, praying for the restoration of the London Company. Much important business was transacted at this session of the assembly. The punishment of temporary slavery, which had existed from the foundation of the colony, was abolished. The trials of causes were made to more nearly conform with those of England. Laws were passed regulating land titles. A treaty was made with Maryland respecting trade on the Chesapeake Bay. Taxation was rendered more uniform, and the tax for the support of the governor was abolished. This was the first meeting of the assembly the acts of which were published.

THE ENGLISH REVOLUTION OF 1642.

The war clouds which had darkened the political horizon of England for many years now broke forth in a storm of uncontrolled fury. Civil war drenched the island in blood. The Royalists were defeated; Charles went to the scaffold; monarchy was overthrown, and Oliver Cromwell declared Protector of the Commonwealth of England, the destinies of which he controlled until the year 1658, when he was succeeded by his son, Richard, who held the reins of government until the restoration of monarchy in 1660.

Throughout the period of the revolution the Virginians continued loyal to the royal cause, not because they loved monarchy, but because they cherished the liberties secured under the constitution which Charles I. had given them, and after the execution of Charles I. they recognized his fugitive son as their rightful sovereign—then an exile in Holland. The loyalty of Virginia to the father did not escape the notice of his son, and from a foreign shore he transmitted to Berkeley a commission as governor, signed by his royal highness. Thus the fugitive from England, the refugee to Holland, was still the sovereign of Virginia.

In the meantime the last opposition to the Parliamentary army in Britain had been overcome, and Cromwell now turned his attention to his distant colony, determined to force it to submit to the new government.

Virginia was now rapidly becoming a nation. Under the influence of her salutary laws, the products of a virgin soil, wrought by willing hands, and the advantages which her foreign trade had given her, she had increased her population from a few hundred to twenty thousand, and there were trading to her ports ten ships from London, two from Bristol, twelve from Holland, and seven from New England. Such was the colony which Cromwell now proposed should submit to the government of the Commonwealth.

A fleet, together with a considerable land force, sailed for Virginia, and cast anchor before Jamestown. But the colonists, in anticipation of the projected conquest, had not been idle. Many veterans from the shattered royal army had taken refuge in Virginia. The colonial army, thus augmented, was a power of which the Commonwealth was ignorant. In addition, several Dutch merchant ships were lying in the river, trading in violation of the acts of Parliament, and of course were armed, that they might defend themselves against the fleets of the Commonwealth. They now allied themselves with the colonial forces. The commissioners of Cromwell, surprised at such a show of resistance, hesitated, and offered fair and honorable terms to the colonists. By them was insured a continuation of their liberties, the preservation of their constitution intact, and a full and complete pardon for all past offenses. Thus the colonists could gain by treaty all that they could hope to gain by the most successful resistance. The articles were signed by the commissioners on the part of the Commonwealth, and the council on the part of the State of Virginia, "as equals treating equals."

From this time to the Restoration, Virginia governed herself, and obtained unlimited liberty of commerce, which was regulated by independent laws. The famous Navigation Acts of Cromwell were not designed for her oppression, and were never enforced on her shores. A trade was opened between Virginia and Denmark, and finally with "every Christian nation in amity with England." When the colony recognized the authority of Cromwell, Berkeley, who held his commission from the exiled king, was too loyal to continue in office, and Richard Bennett, one of the commissioners, was chosen to succeed him. A council was also chosen to act in accordance with instructions from Parliament, and to exercise such powers as the assembly might delegate to it. Bennett retired from office in March, 1655, and Edward Digges became his successor. He served two years, when an election was held, and the choice fell upon "worthy Samuel Mathews, an old planter of nearly forty years' standing, a most deserving Commonwealth's man, who kept a good house, lived bravely, and was a true lover of Virginia."

He, like most Virginians since, was opposed to long sessions of the legislature, and in the spring of 1659, threatened to dissolve that body unless it speedily adjourned. The worthy Samuel had forgotten that it was the legislature that made the governor. His attention was, however, called to the fact by the reply of the Speaker to the effect that "the House of Burgesses, the representatives of the people, were not dissolvable by any power yet extant in Virginia, except their own; and, that the former election of the governor and council was void." The old governor thus learned that Virginia, then—as well as now—regarded her officers as servants and not dictators.

VIRGINIA AT THE TIME OF THE RESTORATION.

Richard Cromwell resigned the Protectorate in 1660. Virginia, too, was without a head. The assembly at once convened and again elected Berkeley governor, with the understanding that he should call the assembly together at least once in two years, and that it should not be dissolved save by its own consent. The old monarchist, now aware that Charles, his beloved prince, would shortly be placed upon the throne, accepted the office and acknowledged himself the people's servant.

Virginia now had a population of thirty thousand. She had established upon her soil the supremacy of the legislative branch of representative government; had secured freedom of trade, security against foreign taxation, and a universal elective franchise. Prosperity kept pace with freedom. The social condition of the emigrants now coming to her shores was vastly improved, and her hospitality was already proverbial. Such was Virginia in the year 1660.

BACON'S REBELLION.

No sooner had intelligence of the Restoration reached Virginia than Berkeley issued a proclamation calling for the election of a new assembly, declaring that the acts of that body during the existence of the Protectorate, were illegal and no longer in force. The people still indulged the hope that all would yet be well; but they had yet to learn that Charles II. was the worst monarch of modern times, and that in enforcing his tyrannical edicts he would find in Berkeley a most willing tool.

The new statute was a death-stroke at colonial liberty. It provided that all trade should be restricted to English ports and carried only in English vessels. A heavy tax was imposed for the support of the government. The colonists remonstrated and petitioned, but the king turned a deaf ear to complaints, and the oppressive laws were rigorously enforced.

But legislative tyranny sank into insignificance when compared with the recklessness of granting large tracts of land to the ignoble and profligate courtiers who thronged his court. No matter whether these lands were on the distant frontier, or the best and most highly cultivated in the colony. Whole hamlets and entire counties were thus given away, and in 1673 the king became a bankrupt in the matter of lands by granting to Lords Culpeper and Arlington a patent for the *entire State of Virginia*, together with all its rights and privileges for a period of thirty-one years.

At the gay court of Charles II. this may have been regarded a small bounty to a royal favorite, but to the forty thousand Virginians thus transferred to a proprietor from whom nothing was to be hoped, and everything feared, it appeared in a very different light. Messrs. Ludwell, Moryson and Smith went to England and presented a remonstrance, but to no purpose.

In the meantime a war broke out with the Susquehanna Indians. The legislature raised and equipped an army of five hundred men for service in the war, but just as they were ready to march they were disbanded by the governor, who refused to assign any reason for the act. Volunteers then flocked to Jamestown and offered to serve without any remuneration if the governor would only appoint a leader. This he refused to do. Then they determined to march to the defenseless frontier without the governor's consent, and looking about for a leader, they found a young man from Henrico county who had just returned from England, whither he had gone to complete his education. The name of that young man was Nathaniel Bacon. When he took command of the volunteer army he made application to Berkeley for a commission, but it was refused, and Bacon marched to the frontier authorized only by the will of the people and the danger of his country. No sooner had the army began its march than Berkeley declared Bacon a rebel and his followers traitors, and collecting as great a force as he could raise among the wealthy aristocrats residing in and about Jamestown, he marched in pursuit of Bacon, with the proclaimed intention of suppressing the rebellion. Bacon continued his march to the frontier, defeated the Indians, drove them far into the interior, and was returning homeward when he heard of the action of the governor. Leaving the greater part of his army, he continued by forced marches towards Jamestown, to which place the governor had fallen back; but he was made prisoner by one Gardiner, and carried before Berkeley. He was finally pardoned and allowed to take his seat in the assembly on condition that he would confess the impropriety of his conduct, and promise obedience for the future. His soldiers, however, were not satisfied with the humility to which their leader was subjected, and marched to Jamestown and compelled the governor to give him a commission, and he again marched to the frontier. But no sooner was he gone than Berkeley retired into Gloucester and a second time declared Bacon a rebel; who when he heard the news, fell back towards Gloucester, and forced the governor with his forces to retreat into Acomac. This county, located on the eastern shore, was considered a distinct territory, although tributary to Virginia. Bacon once more marched up the Potomac, and Berkeley crossed the bay and entered Jamestown. No sooner had Bacon heard of the governor's movements, than he wheeled his van and shortly appeared in front of Jamestown, attacked the place and drove Berkeley on board the ships in the river. The torch was applied, and in twelve hours the oldest town in British America was in ruins.

We know little of Bacon after this, more than that he died of disease contracted during his campaigns. With him died the cause for which he fought. The patriots disbanded, and Berkeley's authority was soon restored, and his vengeance glutted by hanging twenty-three of the followers of Bacon.

Thus ended Bacon's rebellion. The only difference between that struggle and the one of a hundred years later being that the first was an effort to establish a free government *subject* to Great Britain, which could not be done; and the second was an effort to establish a free government *independent* of Great Britain, which was done.

Berkeley resigned his commission and went to England, where he found his actions towards the colony universally disapproved, even by the king himself. This the governor could not withstand, and he soon sank beneath his load of crime, and died, despised in England and execrated in Virginia.

From this time onward, for a period of nearly fifty years, there is little of interest in the history of Virginia, save the succession of governors, and a desultory Indian war carried on upon her western frontier.

VIRGINIA AND VIRGINIANS.

Sir Herbert Jeffries came over as the successor of Berkeley, but was in a short time relieved by Sir Henry Chichely. In 1678 Lord Culpeper, who, together with Lord Arlington, held a patent for the entire State, came over and assumed the government, made many fair promises, one of which was to secure the redress of grievances demanded by the colony; then leaving the government in the hands of Chichely, he returned to England. In 1683 Arlington surrendered his claim to Culpeper, who thus became sole proprietor of Virginia. He came over and began his government on the principle that he owned Virginia, and the Virginians were his slaves; but before his acts could accomplish much mischief, Charles II. revoked his charter because of a failure to comply with its terms. Thus, in 1684, Virginia again became a royal province, with Lord Howard of Effingham as royal governor.

James II. came to the throne in 1685, but there was no change in the government of the colony for the next three years, when William, Prince of Orange, drove James from the English throne and mounted it himself. He referred all complaints of the Virginians to his privy council, with orders that they should receive prompt attention. Sir Francis Nicholson came over and assumed the government. By his mild and conciliatory administration of the affairs of the colony he became more popular than any of his predecessors.

REMOVAL OF THE CAPITAL OF VIRGINIA.

In the year 1698 the seat of government was removed from Jamestown to Williamsburg, seven miles distant from the old metropolis. The historian of that day assigns as the reason of the removal the fact that Williamsburg was "in a healthier and more convenient location, and freer from moschetoes."

Nicholson was succeeded in 1693 by Sir Edmund Andros, but was restored in 1698, and served until 1705, when Edward Nott became governor. He died shortly after receiving his commission, and the government devolved upon Edward Jennings, the president of the council, until the king's pleasure became known. The Earl of Orkney received the commission, but sent out Brigadier-General Hunter to rule in his stead. He was captured by the French while on his way to America, and the illustrious

COLONEL ALEXANDER SPOTSWOOD

became governor. He was the most distinguished individual that controlled the destinies of Virginia prior to the Revolution. He had won distinction on many bloody fields during the campaigns of Marlborough, and thus secured the appointment of colonial governor of Virginia.

THE UNKNOWN REGIONS OF THE WEST.

One hundred and three years had passed away since the founding of Jamestown, and the little colony of one hundred and five souls had grown to nearly one hundred thousand. Hardy pioneers had extended the domain of civilization far into the interior. There were now twenty-four counties in Virginia, and settlements were approaching the eastern base of the Blue Ridge, but of the country beyond the "rocky barrier" nothing whatever was known, The most daring adventurer had not dared to penetrate this unknown wilderness. But the conquest of the wilderness was the mission of those determined spirits who had fled from oppression in the Old World to find a home of freedom on the shores of the New. Governer Spotswood determined to know something more of this region, and accordingly equipped a company of horsemen, and heading it in person began his march from Williamsburg through a dense wilderness inhabited by wild beasts and savage men. Toiling on for several days, the expedition at last reached the base of the Alleghanies, and pushing upward through the narrow defiles the intrepid governor and his little party reached the summit and stood upon one of the loftiest peaks of the Appalachian range. What a spot! Never before, perhaps, had the footsteps or the voice of civilized man been heard amid this mountain fastness. As that little band stood there gazing westward into an illimitable wilderness, they there resolved that its vast extent should be peopled, redeemed from the sway of savage men, and the forest be made to blossom as the rose. How well that resolution has been carried into effect, let the fifteen millions of happy and prosperous people who now throng the great valley of the Mississippi answer.

The party returned to Williamsburg and gave the most glowing description of the country which they had visited. Amid forests of fragrant trees and perfumed alcoves, spots more enchantingly beautiful than were ever graced by Calypso and her nymphs, they had discovered those mysterious hygeian fountains from which flowed these life-giving waters which have since obtained a world-wide fame. In order to induce emigration to the West, the governor established the "Transmontane Order, or Knights of the Golden Horseshoe," giving to each of those who accompanied him a miniature golden horseshoe bearing the inscription, "*Sic Jurat transcendere Montes*" (thus he swears to cross the mountains). These were given to whoever would accept them, with the understanding that he would comply with the inscription. (See De Hass, page 35.)

SILVER MEDAL PRESENTED THE INDIAN POTENTATE, THE
"KING OF PAMUNKIE,"
By the Colonial Authorities of Virginia.

FIRST SETTLEMENTS WEST OF THE MOUNTAINS—"WESTWARD THE STAR OF EMPIRE TAKES ITS WAY."

Many daring adventurers crossed the rocky barrier during the succeeding years, but it was not until the year 1732 that a permanent settlement was made west of the mountains. In this year sixteen families from Pennsylvania came over and began a settlement near where Winchester now stands. They were guided to the location by a gentleman named Joist Hite, and to them is due the credit of having first planted the standard of civilization in Virginia, west of the mountains. (Kerchevel, page 65.)

The second settlement was made in 1734 by Benjamin Allen and three others on the north branch of the Shenandoah, about twelve miles south of the present town of Woodstock. Other adventurers pushed on and settlements gradually extended west, crossing the Capon river, North Mountain and the Alleghany range, until finally they reached the tributaries of the Monongahela (MS. volume of Dr. Ruffner). For twenty years after the settlement about Winchester, the natives inhabiting the mountains and intervening vales remained in a state of comparative quiet; but about this time a circumstance occurred which led to a much better acquaintance with the vast and unexplored regions of the West. Two men, Thomas Morlen and John Salling, determined to explore those unknown regions, and accordingly set out from Winchester. They journeyed up the Shenandoah, crossed the James river near the Natural Bridge, and had progressed as far as the Roanoke, when they were attacked by a party of Cherokees, and Salling was made prisoner. Morlen made his escape from them and returned in safety to the settlement. Salling was carried captive into what is now called Tennessee, where he remained with them for several years. While on a hunting expedition with some of his tribe, they were attacked by a party of Illinois Indians, who were the deadly enemies of the Cherokees, and Salling was a second time borne off a prisoner.

This occurred in what is now the State of Kentucky, which was at that time the favorite hunting-ground of all the tribes of the Mississippi Valley. Salling was taken by his new captors to Kaskaskia, and was afterward sold to a company of Spanish traders on the Lower Mississippi, who in turn sold him to the governor of Canada, and he transferred him to the Dutch authorities at Manhattan; thence he succeeded in reaching Williamsburg, after an absence of more than six years. (De Hass, page 38.)

About the time that Salling returned to Williamsburg, a considerable addition was made to the population of Virginia by the arrival of emigrants at Jamestown, among whom were John Lewis and John Mackey, both of whom were desirous of securing land in the West. Struck with Salling's description of the country which he had traversed, where mighty rivers, flowing from unknown sources amid the icy fountains of the far North, rolled their transparent waters in majestic grandeur to the South; where stretched away vast plains fringed with primeval forests which seemed to be the culminating point of the plant regions of the Northern Hemisphere, they determined to visit it, having first engaged Salling as a guide. The three crossed the mountains, and descending the western declivities, they were so much pleased with the country that they decided to locate and take up their final abode. Accordingly they both set about finding a suitable location. Lewis selected as the place of his future residence a site on a stream which still bears his name. Mackey chose a spot on the Shenandoah; and Salling, having concluded to remain, chose a tract of land on the waters of the James, where he built his cabin.

Lewis made application for and received a grant of one hundred thousand acres of land; and while in Williamsburg perfecting his claim, he met with Benjamin Burden, who had just arrived from England as the agent of Lord Fairfax, to whom James II. had granted five hundred thousand acres of land to be located west of the Blue Ridge, and prevailed upon him to accompany him to his home. Burden remained at Lewis' the greater part of the summer, and on his return to Williamsburg took with him a buffalo calf which he and Andrew Lewis (afterward General Lewis) had caught and tamed. He presented it to Governor Gooch, who was so much pleased with his mountain pet that he entered on his journal a patent authorizing Burden to locate any quantity of land not exceeding five hundred thousand acres on any of the waters of the Shenandoah or James rivers west of the Blue Ridge. One of the conditions of this grant was that he should settle one hundred families in ten years within its limits, and for this purpose Burden sailed for Europe in the year 1737, and upon his return to Virginia brought with him upward of one hundred families of adventurers to settle upon his grant. Among these emigrants were many who became the founders of some of the most distinguished families of Virginia. Of these were the Alexanders, Crawfords, McDowells, McLures, Moores, Matthews, Pattons, Prestons, Tolfords, Archers and others.

ORGANIZATION OF THE FIRST COUNTIES OF THE BLUE RIDGE.

In the year 1738 the Colonial Legislature of Virginia passed a bill providing for the organization of a new county west of the Blue Ridge, and accordingly Orange county was divided into two parts, and the new county named Augusta. The pioneers of this county were so much distinguished for their heroism, which struck terror and dismay into the Indians, that during the darkest days of the Revolution, when the Pennsylvania and New Jersey troops had mutinied, and it seemed that all was lost, Washington was heard to exclaim: "Leave me but a banner to place upon the mountains of West Augusta, and I will rally around me the men who will lift our bleeding country from the dust and set her free."

THE FRENCH AND INDIAN WAR.

ENGLAND AND FRANCE—CLAIMS OF THE TWO NATIONS TO THE OHIO VALLEY.

As has been seen, France had taken possession of that part of the continent lying far away towards the Arctic Circle, and had planted settlements along the St. Lawrence; her discoverers, Jolliette and Marquette, had explored the country from the extreme north-east to the Gulf of Mexico, and upon these discoveries she based her claim to all that part of the continent drained by the Mississippi river and its tributaries. And when the English crossed the rocky barrier and began to penetrate into the Ohio Valley, she viewed these encroachments upon her soil with a jealous eye, and at once determined to oppose them at all hazards. France rested her claim to the Ohio and Kanawha valleys upon the recognized law of nations that "The discovery of the mouth of the river should entitle the nation making the discovery to the country drained by that river and its tributaries." The claim thus set up by France and resisted by Great Britain is exactly the same as that upon which the United States subsequently based their claims to the Territory of Oregon. England claimed that aside from her title by purchase, she held, under the discovery of John and Sebastian Cabot (1498), the entire region lying between the 38th and 64th parallels of north latitude, a zone extending across the continent from ocean to ocean. She also set up another claim—priority of discovery, a claim uttterly absurd and entirely untenable.

France, convinced of the justness of her claims, after addressing an appeal to the nations of the world, determined not to yield before the threatening attitude of her powerful rival, and immediately set about adopting the most effective measures for maintaining her claim to the great Valley of the West, and accordingly began the erection of a cordon of forts extending from the St. Lawrence to the Gulf of Mexico, the most important of which were those at Fontinac, Niagara, Detroit, Green Bay, Vincennes, Kaskaskia, Natchez and Biloxi. In the year 1720 she erected Fort Chatres, in what is now Illinois. It was constructed by an engineer of the Vauben school, and was one of the strongest fortifications ever erected on the continent of North America.

In 1748 the British parliament passed laws authorizing the formation of many new settlements and issued many land grants, in which the interests of British commerce were consulted, rather than the articles of the treaty of Aix-la-Chapelle. Prominent among these movements was the organization of the Ohio Company, the settlement of the Upper Ohio, and several others of an aggressive character, the most important of which was the sending of a regiment of British soldiers into the Ohio Valley, where they took post at the mouth of the Monongahela.

When the French authorities heard of this movement on the part of the English, the home government authorized the governor-general of Canada to remonstrate against the aggressive invasion of French territory, and a summons was accordingly addressed to the English commander. The following is an extract:

"Sir—Nothing can surprise me more than to see you attempt a settlement upon the lands of the king, my master, which obliges me now, sir, to send you this gentleman, Chevalier Le Mercier, captain of the artillery of Canada, to know of you, sir, by virtue of what authority you are come to fortify yourself within the dominions of the king, my master. This action seems so contrary to the last treaty of peace, at Aix-la-Chapelle, between his most Christian majesty and the King of Great Britain, that I do not know to whom to impute such an usurpation, as it is uncontested that the lands situated along the beautiful river belong to his most Christian majesty.

"Your obedient servant,
"CONTRECOEUR,
"Captain of French Marine."

(See De Hass, page 61.)

In the year 1749, as a preliminary step in taking formal possession of the Ohio and its tributaries, the Marquis de la Galisoniere, governor-general of Canada, determined to place along the "Oyo," or *La Belle Riviere*, a number of leaden plates suitably inscribed, asserting the claims of France to the lands on both sides of the river, even to the source of its tributaries. The command of the expedition whose duty it was to deposit those plates was given to Captain Bienville de Celeron, and consisted of eight subaltern officers, six cadets, an armorer, twenty soldiers, one hundred and eighty Canadians, and fifty-five Indians—two hundred and seventy in all. The expedition left Montreal on the 15th of June, 1749, and on the 29th reached the *La Belle Riviere* at the junction of the Monongahela and Alleghany rivers, where the first plate was buried. The expedition then descended the river, depositing plates at the mouths of the principal tributaries, and on the 18th of August reached the mouth of the *Chinodashichetha* (Great Kanawha), and on the point between the two rivers the fifth plate was buried. It was found in 1846 by a son of Mr. John Beale, of Mason county, West Virginia, afterwards of Kentucky, and removed from the spot in which it had remained for a period of ninety-seven years. The following is a translation of the inscription on the plate. We have compared it with that made recently by Professor O. S. Marshall, from the original copy-plate now preserved in the archives of the *Departement de la Marine*, in Paris, and find them to agree in every particular.

TRANSLATION.

"In the year 1749, reign of Louis XV., King of France, we, Celeron, commandant of a detachment sent by Monsieur the Marquis de la Galisoniere, commandant-general of New France, to re-establish tranquillity in some Indian villages of these cantons, have buried this plate at the mouth of the river *Chinodashichetha*, the 18th of August, near the river Ohio, otherwise Beautiful River, as a monument of renewal of possessions, which we have taken of the said river Ohio, and of all those which fall into it, and of all the land on both sides, as far as to the sources of said rivers, the same as were enjoyed, or ought to have been enjoyed, by the preceding kings of France, and that they have maintained it by their arms and treaties, especially by those of Ryswick, Utrecht and Aix-la-Chapelle."

From the mouth of the Great Kanawha the voyage was continued down the Ohio, and on the 30th day of August the expedition reached the mouth of the *Riviere a la Roche* (Great Miami), and the voyage on the Ohio ended. The following is an extract from Celeron's journal, now deposited in the archives at Paris, as translated by Marshall: "Buried on the point formed by the intersection of the right bank of the Ohio with the left bank of the Rock river, the sixth and last plate, August 31, 1749." This plate has never been found. After journeying up the Miami some distance, the detachment began its homeward march, and reached Montreal on the 10th day of November.

In the same year George II., who regarded the British possessions as personal property, granted to a corporation known as "The Ohio Company," a title to five hundred thousand acres of land, to be located in the Ohio Valley. The company was composed of twelve gentlemen, all residents of Virginia and Maryland, except a Mr. Hanbury, of London. This land was to be located partly south of the Ohio, between the Monongahela and Great Kanawha rivers, and partly north of the Ohio. In 1750 Christopher Gist was sent out by the company for the purpose of exploring and locating these tracts of land in the west. He traversed the country beyond the Ohio, and returned by way of the Kanawha, making thorough exploration of the country east of that river. This was the first exploration made by the English in the Kanawha Valley, and Gist the first Englishman who reached the mouth of the Kanawha. His journal is now in the library of the Historical Society of Massachusetts. Thus it will be seen that the two great rival powers beyond the Atlantic were each determined to hold possession of the great valley, and it became evident that the final struggle for territorial supremacy in America was near at hand. The English, acting upon the principle of action that "They should *take* who have the power," and the French upon nearly a similar one, that "They should *keep* who can," were both resting from an eight years' war, under the truce secured by the treaty of Aix-la-Chapelle, while their commissioners were trying to outwit each other in the matter of the disputed lands in the west. (Smollett's George II., chapter 8.) But the calm was similar to that which precedes the storm. The cloud of war which had for a time disappeared from Europe was now hanging over the wilds of North America. Here was to be heard the clash of arms, the "Forward, march," the daily reveille, the battle cry, the strains of martial music—sounds so strange beneath the dark shades of an American forest. The storm burst with all its fury, and continued to rage for six long years—years characterized by acts of the most savage cruelty known to the annals of warfare; years in which the two leading nations of the world employed against each other the ruthless savages, whose bloodthirsty dispositions incited them to deeds too horrible to contemplate—deeds the record of which will ever remain as the darkest blots upon the pages of the history of these nations.

But the struggle ended, and the world knows the result. The dominion and power of France have disappeared, and no traces of her lost sovereignty exist save in the few names she has left on the prominent streams and landmarks of the country, and in the leaden plates which, inscribed in her language, still lie buried on the banks of the beautiful river. Her temporary occupation of the country, the voyages of her navigators, and the discoveries of her discoverers, live only on the pages of history and in her archives, where she has carefully preserved them. Thus the Ohio Valley, together with all of South-western Virginia, passed from under the dominion of France to that of the Island Empire. But another title to the valley was yet to be abrogated, that of the original owners—the Indians, who, for perhaps a thousand years, had roamed over its hills and vales in pursuit of game; who had made it their principal thoroughfare in their missions of blood and rapine ever since the Anglo-Saxon set foot on these shores and had began his march in pursuit of the empire star. This title was yet to cost the lives of many hundreds of those sturdy pioneers who had braved the perils of the wilderness. Over its entire extent was to be heard the frightful war-whoop of the savage, and night was to be made lurid by the flames of burning homes. Then, to record an account of these scenes will next be our province.

INDIAN WARS ON THE WESTERN FRONTIER.

In presenting an outline of the annals of the settlement of the western frontier, we must remember that a dreary uniformity of incident marks all the story of the primitive settlements in every part of our country, from Plymouth to Jamestown, and from the northern lakes to the Mexican gulf, and that to enter into a narration of individual efforts and sufferings, and less important triumphs and defeats, would only render our chronicles a confused mass of rencounters of the rifle and tomahawk, of burnings, murders, captivities and reprisals, which confound by their number and weary by their monotony and resemblance. A few more prominent events only can be selected as samples of the many others. A few names only, from the long catalogue of pioneers, can be mentioned. The memory of the hundreds necessarily omitted lives where they would have wished it to live—in the winter evening's recital, in the rustic mountain ballad, and in the rude but interesting tradition of border warfare.

The first white woman who saw the Kanawha river was

MRS. HANNAH DENNIS.

In the summer of 1761 a war party of Shawnee Indians penetrated the settlements on James river, murdered many of the settlers and carried a number of others into captivity, among the latter Mrs. Dennis. She, with about twenty others, was carried to the towns north of the Ohio, and upon arriving there the captives were separated by their captors, and it was decided Mrs. Dennis should live at the Chillicothe towns, where she remained more than two years, during which time she learned their language, painted herself, and in many respects conformed to their manners and customs. She devoted herself to the sick, and was highly esteemed by the Indians as one skilled in the art of curing disease. Having discovered that they were very superstitious and believed in necromancy, she professed witchcraft and affected to be a prophetess. Notwithstanding this, Mrs. Dennis was always determined to effect her escape when a favorable opportunity should present itself, and having so long remained with them, apparently well satisfied, they ceased to entertain any suspicions of such a design. In June, 1763, she left the Chillicothe towns, *ostensibly* to procure herbs for medicinal purposes, but *really* to make her escape. As she did not return that night her intention was suspected, and early next morning several warriors were sent in pursuit of her. In order to leave as little trail as possible, she had crossed the Scioto river three times, and was just getting over the fourth time, forty miles below the towns, when she was discovered by her pursuers. They fired at her across the river without effect, but in endeavoring to make rapid flight she cut one of her feet upon a sharp stone.

MEDAL OR FRONTLET PRESENTED TO THE INDIAN
"QUEEN OF PAMUNKEY,"
By the Colony of Virginia, about 1676, and worn by her.

The Indians then rushed across the river to overtake her, but she eluded them by crawling into the hollow of a large fallen sycamore. They searched around for her for some time, frequently stepping on the log which concealed her, and encamped near it that night. On the next day they went on to the Ohio river, but finding no trace of her they returned home.

Mrs. Dennis remained at that place three days, waiting for her wound to heal, and then set off for home. She reached the Ohio river, opposite the present site of the town of Mount Pleasant, and crossed that river on a drift log, then began her journey up the Kanawha to the settlements in the Greenbrier country, which she knew to be nearest her. She traveled only during the night, for fear of discovery, and at last, having subsisted on roots, herbs, green grapes, wild cherries and river muscles for several days, and exhausted by fatigue and hunger, she sat down by the side of Greenbrier river with no expectation of proceeding further. In this situation she was found by Thomas Athol and three others, from Clendenin's settlement, which she had passed without knowing it. She had been then more than twenty days on her disconsolate journey, alone, on foot, but till then cheered with the hope of again being with her friends. She was taken back to Clendenin's, where they kindly ministered to her until she became so far invigorated as to travel on horseback with an escort to Fort Young, on Jackson's river, and from there was carried to her relatives on the James river. (The above we subjoin from the very interesting work of Withers.)

MURDER OF THE CLENDENIN FAMILY.

Shortly after Mrs. Dennis had gone from Clendenin's, a party of Shawnees penetrated into the Greenbrier country, led on by the distinguished warrior Cornstalk, and in two short days succeeded in destroying every settlement in that section of the State. After having murdered the inhabitants at Muddy creek, they passed over into the Levels and attacked the house of Archibald Clendenin, in which from fifty to one hundred persons had taken refuge. Of the whole number of men at Clendenin's but one escaped. He, being at some distance from the house, heard the screams of the women and children, and fled to Jackson's river, where he gave the alarm in time to save the settlers from destruction. The scene in and about the house was one that beggars description; men, women and children lying in a confused mass, weltering in each other's blood, while the shrieks and groans of the dying rent the air. One colored woman, who was endeavoring to escape, killed her own child, which was following her, crying, lest her whereabouts might be discovered by its cries. Stuart says in his Memoir that Mrs. Clendenin did not fail to abuse the Indians with terms of reproach, calling them cowards, etc., although the tomahawk was drawn over her head, accompanied with threats of instant death, and the scalp of her murdered husband was lashed about her face. The prisoners were all taken to Muddy creek, and a party of Indians retained them there until the return of others from Carr's creek, when the whole were started off together to spend a hopeless captivity beyond the Ohio.

On the day they started from the foot of Keeney's Knob, going over the mountain, Mrs. Clendenin gave her infant child to a woman, who was also a prisoner, to carry, and as the prisoners were marching in the center and the Indians in front and rear, she stepped aside into a thicket until all had passed by. The cries of the child soon made the Indians inquire for the mother, who was missing, and one of them said he would soon bring the cow to the calf, and taking the child from the woman he dashed its brains out against a tree, and then threw the body down in the path, where it was trampled to pieces by the horses. Mrs. Clendenin remained until nightfall, and then returned to her own house, a distance of more than ten miles, where she found the mangled remains of her husband lying in the yard, which she covered over with rails, after which she went into a corn-field and remained until morning, when she resumed her flight, and, after many toils and privations, reached the settlements on Jackson's river. It has been supposed that the Indians perpetrating these dreadful outrages were in pursuit of Mrs. Dennis, and, if it be true, how dearly were others made to pay the price of her deliverance!

OTHER INDIAN DEPREDATIONS.

In October, 1764, a party of Mingo and Delaware Indians crossed the Ohio, and, ascending the Big Sandy, crossed over on New river, where they separated into two parties and directed their steps toward different settlements—one party going toward Roanoke and (Catawba), and the other in the direction of Jackson's river. They had not long passed when their trail was discovered by three men, named Swope, Pack and Pitman, who were then engaged in trapping on New river. These men followed the trail until they came to the place where the Indians divided, and judging from the routes taken that the Roanoke and Jackson's river settlements were the objects of their vengeance, they determined to apprise the inhabitants of these places of their danger. Swope and Pack started for Roanoke, and Pitman for Jackson's river, but before they could accomplish their object the Indians had reached the settlements on the latter river and on the Catawba. The party whose destination was Jackson's river traveled down Dunlap's creek and crossed the James river a short distance above Fort Young in the night and unnoticed, and going down this river to the residence of William Carpenter, at which place was a stockade fort, commanded by a Mr. Brown. They met Carpenter just above the house and killed him, then immediately proceeded to the house and made prisoners of a son of Mr. Carpenter and two sons of Mr. Brown (all children) and one woman. The others belonging to the house were in the field at work, and thus escaped a terrible fate. The Indians then despoiled the house, and, taking some horses, commenced a precipitate retreat, fearing discovery and pursuit.

When Carpenter was shot, the report of the gun was heard by those at work in the field, and Brown carried the alarm to Fort Young. In consequence of the weakness of this fort a messenger was dispatched to Fort Dinwiddie with the intelligence. Captain Paul, commandant there, immediately began the pursuit with about twenty of his men, and passing out of the head of Dunlap's creek descended Indian creek and New river to Piney creek, without making any discovery. On Indian creek they met Pitman, almost exhausted, who had been running all the day and night previous for the purpose of apprising the garrison at Fort Young of the approach of the Indians. Pitman joined in the pursuit, which was continued down the Kanawha river until it was ascertained that the Indians had crossed the Ohio.

As Captain Paul and his party were returning they accidentally met with the other party of Indians, which had been to Catawba and committed some depredations and murders there. They were discovered about midnight, encamped on the north bank of New river, opposite an island at the mouth of Indian creek. Excepting some few who were watching the prisoners whom they had taken on the Catawba, they were lying around a small fire, wrapped in skins and blankets. Paul's men, not being aware that there were prisoners among them, fired into their midst, killed three of the Indians and wounded several others, one of whom ran into New river and drowned himself to preserve his scalp. The rest of the party fled hastily down the river and escaped.

In an instant Captain Paul and his men rushed forward to secure the wounded and prevent further escapes. To show the deadening effect that scenes of murder and bloodshed has on the human intellect, we here introduce the reply of a prisoner, rescued at this time. She was a Mrs. Catharine Gunn, an English lady, who had known Captain Paul years before. Recognizing his voice, she called him by name, just as one of his men was in the act of tomahawking her. She made no resistance, and when asked the reason, replied: "I had as soon be murdered as not. My husband is murdered, my children are slain, my parents are dead. I have not a relative living in America. Every thing dear here to me is gone. I have no wishes, no hopes, no fears. I would not have risen to my feet to save my life." (See De Hass.) Such were some of the horrible realities experienced by the early settlers of South-western Virginia.

CESSATION OF HOSTILITIES.

But now, 1764, the inhabitants of the western frontier were to enjoy a brief respite from savage barbarity, the first since the Anglo-Saxon had dared to venture west of the mountains. In that year the British government, anxious to secure an amicable adjustment of the difficulties growing out of the French and Indian war, resorted to various modes for effecting so desirable an object. Hoping to conciliate by fair words and fine promises, one of the first movements was to issue, through Colonel Boquet, a proclamation in which the desires for peace on the part of the government were made known. Thirty Indian tribes signified a willingness to treat for peace. General Bradstreet, accompanied by Sir William Johnson, repaired to Niagara for the purpose of opening negotiations with the northern tribes, while Colonel Boquet was sent to the Muskingum to treat with the Ohio Indians, and there, on the 9th of November, 1764, he concluded a treaty of peace with the Delawares and Shawnees, and received from them two hundred and six prisoners, ninety of whom had been carried away from the frontier of Virginia.

THE WESTERN FRONTIER IN 1772.

Eight years had passed away since the close of the French and Indian war. During this time the savages had remained faithful to the terms of Boquet's treaty, and emigration was fast pouring over the mountains; the cabin of the pioneer dotted the wilderness along the western declivities of the Alleghanies. The great object of the western emigrant has ever been to obtain land, and wherever that object could be accomplished, there arose the log cabin, and there was the home of the pioneer.

The result of the last war had forever settled the title of Virginia to all that portion of country lying between the Blue Ridge and the Ohio river, and she now freely granted portions of it to any or all who would undertake to found a home in the then "far west." From her eastern part, from Pennsylvania, and from Maryland, came the conquerors of the wilderness, either a single family, or in companies of a dozen or more, and from Southern Pennsylvania to the Big Sandy river settlements were being made.

As early as 1754, the first settlement in North-western Virginia was made. In that year David Tygart and a man named Files brought their families across the mountains and located themselves—Tygart in the beautiful valley which still bears his name, and Files near where Beverly, the county seat of Randolph, now stands. These were the first settlements in that part of Virginia, and the family of Files was to be the first in the long list of those who were to fall victims to savage cruelty. The Tygart family escaped and returned east of the mountains.

In the above year, Christopher Gist, the agent and surveyor of the Ohio Land Company, and who was the first to make surveys west of the Ohio river, settled upon a tract of land in what is now Fayette county, Pennsylvania, but was then supposed to be in Virginia. His was the first actual settlement on the waters of the Upper Ohio, and his presence there soon induced several other families to come out and settle around him.

In 1758 Thomas Decker and several others located at the mouth of Decker's creek, but early the next spring they were all murdered by a party of Mingo and Delaware Indians, who were determined that their hunting-grounds should not become the home of the invaders with whom they had disputed possession for more than a hundred years.

The next attempt at settlement was made in 1768 by a number of persons on Buckhannon, a tributary of Tygart Valley river. Among them were Samuel Pringle, John Pringle, John and Benjamin Cutnight, Henry Rule, John Hacker, and John and William Ratcliff.

In 1770 many emigrants reached the Monongahela and Ohio rivers. In that year Captain Cresap erected a cabin at the mouth of what is now Dunlap's creek. Captain Parsons settled on the Horse Shoe bottom, on Cheat river, and many other enterprising men, whose names were to be rendered prominent by their posterity, "took up" large tracts of these fertile lands. Among them were Cunningham, Butler, Minear, Goff, Fink, etc.

SETTLEMENT OF WHEELING.

In this year, too, the foundation of "Virginia's Metropolis of the West" was laid. The Zanes made the first settlement on the banks of *"La Belle Riviere"* (Ohio) below Fort Pitt, at the mouth of Wheeling creek, and Joseph Tomlinson made the second at the mouth of Grave creek shortly after. They were soon joined by Bonnett, Wetzel, Messer, George Leffler, Benjamin Biggs, Joshua Baker, Zachariah Sprigg, Andrew Swearengen, David Shepherd, the McCollochs, Mitchells, Van Meters, Millers, Kellers, etc., etc. These were the men who founded Wheeling, and whose means and determined bravery went far towards breaking the power of the savage and thus opening the country to civilization.

In 1772, settlements were made on Elk river, and in the vicinity of Clarksburg, and at other points in South-western Virginia. Among these pioneers were the Hickmans, the Powers, Andersons, Webbs, Nutters, Collrials, Beards, Davisons, and a host of others prominent in pioneer history.

These were the principal settlements made in Western Virginia prior to the year 1773; but tidings of this fertile land had already reached the far east, and hundreds prepared to find homes in the exhaustless domain that stretched out before them.

But through all these years a jealous eye was watching the march of the Anglo-Saxon in his conquest of the wilderness. It was the Indian who saw in it all the extinction of his own race; his immediate ancestors had been forced to leave the shores of the Chesapeake, and the banks of the James and Potomac, and to take refuge west of the mountains, in the very country which he now saw passing into the possession of his enemies. He resolved to defend it against the encroachments of his conquerors east of the mountains, and only awaited an opportunity to commence his favorite work of murder. That opportunity, through the indiscretion of the English, soon presented itself.

ENGLISH FOLLY—DUNMORE'S WAR.

The treaty which had continued inviolate since 1765, was now to be broken on the part of the English. In the early part of 1774 several Indians were murdered on the South Branch of the Potomac, by one Nicholas Harpold and his associates. About the same time Bald Eagle, an Indian chief of considerable notoriety, not only among his own tribe, but along the whole western frontier, was in the habit of hunting with the English, and on one of his visits was murdered by Jacob Scott, William Hacker and Elijah Runner, who, reckless of consequences, committed the act simply to gratify their thirst for Indian blood.

There was at this time an Indian town on the banks of the Little Kanawha river, not far from the present site of the town of Elizabeth, in Wirt county, West Virginia. It was called Bulltown, and was inhabited by five families of friendly Indians, who were in intercourse with the settlers on Buckhannon, frequently visiting and hunting with them. There was likewise a German family named Strowd residing on Gauley river, near its junction with the Great Kanawha. In the summer of this year, when Mr. Strowd was absent from home, his family were all murdered, his house plundered, and his cattle driven off. The trail left by the perpetrators of this outrage led in the direction of Bulltown; this led to the supposition that its inhabitants were the authors of these murders, and several parties resolved to avenge the crime upon them. A party of five men expressed a determination to proceed forthwith in search of the supposed murderers. They were absent several days, and, upon their return, denied having seen an Indian in their absence. Future developments, however, proved that they had murdered every inhabitant—man, woman and child—at Bulltown, and had thrown their bodies in the river that their acts might never be known. Here, then, was a sufficient cause to justify retaliation, and forthwith there broke out a savage war along the entire western frontier.

To meet this general uprising of the confederated tribes of the Northwest, who had now determined to annihilate the inhabitants of the whole western frontier, Virginia, ever ready with her treasure and the services of her people, responded to the call of his excellency, Governor Dunmore, and forthwith three thousand soldiers, chiefly from the counties of Augusta, Botetourt, Frederick and Shenandoah, enrolled their names and shouldered their rifles in defense of the defenseless frontier.

These troops were divided into two bodies, called the Northern and Southern divisions. The Northern division was led by Governor Dunmore in person, and the command of the Southern was given to General Andrew Lewis. His command rendezvoused at Camp Union (afterward Fort Savannah), now Lewisburg, in Greenbrier county, and by the first of September General Lewis only awaited the arrival of Colonel Christian and others from Lord Dunmore to begin his march against the Indian towns north of the Ohio. In a few days a messenger arrived with orders from Dunmore, who was then at the head of the Northern division, at Williamsburg, to meet him on the 2d of October at the mouth of the Great Kanawha. On the 11th the tents were struck, and the army commenced its line of march through an unknown and trackless wilderness.

Captain Matthew Arbuckle, who had traversed the Kanawha Valley in 1764, acted as guide and conducted the expedition to the Ohio river, which was reached after a dreary march of nineteen days. Some days after the march began several of the command were attacked with smallpox, and were left where the city of Charleston now stands. Among the number was Alexander Clendenin, brother of Captain William Clendenin, and father of Andrew Clendenin, Esq., now of Mason county. When General Lewis reached the mouth of the Kanawha, he was greatly disappointed in not meeting Governor Dunmore, and still more so at not hearing from him. In the absence of orders it was determined to go into camp, and accordingly the tents were pitched upon the triangular point of land between the right bank of the Kanawha and the left bank of the Ohio, accessible only from the rear. This place was called by the Indians, "*Tu, enda, wie,*" signifying in the Wyandotte language, "The junction of two rivers." The ground thus occupied by the Virginia army is the same upon which the town of Point Pleasant has since been built. Little did that band of sturdy Virginians think that ere they left that place they were to fight the most fiercely-contested battle ever fought with the Indians in Virginia, if not on the continent. It was not until Sunday, October 9th, that a messenger reached General Lewis, informing

SCENE ON THE GREAT KANAWHA.

him that the plan of the campaign had been changed, and ordering him to march direct to the Indian towns on the Scioto, at which place the Northern division would join him.

THE BATTLE OF POINT PLEASANT.

Accordingly arrangements were made preparatory to leaving on the following morning (Monday, 10th); but early on that morning two soldiers, named Robertson and Hickman, went up the Ohio in quest of deer, and after having gone a short distance they discovered a large body of Indians, just arising from their encampment. The soldiers were fired upon and Hickman was killed, but Robertson escaped and ran into camp, hallooing, as he ran, that he had seen a "body of Indians covering four acres of ground." This force consisted of the flower of the confederated tribes, who had abandoned their towns on the Pickaway plains to meet the Virginia troops and give them battle before the two corps could be united. Within an hour after the presence of the Indians had been discovered, a general engagement took place, extending from the bank of the Ohio to that of the Kanawha, and distant a half a mile from the point.

General Lewis, who had witnessed a similar scene at Braddock's defeat, acted with steadiness and decision in this great emergency. He arranged his forces promptly and advanced to meet the enemy. Colonel Charles Lewis (brother of the General), with three hundred men, formed the right line, met the Indians at sunrise, and sustained the first attack. He fell, mortally wounded, in the first fire, and was carried to the rear, where he shortly after expired. His troops, receiving almost the entire weight of the charge, were broken and gave way. Colonel Flemming, commanding the left wing, advanced along the bank of the Ohio, and in a few moments fell in with the right wing of the Indian line, which rested upon the river. The effect of the first shock was to stagger the left wing as it had done the right, and its commander was severely wounded at an early stage of the conflict. But his men succeeded in reaching a piece of timber land and maintained their position until the reserve under Colonel Field reached the ground. It will be seen by examining Lewis' plan of the engagement, and also the ground on which the battle was fought, that an advance on his part and a retreat on the part of his opponents necessarily weakened their lines by constantly increasing their length, and if it extended from river to river, he would be forced, eventually, to break his line or leave his flanks unprotected. Writers upon the subject of Indian tactics inform us that it was the great object of his generalship to preserve his flanks and overthrow those of his enemy. They continued, therefore, contrary to their usual practice, to dispute the ground with the pertinacity of veterans along the whole line, retreating slowly from tree to tree until 1 o'clock P. M., when they reached a strong position. Here both armies rested within rifle range of each other until late in the evening, when General Lewis, seeing the impracticability of dislodging the Indians by the most vigorous attack, and sensible of the great danger which must arise to his army if the contest were not decided before night, detached the three companies commanded by Captains Isaac Shelby, George Mathews and John Stewart, with orders to proceed up the Kanawha river, and under cover of the banks of Crooked creek (a stream emptying into the Kanawha about half a mile from the point) to attack the Indians in the rear. The maneuver thus planned and executed had the desired effect, and gave to the colonial army a complete victory. The Indians, finding themselves suddenly encompassed between two armies, attacked in front and rear, and doubtless believing that in the rear was the long expected reinforcement under Colonel Christian, soon gave way, and about sundown commenced a precipitate retreat across the Ohio, toward their towns on the Scioto.

The desperate nature of this conflict may be inferred by the deep-seated animosity of the parties toward each other, the high courage which both possessed, and the consequences which hung upon the issue. The victory was indeed most decisive, and many were the advantages obtained by it; but they were dearly bought. One-half of the commissioned officers had fallen, seventy-five men lay dead upon the field, and one hundred and forty wounded. Among the slain were Colonels Lewis and Field; Captains Buford, Morrow, Wood, Cundiff, Wilson and McClanahan, and Lieutenants Allen, Goldsby and Dillon. The loss of the Indians could never be ascertained, nor could the number engaged be known. Their army was composed of warriors from the different nations north of the Ohio, and comprised the flower of the Shawnee, Delaware, Mingo, Wyandotte and Cayuga tribes, led on by their respective chiefs, at the head of whom was Cornstalk, Sachem of the Shawnees, and King of the Northern Confederacy. Never, perhaps, did men exhibit a more conclusive evidence of bravery in making a charge and fortitude in withstanding a charge than did these undisciplined soldiers of the forest on the field at Point Pleasant. Such, too, was the heroic bravery displayed by those composing the Virginia army on that occasion that high hopes were entertained of their future distinction. Nor were these hopes disappointed, for in the various scenes through which they subsequently passed, the pledge of after eminence then given was fully redeemed, and the names of Shelby, Campbell, Lewis, Mathews, Moore and others, their compatriots in arms on the bloody field at the mouth of the Great Kanawha, have been inscribed in brilliant characters upon the roll of fame. The following gentlemen, with others of high reputation in private life, were officers in the battle of Point Pleasant: General Isaac Shelby, the first Governor of Kentucky, and Secretary of War during Monroe's administration; General William Campbell and Colonel John Campbell, heroes of King's Mountain and

Long Island; General William Shelby, one of the most favored citizens of Tennessee, often honored with confidence of that State; General Andrew Moore, of Rockbridge county, the only man ever elected by Virginia to a seat in the United States Senate from the country west of the Blue Ridge; Colonel John Stewart, of Greenbrier; General Tate, of Washington county, Virginia; Colonel William McKee, of Lincoln county, Kentucky; Colonel John Steele, afterward a Governor of Mississippi Territory; Colonel Charles Cameron, of Bath county, Virginia; General Bazaleel Wells, of Ohio; General George Mathews, a distinguished officer in the war of the Revolution, the hero of Brandywine, Germantown and Guilford, a Governor of Georgia, and a Representative from that State in the Congress of the United States; Captain William Clendenin, the first Representative from Mason county in the Legislature of Virginia; General Andrew Lewis, a Brigadier-General during the Revolution, twice wounded at the siege of Fort Necessity, the commandant of the troops that drove Lord Dunmore from Gwynn's Island in 1776, and announced his orders of attack by putting the match to the first gun, an eighteen-pounder, himself. Robertson, who gave the first alarm at Point Pleasant, afterward rose to the rank of Brigadier-General in Tennessee.

The day after the battle Colonel Christian, at the head of three hundred Fincastle troops, arrived at Point Pleasant and at once proceeded to bury the dead. A fort was hastily erected and named Fort Randolph, in which a garrison of one hundred men were left. The Virginia army, made eager by success and maddened by the loss of so many brave officers, crossed the Ohio and dashed away in pursuit of the beaten and disheartened savages. Our next information of the Virginians is that a march of eighty miles through an untrodden wilderness has been performed, and on the 24th of October we find them encamped on Congo creek, in what is now Pickaway township, Pickaway county, within striking distance of the Indian towns, but there again compelled to await the movements of the Tory governor, at the head of the left wing, who was then encamped further north, at a point called Camp Charlotte, and from which place he sent a messenger to General Lewis, forbidding his further advance into the hostile country, as he (Dunmore) was now negotiating for peace with the Indians. The peace was concluded, a junction of the two divisions was formed, and the whole army returned by way of Fort Gower (at the mouth of the Muskingum) to Virginia. Thus ended Dunmore's war.

To the student of history no truth is more patent than this—that the battle at Point Pleasant was the first in the series of the Revolution, the flames of which were then being kindled by the oppression of the mother country, and the resistance of the same by the feeble but determined colonies. It is a well-known fact that emissaries of Great Britain were then inciting the Indians to hostilities against the frontier for the purpose of distracting attention, and thus preventing the consummation of the union which was then being formed to resist the tyranny of their armed oppressors. It is also well known that Lord Dunmore was an enemy of the colonists, by his rigid adherence to the royal cause and his efforts to induce the Indians to co-operate with the English, and thus assist in reducing Virginia to subjection. It has been asserted that he intentionally delayed the progress of the left wing of the army that the right might be destroyed at Point Pleasant. Then, at the mouth of the Great Kanawha river, on the 19th day of October, 1774, there went whizzing through the forest the first volley of a struggle for liberty which, in the grandeur and importance of its results, stands without a parallel in the history of the world. On that day the soil upon which Point Pleasant now stands, drank the first blood shed in defense of American liberty, and it was there decided that the decaying institutions of the Middle Ages should not prevail in America, but that just laws and priceless liberty should be planted forever in the domains of the New World.

Historians, becoming engrossed with the more stirring scenes of the Revolution, have failed to consider this sanguinary battle in its true import and bearing upon the destiny of our country, forgetting that the colonial army returned home only to enlist in the patriot army, and on almost every battle-field of the Revolution represented that little band who stood face to face with the savage allies of Great Britain at Point Pleasant. But all did not return. Many thus early paid the forfeit of their lives, but they were not forgotten. Though no marble marks their place of rest, and no historian has inscribed their names on the roll of the honored dead, yet their memory lives in the rehearsal around the cabin fires of the mountains of West Augusta, and in the rustic mountain ballads which were chanted many years after the storm of the Revolution had spent its force and died away.

LAST SURVIVOR OF THE BATTLE.

Belonging to General Lewis' army was a young man named Ellis Hughes. He was a native of Virginia, and had been bred in the hot-bed of Indian warfare. The Indians having murdered a young lady to whom he was very much attached, and subsequently his father, he vowed revenge, and the return of peace did not mitigate his hatred of the race. Shortly after Wayne's treaty with the Indians in 1795, he forsook his native mountains, and, in company with one John Ratliff, removed north of the Ohio, where they became the first settlers in what is now Licking county in that State.

Hughes died near Utica, that county, in March, 1845, at an advanced age, in the hope of a happy future; claiming, and accredited by all who knew him, to be the last survivor of the battle of Point Pleasant. He was buried with military honors and other demonstrations of respect.

VIRGINIA IN THE WAR OF THE REVOLUTION.

It was the year 1775, and the soldiers engaged in Dunmore's war returned to Virginia only to find the affairs between Great Britain and her American colonies rapidly verging to a crisis. Patrick Henry was holding public meetings spellbound by his matchless oratory in denouncing the tyrannical policy of the mother country toward her subjects on this side of the Atlantic.

On the 19th of April there had been discharged a volley which was being echoed and re-echoed along the coast from the St. Lawrence to Florida—a volley, the first of a struggle which was to give the American continent to liberty and make it ever after the home of the oppressed of all foreign lands. Virginia at once prepared to play her part on the theater of the Revolution, and her first task was to rid herself of Dunmore, her Tory governor.

Early in the year the British government, uneasy because of the hostile attitude of the colonies, issued orders to the various governors to remove all military stores to a place of safety, and thus prevent them from falling into the hands of the colonists. In compliance with these orders, Dunmore, on the 20th of April, secretly removed the gunpowder from Williamsburg to the Magdalen, a British man-of-war lying at anchor off Yorktown. No sooner had the act become known than the people of Williamsburg flew to arms, and it was with difficulty that they could be restrained from seizing the person of the governor. A deputation was sent to him, who remonstrated with him for the act. His reply "was everywhere considered as a mean and scandalous evasion." He became alarmed and placed a guard of negroes around his residence, and then swore "by the living God" that if any violence was offered him he would proclaim freedom to every slave in Virginia and lay Williamsburg in ashes. These threats wrought the indignation of the people up to the highest pitch. Six hundred men armed themselves and repaired to Fredericksburg, ready to march to Williamsburg and defend it from the threatened attack of Dunmore, while thousands of others in all parts of Virginia stood ready to render aid.

Virginia has ever had patriots and statesmen within her borders to whom she has turned a listening ear, and it was so now. Peyton Randolph and Edmund Pendleton transmitted their advice to Fredericksburg, requesting the people there assembled to abstain from hostilities until the Continental Congress should decide upon a general plan of resistance. This had the desired effect at Fredericksburg, and the people there collected dispersed after passing a resolution that they *would defend by force of arms this or any other sister colony from unjust or wicked invasion.*

But with the volunteers collected at Hanover Court House it was different. They resolved *to recover the gunpowder or die in the attempt.* Patrick Henry was chosen leader, and the company marched toward Williamsburg and halted at Doncastle's inn, within sixteen miles of that place. Dunmore knew Patrick Henry, and for that reason sent Corbin, the king's receiver-general, out to meet the patriots. The result was that that officer made full compensation for the powder. Henry disbanded the company on the 4th of May, and all returned to their homes. Two days later Dunmore issued a proclamation against "a certain Patrick Henry, of the county of Hanover, and a number of deluded followers," and forbade all persons to recognize or harbor him or "any other concerned in like combinations." On the 11th, Henry left Virginia to attend the meeting of the Continental Congress at Philadelphia, to which he had been chosen a member.

The Virginians read the governor's proclamation and received news of the battle of Lexington at the same time, the combined effect of which was to thoroughly arouse the people of every county in Virginia to a sense of the dangers which beset them. A company was organized which secretly entered the government arsenal and carried away a great number of arms and military equipments, after which act, when the governor heard of it, he sent a messenger to Captain Montague, commanding the Fowey, a British man-of-war lying off Yorktown, asking assistance. In compliance with this request, forty marines were sent to Williamsburg. A letter from Montague also came to Colonel Nelson, commanding the Virginia troops, informing him that if the marines were molested he would at once bombard the town. This only had the effect of still further increasing the indignation of the people, and on the 8th of June Dunmore and his family took refuge on board the man-of-war off Yorktown, fearful of his safety at Williamsburg. Here he remained, and "refused upon invitation of the assembly to return to his place or to sign bills of the utmost importance to the colony," unless that body would hold its meetings under the guns of his ship at Yorktown. This that body refused to do, communications ceased, and, on the last of June, Dunmore sailed down the river, and thus forever ended the royal government in Virginia.

The assembly then declared the governor to have abdicated, and, after issuing a call for a convention to meet in the city of Richmond, on the 17th of July following, adjourned.

On the day appointed the convention met, its object being "to organize a provincial form of government and a plan of defense for the colony." A committee of safety was appointed, consisting of the following illustrious gentlemen: Edmund Pendleton, George Mason, John Page, Richard Bland, Thomas Ludwell Lee, Paul Carrington, Dudley Digges, James Mercer, Carter Braxton, William Cabell and John Tabb. The convention then made arrangements to raise troops for defense, and ordered that the force already enrolled be augmented to 9,000, there being at that time two regiments already in the field. The other regiments were speedily mustered and officered as follows:

REGIMENT.	COLONELS.	LIEUTENANT-COLONELS.
First	Patrick Henry	Robert Howe
Second	William Woodford	Adam Stephen
Third	Hugh Mercer	George Wheedon
Fourth	Adam Stephens	Isaac Reed
Fifth	William Peachy	William Crawford
Sixth	Mordecai Buckner	Thomas Elliott
Seventh	William Dangerfield	Alexander McClanahan
Eighth	Peter Muhlenberg	A. Bowman
Ninth	Thomas Flemming	George Mathews

Of this force, six regiments were placed upon the continental establishment, and the remaining three were retained as provincial guards.

The committee of safety ordered the army contractors to provide a stand of colors, to be borne at the head of the various regiments, bearing on one side the name of the district in which the regiment had been raised, and on the other, "*Virginia for Constitutional Liberty.*" This was the first banner of liberty unfurled in the New World.

In October, Dunmore sent a party on shore at Norfolk, under cover of the men-of-war lying in the harbor, who demolished Holt's printing office, from which there had issued a newspaper imbued with the patriotic principles of the day. The corporation of the town remonstrated against the outrage, but Dunmore answered by saying, he "could not have done the people of Norfolk a greater service than by depriving them of the means of having their minds poisoned, and of exciting in them the spirit of rebellion and sedition." Holt, however, was not to be thus beaten. He published an eloquent philippic against the governor in the Williamsburg papers, and declared his intention to establish another paper to promulgate the same principles as the one which had been destroyed.

Dunmore having heard that a force was collecting in Princess Anne county, left Norfolk on the 16th of November, marched into that county, attacked the provincials and completely routed them. He then returned to Norfolk, where he established his head-quarters, and from here he issued his celebrated proclamation, in which he proclaimed martial law throughout Virginia; declared all able to bear arms traitors, who did not resort to the king's standard, and offered freedom to all slaves "appertaining to rebels," who would join his master's cause. On this, Dunmore staked his last hopes of subjugating Virginia. Had he possessed at his command a sufficient force to have enabled him to carry his threats into execution some apprehensions might have been aroused. But, as it was, his course only aided to harmonize public opinion, and proportionately to increase public irritation.

About the 20th of November, Colonel Woodford, with a portion of the second regiment, marched within twelve miles of Norfolk, where he halted and began the erection of breastworks, and here, on the 9th of December, he was attacked by a body of grenadiers, commanded by Captain Fordyce, who attempted to storm the works, but were repulsed by a most destructive fire from the Virginians. Fordyce retreated to Norfolk, and Dunmore and his entire force fled for safety to the vessels lying in the harbor. The Virginians entered the city and began a desultory fire on the vessels, which was continued for several days. In retaliation, Dunmore, on the 1st day of January, bombarded the town and set fire to the buildings along the shore. Orders were then received by Colonel Woodford from the committee of safety to burn the remainder of the town, and thus prevent the British from making it a permanent post. The orders were executed, and Norfolk, containing 6,000 inhabitants, and then the most populous town in Virginia, was laid in ashes.

The General Convention of Virginia met at the capital on the 6th of May. Edmund Pendleton was chosen president and John Tazewell secretary. Its work was plain. The tottering fabric of royal government in Virginia had fallen, and to rear upon its ruins a structure more elegant, more solid and more lasting, was now the task to be performed.

On the 15th of this month, after appealing to the "Searcher of Hearts," the convention unanimously adopted the following resolution:

"That the delegates appointed to represent this colony in general congress, be instructed to propose to that respectable body *to declare the United Colonies free and independent States,* absolved from all allegiance to, or dependence on the crown or parliament of Great Britain; and that they give the assent of this colony to such declaration, and whatever measures may be thought necessary by Congress for forming foreign alliances, and a confederation of colonies, at such time and in the manner that to them shall seem best; provided, that the power of forming governments for, and the regulation of the internal concerns of each colony, be left to the colonial legislatures."

Thus Virginia furnished the draft of the future declaration of independence.

On the 29th a constitution was adopted, the first which was framed with view to a permanent separation from Great Britain, since those of South Carolina and New Hampshire, which alone preceded it, were to continue only until a reconciliation could be effected between the mother country and the colonies. The plan of government was proposed by the distinguished George Mason, and with the addition of a preamble written by Thomas Jefferson, unanimously adopted by the convention, and the following officers appointed in compliance with its provisions: Patrick Henry, governor; John Page, Dudley Digges, John Taylor, John Blair, Benjamin Harrison of Berkeley, Bartholomew Dandridge, Charles Carter, and Benjamin Harrison of Brandon, counselors of State; Thomas Whiting, John Hutchings, Champion Travis, Thomas Newton, Jr., and George Webb, commissioners of admiralty; Thomas Everard and James Cocke, commissioners for settling accounts; Edmund Randolph, attorney-general.

In the meantime Virginia had sent her representatives to the general congress then in session at Philadelphia; and they, in compliance with instructions from their constituency, were standing shoulder to shoulder battling for the Declaration of Independence, and when, on the 4th day of July, 1776, the immortal band signed that document, no less than seven of her honored sons were among the number. The names of those who thus signed the charter of American Liberty, were as follows: George Wythe, Richard Henry Lee, Thomas Jefferson, Benjamin Harrison, Thomas Nelson, Jr., Francis Lightfoot Lee, and Carter Braxton.

In the early days of June, Dunmore, with his fleet, had left Hampton Roads, landed and erected fortifications on Gwynn's Island, within the limits of what is now Matthews county. Here he was attacked on the 9th of July by a body of Virginians under Brigadier-General Andrew Lewis (who was in command at the battle of Point Pleasant in 1774), and forced to abandon the island. Dunmore, now having despaired of ever swaying the scepter over the province again, dispatched the remnant of his followers to Florida and the West Indies, and sailing himself away to the north, left the shores of Virginia, never to return.

On the 25th of the month the adoption of the Declaration of Independence was officially announced at Williamsburg amid the acclamations of the people, the roar of artillery and rattle of musketry. The Assembly met on the 7th of October for the first time under the new government; Edmund Pendleton was elected Speaker of the House of Delegates, and Archibald Casey, President of the Senate. The first act passed by that body was one repealing all acts of Parliament against dissenters, and thus was the first blow struck at the Established Church in Virginia. Another act was passed providing for the appoint-

MEREWETHER LEWIS,
Of the Lewis and Clarke Expedition,
(In Indian costume.)

ment of a committee to revise the State laws, and prepare a code "more suitable to the new state of affairs." The committee was appointed as follows: Edmund Pendleton, George Wythe, George Mason, and Thomas Ludwell Lee. All the work, however, was performed by the first three.

The seat of war had now been transferred to the North, where Washington, Virginia's distinguished son, on whom the Continental Congress had bestowed the commission of Commander-in-Chief of all the forces raised in defense of American liberty, was drawing Burgoyne in a trap into which he was destined to fall.

During this brief respite from war, Virginia renewed her labors in behalf of literature and society, as well as in the improvement of civil relations. Dr. Small, the learned professor of William and Mary College, continued his efforts in the diffusion of knowledge, which he had commenced before the beginning of hostilities, under the patronage of James Fauquier, "the ablest character who had then ever filled the chair of government in Virginia." A literary and scientific society was formed at this time, of which John Page was president, and Professor James Madison one of the secretaries. This body held its meetings in the capitol at Williamsburg, and many philosophical papers were read, and many interesting lectures delivered, but unfortunately the continuation of war prevented the ripe development of the association.

ALLIES OF GREAT BRITAIN.

While Virginia was battling with her oppressors on her eastern shores, she was also compelled to defend her frontier against the savage hordes employed by the emissaries of Great Britain to whom she paid a premium for the scalps snatched from the heads of helpless women and children. Thus Christian England, then boasting of the splendors of her civilization, turned loose the ruthless savage to murder and burn at the stake the people of her own blood.

MURDER OF CORNSTALK AT POINT PLEASANT.

One of the most atrocious acts recorded in border warfare was committed at Point Pleasant, at the mouth of the Great Kanawha, in the summer of 1777. This was the shocking murder of Cornstalk, the celebrated Shawnee chief, whose nobleness of character every student of pioneer history has learned to admire. In the spring of the above year, Cornstalk and Redhawk came to Fort Randolph at the mouth of the Great Kanawha and declared that he and all his tribe were opposed to engaging in the war on the side of the British; but, that all the other tribes north of the Ohio were determined to do so, and that his people would be compelled to do likewise. Captain Arbuckle, commandant at Point Pleasant, detained his visitors as hostages, hoping thus to prevent their tribe from becoming allies of Great Britain. We subjoin an account of the murder from the memoir of Colonel John Stewart, who was an eye-witness of the scene:

"During the time of our stay [at Point Pleasant] two young men named Hamilton and Gilmore went over the Kanawha one day to hunt for deer. On their return to camp some Indians had concealed themselves on the bank among the weeds, to view our encampment, and as Gilmore came along past them, they fired on him and killed him on the bank. Captain Arbuckle and myself were standing on the opposite bank, when the gun was fired, and while we were wondering who it could be shooting contrary to orders, or what they were doing over the river, we saw Hamilton run down to the bank, who called out that Gilmore was killed. Gilmore was one of the company of Captain John Hall, of that part of the country now Rockbridge county. The captain was a relative of Gilmore's, whose family and friends were chiefly cut off by the Indians, in 1763, when Greenbrier was cut off. Hall's men instantly jumped into a canoe and went to the relief of Hamilton, who was standing in momentary expectation of being put to death. They brought the corpse of Gilmore down the bank, covered with blood, and scalped, and put it into the canoe. As they were passing the river, I observed to Captain Arbuckle that the people would be for killing the hostages, as soon as the canoe would land. He supposed that they would not offer to commit so great a violence upon the innocent, who were in no wise accessory to the murder of Gilmore. But the canoe had scarcely touched the shore until the cry was raised, 'Let us kill the Indians in the fort!' and every man with his gun in his hand, came up the bank pale with rage. Captain Hall was at their head and leader. Captain Arbuckle and I met them, and endeavored to dissuade them from so unjustifiable an action; but they cocked their guns, threatened us with instant death if we did not desist, rushed by us into the fort and put the Indians to death.

"On the preceding day Cornstalk's son, Elinipsico, had come from the nation to see his father, and to know if he were well, or alive. When he came to the river, opposite the fort, he hallooed. His father was at that instant in the act of delineating a map of the country and the waters between the Shawnee towns and the Mississippi, at our request, with chalk upon the floor. He immediately recognized the voice of his son, went out and answered him. The young fellow crossed over, and they embraced each other in the most tender and affectionate manner. The interpreter's wife, who had been a prisoner among the Indians and had recently left them, on hearing the uproar the next day, and hearing the men threatening that they would kill the Indians, for whom she retained much affection, ran to their cabin and informed them that the people were just coming to kill them, and that because the Indians who killed Gilmore had come with Elinipsico the day before. He utterly denied it; declared that he knew nothing of them, and trembled exceedingly. His father encouraged him not to be afraid, for that the *Great Man above* had sent him there to be killed and die with him. As the men advanced to the door, Cornstalk rose up and met them; they fired upon him, and seven or eight bullets went through him. So fell the great warrior, Cornstalk, whose name was bestowed upon him by the consent of the nation as their great strength and support. His son was shot dead as he sat upon the stool. The Redhawk made an attempt to go up the chimney, but was shot down. The other Indian was shamefully mangled, and I grieved to see him so long in the agonies of death."

Point Pleasant did not flourish for many years. There was no church—its social condition was at the lowest ebb. Judging from the accounts of travelers who visited the place in its earlier days, one would suppose that Goldsmith's "Deserted Village" was a paradise in comparison. The popular superstition was that a curse had been laid upon the place to continue for one hundred years—a punishment for the fiendish murder. Patrick Henry, then governor, offered a reward for the apprehension of the murderers, but without effect.

WAR CLOUDS AGAIN HANGING OVER VIRGINIA.

In the year 1779 the British determined upon the conquest of the Southern States, and Sir Henry Clinton, aware that their resistance would very much depend upon Virginia, resolved to humble her pride and destroy her resources. Accordingly, early in May a portion of the British fleet anchored in Hampton Roads, where they compelled the surrender of Fort Nelson, and on the 11th, the British General Mathews took possession of Portsmouth. They then destroyed great quantities of military stores at Gosport and Norfolk; burned the town of Suffolk; marched far into the interior, burning private residences, barns, and scattering destruction far and wide. Their men-of-war destroyed in the meantime more than one hundred vessels, thus entirely ruining the coasting trade of the colony. The army then re-embarked and sailed away to New York, having finished, in a masterly manner, the work assigned them to do.

The triumph of the British arms in the South portended great evil to Virginia. Clinton determined to make her feel the effects of her continued resistance to a greater extent than ever before, and for that purpose sent General Leslie with a force of three thousand men to complete her destruction. He appeared in the Chesapeake Bay in October, 1780, landed at Portsmouth and destroyed the vessels and all other property which he found along the coast. Meantime, Thomas Jefferson, who had succeeded Patrick Henry as governor of the State, was, with the assistance of the best men in the State in the assembly, concentrating every force to oppose the invaders. At this time General Gates, who had been beaten by Cornwallis in the South, was relieved of his command, and General Greene appointed in his stead. The British, fearing that a change of officers might also change the fortunes of Cornwallis' army, ordered Leslie to withdraw from Virginia and at once form a junction with the army in South Carolina. This he did just in time to assist in driving Greene back into Virginia. The day after the Americans crossed the Dan—the dividing line between Virginia and North Carolina—Greene wrote to the Governor and also to Baron Steuben informing them of his situation and asking for reinforcements.

Early in December, 1780, Governor Jefferson also received a letter from Washington, informing him that the British were preparing to send an expedition south, the objective point of which was most probably Virginia. This prediction proved correct, for on the 30th, Benedict Arnold, who had attempted the betrayal of the American army at West Point, for which he received ten thousand pounds and a brigadier-general's commission in the British army, arrived with fifty sail in the Chesapeake, and after embarking in lighter vessels, ascended the James river. When Jefferson heard of the approach of Arnold's squadron, he sent General Nelson into the interior counties to raise as large a force as possible, while Baron Steuben was dispatched to Petersburg with a force of about two hundred men. On the 4th of January, 1781, Arnold landed his force near Westover, and marched to Richmond without opposition. No sooner was the capital in possession of the traitor than her stores were plundered, her archives destroyed, and the governor forced to seek safety in rapid flight. From Richmond, Arnold sent a detachment under Colonel Simcoe to Westham, where they destroyed the only cannon foundry in Virginia.

The British, now fearing an attack from the combined forces of Steuben and Nelson, the latter of whom had succeeded in raising a considerable force, commenced their voyage down the river, destroying all property, public and private, on both sides of the river. Virginia was truly in a defenseless state. All her regular force was with General Greene, in the southern part of the State, who was disputing the passage of the Dan with Cornwallis. Her whole dependence was in her militia, of which only about two thousand were in the field, and with this force she could not hope to resist invasion.

No sooner had Arnold gone than another invasion occurred, at the head of which was General Phillips, who, with one thousand men, again ascended the James, ravaged Yorktown, City Point, Petersburg, and spread desolation and terror—ever the followers in the wake of the British army—on every side. He conceived the idea of marching to Richmond a second time, but the fortunate arrival of Lafayette with a considerable force of regulars saved the metropolis, and hastened Phillips in his descent of the river. Lafayette followed, closely watching his movements, until he reached Brandon, where he suddenly landed, and marched again in the direction of Petersburg. The French marquis, however, divined his true intention to be that of forming a junction with Cornwallis, who in the meantime had forced Greene from the banks of the Dan, and was now marching northward through Virginia. The two forces were united at Petersburg on the 20th of May, and Lafayette, whose force was now augmented to four thousand men, remained in the vicinity of Richmond, awaiting reinforcements or an opportunity to join General Greene. Meanwhile, General Wheedon collected a force of several hundred militia, and lay at Falmouth guarding the arms manufactory at that place. In addition to these forces, General Wayne was on his way to Virginia with nine hundred veterans from the frontier. The strength of the united British armies was too great for any force which Virginia could raise, and her fate now seemed to be decided.

From this point Cornwallis sent out detachments to ravage the various parts of the State which had not before been visited by the ruthless Briton, and in two months property to the value of fifteen million dollars had been destroyed.

Colonel Tarleton, at the head of one of these raiding parties, advanced to Charlottesville, where he hoped to capture a republican legislature, the assembly being in session there at the time. That body, however, received information of his approach, and all of the members, except seven who were made prisoners, saved themselves by flight. Governor Jefferson made his escape by riding into the mountains on horseback. Lafayette, although unable to meet the British in the open field, watched their every movement with sleepless vigilance. Acting under orders from Sir Henry Clinton, then at New York, Cornwallis descended the James and halted at Green Springs, within eight miles of the site of Jamestown. Lafayette followed closely upon his rear. From the above place Cornwallis moved to Portsmouth, where he would have fortified himself had not Clinton ordered him to re-embark and take post at Yorktown, which he did on the 1st of August. The position thus taken was situated on the York peninsula on the southern bank of York river, a few miles from its mouth.

A few days later Lafayette, with the entire available force of Virginia, took post a few miles north of the British position, and from here sent messengers with dispatches to Washington, requesting him to hasten to Virginia and assist in the overthrow of the entire British force. A powerful French fleet was daily expected in the Chesapeake, and the American commander saw that Cornwallis, with his retreat cut off by land and sea, would be compelled to surrender, and thus the fatal blow to the British arms would be struck. On the 30th of August the expected fleet, with four thousand men on board, arrived and anchored at the mouth of York river; and on the 2d of September Count de Barras, commanding the French fleet at Newport, sailed into the Chesapeake with eight men-of-war and a number of transports. Three days later Admiral Graves, with a large fleet of ships-of-the-line, appeared in the bay. A naval battle ensued, in which the ships of the English were so roughly handled by the French flotilla that Graves was compelled to withdraw from the bay and sail away to New York.

On the 14th General Washington arrived at the head-quarters of Lafayette, and on the next day visited the flag-ship of Count de Grasse, where the plan of the siege was arranged. On the 25th the Army of the North, which had been preceded by the commander-in-chief, arrived, and on the 6th of October the combined forces of America and France opened fire on the walls of the now beleaguered army, and on the night of the 14th carried the outer works by storm. Early in the morning of the 16th the English made a sortie, but were hurled back into their intrenchments. The next day Cornwallis proposed a surrender; on the 18th the terms of capitulation were signed; and on the 19th Major-General O'Hara, who appeared instead of Cornwallis, who feigned illness, marched the whole force out into the open field, where in the presence of the united forces of France and America, 7,247 English soldiers laid down their arms and became prisoners of war. Thus ended the war in Virginia, and here, on her soil, the power of the Briton in America was forever broken.

Had Virginia done her part in that mighty struggle? Let history answer. She had been the first to adopt an independent constitution; she was the first to recommend the Declaration of Independence; she had sent her noble son to become the first among the leaders of the armies of the nation; her officers and soldiers which she kept in the field for eight long and weary years, whether in the shock of battle, or marching half-clad, half-starved, and barefooted amid the snows of the North, or through the pestilential swamps of the South, had ever evinced unsurpassed bravery and fortitude. She had furnished the voice of Henry, the pen of Jefferson, the sword of Washington, and that was enough. What other American State can show such a record?

VIRGINIA AFTER THE REVOLUTION.

The most important act in the history of the State in the year 1781, was the cession of her immense territory north-west of the Ohio to the general government. The feeble colony of 1607, now grown to a powerful State, stands on the banks of the Ohio and cedes to the general govment her vast empire beyond. To this liberal act she was induced by her desire to accelerate the general ratification of the Articles of the Confederation of the Union.

The war was now past, and it was seen by the ablest statesmen of the nation that the Articles of Confederation, under which the colonies had achieved their independence, were not suited to bind together a union of States whose territory extended over half a continent, and whose desire was to be held together by bonds of union which could never be severed; and now, for the first time, the subject of a federal or national constitution began to be thought of. This plan of remodeling the government originated in Virginia.

After Washington resigned his commission as commander-in-chief of the army to the Continental Congress, he retired to his home at Mount Vernon, and it was here, in the year 1785, during the visit of several distinguished statesmen, that the proposition was first made. They then prepared and issued a call for a convention to meet at Annapolis, in Maryland, the following year, " to consider the subject of a national constitution." In September, 1786, the convention met, but only five States were represented. This being a minority of the States, the body, after passing a resolution urging the several legislatures to appoint delegates to a national convention, to meet at Philadelphia on the second Monday in May, adjourned.

In compliance with that resolution, the convention met at the appointed place and time, every State being represented except Rhode Island. To that convention Virginia sent as her representatives, George Washington, John Blair, James Madison, Jr., George Mason, James McClurg, Edmund Randolph and George Wythe, the first of whom was elected president of the convention.

From the day of meeting to the 29th, a discussion was kept up in relation to the revision of the articles of confederation, when, on the latter day, Edmund Randolph moved to set aside the articles and prepare a new constitution. The motion prevailed. A committee was appointed, which reported early in September. Their report was the *Constitution of the United States.* Copies of the new instrument were sent to the several legislatures for ratification or rejection.

The Virginia convention called to ratify the Federal compact met in the city of Richmond in June, 1788, and was composed of men whose names were already illustrious, or destined to become so in the future history of the State and nation. Among them sat Marshall, Madison, Monroe, Mason, Nichols, Henry, Randolph, Pendleton, Lee, Washington, Wythe, Innes, Bland, Grayson, and many others "whose sound reasoning and eloquence shed a lustre upon the deliberations of that august body which has never been surpassed in the annals of the commonwealth." On the 25th an ordinance was passed ratifying the Federal Constitution, and the new government at once went into operation, nine States having previously adopted that instrument.

It was then that Virginia began her career as the central figure in the galaxy of States, and for fifty years her progress was such that it won for her the proud title of "the Old Dominion." But our space forbids us to notice in detail the minor events in her history during that period, and we must content ourselves with a brief mention of the most important only.

BURNING OF THE RICHMOND THEATER.

The saddest event recorded in the annals of the State is that of the burning of the Richmond theater on the night of the 26th of December, 1811. This terrible catastrophe carried heart-rending sorrow to many heretofore happy homes, and cast a gloom over the entire State.

On that evening a popular play was to be introduced, and an audience numbering six hundred, composed of the *elite* of the city, together with many others from distant parts of the State who were spending the holidays at the capital city, had collected to witness the performance, and just at the time the play was to commence the scenery in the rear of the stage became ignited by coming in contact with a chandelier. The alarm was given, and then at once began such a scene as has rarely, if ever, been witnessed. We let the editor of the Richmond *Standard*, who was an eye-witness, describe it:

"The performers and their attendants in vain endeavored to tear down the scenery; the fire flashed in every part of the house with a rapidity horrible and astonishing; and, alas! gushing tears and unspeakable anguish deprived me of utterance. No person who was not present can form any idea of this unexampled scene of distress. * * * There was but one door for the greatest part of the audience to pass. Men, women and children were pressing upon each other, while the flames were seizing upon those behind. The editor went to different windows, which were very high, and implored his fellow-creatures to save their lives by jumping out of them. Those nearest the windows, ignorant of their danger, were afraid to leap down, while those behind them were seen catching on fire and writhing in the greatest agonies of pain and distress. At length those behind, urged by the pressing flames, pushed those who were nearest to the windows, and people of every description began to fall one upon another, some with their clothes on fire, some half roasted. Oh, wretched me! Oh, afflicted people! Would to God I could have died a thousand deaths in any shape, could undivided suffering have purchased the safety of my friends, my benefactors, of those whom I loved! The editor, with the assistance of others, caught several of those whom he had begged to leap from the windows. One lady jumped out when all her clothes were on fire. He tore them burning from her; stripped her of her last rags, and, protecting her nakedness with his coat, carried her from the fire. Fathers and mothers were deploring the loss of their children; children the loss of their parents; husbands were heard to lament the loss of their companions; wives were bemoaning their burnt husbands. The people were seen wringing their hands, beating their hands and breasts, and those that had secured themselves seemed to suffer greater torments than those enveloped in the flames.

"Oh, distracting memory! Who that saw this can think of it again and yet retain his senses! Do I dream? No, no! Oh, that it were but a dream! My God! who that saw his friends and nearest connections devoured by fire and laying in heaps at the door, will not regret that he ever lived to see such sights? Could savages have seen this memorable event, it would even soften their hearts.

"A sad gloom pervades this place, and every countenance is cast down to earth. The loss of a hundred thousand friends on the field of battle could not touch the heart like this. Enough. Imagine what can not be described. The most distant and implacable enemy, and the most savage barbarians, will mourn our unhappy lot."

* * * * * * * *

About one hundred and twenty perished in the flames, among whom were the Hon. George W. Smith, governor of the State; Abraham B. Venable, United States ex-senator and president of the State Bank of Richmond, and many other distinguished persons. Lieutenant J. Gibbon, of the regular army, lost his life in an attempt to save that of a Miss Conyers, his affianced.

SECOND WAR WITH GREAT BRITAIN.

When the war of 1812 came, Virginia was ready. She contributed liberally of her treasure, and thousands of her sons from her eastern shores and from her wide western domain enrolled themselves in favor of "Free Trade and Sailors' Rights," and went to join the land and naval forces of the nation; and when the vandals of Ross, who laid the Federal capital in ashes, were ravaging her shores, her citizens rose *en masse* to repel the ruthless invader. At Hampton, at Craney Island, at Norfolk, at Fort Meigs, and along the shores of the Northern lakes, hundreds of her sons fell upon the battle-field, and other hundreds paid the forfeit of their lives in a climate which, to them, habit and nature had rendered uncongenial and fatal.

REVOLUTIONARY RELICS.

GRAVE OF GENERAL DANIEL MORGAN,
of the Revolution, at Winchester, Va.

CONSTITUTIONAL CHANGES.

As already noticed, Mr. Archibald Cary, from the committee appointed for the purpose, reported, on the 24th of June, 1776, a plan of government for the colony. It was read a second time, on the 26th, and considered in committee of the whole on that day, and on the 27th and 28th. It was then reported to the House, with amendments, which were read twice and agreed to. After being fairly transcribed, it was read a third time on the 29th and passed unanimously.

This constitution or form of government was originally drawn up by George Mason. Mr. Jefferson had put a draft of one into the hands of Mr. Wythe, who reached Williamsburg after the other was committed to the committee of the whole. Two or three parts of Mr. Jefferson's plan were, with little alteration, inserted in the other, and his preamble was also adopted. This constitution was in force until superseded by the amended constitution or form of government for Virginia which, on the 15th of January, 1830, was submitted and proposed to the people of Virginia by their delegates and representatives in convention assembled.

This amended constitution continued in force until January, 1852. A convention to form a new constitution was called in 1850. It assembled on the 14th of October of the same year, and the constitution which continued in force until the time of the civil war was adopted on the 1st of August, 1851. It was submitted to the people, who ratified it on the fourth Thursday in October following. On the second Monday of the succeeding December an election was held for the legislature, governor, lieutenant-governor and attorney-general. The first general assembly under the new constitution convened on the second Monday in January (the twelfth day of the month), and the first governor and lieutenant-governor took the oath and entered upon the discharge of the duties of their respective offices on the 16th of January, 1852. Under the now liberal provisions of this constitution, the State entered upon a decade of unexampled prosperity. These were the halcyon days of Virginia, but the storm came on apace and civil war hovered near.

JOHN BROWN'S RAID UPON HARPERS FERRY, VIRGINIA, 1859.

On the 16th day of October, 1859, an event occurred at Harpers Ferry, Virginia, which sent a thrill of terror throughout the State and astonished the entire nation, an event which was but the forerunner of mightier ones; it was the muttering of the storm in the distance, the rumbling of thunder below the horizon where lay the storm which was destined, erelong, to break forth in all its fury and scatter destruction far and wide throughout the country.

May 8th, 1858, a conference was held at Chatham, Canada, composed of numerous representatives from various parts of the United States and British America, the object of which was to consult upon and determine the best plans for bringing about a consummation of their long-cherished hope, the abolition of slavery in the Southern States. The moving spirit of that body was John Brown, or "Old Ossawattamie Brown," so called because of his participation in the battle fought at Ossawattamie, Kansas, during the troubles in that State. What the action of that convention was, never has been, and never will be known, but an inference may be drawn from the immediate action of its principal leader.

Shortly after, Brown and his two sons, Oliver and Watson, appeared in the vicinity of Harpers Ferry, Virginia, and under the assumed name of Smith, leased a farm in Maryland, only a few miles distant from the place selected as the scene of their future operations. Here a considerable quantity of arms and ammunition, shipped from an unknown source, was collected, and a force of twenty-two confederates joined him, of whom seventeen were white and five were colored. Brown's courage and resolute daring displayed in the long and bloody war which ended in making Kansas a free State, secured for him the leadership in the dangerous enterprise now to be undertaken. At length the day for action arrived; Brown issued his instructions to his followers and concluded by saying, "And now, gentlemen, let me press this one thing upon your minds. You all know how dear life is to you, and how dear your lives are to your friends; and remembering that, consider that the lives of others are as dear to them as yours is to you. Do not, therefore, take the life of any one, if you can possibly avoid it; but, if necessary to take life in order to save your own, then make sure work of it."

The hour was 10 o'clock P. M., when William Williamson, the arsenal guard on the Potomac bridge, while walking his beat, was seized and made a prisoner. The guard thus removed, Brown and his men quietly took possession of the armory buildings, in which were stored an immense quantity of arms and ammunition. When the midnight relief came to the bridge and found the lights out and the guard gone, he supposed it to be an attempt at robbery, and hastened away to give the alarm. About 1 o'clock in the morning several of the invaders went to the house of Lewis Washington, an extensive farmer and slave owner, and, arousing him from his bed, made him a prisoner, and after securing his arms and carriage and proclaiming freedom to his slaves, carried him to the arsenal. A similar visit was made to the residence of Mr. Alstatt, who, together with his son, was made a prisoner and his slaves likewise proclaimed free. Several other prisoners were also brought in, some of whom interrogated Brown as to the object of the proceedings, to which he answered, "*To free the slaves;*" and when asked by whose authority the reply was, "*By the authority of God Almighty.*"

At the usual hour the mail train on the Baltimore & Ohio road arrived, but was warned not to pass over the bridge, but after considerable detention was permitted to proceed. So quietly had everything been managed that the town was not aroused until after daybreak, when it was discovered that the government buildings were in possession of a band of insurgents, who, with armed sentinels, guarded every approach to the town, thus rendering its inhabitants prisoners. At daylight the workmen engaged on the buildings, not yet aware of the proceedings, went as usual to their work and were made prisoners and confined in a large building in the yard; the other prisoners being confined in the engine-house which the invaders after made their chief fortress.

When the true state of affairs became known the wildest confusion prevailed; messages were hastened off to the surrounding towns, and by noon military companies began to arrive. Colonel Baylor, with a company of Charlestown troops, was the first to arrive; they made a dash toward the bridge, the invaders falling back and taking refuge in the armory, where they checked the military and compelled them to fall back; a desultory fire was kept up during the remainder of the day, by which Mr. Beckham, mayor of the town, was killed; also Brown's son, Oliver, Kagi, his secretary, and Leeman, one of his captives, fell within the armory. In the evening a considerable force arrived from Martinsburg, which at once stormed and carried the building in which the workmen were imprisoned; they were all liberated and an attack was then made upon the engine-house, which was repulsed with considerable loss.

Brown had taken the precaution to have the wires cut, so that the outside world should not be aware of his proceedings until he should have firmly established himself; but late in the evening messengers bore dispatches beyond the damage to the wires, and transmitted them to Washington, Baltimore, Richmond, and other points, at all of which the intelligence produced the wildest excitement and throughout the South it amounted to almost a "reign of terror." Col. Robert E. Lee, with one hundred United States marines and two pieces of artillery, was at once dispatched from Washington to the scene of action, and upon the arrival Colonel Lee sent Lieutenant J. E. B. Stuart to demand an unconditional surrender; only promising the insurgents protection from immediate violence, and a trial under the civil laws, but Brown refused to capitulate on any terms other than these: "That they should be permitted to march out with their men and arms, taking their prisoners with them; that they should proceed, unpursued, to the toll-gate, when they would free their prisoners; the soldiers would then be permitted to pursue them, and they would fight if they could not escape." To these terms Lieutenant Stuart could not consent; he withdrew, and an attack was at once made which resulted in the capture of Brown and several of his followers, all of whom were forced to surrender only at the point of the bayonet. One of the soldiers struck Brown, after he had thrown down his arms, in the face with his saber, and another soldier ran a bayonet twice into his body.

Captain Brown was carried out into the yard, where he soon revived, and talked freely to those around him, defending his action, and declaring that he had done only what was right. The following conversation took place between himself and one of the officers:

"Are you Captain Brown of Kansas?"
"I am sometimes called so."
"Are you Ossawattamie Brown?"
"I tried to do my duty there."
"What is your present object?"
"*To free the slaves from bondage.*"
"Were any other persons but those with you now, connected with the movement?"
"No."
"Did you expect aid from the North?"
"No; there was no one connected with the movement but those who came with me."
"Did you expect to kill people in order to carry your point?"
"I did not wish to do so, but you have forced us to do it."

An indictment for treason and murder was at once found against Brown by the authorities of Virginia, and from this time until his trial, he was closely confined in prison. Several of his followers were also confined to await trial, all of whom demanded to be tried separately; the authorities consented, and Brown was placed on trial for his life, upon the charge preferred in the indictment. The case came up for hearing on the 26th of October, at Charlestown, Virginia. He asked for a continuance because of his severe wounds, but it was denied him. Throughout the trial, being unable to sit, he lay upon a mattress. The trial continued three days; a verdict of guilty upon all the charges preferred was found against him, and he was sentenced to be hanged on the 2d of December.

During the period of Brown's confinement from the time his sentence was pronounced until the day of his execution, he was visited by many distinguished persons, and letters of sympathy and condolence from eminent editors and politicians poured in upon him. When the day of his execution arrived he walked forth from the jail with a calm expression upon his face, and a firm and steady step; mounted the wagon which was to convey him to the gallows, and seated himself between Mr. Avis, the jailer, and Mr. Saddler, the undertaker. On the way to the gallows he conversed as cheerfully as if he had only been taking a morning drive with the object of viewing the surrounding mountain scenery. Arrived at the place of execution, he descended from the wagon and mounted the scaffold, the first man to stand upon it. A white cap was then drawn over his eyes and the fatal noose adjusted. Said the sheriff: "Captain Brown, you are not standing upon the drop; will you step forward?" Brown replied: "I can not see; you must lead me." Sheriff Avis then led him to the center of the drop; the fatal signal was given and the body was dangling in the air. After hanging thirty-eight minutes it was cut down, given to the undertaker, who placed it in a walnut coffin, after which it was conveyed to North Elba, New York, where an eloquent eulogy was pronounced over it by Wendell Phillips. That thus died a fanatic, a victim to a delusion which entirely possessed him, none will deny; but that he was a brave man, possessing determined resolution, we have the testimony of Governor Henry A. Wise, who said of him: "Brown was as brave a man as ever headed an insurrection. He is the farthest possible remove from the ordinary ruffian, rake or madman."

Six of Brown's companions were also executed: Cook, Coppoc, Copeland and Green, on the 16th of December, and Stephens and Haslitt on the 16th of the following March. Thus ended the most tragic scene in the history of Virginia.

THE WAR BETWEEN THE STATES.

We have followed the fortunes of Virginia through the old French and Indian war; through two hundred years of border warfare; through the stormy scenes of the Revolution; through the second war with Great Britain; we know how her sons marched with alacrity to the distant fields of Mexico; but now we are to see her plunged into a civil war, the equal of which has not been recorded in the annals of nations. Virginia, owing to her geographical position, was destined to become one great battle-field. On her soil was to be marshaled the hosts of the contending armies, and her mountains and valleys were to be crimsoned with the best blood of the nation. Within her domain was to arise a new commonwealth, and both the mother and the daughter were to reside upon the ancient estate. The year 1861 found Virginia in a state of civil commotion, unparalleled in history except it be France in the early days of the French revolution.

On the one hand lay the States still composing the Federal Union, while on the other were those which had cast their fortunes with the Southern Confederacy. Virginia hesitated long. A majority of her people in the east favored secession, while in the west, a large majority was opposed to such action. But the time for final action had come. Early in the year Governor John Letcher, influenced by the pressure of the times, issued a proclamation, convening the State Legislature in extra session; and, in obedience to the summons, that body convened in the city of Richmond, January 7, 1861. Then commenced the stormiest session in the history of that body.

Seven days after the meeting, a bill was passed calling for a convention of the people of Virginia, the delegates to which were to be chosen in the manner prescribed for the election of members of the legislature. The convention was to consist of one hundred and fifty-two members equal to the number of members composing the house of delegates.

In compliance with the above act, the election of delegates was held on the 4th day of February, 1861, and the convention met at Richmond on the 13th of the same month.

THE CONVENTION.

Never before, in the history of the State, had a body convened presenting such an array of talent. Among its members sat John Tyler, ex-president of the United States; Henry A. Wise, ex-governor of Virginia, and many others who had held positions of cabinet ministers in the Federal government, or had been representatives in the councils of the nation. There sat her most renowned jurists by the side of her profoundest philosophers and literary characters.

That body organized by electing John Taney, Esq., a delegate from Loudoun county, president of the convention, and John L. Eubank secretary of the same. A committee on Federal Relations was appointed, consisting of Messrs. Robert Y. Conrad, A. H. H. Stewart, Henry A. Wise, Robert E. Scott, W. B. Preston, Lewis L. Harvie, Sherrard Clemens, W. H. McFarland, William McComas, R. L. Montague, Samuel Price, Valentine W. Southall, Waitman T. Willey, James C. Bruce, W. W. Boyd, James Barbour, S. C. Williams, William C. Rives, Samuel McD. Moore, George Blow, Jr., and Peter C. Johnson. Stewart and Clemens asked to be, and were, excused from serving.

On the 18th day of February there appeared before the convention the commissioners on the part of South Carolina, Georgia and Mississippi, to ask the co-operation of Virginia in establishing an independent government for the seceded States. The first speaker was the Hon. Fulton

Anderson, of Mississippi, followed by Hon. Henry L. Benning, from Georgia. Then came the commissioner from South Carolina. All, in speeches resplendent with rhetorical flourish and literary excellence, held up to view a new government, of a new union, in which Virginia, should she pass an ordinance of secession, would become the chief corner-stone. The effect produced by this visit of the commissioners was truly powerful, and, in fact, determined the future action of the convention.

On the 9th of March, the committee on Federal Relations submitted a lengthy report, in which it was set forth that any State had a constitutional right to withdraw from the federative union whenever a majority of the people of that State chose to do so. One of the most spirited debates of modern times now began, and continued until the 17th of April, when the ordinance of secession was voted upon. The vote stood eighty-one for, and fifty-one against it. Nearly all the delegates voting against it were from the western part of the State. The following is a verbatim copy of that document, now the most remarkable State paper in the archives of Virginia:

"AN ORDINANCE, To repeal the ratification of the Constitution of the United States by the State of Virginia, and to resume all the rights and powers granted under the said constitution.

"THE PEOPLE OF VIRGINIA, in their ratification of the Constitution of the United States of America, adopted by them in convention on the twenty-fifth day of June, in the year of our Lord one thousand seven hundred and eighty-eight, having declared that the powers granted under the constitution were derived from the people of the United States, and might be resumed whenever the same should be perverted to their injury and oppression, and the Federal Government having perverted said powers, not only to the injury of the PEOPLE OF VIRGINIA but the oppression of the Southern slave-holding States:

"*Now, therefore, we, the People of Virginia, do* DECLARE and ORDAIN, That the ordinance adopted by the people of this State in convention on the twenty-fifth day of June, in the year of our Lord one thousand seven hundred and eighty-eight, whereby the Constitution of the United States of America was ratified; and all the acts of the General Assembly of this State ratifying or adopting amendments to said constitution are hereby *repealed and abrogated;* that the union between the State of Virginia and the States under the constitution aforesaid, is hereby dissolved, and that the State of Virginia is in the full possession and exercise of all the rights of sovereignty which belong and appertain to a *free* and *independent* State. And they do further *declare,* that said Constitution of the United States of America is no longer binding on any of the citizens of this State.

"This ordinance shall take effect and be an act of this day, when ratified by a majority of the votes of the people of this State cast at a poll to be taken thereon on the fourth Thursday in May next, in pursuance of a schedule hereafter to be enacted.

"Done in convention, in the city of Richmond, on the seventeenth day of April, in the year of our Lord one thousand eight hundred and sixty-one, and in the eighty-fifth year of the Commonwealth of Virginia.
"Attest: JNO. L. EUBANK,
"Secretary of the Convention."

One hundred and forty-two signatures were attached to the ordinance. At the election in May a majority of the votes cast were in favor of secession. The governor issued a proclamation declaring Virginia out of the Union, and placing the whole military force, offensive and defensive, of the commonwealth under the chief control and direction of the president of the Confederate States. Thus Virginia withdrew from the Union.

MILITARY OPERATIONS.

Pending the final action at Richmond, companies and regiments were being mustered and armed all over the State, ready for service in the Confederate army. Early in the spring of 1861, a considerable force, under command of General Joseph E. Johnston, was concentrated at Harper's Ferry, where possession of the government property was taken. Other forces were collected at Philippi, under command of Generals Pegram and Garnett. But while the forces were being collected in Western Virginia, events of much greater magnitude were occurring in the East. Regiment after regiment reported ready for the fray and took post along the Potomac, ready to repel any invasion.

FIRST FEDERAL TROOPS IN VIRGINIA.

The day after the fall of Fort Sumter, President Lincoln issued a proclamation calling for 75,000 men. The call was responded to with alacrity by the Northern States, and by the first of May the required number had been raised and concentrated at Washington and other points along the borders of the seceded States; and although by far the greater number lay at the capital, yet no advance was made until the 23d of May. The force destined for the invasion of Virginia consisted of 8,000 infantry, two companies of cavalry, and two sections of Sherman's artillery battalion, the whole under the command of General Mansfield. Four thousand New York troops, under command of General McDowell, were to co-operate with Mansfield's force. The object of the advance was to take possession of Alexandria and drive the Confederates from their position on Arlington Heights. The 1st Michigan regiment was the first to enter Alexandria. They immediately took possession of the depot and made prisoners of one hundred Confederate cavalry stationed at that place. A Zouave regiment under Colonel Ellsworth was the second that reached Alexandria, and at once began to tear up the Richmond railroad. As they passed the Marshall hotel, Ellsworth discovered a Confederate flag flying from the balcony. He rushed through the hall, up a flight of stairs, pulled down the flag, and was returning, when he was met by Jackson, the enraged proprietor, who discharged the contents of a double-barreled shot-gun into his body. Ellsworth fell to rise no more; but no sooner had the fatal shot been fired than a private, named Brownell, shot Jackson through the heart, and he and his victim expired at the same moment.

The first engagement of a serious nature occurred at Big Bethel, near Fortress Monroe. Early in June, General Pierce with four regiments was sent by General Butler to occupy Newport News. From here they pushed on to Big Bethel, where they were met and defeated by a body of Confederates. Pierce fell back with a loss of forty killed and wounded.

MILITARY MOVEMENTS IN WESTERN VIRGINIA.

The first engagement west of the mountains took place at Philippi, in Barbour county, on the 3d day of June, between a Confederate force of two thousand, under Colonel Potterfield, and a Federal force numbering four thousand, commanded by Colonels Lander and Kelley. The Confederates were beaten, and retreated with heavy loss. Colonel Kelley was severely wounded, but afterwards recovered and was promoted to the rank of brigadier-general

BATTLE OF RICH MOUNTAIN.

On the 23d day of June, General McClellan assumed command of all the Federal forces in Western Virginia, and immediately began a series of movements which met with no successful resistance until the Confederates were compelled to retreat beyond the mountains. He at once marched against General Pegram, who, with a force of 4,000 infantry, had taken up a strong position on Rich Mountain. McClellan, after reconnoitering the position, sent General Rosecranz with two Indiana regiments, and one from Ohio, together with a body of Cincinnati cavalry, to take position in their rear. The Federals intended to keep the Confederates in ignorance of the movement, but a messenger with dispatches and a copy of the diagram of the route was captured, and the plan of attack thus revealed. Pegram sent 2,500 men and a battery of artillery to resist the advance of Rosecranz. They were the first to reach the summit of the mountain, and here the Federals were

LARGE PENDANT, OR BROAD SEAL OF THE COLONY
of Virginia, in the reign of Queen Anne, 1710.

greeted by a discharge of artillery, and their advance checked. Soon, however, they were reinforced by an Indiana regiment, a charge was made along the entire line, the Confederates fell back, and at once began a hasty retreat. The mountain was strewn with the dead and wounded, 150 being buried on the field. Pegram, finding no way of escape, a few days later surrendered his entire force prisoners of war.

ENGAGEMENT AT CARRICKS FORD.

At this time General Garnett was lying near Beverly, in Randolph county, with a force of 6,000 men, and when he heard of Pegram's defeat, began a retreat through the mountains to the east. He was hotly pursued until he reached Carricks Ford, on Cheat river, where he made a stand, but his forces were defeated, and he was left on the field among the slain. He was a brave and meritorious officer, having won distinction in the Mexican war.

The whole Confederate army in Western Virginia was at this time (July 1) estimated at 10,000 strong. Of this force a considerable portion was in the Great Kanawha Valley, under command of ex-Governor Henry A. Wise. He made an advance down the river, but was confronted by a Federal force commanded by General Cox, of Ohio. Wise fell back toward the mountains, was overtaken at Gauley Bridge, but continued his retreat without risking a battle.

ALONG THE POTOMAC —"ON TO RICHMOND."

While these events were transpiring in Western Virginia, two powerful armies were being concentrated on the banks of the Potomac, and were quietly preparing for a great battle. General Beauregard, who had taken command in Virginia, after the fall of Fort Sumter, was at the head of a powerful army at Manassas Junction, while General Joseph E. Johnston was in command of 30,000 men in the neighborhood of Harpers Ferry. General Patterson was in command of a Federal force concentrating at Hagerstown, Maryland, for the purpose of preventing Johnston from joining Beauregard when an attack should be made upon the latter. An army of 40,000 men had now been collected at Washington, and public opinion at the North demanded that an attack be made at once upon the forces of General Beauregard, who had changed his location and taken a strong natural position at Bull Run, about thirty miles from the national capital.

General Irwin McDowell was placed in command, and on the 17th of July all things were in readiness. It was Saturday, and at 4 o'clock A. M. the orders to march were given. Forty thousand men filed out from Washington on the road leading to Centreville. It was the grandest pageant that had yet been witnessed on the continent. Banners were flying in every direction, and strains of martial music filled the air. Little thought any one that ere thirty-six hours had passed away, that magnificent army would be but a shattered fragment of its former self. But behind the fortifications at Bull Run lay 30,000 brave men awaiting the shock of battle. With the rising of the sun on that Sabbath morning, came the sound of battle, and for thirteen dreadful hours 70,000 men struggled for the mastery. As the day waned away, so appeared to wane the cause of the Southern arms, and just when the victory of the Federals seemed assured, a long-expected reinforcement arrived and turned the tide of battle. As Blucher slipped away from Grouchy at Wavres, to decide the fate of Napoleon at Waterloo, so Johnston had stolen away from Patterson, and by forced marches arrived just in time to save the day and make a Waterloo for the Federal arms at Bull Run. He poured 10,000 fresh troops in upon the now exhausted regiments, and then at once began one of the most disastrous retreats an account of which is recorded in history. The Federal army fell back to Washington and the Confederates remained in possession of Bull Run. Four thousand men lay dead upon the field. Thus terminated the first great battle of the Civil War.

BATTLE OF CARNIFEX FERRY.

The Great Kanawha Valley was the principal salt-producing region of the South, and hence of vast importance to the Confederate government. After Wise was compelled to leave the valley, another force was sent to Western Virginia, under ex-Secretary Floyd, who took position at Carnifex Ferry, on Gauley river. General Rosecranz, with several regiments, among which was the 12th Ohio, was sent against him. Detachments of the two armies met at Summerville, near the county-seat of Nicholas county, and a severe engagement ensued. The Federals retreated with a loss of 200 killed and prisoners. On the 10th of August, Rosecranz attacked Floyd's forces and a general engagement followed, lasting four hours, when night put an end to the action. Floyd took advantage of the darkness and fell back into the mountains. The Federal loss was 225, among which was Colonel Lowe, of the 12th Ohio, who fell at the head of his regiment.

GENERAL ROBERT E. LEE SENT TO WESTERN VIRGINIA.

Wise and Floyd both having shown themselves unable to hold a position in West Virginia, General Lee, the ablest officer in Virginia, marched at the head of 9,000 men against General Reynolds, who was lying with a considerable force at Cheat Mountain. The attack was made on the 14th of September, and after several hours' severe fighting

Lee was forced to retreat, leaving 100 dead upon the field. Among the latter was Colonel John Washington, a recent proprietor of Mount Vernon. Lee's army halted on the banks of Greenbrier river, and began to intrench itself. General Reynolds, after receiving reinforcements, set out on the 2d of October from Cheat Mountain with a force of 5,000 men to drive Lee from his position. Colonel Kimball, with the 14th Indiana, led the advance, while General Milroy, with a portion of his brigade, was to deploy to the left, drive in the pickets and force the Confederates within their intrenchment. At daylight he arrived at Greenbrier bridge and found it occupied. A charge was made, the bridge carried, and a crossing effected. Then began an artillery duel which fairly shook the surrounding mountains. Soon, however, three of Lee's guns were disabled, and he again retreated. The Federal loss was eight killed and thirty-two wounded.

Lee left General Johnston, of Georgia, with 2,000 men on the summit of the Alleghanies and continued his march to Staunton. Milroy marched against Johnston, taking with him the 13th Indiana and two other regiments, and on the 15th of December reached Camp Alleghany, where he found the Confederates strongly fortified. An engagement took place, the results of which were not advantageous to either side, the loss being about 130 on both sides. Milroy withdrew and fell back to Cheat Mountain. This practically put an end to the war in Western Virginia.

ALONG THE POTOMAC.

After the reverse at Bull Run, it became evident that a war of gigantic proportions was now in progress. Throughout the North regiments were equipped and hurried to the seat of war. Recruiting went on with equal rapidity in the Southern States, so that by the first of October two of the largest armies ever mustered on the continent were fronting each other on the banks of the Potomac, and it seemed as if another was to be added to the list of the great battles of the world. But such was not to be, for a masterly inactivity seemed to characterize both.

FIGHT AT BOLIVAR HEIGHTS.

The extreme left of the Confederate line now lay near Leesburg, on the Potomac. On the 8th of October, Major Gould crossed the river at Harpers Ferry for the purpose of seizing a quantity of wheat, and when about to recross, on the 16th, he was attacked by a force of Confederates on Bolivar Heights, and, at the same time, a battery of artillery opened fire from Loudon Heights, within cannon range of the Ferry. Then a cavalry charge was made, but was repulsed by the 13th Massachusetts regiment, under Colonel Schriber. Major Gould had sent for reinforcements, and Lieutenant Martin with a battery of artillery now arrived upon the scene. Unlimbering his guns in the street, he poured such a destructive fire upon the Heights that the line stationed there began to waver, and by a bayonet charge on the part of the Federals were compelled to retreat and leave the field, with a loss of 100 killed and wounded. A few days later an engagement took place at Balls Bluff, in which Colonel Baker, a United States ex-senator from Massachusetts, was killed and the Federal troops defeated with great slaughter.

DRAINSVILLE.

The battle of Drainsville, near Washington, took place on the 20th of December. It was the first engagement of any importance in which the army of the Potomac was successful. On the above date General Ord, with his brigade, advanced toward Drainsville for the purpose of securing forage for his animals. With him were the Pennsylvania Bucktails, commanded by Lieutenant-Colonel Kane, brother of E. K. Kane, the Arctic explorer, and an Eastern battery of light artillery. When near Drainsville they encountered a force about 6,000 strong. A battle ensued, which lasted about five hours, and resulted in a complete rout of the Confederates. Federal loss was sixty-seven, while that of the Confederates was 240. This, with the exception of a slight engagement at New Market bridge, near Newport News, was the last fighting in Virginia during the year 1861.

FORMATION OF THE NEW STATE OF WEST VIRGINIA.

We must now turn aside from the records of war, and notice the rise of a new commonwealth—the only one ever formed within the territory of an organized State.

As has been stated, the people of the western portion of Virginia were opposed to the sessation of the State; this was evidenced by the vote upon that question, a majority of which in all the western counties was against it, and in several the negative vote was almost unanimous. Soon after the election of 1860, the inhabitants of this section began to express their feelings upon the questions which then agitated the country.

The first meeting that was held to give expression to the sentiments of the people, took place in Preston county, on the 12th of November, 1860. Men of all shades of political opinion participated in the proceedings. Resolutions were adopted opposing sessation, and declaring that any attempt on the part of the State to sever her connection with the Union, would meet with the disapproval of the people of that county.

On the 24th of November, a meeting was held in Harrison county, which declared that they would exhaust all constitutional remedies for redress, before they would resort to any violent measures; that the ballot-box was the only medium known to the Constitution for a redress of grievances, and to that alone would they appeal. The people of Monongalia county convened at their court house on the 26th of November, and passed a series of resolutions declaring that the election of the candidates of the Republican party did not justify sessation, and that the Union as it was, was the best guarantee of the people's future welfare. A meeting of the people at the court house of Taylor county, on the 3d of December following, declared that they were opposed to any action looking to the dissolution of the Union for existing causes.

The citizens of Ohio county convened in the city of Wheeling on the 14th of the same month and adopted resolutions similar to the foregoing. In many other western counties meetings of like import and significance were held.

The Virginia Convention passed the Ordinance of Secession on the 17th of April, 1861, and then began a series of meetings and an expression of public sentiment, before unparalleled in the history of Virginia. All united in a solemn protest against the sessation of the State and asserted that the Union was the object of their undying attachment, and that they would cling to it, despite the efforts of the East to plunge them into the gulf of sessation and consequent ruin; that sessation was only unmitigated treason against the Constitution and the government of the United States; that Western Virginia, for a half century, had patiently submitted to the oppression of Eastern Virginia, but that now the measure of tyranny was full, and that if, as was claimed, sessation was the only remedy for supposed State wrongs, the day was not far distant when the West would arise in its majesty, sever all political and civil relations with the East, organize a new State, and remain firmly attached to the Union.

A mass meeting of the citizens of Taylor county, held on the 13th of April, declared that the government of the United States ought to be maintained, and all constitutional laws enforced; and if the eastern part of the State should secede from the Union, then they were in favor of establishing an independent government in the western portion of the State. Moved by a similar sentiment, the people of Wetzel county, on the 22d of the same month, resolved that if the State cast her fortunes with those of the Gulf States, then, as citizens of Western Virginia, they would deem it a duty to themselves and posterity to use such measures as would result in a division of the State.

VIRGINIA AND VIRGINIANS.

CONVENTION AT CLARKSBURG.

Up to this time all had been independent action on the part of the several counties, but now a united effort was to be made. On the 22d of April, 1861, a meeting of twelve hundred citizens, held under the auspices of John S. Carlisle, the late delegate from Harrison county in the Richmond convention, met at Clarksburg, and in a long preamble declared that the means resorted to by the secessionists to transfer the State from its allegiance to the Federal Government to the so-called Confederate States, was wholly unjustifiable, and resolved that they would resist such action to the last extremity. Before adjournment the convention recommended to the people in each of the counties composing Western Virginia, to appoint not less than five delegates of their "wisest, best and discreetest men," to meet in convention at Wheeling, on the 13th day of May following, "to determine upon such action as the people of Western Virginia should take in the present fearful emergency."

THE FIRST WHEELING CONVENTION.

In compliance with the foregoing, the delegates were chosen by the various counties, and the 13th day of May saw a swarming and excited multitude thronging the streets of Wheeling. The delegates convened at Washington Hall at 11 A. M., and the meeting was called to order by Chester D. Hubbard, of Ohio county, on whose motion William B. Zinn, of Preston county, was chosen temporary chairman, and George R. Latham, of Taylor county, was appointed temporary secretary. Rev. Peter T. Laishley, of Monongalia county, himself a delegate, then invoked Divine guidance in the deliberations of the convention. A committee on permanent organization, and also one on credentials, was appointed, after which the body adjourned to meet at 2 P. M.

Upon reassembling, the committee on permanent organization reported John W. Moss, of Wood county, for permanent president, and Colonel Charles B. Waggener, of Mason, Marshall M. Dent, of Monongalia, and J. G. Chandler, of Ohio county, secretaries. Two door-keepers and a sergeant-at-arms were then appointed. The committee on credentials reported accredited delegates from twenty-six counties, as follows: Hancock, Brooke, Ohio, Marion, Monongalia, Preston, Wood, Lewis, Ritchie, Harrison, Upshur, Gilmer, Wirt, Jackson, Mason, Wetzel, Pleasants, Barbour, Hampshire, Berkeley, Doddridge, Tyler, Taylor, Roane, Frederick, and Marshall.

A committee on State and Federal relations was appointed, consisting of the following named gentlemen: Campbell Tarr, Brooke county; W. T. Willey, Monongalia; John S. Carlisle, Harrison; J. J. Jackson, Wood; Charles Hooton, Preston; Daniel Lamb, Ohio; George McC. Porter, Hancock; Joseph H. Machir, Mason; D. D. Johnson, Tyler; James Scott, Jackson; G. W. Bier, Wetzel; R. C. Holliday, Marshall;

A. S. Withers, Lewis; E. T. Trayhorn, Wirt; F. H. Pierpont, Marion; S. Dayton, Barbour; G. S. Senseney, Frederick; J. S. Burdett, Taylor; A. R. McQuilkin, Berkeley; S. Cochran, Pleasants; J. E. Stump, Roane; S. Martin, Gilmer; A. B. Rohrbough, Upshur; O. D. Downey, Hampshire; Mr. Foley, Ritchie.

Everything was now in complete working order. The fact that the convention was divided upon the subject of immediate action very soon became apparent from the spirited discussion which characterized the early days of the session. One party, led by the Hon. John S. Carlisle, was in favor of an immediate division of the State, and the formation of a government for the counties represented, all offices to be filled by temporary appointment. Another party, headed by Hon. W. T. Willey, declared that this was but an informal meeting of the people, no action of which could be made binding upon them; that no vote had yet been taken upon the ordinance of secession, therefore the State of Virginia still had a government recognized by the Constitution of the United States; hence any action tending in the direction of a new government could not be other than revolutionary in its nature. An acrimonious debate continued throughout the second and third days, and it seemed that an adjournment would take place before the objects for which the body had met could be accomplished; but late at night the discussion was interrupted by the committee on State and Federal relations begging leave to report. Campbell Tarr, the chairman of said committee, read the report. It was a skillful production, a blending of all opinions, a happy mean between spasmodic disruption and authorized resistance. The first part was a review of the secession movement from its incipiency to that time. Then followed declarations of loyalty to the Union, which should continue on the part of the people here represented, despite all efforts of the east to drag them out of the Union. A recommendation was made to the people of the various counties, that, in the event of the ratification of the ordinance of secession, they appoint delegates on the 4th day of June to meet in a general convention on the 11th of the same month, at some place to be hereafter designated. A last suggestion was that a central committee, consisting of nine members, be appointed, with power to carry into effect the objects of the convention.

The report, after a short discussion, was almost unanimously adopted, but two votes being recorded against it. The central committee was then appointed, consisting of John S. Carlisle, James S. Wheat, Chester D. Hubbard, Francis H. Pierpont, Campbell Tarr, George R. Latham, Andrew Wilson, L. H. Woodward, and James H. Paxton. Prayer was then offered, imploring blessings upon the work performed. A thousand voices united in singing the "Star Spangled Banner," and the convention adjourned *sine die*.

VIRGINIA AND VIRGINIANS. 359

THE SECOND WHEELING CONVENTION — THE RESTORED GOVERNMENT.

On the 23d day of May, 1861, the vote was taken on the ordinance of secession. The result showed the sentiment of the people west of the Alleghanies. Out of about 44,000 votes polled in the counties now comprising West Virginia, 40,000 were recorded against secession. Delegates were elected on the 4th of June, and what is known as the second Wheeling convention met on the 11th of the same month at Washington Hall, in that city. Seventy-seven delegates, representing thirt-yfive counties, were present. The committee on permanent organization reported the names of Arthur J. Boreman, of Wood county, for president, and G. L. Cranmer, of Ohio county, for secretary. A committee consisting of thirteen members was appointed, to report business to the convention. The members of that committee, the report of which became the foundation for the new State, were as follows: Carlisle, of Harrison; Lamb, of Ohio; Pierpont, of Marion; Hagans, of Preston; Van Winkle, of Wood; Berkshire, of Monongalia; Polsley, of Mason; Boreman, of Wood; Caldwell, of Marshall; Frost, of Jackson; Porter, of Hancock; Farnsworth, of Upshur; and Copley, of Wayne.

On the third day they submitted a report entitled "*A Declaration of the People of Virginia, represented in convention at the city of Wheeling, Thursday, June 13, 1861.*" Among many other things set forth, it was declared that "the preservation of the dearest rights and liberties, and security in person and property, imperatively demand the reorganization of the government of the commonwealth." * * * "And that the offices of all who adhere to the said convention [that of Richmond], whether legislative, executive or judicial, are vacated."

The report was adopted on the 17th, and the convention at once proceeded to reorganize the government of Virginia.

On the 19th, an ordinance for the reorganization of the State government was passed, as follows:

"The people of the State of Virginia, by their delegates assembled in convention at Wheeling, do ordain as follows:

"1. A governor, lieutenant-governor and attorney-general for the State of Virginia, shall be appointed by this convention to discharge the duties and exercise the powers which pertain to their respective offices by the existing laws of the State, and to continue in office for six months, or until their successors be elected and qualified; and the general assembly is required to provide by law for an election of governor and lieutenant-governor by the people as soon as in their judgment such an election can be properly held." * * * * *

The following oath was prescribed to be taken by the various officers elected by the convention before entering upon the discharge of the duties of their respective offices:

"I solemnly swear (or affirm) that I will support the Constitution of the United States, and the laws made in pursuance thereof, as the supreme law of the land, anything in the constitution and laws of the State of Virginia, or in the ordinances of the convention which assembled at Richmond on the 13th of February, 1861, to the contrary notwithstanding; and that I will uphold and defend the government of Virginia as vindicated and restored by the convention which assembled at Wheeling on the 11th of June, 1861."

In compliance with the first clause of the ordinance, the convention, on the 20th of June, proceeded to the election of officers. Francis H. Pierpont, of Marion, was chosen governor of Virginia, and Daniel Polsley, of Mason, lieutenant-governor. On the 24th, James S. Wheat, of Ohio county, was chosen attorney-general.

The convention, having thus restored the government, elected a chief executive and provided for the election of all other officers pertaining to the State government, adjourned to meet again on the first Tuesday in August ensuing.

MEETING OF THE PROVISIONAL LEGISLATURE.

The third clause of the ordinance passed June the 19th, provided for the meeting of the General Assembly on the 1st day of July, the members of which had been duly chosen at the general election on the 23d day of May, and in pursuance of the ordinance that body convened at Wheeling on the day appointed. The session was held in the custom-house, in which the offices of the governor and other State officers had been located. Upon calling the roll, it was ascertained that there were thirty-one members present. A speaker and clerk were chosen, after which the governor's message was received. In it he reviewed, at considerable length, the action of the Richmond convention, the history of the movements which led to the reorganization of the State governments and his own election. He informed the house that he had entered into a correspondence with the President of the United States, and informed him of the circumstances surrounding the loyal government of Virginia, and had received from him, through the secretary of war, assurances that all constitutional aid would be promptly rendered.

Accompanying the message were copies of communications received from the Secretary of the Interior certifying to the apportionment of representation to which Virginia was entitled in the Thirty-eighth Congress, according to the census of 1860. The attention of the Assembly was called to the fact that the President, in a proclamation issued on the 4th inst., had declared vacant the seats of all representatives from Virginia in the Congress of the United States by reason of their active participation in the effort to overthrow the Federal government, and he recommended that the house proceed at once to fill such vacancies by

TOMB OF MARY, MOTHER OF WASHINGTON,
At Fredericksburg, Virginia.

the election of members who should at once apply for seats in the national Congress as representatives of Virginia under the restored government.

The General Assembly, on the 9th of July, went into an election, and on joint ballot elected L. A. Hagans, of Preston county, secretary of the commonwealth; Samuel Crane, of Randolph, auditor of public accounts, and Campbell Tarr, of Brooke, treasurer. They then proceeded to ballot for United States Senators, which resulted in the election of John S. Carlisle, of Harrison, and W. T. Willey, of Monongalia. They, together with the representatives from the three congressional districts west of the mountains, who had been elected at the same time the members of the General Assembly were chosen, at once proceeded to Washington, where "they were admitted to seats in the respective houses as senators and representatives from Virginia." On the 24th of July, the Assembly, having finished the business before it, adjourned.

Thus the machinery of the restored government was in complete working order; but this did not satisfy the people, many of whom had for years entertained the fond hope that at some time their relations with the east should be severed, and a new State, independent of Virginia, should rise west of the Alleghanies. All felt that the auspicious moment had now come, and it was impressed upon the

THIRD WHEELING CONVENTION,

Which convened on the 6th of August, 1861, that there was but one duty to perform, and that was to perfect the organization of a new State.

At this meeting a number of delegates from the Kanawha Valley counties, who had not attended the second convention, were present, and took an active part in the labor now to be performed, which was none other than the partition of the old State and the formation of a new one.

On the 20th an ordinance was passed, with the following preamble:

"Whereas, it is represented to be the desire of the people inhabiting the counties hereinafter mentioned, to be separated from this commonwealth, and to be erected into a separate State, and admitted into the Union of States, and become a member of the government of the United States."

The new State was to be called "Kanawha," the boundaries of which were to include the following counties, viz: Logan, Wyoming, Raleigh, Fayette, Nicholas, Webster, Randolph, Tucker, Preston, Monongalia, Marion, Taylor, Barbour, Upshur, Harrison, Lewis, Braxton, Clay, Kanawha, Boone, Wayne, Cabell, Putnam, Mason, Jackson, Roane,

Calhoun, Wirt, Gilmer, Ritchie, Wood, Pleasants, Tyler, Doddridge, Wetzel, Marshall, Ohio, Brooke and Hancock.

It was also provided that the boundaries might be so changed as to include within the boundaries of the proposed State the counties of Greenbrier, Pocahontas, Hampshire, Hardy, Morgan, Berkeley, and Jefferson, or either of them, or any other contiguous counties, in case a majority of the votes cast at an election to be held for the purpose, should declare their wish to become a part of the new State; and at the same time elect delegates to the proposed constitutional convention, which was to meet at Wheeling on the 26th of November, should a majority of the votes cast at an election to be held on the fourth Thursday in October be in favor of the formation of the new State. The convention, after submitting the question of the organization of the State to the people, adjourned on the 21st of August.

THE CONSTITUTIONAL CONVENTION.

The October election was held in nearly every county of the proposed State; 19,189 votes were polled, of which 18,408 were in favor of the new State, and 781 against it.

Delegates to the constitutional convention were chosen at the same time, and on the 26th of November, 1861, that body convened in the Federal court room at Wheeling, all the counties then within the limits of the proposed State being represented except Jefferson, Berkeley, Webster and Monroe. The session continued eighty-two days, during which time a constitution was framed and submitted to the people, to be voted upon on the 3d day of April, 1862. The convention adjourned on the 18th of February.

The constitution thus submitted was voted upon, on the day appointed, and resulted in its adoption by a vote of 18,862 for it, and 514 against it. By the census of 1860 it will be seen that the counties voting had a population of 334,921 whites, and 12,771 colored. The reader will have noticed the decrease in the number of votes polled at the above election, from that polled at the time of the vote polled upon the ordinance of secession, which was more than 54,000; but we must remember that up to this time 10,000 men from Western Virginia were enrolled in the Federal army, and several thousand had gone South, and were fighting the battles of the Confederacy. Hence the difference in the number of votes polled at the two elections.

THE NEW CONSTITUTION—THE WORK COMPLETED.

The General Assembly of the reorganized government convened on the 6th of May, 1862, and gave its formal assent to the formation of the new State of West Virginia within the territory of the State of Virginia, according to the provisions of the constitution, recently ratified by the people. A memorial, together with the bill granting assent to the erection of the State, and a copy of the donstitution, was transmitted to Congress, praying for the admission of West Virginia into the Union. Senators Carlisle and Willey presented the bill in the United States Senate on the 27th of May, 1862. No action was taken until December 31st, following, when it was again taken up and passed by both houses with the understanding that "West Virginia was and should be one of the members of the Federal Union" whenever she struck out from her constitution the seventh section, known as the Battelle provision for the gradual extinction of slavery within the State. On the 12th day of February, 1863, the convention reassembled and amended the constitution according to the requirements of Congress; submitted it to a vote of the people, who a second time ratified it by a majority of about 17,000. The result was certified to President Lincoln, and on the 19th of April he issued his proclamation to the effect that after sixty days "West Virginia should be one of the United States of America; admitted into the Union on an equal footing with the original States in all respects whatever."

The convention, before adjourning in February, provided that in case the revised constitution should be ratified, an election should be held on the fourth Thursday of May following, for the purpose of electing members of both houses of the Legislature, a Governor, and other State officers, Judges of the Supreme Court of Appeals, etc.

The election was held at the appointed time. Hon. Arthur I. Boreman, of Wood county, was chosen Governor, and thus became the first chief executive of West Virginia; Samuel Crane, of Randolph was elected Auditor; Campbell Tarr, of Brooke, Treasurer; J. Edgar Boyers, of Tyler, Secretary of State, and A. Bolton Caldwell, of Ohio, Attorney-General. Hons. Ralph L. Berkshire, of Monongalia, William A. Harrison, of Harrison, and James H. Brown, of Kanawha, were elected Judges of the Supreme Court of Appeals.

When, therefore, the sixty days after the President's proclamation had elapsed, on the 20th of June, 1863, West Virginia, "the daughter of the rebellion," born amid the throes of civil war, entered upon her career as one of the members of the Sisterhood of States.

THE RECORD OF WAR AGAIN.

We have seen West Virginia—the daughter, become "the adopted child of the Republic," and we must now return to Virginia, the mother, whom we left at the close of the year 1861, amid all the horrors of a sanguinary war.

1862.

During the early months of this year but few military movements occurred in Virginia. The first action of the year occurred at Huntsville, in Nicholas county, January 3d, whither General Milroy had sent Major Webster, with a force of seven hundred and thirty-eight men, to destroy a quantity of Confederate stores known to be deposited at that place. The work was successfully performed, six buildings filled with provisions being burned.

On the 4th, General Jackson, stationed at Winchester, in the Shenandoah Valley, made a dash toward the Potomac for the purpose of tearing up the Baltimore & Ohio railroad. The Federals were driven north of the river, and Jackson, after destroying several miles of the road, fell back toward the valley.

An engagement took place on the 7th between a portion of General Kelly's forces lying at Romney, in Hampshire county, and a body of Confederates at Blues Gap. Colonel Dunning, with the 5th Ohio, won the day. The loss on either side was slight.

THE CAPITAL OF VIRGINIA BECOMES THE CAPITAL OF THE CONFEDERACY.

In the meantime the seat of government of the Confederacy had been transferred from Montgomery, Alabama, to Richmond; and here, on the 22d day of February--Washington's birthday--Jefferson Davis, of Mississippi, and Alexander H. Stephens, of Georgia, having been unanimously chosen President and Vice-President, respectively, by the votes of the convention of every Southern State, were duly inaugurated for the term of six years. The oath of office was administered to the President by the Hon. J. D. Halyburton, chief Confederate Judge, and to Alexander H. Stephens by the President of the Confederate Senate. On the next day President Davis sent to the Senate for confirmation, a list of cabinet appointments, as follows: Secretary of State, Judah P. Benjamin, of Louisiana; Secretary of War, George W. Randolph, of Virginia; Secretary of the Navy, S. R. Mallory; Secretary of the Treasury, C. G. Memminger, of South Carolina; Postmaster-General, Mr. Henry, of Kentucky; Attorney-General, Herschel V. Johnson, of Georgia; all of which were speedily confirmed. Thus, on the soil of Virginia, was located the capital of the then existing Southern Republic. The city thus occupied had been the seat of government of Virginia for a period of eighty-five years, the State troops, arms and ammunition, and public records having been removed from Williamsburg to that place in 1777, to prevent their falling into the possession of the British army, then ravaging Virginia. In May, 1779, the Assembly passed an act making it the permanent capital of the State. It was called Richmond because of the fancied resemblance of its location to that of Richmond-on-the-Thames, in England.

Six days after the inauguration ceremonies, on the 1st of March, the right wing of the army of the Potomac, commanded by General Banks, crossed the river, advanced into Virginia, and occupied Bolivar, Charlestown and Martinsburg. This was the first movement of a series in which the Federal armies were intended to approach Richmond and attack its defenses. Banks continued his march in the direction of Winchester, where Stonewall Jackson was posted with a considerable force.

On the 11th of March the Confederates evacuated Manassas and fell back beyond the Rappahannock, and the Federals at once took possession of the abandoned position. It was expected that Banks would drive Jackson toward Richmond, and that the army at Manassas would cut off his retreat, and thus capture his entire force; but instead the wily Jackson retreated up the Valley, closely pursued by Banks. At Strasburg he halted and took a strong position at New Market, within supporting distance of Johnston.

BATTLE OF WINCHESTER.

Banks now fell back to Winchester, and was in turn pursued by Jackson. Here, on the 22d of March, was fought one of the most fiercely contested battles of the war. Both armies exhibited the most determined bravery. The 5th Ohio had five color-bearers killed. The battle waged until nightfall, when the Confederates withdrew, leaving the field in possession of their enemies. The loss on both sides has been variously estimated at from 900 to 1300, of which the greater part was that of the Confederates.

During the night Jackson received a reinforcement of five regiments of infantry and two batteries of artillery. With his forces thus augmented, he determined to risk another battle, and accordingly formed his lines near the village of Kernstown. Early on the morning of the 23d, Banks sent forward General Tyler's brigade to open the action. He was supported by two other brigades of Ohio and Michigan troops, all of which soon became engaged. Here again were re-enacted the scenes of the previous day. The result was similar. The Federals were again victorious, completely routing the forces of Jackson, who now retreated rapidly towards Staunton.

OPERATIONS ON THE PENINSULA.

After the evacuation of Manassas by the Confederates, they took position near Yorktown on the peninsula, and erected the strongest fortifications yet built in the New World. The early part of April saw the Federal army, 100,000 strong, anchored off Fortress Monroe, and McClellan found that the fortifications extended entirely across the peninsula, from the York to the James river, and he at once concluded that one of two things was certain: here the Confederates could be cooped up on the peninsula, and be compelled to surrender, or they must evacuate the stronghold, and take refuge behind their batteries at Richmond. The forces were landed, and after an examination of the works, McClellan was confident that with his artillery—a thousand pieces—he should be able to level these works. He had seen the telling effects of artillery upon similar ones at Sebastopol during the Crimean war. General Robert E. Lee, of Virginia, the ablest leader of the Southern armies, knew the same, and at once recommended to the government the evacuation of the peninsula. Accordingly on the 3d of May the whole Confederate army, numbering 70,000 men, marched out on the road to Richmond, and left these works, as they had left those of Manassas, in possession of their enemies. A rapid pursuit was at once begun, and, on the 4th, General Stoneman's command came up with the rear of the retreating army at Williamsburg, about fifty-eight miles from Richmond. Here the Confederates made a stand, and, with the pertinacity of veterans, disputed the Federal advance. It was the 5th of May, at seven o'clock in the morning, when the battle began, and it raged until late in the evening, when Lee's forces were again compelled to continue their march toward their capital, leaving 700 dead on the field. The loss of the Federals was 1100.

On the next day a bloody engagement occurred at West Point, on the York river, between the forces of General Franklin and a body of Confederates under General Magruder. After a spirited contest of three hours, victory again declared in favor of the Federals, their loss being 80 killed, 300 wounded, and 500 taken prisoners. The loss on the other side was about 900.

McClellan continued his march toward Richmond; at the same time a fleet of gunboats entered the Chesapeake Bay for the purpose of cooperating with the land forces in the attack upon the Confederate capital. On the 15th of May the fleet steamed up the James within eight miles of Richmond, where the guns of Fort Darling opened fire, and the Federals met their first reverse before Richmond. After a splendid artillery fight of five hours the gunboats were compelled to withdraw down the river to their former anchorage. This did not delay for a moment the progress of the land forces, and on the 20th of May, McClellan occupied a position within eight miles of Richmond.

In the meantime General Banks had again marched into the Shenandoah Valley, where he was opposed by a force of about 25,000 men under Generals Early and Jackson. For weeks the possession of the "Garden of Virginia" was disputed by the contending armies; but on the 25th of May, Banks was attacked, defeated at Winchester, and forced to abandon the valley. His retreating columns were closely pursued to Williamsport, where they crossed the Potomac and took refuge in Maryland.

TIDEWATER VIRGINIA MADE THE BATTLE-GROUND.

In all historical struggles of the past between nations, it is exhibited that the final contest has been limited to a few localities, in which the resources of the combatants were concentrated and the operations more colossal than any preceding them. This was exemplified in the late civil war, the crisis being reached in 1862, and the period was signalized by contests more sanguinary than had ever before been witnessed on the American continent. The first of these encounters between the opposing armies before Richmond was the

BATTLE OF SEVEN PINES,

On the 31st of May, in which the Federal loss was 6,000 greater than the Confederate, with arms, stores, etc. A demonstration by McClellan on the next day which was repulsed by General Pickett, magnified in the Federal reports as the battle of *Fair Oaks*, was an action of no consequence. Our limits forbid a minute detail of the events of the momentous three years succeeding, and confine us to a general view of the war in Virginia. On the first of June the armies confronting each other on her soil aggregated quite 200,000 men. The struggle around the beleaguered capital of the Confederacy commenced with the

SEVEN DAYS' BATTLES

In the region of the Chickahominy, which were inaugurated on the 26th of June, by the

BATTLE OF MECHANICSVILLE.

General Johnston had been severely wounded at Seven Pines, and General R. E. Lee was now in chief command of the Confederate forces around Richmond. General McClellan had recently assumed the command of the army of the Potomac, then concentrated on the banks of the Chickahominy.

In order that the reader may better understand the movements now to be noticed he should study carefully the geography of the Tidewater district of Virginia. By an inspection of the map it will be seen that the Chickahominy river has its source in the north-western portion of Henrico county, whence it flows in a south-western direction—its course in the neighborhood of Richmond closely resembling the arc of a circle—until it reaches the south-eastern portion of Charles City county, where it suddenly turns to the south and flows into the James, about seventy-five miles below Richmond. Mechanicsville is situated on the northeast bank of this river, distant five miles from Richmond, and marks the point of McClellan's nearest approach to that city.

At the time of the engagement a portion of the Federal army had crossed the Chickahominy and held a fortified position on the Williamsburg road, but far the greater portion lay on the north side, the line extending many miles up and down the stream.

It was at 3 P. M. Thursday, June 26th, that Major-General Jackson—flushed with recent victories in the Shenandoah Valley—took up his line of march from Ashland and proceeded south-east through the country lying between the Chickahominy and Pamunkey rivers. Brigadier-General Branch, crossing the former, directed his march so as to form a junction with the corps of General A. P. Hill. Jackson kept well to the Pamunkey until he reached the village of Raleigh, when he turned suddenly to the west and attacked the fortified Federal position at Mechanicsville; at the same time General Hill with a force of fourteen thousand joined in the attack, and, after a short but desperate contest, night settled down upon the scene, both armies holding their position, but under cover of darkness the Federals withdrew and fell back down the river to Powhite swamp.

Friday morning dawned clear and bright, and the sun arose to shed his rays upon such a scene as had not yet been witnessed on this continent. The way had been cleared at Mechanicsville, and General Longstreet's *corps d' armée,* composed of his veteran division of the Old Guard of the Army of the Potomac and General D. H. Hill's command, emerged from the forest on the south side of the Chickahominy and crossed that river. A general advance on the part of the Confederates now began; the command of General A. P. Hill in the centre marching in the direction of Cold Harbor; Generals Longstreet and D. H. Hill on the right, proceeding down the Chickahominy, and the veteran Jackson marching far to the left, but converging toward the river.

The position of the Federal army was now a peculiar one: that portion lying south of the river was confronted by the command of General Magruder, while that on the north side had fallen back to a new line of defenses, and here McClellan had decided to make a decisive battle.

Jackson's arrival at Cold Harbor was announced by the roar of his guns, which was the signal of battle, and in compliance with that signal the forces of Generals Lee, Longstreet, A. P. Hill and D. H. Hill were simultaneously engaged. From four o'clock until eight, the battle raged with terrible fury, and a wonderful display of daring and intrepidity on the part of the Confederates. At last the Federals gave way, and night covered the retreat of their broken and shattered lines to the south bank of the Chickahominy.

A memorable part of the day's fighting was that known as the

BATTLE OF GAINES MILLS,

And the repeated charges made here deserve to rank with the most glorious deeds of the war. The corps of General A. P. Hill had made the first charge upon the Federal intrenchments at this place, and a terrible struggle had continued throughout the day, neither side seeming to have the advantage—the Federals holding their position, but powerless to keep at bay the Confederates, whose dauntless successive charges were ineffectual to carry the works. An eye-witness says that Hill's division made repeated charges, but were as often driven back by the murderous sheet of fire from the formidable works. Twenty-six pieces of artillery were belching forth their thunders, and a perfect leaden hail-storm fell thick and fast around them. In front stood earth-works stretching for miles away; and drawn up in line of battle were three full divisions, commanded by Generals McCall, Porter and Sedgwick. Banners everywhere filled the air; artillery vomited forth incessant volleys of grape, canister and shell, and the angel of death hovered over the field amid the sulphurous atmosphere of battle. But at last as the sun was descending behind the western hills Pickett's brigade, from Longstreet's division, came to Hill's support. Then came Whiting's division, consisting of the "Old Third" and the Texan brigades; they advanced at a double quick, charged the batteries, and drove the Federals from the intrenchments which they had defended with such obstinacy throughout the day. Belonging to the last mentioned brigade was the 4th Texas regiment commanded by a gallant Virginian, Colonel Bradfute Warwick; this was his last charge; just as the works were carried his breast was pierced by a minie-ball, and he fell to rise no more. Thus ended the second of the terrible Seven Days. Skirmishing was kept up during Saturday, and on Sunday the 29th was fought the

BATTLE OF SAVAGES STATION.

On the morning of this, the fourth day, a considerable body of the Federals were discovered occupying a strong natural position at the place named, on the York River Railroad. The division of General McLaws, consisting of Kershaw's and Semmes' brigades, supported by General Griffith's brigade, from Magruder's division, made the attack at one o'clock, and were received by a furious cannonade from a park of field pieces. Kemper's battery was ordered to the front, and after a splendid artillery duel which fairly shook the surrounding country, the

EARLY SEAL OF WILLIAM AND MARY COLLEGE, VIRGINIA.
The first established Institution of Learning in America.

Federals were once more forced to retreat. Early in the action General Griffith, a brave and meritorious officer from Mississippi, was struck by a fragment of a shell and instantly killed. He was the only general officer lost by the Confederates during that sanguinary week. The gallant 10th Georgia led the charge, and its depleted ranks told but too well of the raking fire to which it had been exposed.

THE BATTLE OF FRAYSERS FARM.

Monday was the fifth in the bloody list, and on that day was fought the battle known as Fraysers Farm. At daybreak the whole Confederate army was moving in pursuit of McClellan's retreating regiments. D. H. Hill, Whiting, and Ewell, under the command of Jackson, passed the Chickahominy at Grapevine Bridge, and marched along the Williamsburg road; while Longstreet, A. P. Hill, Huger and Magruder followed by the way of the Charles City road, with the design of intercepting the retreating columns. This disposition of the troops soon brought General Longstreet's division in front of the Federals. He was supported by Hill's division, consisting of six brigades. When he came up with the Federals, he found that they had taken position about five miles north-east of Darbytown, on the New Market road, the immediate vicinity being locally known as Fraysers Farm. The attack was at once brought on by the division of General Hill, and for three dreadful hours it is doubtful if on any one of the bloody fields of Virginia more heroic bravery was ever witnessed than was displayed by both armies. The roar of artillery and the rattle of musketry resounded far and wide, the air was filled with the missiles of death, and every spot presented a sight of ghastly destruction and horror. The dead and wounded were strewn thickly upon the field. But at last, above the roar and din of battle, came the orders along the Federal lines to retreat. No order was ever obeyed with more alacrity upon any field. In three minutes the shattered ranks were once more in full retreat, and the Confederate forces occupied the field and rested for the day. The sixth day, Tuesday, was to become memorable because of the terrible

BATTLE OF MALVERN HILL.

Early Tuesday morning, the sixth day in the awful series, McClellan's forces continued their retreat in a south-western direction toward his gunboats in the James. No sooner was the movement discovered than the Confederates began the pursuit. General Magruder was ordered to march by the Quaker road, and take position on the right of Jackson, but owing to a misunderstanding as to which was this road, the wrong route was taken, and, by the necessary change, his troops were formed on the right wing of Huger instead of that of Jackson, as at first designed.

The Federal commander having learned from the rapid march of the Confederates that he must fight again before he could reach the naval force lying in Turkey Island bend of the James, took position on an eminence known as Malvern Hill, upon the summit and declivities of which he placed in position his batteries, supported by strong columns of infantry. General Magruder advanced to the attack, shelling the woods and swamps as he proceeded, and at 5 o'clock P. M., when he had reached a point sufficiently near, he gave the order to charge and drive the Federals from their position. The order was received with a shout, and instantly the entire command were crossing the plain which lay at the base of the hill at a full run. But now, had that hill been torn asunder by some mighty volcanic force, the deep intonations could scarce have been greater. One hundred pieces of artillery opened a simultaneous fire and belched forth a murderous storm of grape and canister which swept the charging columns with the most terrible effect. Officers and men fell by the hundred; but yet unwavering, that charging column rushed on until two-thirds of the distance across the field had been passed. But wholesale carnage now prevailed on every hand. No body of men could stand before so withering a fire, and the column gave way and took refuge in the woods near by. Twice again those charging squadrons presented a living wall to that deadly fire, and twice again were they forced back. Around that hill was a steady flame, and at sunset it quivered with the terrific concussion of artillery and huge explosions. Shells were flying in every direction and bursting into deadly iron hail. Columns of black smoke shot skyward and darkened the air. But the day waned, the battle abated, and both armies rested on their arms and upon the field. That night a sulphurous smoke hung around the summit of Malvern Hill and settled away in dense columns over the valley of the historic James. Soon dark, ominous clouds covered the sky and the rain descended in torrents, which washed the blood-stained slopes of the little hill, carrying the sanguinary tide into the copses and woodlands which surrounded the base below. As twilight began to streak the eastern sky, the Confederate officers arose ready to renew the attack, but, upon turning their eyes to the hill from which they had been repulsed, they were filled with inexpressible astonishment. No enemy was there: the volcano was still, and McClellan's army was already far away on its

RETREAT TO HARRISONS LANDING.

In less than two hours after the roar of artillery had died away, the entire Federal army was stealing away from its enemy, and at midnight it presented all the confusion of a fleeing and routed army; and although the distance to Harrisons Landing was but seven miles, the rear of that broken and dispirited army did not reach its destination until noon of the next day. The mud was in many places more than ankle-deep. This prevented the Confederates from bringing up their artillery, and this fact alone, doubtless, saved McClellan's army from complete destruction.

On the 8th of July the Confederates returned to Richmond, and the Federals lay at Harrisons Landing until the 4th of August, when, as we shall see, it became necessary for them to move again. The terrible seven days were past and the Peninsular Campaign ended; and what were the results? McClellan reached the banks of the Chickahominy with 159,500 men, and ten days later, when he reached Harrisons Landing, he telegraphed to the Secretary of War that he presumed he had not "over 50,000 men left with his colors;" but on the 7th of July, when President Lincoln visited the camp, he found 86,000 men on the field, thus showing a loss of 73,500 men in ten days. General Lee, in his report to the Confederate Secretary of War, said:

"The siege of Richmond has been raised, and the object of a campaign, which had been prosecuted after months of preparation at an enormous expenditure of men and money, is completely frustrated. More than 10,000 prisoners, including officers of rank, fifty-two pieces of artillery, and more than 35,000 stand of small arms were captured. The stores and supplies of every description which fell into our hands were great in amount and value, but small in comparison with those destroyed by the enemy. His losses in battle exceeded our own, as attested by the thousands of dead and wounded left on every field, while his subsequent inaction shows in what condition the survivors reached the protection to which they fled."

As before mentioned, on the 4th of August McClellan received orders from Washington to remove his army to Acquia creek to aid in repelling the Confederate movement toward the National Capital. The bulk of his army removed to Fortress Monroe, which place he left on the 23d of August, and reached Acquia creek the next day.

BATTLE OF CEDAR MOUNTAIN.

No sooner had the Washington Government learned of the reverses on the Peninsula, than General Pope was sent to Virginia to occupy the Shenandoah Valley. His advance consisted of two divisions under command of General Banks. General Lee, ever vigilant, sent a strong force to repel this invasion, and on the evening of the 8th of August a portion of General Jackson's corps, consisting of the 1st, 2d and 3d brigades, commanded by General Charles S. Winder, forded the Rapidan river and advanced into Culpeper county. The next morning it was reported that the Federals were advancing to the attack, and Ewell's division moved out three miles on the road leading from Orange

Court House to Culpeper Court House, where it took position, with the left flank resting on South Mountain.

At 12 M. cannonading began; at 3 P. M. General Early's brigade of Ewell's division made a circuit through the woods and attacked the Federals on the right, the 13th Virginia regiment marching in the advance. At 4 P. M. the action became general, and as General Jackson's division, under command of General Winder, was advancing to the attack, it was subjected to a galling fire poured forth with great precision from the mountain side. General Winder had his left arm shattered, and a few minutes later received a wound in the side, from which he died in an hour. The battle raged until nightfall and victory seemed to hang in the balance, but just as the full-orbed moon was lighting up the mountain tops, the Federals gave way and retreated, leaving their dead and wounded upon the field.

SECOND BATTLE OF MANASSAS.

After the battle of Cedar Mountain, the Federals returned to the Potomac river, and Jackson took position on the already historic plains of Manassas, where, on the 27th of August, 1862, the soil was a second time bathed in the best blood of the nation. On the morning of that day, General Taylor's brigade of Major-General Slocum's division of the Army of the Potomac, composed of the 1st, 2d, 3d, and 4th New Jersey regiments, proceeded by rail from Camp Ellsworth, near Alexandria, and reached Manassas about 11 o'clock A. M. Upon arriving, General Taylor marched his men to the summit of the hill above the valley of Bull Run, when he encountered a skirmish line, which fell back before him. He continued onward until near the Junction, where his command was met by a heavy enfilading fire of artillery. Unable to withstand it, he fell back and took shelter behind the crest of a ridge, but from which he was soon driven, and forced to a precipitate flight in the direction of Fairfax. The Confederates followed in hot pursuit, which was kept up until the fugitive army was beyond Centreville. General Taylor himself, his son, of his staff, and his nephew, were all severely wounded. Thus ended the second battle of Manassas —not on such a gigantic scale, but in as complete a rout as the first.

GENERAL LORING IN THE KANAWHA VALLEY.

It was now September, and the Federal army had been driven completely out of Virginia. General Loring was sent to the Kanawha Valley to take possession of that great salt-producing region. On the 10th he reached Fayette Court House, where he found the Federals posted in considerable force. An attack was at once made, and after an engagement lasting six hours, the place was captured, the Federals falling back to Cotton Hill, where they made a stand; but after a few hours' fighting the next day, they were driven again, and this time continued their retreat to Charleston, the county-seat of Kanawha. General Loring followed on down the Kanawha river, and two days later occupied Charleston, from which the Federals had fled after firing it. At Point Pleasant they were largely reinforced, and marching back to Charleston, compelled General Loring, whose forces were greatly inferior, to evacuate the town and fall back to Staunton, in Augusta county.

GENERAL LEE IN MARYLAND.

The progress of events, now, for the first time during the struggle, leads us to a new theater of war within the recognized dominion of the Federal Government.

On the 4th of September General Lee took the offensive, and leaving on his right Arlington Heights, whither the shattered forces of General Pope had been driven from the valley, crossed the Potomac river and entered Maryland. Two objects were in view: the first, the capture of Harpers Ferry; and the second, to test the spirit of the Marylanders, and thus learn whether their proffered aid in support of the Confederacy could be relied upon. Attention was diverted from this expedition by a demonstration upon Pennsylvania, which so alarmed its governor, Curtin, that he called out the entire available force of the State, and made every preparation for defense. During the consequent excitement which prevailed throughout the Northern States, General Lee was in reality directing his movements against Virginia, and for the more effectual accomplishment of his purpose, divided his force into three corps, commanded respectively by Generals Jackson, Longstreet and Hill. The first recrossed the Potomac at Williamsport, and having occupied Martinsburg, passed rapidly to the south of Harpers Ferry, the object being the capture of the arms and stores there. In the meanwhile the commands of Hill and Longstreet were stationed to cover the movements of Jackson, and thus hold at bay the forces of McClellan, which were marching to the relief of Harpers Ferry, then held by a force of ten or twelve thousand men under General Miles. General Lee, foreseeing that the design of the Federal officers was to attack and defeat the Confederates in detail before their forces could be reunited, to frustrate this expectation, sent the division of General D. H. Hill to take a position at the mountain post known as Boonesboro Gap. Here, on the 14th of September, was fought the

ARMORIAL BOOK-PLATE

Of Colonel WILLIAM BYRD, of "Westover," James River, who founded Richmond in 1737.

BATTLE OF SOUTH MCUNTAIN.

At 8 A. M. of that day, General Cox's division, of Reno's corps, moved up the country road leading toward the summit, which in the meantime had been occupied by General Hill, and the conflict at once began. The brigade of General Garland, of Virginia, received the first fire, and its brave commander fell, fatally pierced by a musket ball, and very nearly at the same moment General Reno, a distinguished Federal officer, was mortally wounded, dying upon the field. The battle continued to rage with unabated fury, and reinforcements to arrive and engage at once in the deadly fray. That morning the corps of General Longstreet was lying at Hagerstown, distant fourteen miles from the scene of action. Hurrying forward with all speed, it reached and joined the wearied ranks of Hill at 3 P. M., and an hour later the brigades were in position, and that of General Toombs engaged. Evans occupied the extreme left, Drayton the right, and Hood, with the "ragged Texans," the center. At the same hour the Federals received powerful reinforcements. Hooker's corps of Burnside's column moved to the right, Meade's division to the left, and Rickett's to the center. The first was supported by Patrick, the second by Doubleday, and the third by Phelps. It was a living human wall against which no force could prevail, and at dark the Confederates withdrew from the field, but they had accomplished their object—they had held the entire army of McClellan, outnumbering them five to one, back, while General Jackson succeeded in the

CAPTURE OF HARPERS FERRY.

At midnight on the 14th, Jackson massed his batteries on the heights overlooking Harpers Ferry, and at daylight on the morning of the 15th opened a fire which fairly shook the surrounding mountains. Just at sunrise General Miles, the Federal commander, was struck by a shell and his left leg carried away. At twenty minutes past seven the white flag was waving over the Federal position, and a few minutes later Miles surrendered 11,583 men, 73 pieces of artillery, 13,000 small arms, 200 wagons, and an immense quantity of supplies. But Jackson did not wait to receive the surrender; leaving that to Hill, he hurried across the Potomac into Maryland to join Lee, and assist him at the

BATTLE OF ANTIETAM, OR SHARPSBURG,

Which was fought two days later, on the 17th. Sharpsburg is ten miles north of Harpers Ferry, and eight west of Boonesboro, on the bank of Antietam creek, a sluggish stream emptying into the Potomac eight miles above Harpers Ferry. Here, on the morning of the 17th, General Lee lay with a force of 45,000 men. The Federals were commanded by McClellan in person, and consisted of the entire command of Burnside, McDowell's corps, now under the command of Hooker; Sumner's corps, Franklin's corps, Banks' corps, commanded by Williams, and Sykes' division of Fitz John Porter's corps.

Lee looked anxiously for the arrival of the divisions of McLaws, R. H. Anderson, A. P. Hill and Walker, but they did not come up until late in the day. At dawn the work of carnage began, and continued for twelve hours; 200,000 men struggled for the mastery. Blood flowed in streams, and the field was strewn far and wide with the dead and dying; the deathly grapple was yet indecisive, and at sunset when the worn armies desisted from strife one of the best examples of a drawn battle which history records was presented. Both armies rested upon the field that night, and when on the next morning the Confederates fell back across the Potomac to Shepherdstown, Virginia, McClellan's army was too much demoralized to follow.

The Federal force actually engaged numbered 87,164, of which 4,320 were cavalry; their loss was 2,010 killed, 9,416 wounded, and 1,043 missing—a total of 12,469. The Confederates had during the day 70,000 men engaged, and left upon the field 3,000 dead, and 2,000 severely wounded. Of the killed on both sides many rotted in the sun, and, long after, their bones were bleaching on the mountain sides and in the valley of the little stream.

FROM THE POTOMAC TO FREDERICKSBURG.

For many days after the battle of Antietam the Federal army exhibited a "masterly inactivity." The ever-vigilant Lee was being reinforced, and was rapidly remobilizing his army and getting ready for his adversary, when he should once more invade the soil of Virginia. McClellan's force on the 1st of October numbered 150,000 men, and on the 6th Halleck telegraphed him, saying: "The President directs that you cross the Potomac and give battle to the enemy or drive him South. Your army must move while the roads are good." But two weeks passed away, and still no advance was made. Halleck once more telegraphed him: "The President does not expect impossibilities, but this good weather must not be wasted in inactivity." November 1st the entire force once more crossed the Potomac and entered Virginia. It moved leisurely south along the eastern base of the Blue Ridge, while Lee kept up a parallel movement on the west side. On the 7th a heavy snow storm set in. Everything betokened the beginning of winter. "Patience ceased to be a virtue" with the authorities at Washington, and that night at 12 o'clock Lincoln ordered McClellan to turn over the command of the army to General Burnside. The new commander determined to advance at once to Fredericksburg, masking his intention by a feint towards Gordonsville. Lee readily interpreted his action, and while Burnside marched along the north bank of the Rappahannock to Falmouth, he continued down the south bank and took position at Fredericksburg. Here he destroyed the bridges, and prevented the crossing of Burnside until he had time to surround himself with fortifications.

Fredericksburg lay midway between the contending armies, and it was evident that its destruction was sealed whenever either army should enter it.

THE BATTLE OF FREDERICKSBURG.

On the morning of the 10th of December Burnside's pontoon bridges arrived from Washington, and on the next day an effort was made to cross the river in front of the town, but the fire from the Confederate sharpshooters was persistent and directed with such unerring precision that the place was abandoned; but on the 12th the Federals succeeded in crossing three miles further down the river. Lee was awaiting the advance with 80,000 men lying behind the fortifications. "Stonewall" Jackson commanded on the right, and Longstreet on the left. Of the Federal force, Franklin was on the left, Hooker in the center, and Sumner on the right. The battle began at 11 o'clock A. M.: the first attack was made on the position of General Jackson by Meade with a brigade belonging to Franklin's grand division. It went into the charge with 4,500 men, and was instantly hurled back, leaving on the field 1,760 dead and wounded. The battle raged until nightfall, when Burnside having been repulsed at every point of attack was forced to recross the river, and on the next morning to abandon his position and fall back to Falmouth. His loss was 13,711, while that of the Confederates was only 5,309. The year 1862 closed, and left the two armies lying as at the close of the battle. Here they went into winter-quarters, and Burnside having proven himself no more satisfactory to the Washington Government than his predecessor, was soon after superseded in the command by Major-General Hooker, who gloried in the sobriquet of "Fighting Joe."

THE ARMY OF NORTH-WESTERN VIRGINIA AT THE CLOSE OF THE SECOND YEAR'S WAR.

As the year closed, it was asserted both in the North and South that General Lee's army was rapidly dwindling away from desertion. This elicited a reply from the Commander-in-Chief, in which he likened the sufferings of that army to those of the French in their retreat from Moscow, and closed with the tribute: "This army cut and fought its way to the Potomac, crossed that stream, moved on to Frederick and Hagerstown, had a heavy engagement at Boonesboro, another at Crampton's Gap, fought the greatest pitched battle of the war at Antietam, and then recrossed the Potomac into Virginia. During all this time, covering the full space of a month, the troops rested but four days. And let it be always remembered to their honor that of the men who performed this wonderful feat, one-fifth were barefooted, one-half in rags, and the whole half-famished. * * * * Their difficulties were increased by the fact that cooking utensils in many cases had been left behind, as well as everything else that would impede their movements. It was not unusual to see a company of starving men have a barrel of flour distributed to them which it was utterly impossible for them to convert into bread with the means and in the time allowed them.

"Do you wonder, then, that there should have been stragglers from the army? That brave and true men should have fallen out from sheer exhaustion, or in their efforts to obtain a mouthful to eat along the roadsides? Or that many seasoned veterans—the conquerors in the Valley, at Richmond and at Manassas—should have succumbed to disease, and been forced back to the hospital? * * * * That there has been unnecessary straggling is readily admitted, but in a large majority of cases the men have only to point to their bleeding feet, tattered garments, and gaunt frames for an answer to the unjust charge. No army on this continent has ever accomplished as much or suffered as much as the Army of Northern Virginia within the last three months. At no period during the first Revolutionary war, not even at Valley Forge, did our forefathers in arms encounter greater hardships or endure them more uncomplainingly."

HOOKER HALTS ON THE BANKS OF THE RAPPAHANNOCK.

General Hooker took command of the army, but no advance was made; the condition of the army and the long winter were his excuses, but spring opened and but one engagement broke the long silence of the lines along the banks of the Rappahannock.

That was on the 17th of March, when a Federal force of 3,000 crossed the river at Kelley's Ford and advanced to within six miles of Culpeper Court House, when they were engaged by the brigade of General Fitzhugh Lee. The engagement continued some hours, but at last the Federals were driven from the field after having inflicted a loss of one hundred upon the Confederates, among which number was the gallant Pelham, of Alabama, the "boy Major." He was but twenty-two years of age, and had participated in all the battles of Virginia. His remains were taken to Richmond, where for awhile they lay in state in the Capitol, where they were covered with floral tributes.

THE BATTLES OF THE RAPPAHANNOCK, CHANCELLORSVILLE AND FREDERICKSBURG.

It was now the month of April, and Hooker, the successor of Burnside, busied himself with the reorganization of his powerful army. Its grand divisions were substituted by seven corps: the 1st (Reynolds), 2d (Couch), 3d (Sickles), 5th (Meade), 6th (Sedgwick), 11th (Howard), and 12th (Slocum). His forces numbered 120,000 infantry and artillery, 13,000 cavalry, and 400 pieces of artillery. Confronting him on the south side of the river lay the Army of Northern Virginia, 62,000 strong. It consisted of Jackson's corps in four divisions, commanded respectively by A. P. Hill, Rodes, Colston and Early; two divisions of Longstreet's corps, those of Anderson and McLaws; Longstreet himself, with the remainder of his command, having been sent to the south side of James river. Of Lee's force, the cavalry numbered 3,000 men.

The 27th of April at length arrived, and it seemed that the "grand hesitation" was at an end, for Hooker on that day ordered a general advance. With a view of concealing his real intention he sent Sedgwick, 30,000 strong, to make a feint of crossing the river at Burnside's Ford, three miles below Fredericksburg, while he was to move secretly and rapidly to the right of his column, and, crossing both the Rappahannock and Rapidan above their confluence, take a position near Chancellorsville. This town, consisting of a hotel and several private residences, is situated on the road leading from Orange Court House to Fredericksburg, and is eleven miles north-west of the latter. Here the roads leading from German Mills and Ely's, United States and Banks' Fords, intersect.

The battle-plan of Hooker was not a simple one, but a combined operation consisting of three parts: first, his own movement and flank attack of Lee; second, Sedgwick's attack upon Fredericksburg; and third, Stoneman's cavalry movement to the rear of the Confederate position.

Lee was not slow to divine the designs of his enemy, and at once set about disposing of his little army to the best advantage for repelling the shock of battle which he now knew was at hand. General Barksdale's brigade and General Early's division were left to face Sedgwick's advance upon Fredericksburg, and Lee with his entire remaining available force began the march to Chancellorsville, where by throwing the bulk of his army in front of Hooker, he expected to check his advance.

On Saturday, May 2d, the town was reached, and Jackson in the front began the work assigned him in the mighty contest. For two hours his division passed in review of Sickles' position on the left. The 23d Georgia regiment was guarding the flank of his train, and upon this regiment was poured the first fire. Sickles ordered General Birney to open fire and then charge the passing train; the order was executed

FOLEY'S STATUE OF "STONEWALL" JACKSON,
in the Capitol Grounds, Richmond.

The Inscription reads: "Presented by English gentlemen as a tribute of admiration for the soldier and patriot, THOMAS J. JACKSON, and gratefully accepted by Virginia, in the name of the Southern people. Done A. D. 1875. In the Hundredth Year of the Commonwealth" "Look! there is JACKSON, standing like a Stone Wall."

and the greater part of the Georgia regiment were made prisoners. But Jackson's division was already far to the right and in position; at 5 P. M. the attack was made upon Howard's division, which broke and ran at the first fire. Sickles was preparing to renew Birney's attack with greater force, and for that purpose had just ordered up Pleasanton's cavalry, 1,000 strong, when the movement was changed to check the panic-stricken lines from Howard's right. The action now became general, and the Confederates charged from all points. The 8th Pennsylvania attempted to check the advance of Jackson's column and was entirely overwhelmed. It was the same old story. The Grand Army of the Potomac, in three hours from the first fire, was falling back before the charging columns of that army thrice its victors.

In the meantime Sedgwick with a force of two to one had succeeded in driving Barksdale and Early from their position at Fredericksburg, and they were now slowly falling back to join the main forces at Chancellorsville. Sedgwick was in pursuit, and intelligence of his approach reached Lee just as he was making preparations for a final attack upon Hooker. Something must be done to stay the unexpected force in his rear, and he accordingly dispatched four brigades under McLaws and Anderson to reinforce Barksdale and Early, and check Sedgwick. They encountered his advance near Salem Church, but it was now night and darkness put an end to the conflict, both parties retaining their ground. This movement did not prevent Lee from keeping a furious cannonade on Hooker's front.

On the next morning, Monday, May 4th, Sedgwick sent a messenger to Hooker informing him of his beleaguered condition and asking support from the main army. Hooker replied that no aid could be given. Thereupon Sedgwick fell back rapidly to Banks' Ford, and under a heavy fire from his victorious pursuers succeeded in crossing the river, but leaving 5,000 dead behind him—one-third as many as the commands of Barksdale and Early numbered.

Lee had not given Hooker a moment's rest, and on Tuesday night, having placed straw and brush upon the bridge to prevent a noise, the whole Federal army escaped under cover of the darkness to the other side, and on Wednesday morning when the Confederates moved forward to the attack, no enemy was to be seen. Thus ended the battles on the Rappahannock, in which Hooker lost 17,197 men, of whom 5,000 were unwounded prisoners. He had also lost thirteen cannon and 20,000 stand of small arms. Lee's loss was 13,000, of whom 1,581 were killed, 8,700 were wounded, and nearly 3,000 prisoners. Among the killed was the lamented "Stonewall" Jackson—a sketch of whose life will be found in Volume I of VIRGINIA AND VIRGINIANS.

THE INVASION OF PENNSYLVANIA.

For a month after the battle of Chancellorsville, the two armies lay confronting each other with only the river between them. During the time, Hooker's force had been somewhat reduced by the discharge of several regiments whose term of service had expired, while that of Lee had been augmented by the arrival of several regiments of North Carolina troops. His army too had been thoroughly re-organized, and the question of Jackson's successor settled to the satisfaction of the country. The President, some time in May, commissioned both Major-Generals R. S. Ewell and A. P. Hill as Lieutenant-Generals in the army of Northern Virginia. To the command of each three divisions were assigned, to complete which Anderson's division was taken from Longstreet's corps, and that of A. P. Hill reduced to two brigades, and the command given to Major-General W. D. Pender; to these was added the brigade of Pettigrew and another from North Carolina, forming a corps, the command of which was given to Major-General Heth.

General Lee had for some time entertained a plan for the invasion of the Northern States, being determined that if he could not bring on another engagement in Virginia, by an invasion to induce the withdrawal of the Federal forces from her soil.

On the 3d of June, the preparations being complete, McLaws' division of Longstreet's corps began its march from Fredericksburg toward Culpeper Court House, and the same evening Hood's division, which had been lying near the mouth of the Rapidan, followed on to the same place. By the 8th, the entire army was in motion, with the rear resting at Culpeper. On the 9th, a large force of Federal cavalry and infantry crossed the Rappahannock at Beverly's and Kelley's fords, and attacked General Stuart. The engagement continued throughout the afternoon, and resulted in the retreat of the Federals beyond the river, leaving behind them four hundred prisoners and three pieces of artillery. This engagement is known to Northern writers as the battle of Brandy Station. The principal fighting on the Confederate side was done by the 11th Virginia cavalry, under command of Colonel Lomax.

CAPTURE OF WINCHESTER.

In the meantime, General Jenkins, commanding a brigade of cavalry, was ordered forward toward Winchester, and at the same time General Imboden was directed to make a demonstration toward Romney, for the purpose of covering the movement of General Jenkins against Winchester, and further to prevent the Federals at that place from being reinforced by troops lying along the line of the Baltimore & Ohio railroad.

General Milroy, the Federal commander at Winchester, had a force of 7,000 men. He was either unaware of, or misinformed regarding the force moving against him, and therefore held his position too long. On the 13th, General Rodes drove in a force which was lying at Berryville, and at 5 P. M. on the 14th, General Early was within cannon range of Milroy's position, which it was his purpose to assault ; he at once began preparations for the attack. Twenty pieces of artillery were placed in position and opened fire, and at the same time Hays' Louisiana brigade charged the works, which in a few minutes yielded before the charging columns, and Milroy was defeated and driven from Winchester, with a loss, according to his own account, of 4,000 men, 29 guns, 277 wagons, and 400 horses. Of the fugitives a part escaped to Harpers Ferry, and the remainder into Pennsylvania. General Rodes, having driven the Federals from Berryville, marched to Martinsburg, where he arrived on the 14th, and captured 700 prisoners, 5 pieces of artillery, and a considerable quantity of stores.

THE MARCH INTO PENNSYLVANIA CONTINUED.

These operations had cleared the valley of the Federal forces, those at Harpers Ferry having withdrawn to Maryland Heights; and now the great movement of the war, prefaced by this brilliant introduction, was fairly begun.

Ewell's corps was the first to cross the Potomac. On the 24th it was followed by that of General A. P. Hill, which crossed at Shepherdstown. General Longstreet's corps had previously reached the Maryland shore by the Williamsport ford. The latter was composed of the divisions of McLaws, Pickett, and Hood, while the corps of Hill consisted of those of Pender, Heth, and Anderson, and that of Ewell of the divisions of Rodes, Early, and Johnson. The several columns re-united at Hagerstown, from which place the entire army crossed into Pennsylvania, and on the evening of the 27th encamped near Chambersburg.

Throughout the North this movement produced the wildest excitement. The public records were removed from Harrisburg, and New York and Philadelphia prepared to receive the daring invaders.

On the 15th of June, President Lincoln issued a proclamation calling for 120,000 militia, of which Pennsylvania was to furnish 50,000, Ohio 30,000, Maryland 10,000, West Virginia 10,000, and New York 20,000. In addition, Governor Andrews tendered the entire military strength of Massachusetts in the terrible crisis.

But it was not the rapidly forming battalions of raw militia that claimed the attention of the daring invader, General Lee. He was watching with the gravest interest the movements of that mighty army, a third greater than his own, which he had left on the banks of the Rappahannock, and which along the Potomac had for three years been drilled in the science of war.

Hooker lingered for a short time on the shore of Virginia, unable to determine whether Lee's advance was an invasion of the Northern States or a movement on Washington. Believing it to be the latter, he, on the 13th of June, put his army in motion northward, so as to cover the National Capital, marching along the east side of the Blue Ridge, while the Confederates moved along the west side. He reached the Potomac, and crossing at Edwards' Ferry, moved on to Frederick City. There he yielded to the pressure of public opinion at the North and resigned the command of the army, which was at once given to General Meade. That officer made only such changes as were imperatively necessary. Sykes took the 5th corps, which had been Meade's; Hancock the 2d, in place of Couch, who had been assigned to the department of the Susquehanna; Reynolds retained the 1st, Sickles the 3d, Sedgwick the 6th, Howard the 11th, and Slocum the 12th. The entire cavalry force was placed under Pleasanton. Thus the two armies were constituted on the 27th of June; the Confederate at Chambersburg and the Federal at Frederick — thirty-five miles apart.

BATTLE OF GETTYSBURG.

General Lee designed an attack upon Harrisburg, but on the 29th, learning of the northward movement of Meade, he ordered General Ewell, then on the road toward the capital, to join the army near Gettysburg, and at the same time he put the entire army in motion for the same destination. The march was slow, and it was 10 A. M. on the morning of the 1st of July when Heth's division in the advance reached the town destined henceforth to enduring distinction in American history. Meade had taken advantage of Lee's delay at Chambersburg, and by rapid marching reached the place in time for the 11th corps to engage Heth's division on its arrival.

A day pregnant with momentous issue was at hand. The mighty armies which had ceased to confront each other since leaving the Rappahannock, found themselves face to face at Gettysburg, on Wednesday, July 1st.

Buford's cavalry brought on the attack at a point two miles out on the Chambersburg road, but was soon forced back by the approaching lines of General Heth. General Reynolds then attempted to stay the advance, but he fell mortally wounded in the first fire, and his division in confusion fell back to the town. Another gray line was now moving forward; it was the corps of Ewell from York and Carlisle. He had heard the artillery calling him, and had hastened to the point of attack. Unchecked, they moved into the town, the Federals, under the command of Doubleday since the fall of Reynolds, retiring to the hill beyond. This concluded the first day's fighting.

Let us briefly notice the position of the two armies on the morning of the 2d, which had taken positions during the night of the 1st. Lee's army was arranged along Seminary Ridge and around to the east of Gettysburg in the form of a vast crescent five miles in length, its concavity facing its antagonist. Longstreet was on the right, Hill in the center, and Ewell on the left. Meade's forces were all up by daylight except Sedgwick's corps, which did not arrive until 2 P. M. Slocum was posted on the extreme right; to his left lay the command of Wadsworth; then to his left was Howard, and following in order were Hancock, Sickles and Sykes. The corps of Reynolds was held in reserve.

There lay the forces of General Lee—the Army of Northern Virginia—which had met and defeated the army now before it on many bloody fields. At Mechanicsville, at Malvern Hill, at South Mountain, at Antietam, at Manassas, at Fredericksburg and at Chancellorsville, it had seen the Army of the Potomac routed and fleeing before it. But now a reverse, the most serious of the war, was to be met, but not from any want of intrepidity or the absence of heroic achievement, for here on the field of Gettysburg, though overpowered, it made the grandest stand in its history.

We have not space to follow all the charges and counter-charges, successes and reverses, on that historic field. Such carnage had not before been witnessed on this continent. Well may historians class it as one of the fifteen great battles of the world. Some idea of the terrible struggle may be formed from its casualties. The Federal loss was 23,210, of whom 2,834 were killed, 13,733 wounded, and 6,643 missing. That of the Confederates was 36,000, of whom 5,000 were killed, 23,000 wounded, and 8,000 missing.

On the 4th, Lee began his march to the Potomac, forty miles distant, which he reached on the 7th, expecting to cross at Williamsport, but finding the stream so swollen that pontoons were impracticable, he moved to Falling Waters, where on the 13th he passed into Virginia. The disabled condition of the Federal army may be inferred from the fact that although Lee lingered on the shores of Maryland *nine days* after the battle, and within forty miles of his enemy, no second attack was made, nor was any pursuit attempted save that of the cavalry which followed in his rear.

VIRGINIA TROOPS IN THE SERVICE.

Virginia has ever been ready with her treasure and the lives of her sons in the cause of liberty, and her patriotism and sacrificing spirit was nobly indicated in the stern demands of our late civil war. In the autumn of 1863 it was reported to the General Assembly of the State that she had already furnished 102,915 soldiers to the Confederate service;

that, in addition, thirty thousand conscripts had just passed through the camp of instruction, and that up to that time she had furnished 103,840 muskets, 399 pieces of cannon, and other arms in proportion. The rolls on file in the Adjutant and Inspector-General's office showed that there were then in active service,—

Sixty-four regiments of infantry	52,496
Twenty regiments of cavalry	14,175
Two regiments of artillery	1,779
Twenty-eight battalions of cavalry, infantry and artillery	11,717
Nine battalions of artillery, Army Northern Virginia	4,500
Two hundred and fourteen unattached companies, artillery, infantry, and cavalry	18,248
Total number of men	102,915

ENGAGEMENT AT CHARLESTOWN.

After General Lee crossed the Potomac, he proceeded leisurely up the valley and through the gaps of the Blue Ridge until he reached the Rapidan. General Meade, marching from Gettysburg, passed the Potomac on the 18th, and soon the two armies were again confronting each other in Virginia.

General Imboden was sent with a cavalry force to guard the mountain gaps on Lee's left, and in October advanced upon Charlestown, where a Federal force from Harpers Ferry had taken position. Upon his arrival he found them occupying the court-house, jail, and other contiguous buildings, all of which were loop-holed for musketry, and the court-house yard defended by a strong wall of oak timber. He at once demanded the surrender, but Colonel Simpson, the Federal commander, asked an hour's time for consideration. Imboden offered five minutes, to which was replied, "Take me if you can." The artillery was at once opened at a distance of two hundred yards, and in a few minutes the Federals were driven into the streets, flying towards Harpers Ferry. They had, however, proceeded but a short distance before they were met by the 18th Virginia cavalry and Gilmore's battalions, and forced to surrender. The regiment thus made prisoners was the 9th Maryland infantry. The colonel and a half dozen others, being mounted, made their escape to Harpers Ferry. General Imboden now returned up the Valley and sent his prisoners on to Richmond. This, with the exception of the engagements at Rappahannock Bridge and Germania Ford, ended the operations in Virginia for the third year. Late in the fall the "On to Richmond" cry had been renewed throughout the North, but active operations were deferred until the spring of 1864.

THE GREATEST CAMPAIGN IN AMERICAN HISTORY.

On the morning of the 9th of March, 1864, General Grant was commissioned Commander-in-Chief of the Federal army, which on the 1st of May numbered 662,345 men. This chieftain could boast a phenomenal career. An ex-officer of the United States who had been cashiered for drunkenness, at the opening of the war he was an obscure and improvident tanner at Galena, Illinois. Appointed to the command of a regiment from that State, his promotion had been rapid, and through the unstinted praise of the Northern press he had been elevated in the fitful minds of that people into a hero of the first magnitude. It was, consequently, their sanguine expectation that the recent disasters to the Federal arms under McClellan, Burnside and Hooker, would be speedily retrieved, and that the victorious Stars and Stripes would soon float above the doomed dome of the Confederate Capitol. They had forgotten that the ragged Army of Northern Virginia still lay between them and the last proud consummation.

Before entering upon the history of this, the most momentous campaign recorded in the annals of the American continent, let us consider for a moment the two armies which were to play the prominent parts in the grand drama.

During the winter of 1863-4 they lay confronting each other on the banks of the Rapidan—the Federals on the North and the Confederates on the South. In April the new commander of the Army of the Potomac re-formed that body into three corps, and re-distributed the troops before composing the 1st and 3d corps. Hancock was placed in command of the 2d; Warren of the 5th and Sedgwick of the 6th. The entire force numbered 140,000 men. To oppose this mighty army was that of the Army of Northern Virginia, which now had been reduced to 60,000 men. It, too, consisted of three corps, under the command of Ewell, Hill, and Longstreet, respectively; and at the time of the Federal advance, that of the first named lay upon the banks of the Rapidan, the second at Orange Court House, and the third at Gordonsville.

The early days of May witnessed the beginning of the memorable campaign. On the 4th, orders were given for an advance, and the same day the Federal army moved southward from Culpeper Court House, and on the 5th passed the Rapidan at Ely's and Germania fords, with Burnside's division in the lead, and the

BATTLES OF THE WILDERNESS

At once began. An attempt was made to turn the right flank of Lee's army. The divisions of Heth and Wilcox withstood the assault during

CONFEDERATE STATES SEAL.

the entire day, and successfully too, as even the Northern accounts admit. No shouts of victory echoed through the Wilderness that night.

Late in the evening Hancock's corps moved forward and took a position on the left of the Federal army. At 5 o'clock the next morning (the 6th) the second day's fighting was begun by Hill's and Longstreet's corps attacking both flanks of Hancock's position, which in a short time were turned and forced back. The fighting now became general and continued throughout the day, which closed with a charge by one of Lee's columns and the capture of General Seymour and a large portion of his brigade. Grant's loss was more than 20,000, of which 5,000 were prisoners. Lee had lost 10,000. This is an appalling aggregate, considering that it was a mere incidental engagement, in which the employment of artillery was precluded and strategic maneuver impracticable. The Federal General Wadsworth had been killed and General Longstreet was severely wounded. Such were the first two battles of the Wilderness, the results of which the facts prove to have been in favor of the Confederates. At the North, however, it was claimed that the advantage was with the Federal army.

BATTLES OF SPOTTSYLVANIA COURT HOUSE.

On the 7th, Grant moved slowly toward Spottsylvania Court House, where his army arrived late that evening, and on the next day, the 8th, was fought the first in this locally designated series of battles. The first engagement took place between Longstreet's corps, commanded by Anderson, and the Federal 5th corps, under Warren, who was supported by cavalry. The Federals were repulsed with heavy loss.

On the 9th heavy skirmishing was kept up throughout the day, but there was no general engagement. What may be regarded as the great battle took place on Thursday, the 12th, and for long weary hours it continued. It was a furious and dead-lock conflict. The ceaseless roar of artillery and rattle of musketry continued from early dawn until the darkness of night put an end to the contest. An intelligent writer, who was upon the field and an eye-witness of the terribly sublime scene, says : "It would not be impossible to match the results of any one day's battle with stories from the wars of the old world; but never, we should think, in the history of man, were five such battles as these compressed into six days." The loss on either side was 10,000, and neither gained any advantage.

On the 14th, Grant moved his lines by his left flank, taking a position nearer the Richmond & Fredericksburg railroad; and here he once more assaulted Ewell's line, but was easily repulsed. It was claimed by the Federals that it was but an effort to turn Lee's left flank and not intended as an attack. On the 19th and the 20th, the two armies moved parallel to each other, and on the 21st, Grant's forces took a position at Milford Station and Bowling Green, with the Army of Northern Virginia in his front toward Richmond. During the 23d and the 25th, he made several futile assaults upon Lee's lines. He had now but one alternative, and that was to move his army around from the North Anna, and beyond the Pamunkey. This he did, and on the 27th his advance, under Sheridan, occupied Hanovertown on the Pamunkey, 15 miles north-east of Richmond, but here again the movement was intercepted by Lee. Grant, now despairing of reaching Richmond from that point, turned away to his right, and on the 1st day of June took up his position near Cold Harbor. This was the nearest point to the Capital City yet reached.

BATTLE OF THE CHICKAHOMINY, OR COLD HARBOR.

Grant once more determined to try the strength of Lee's lines. On the morning of the 3d of June, which dawned with a drizzling rain, as soon as it was light enough to see, the word was given, and the commands of Barlow and Gibbon, of Hancock's corps, advanced against the outer Confederate line, which was held by the division of General Breckinridge. It was at once forced back, but the reverse was only momentary, for Milligan's brigade and the Maryland battalion immediately dashed forward and retrieved the lost position, driving the Federals back with frightful loss. Wright and Smith both charged the lines, but met with no better fortune than Barlow and Gibbon. Many of the best officers of these commands were killed. The Federals were repulsed at every point, and Grant's object—a knowledge of the strength of Lee's lines—was attained. The battle lasted but forty minutes, but in that time the Federal loss was 7,000, while that of the Confederate was only 3,000.

GRANT MOVES TO THE SOUTH SIDE OF THE JAMES.

Cold Harbor was the last pitched battle of the campaign north of the James. Grant deciding that the "On to Richmond" route was not from the direction of the Potomac, but from the opposite point, accordingly put his army in motion, and after a march of fifty-five miles over the sandy roads of the Chickahominy, on the 15th reached the bank of the James at City Point, sixty miles below Richmond, and three days later his rear guards passed beyond that river. Lee made no resistance to this movement, but leisurely fell back to Richmond.

The Federal army had been from the 5th of May to the 15th of June—forty-five days—in its marching from the Rapidan to the James; and during that time had fought the battles of the Wilderness, Spottsylvania Court House, North Anna, and Cold Harbor. At the time that Grant reached the James his official reports show that he had lost 54,551 men, of whom 7,289 were killed, 37,406 wounded, and 9,856 missing. Lee had lost 32,000 men, of whom 8,500 were prisoners. He entered Richmond with 58,000 troops, while Grant crossed the James with 150,000, including those of Butler's command. Here is presented by the Virginia Army one among the most remarkable achievements in the history of wars. For a period of forty-five days that little army stood face to face with one nearly three times as great as itself, then necessitating it to a cautious and circuitous progress, as in the arc of a circle, radiating fifty miles from Richmond, and finally compelling it to cross the James sixty miles below its objective point.

HUNTER CAPTURES STAUNTON.

We must now turn away from the theater of war around Richmond and notice for a moment the operations in the Shenandoah Valley. A part of Grant's plan was a joint movement up the Shenandoah under Siegel, and up the Kanawha under Crook, their objective points being Staunton and Lynchburg.

Accordingly, on the 1st of May, Siegel moved up the valley with a force of 10,000 men, but was met on the 15th, at New Market, by the Confederate General Breckinridge and signally routed with the loss of 700 men, 6 pieces of artillery and 1,000 small arms.

Crook was moving easterly from Charleston, on the Great Kanawha, and on the waters of New river he divided his force, sending Averill with 2,000 cavalry to destroy the coal mines at Wytheville, while he advanced further to the north. Averill was met on the 10th by a cavalry force under Morgan and defeated. Crook with a force of 6,000 men moved on toward Dublin Depot, and there repelled an attack, but with the loss of 700 killed and wounded.

Siegel was now relieved of the command, and was succeeded by Hunter, who at once took the offensive, Breckinridge having in the meantime joined Lee. Hunter met the Confederate force at Piedmont on the 5th of June and completely routed it, taking 1,500 prisoners, three guns and 3,000 small arms. He then advanced on Staunton, where he was joined by Crook and Averill, augmenting his force to 20,000. He then moved by way of Lexington toward Lynchburg. Lee foreseeing the inevitable disasters to result upon a capture of that place, sent a strong force to its relief, forcing the retreat of Hunter on the 18th of June. Hotly pursued, Hunter followed the railroad westward to Salem, and thence through Newcastle toward Meadow Bluff. Thus failed the plans of Grant from the west as they had done from the east.

THE SIEGE OF PETERSBURG.

Petersburg is twenty-two miles south of Richmond and nine miles south-west of City Point, and was during the war one of the greatest railroad centers of the South: the Richmond & Petersburg railroad entered it from the north, and the Weldon or Roanoke road from the south, while the Lynchburg or Southside Road came in from the west. Over these lines came the supplies for Richmond, and Grant, without losing a single moment after crossing the river, attempted the capture of the place; but, being disappointed in that, his operations necessarily assumed the features of a siege, knowing, as he did, that upon the capture of Petersburg, depended the reduction of Richmond. The Confederate authorities were fully cognizant of the momentous issue, and to the raw troops and militia now put under arms for the defense of the "Cockade City," General Wise addressed a memorable and thrilling order: "Petersburg," said he, "is to be and shall be defended on her outer walls, on her inner lines, at her corporation bounds, in every street, and around every temple of God, and altar of man."

But the gallant little city was now to be put to a much more severe test than any which it had hitherto experienced. It was now to bear the brunt of the bulk of the mighty besieging army which bore upon it like an avalanche. Butler was ordered by Grant to send Smith's division forward, and at the same time informed that the entire Army of the Potomac would be moved forward as rapidly as possible. Smith, on the morning of the 14th, landed at Bermuda Hundred, but did not get ready to make the attack until near sunset; then, with a portion only of his command, he made the attack, and at 7 P. M. succeeded in carrying the outer line of works on the north-east of the city, capturing fifteen guns and 300 prisoners. Night came on and the moon was shining brightly, when at 9 o'clock Hancock, with two divisions of the 2d corps, reached Smith, and, waiving his precedence in rank, tendered to him the service of his troops. Smith declined the offer, but requested Hancock to hold the captured works.

Another terrible assault was now made on the batteries from nine to twelve inclusive, which were defended by the division of General Hoke, whose heroic troops, after having repulsed three successive assaults, charged over their works and compelled a large portion of one of Smith's brigades to take shelter in a ravine, where they surrendered to the 64th Georgia regiment.

The engagement continued throughout Friday, the 17th, without decisive results. On the 18th an attack was made along the entire line, and during the day three desperate assaults were made—one at four in the morning, another at noon, and a third at four in the afternoon. Each was repulsed, and the attack finally abandoned. Grant's loss in the four days before Petersburg was 9,000 killed and wounded. He, concluding that it was impossible to carry the works by direct assault, determined to resort to "mining," a plan which had worked so admirably at Balaklava and Inkerman Valley during the war of the Crimea.

THE MINE.

The mine, though not devised by Meade, was approved of by him and a majority of the corps commanders. The work was performed by one of Burnside's regiments, who had been Pennsylvania miners. It consisted of a main shaft five feet across and five hundred and twenty feet long, with lateral continuations extending forty feet in either direction. The work began on the 25th of June, and was completed on the 23d of July. The charge placed in it consisted of 8,000 pounds of giant powder.

The explosion was to take place at half-past 3 o'clock A. M. of the 30th of July, and at the same instant Burrside's division was to rush through the breach thus created and seize the works on Cemetery Hill; General Warren was to support him on the right and Ord on the left—the charging columns to consist of 50,000 men.

At the appointed time the fuse was lighted, but the explosion did not take place. Then Lieutenant Douty and Sergeant Rees entered the mine and found the fuse separated within fifty feet of the magazine; the damage was repaired, and they had barely time to escape when the awful explosion took place. The charging columns rushed forward, and behind them opened ninety-five pieces of heavy artillery. But the Confederates were not dismayed, and in a few minutes their own batteries were replying. On came the rushing columns, furiously assaulting the second line of works, but behind them were men who had never flinched from death, which they had faced on many a gory field, and who were not now to be dismayed by the explosion of mines and the thunder of artillery. The Federal advance was led by a brigade of negro troops under the command of General White, who, appalled by the deadly fire, rushed panic-stricken back through the lines of the white troops to the rear. Terrible carnage ensued, and it is doubtful whether all the circumstantial horrors of war were ever before displayed in such awful intensity on any field. At last came the orders to the Federals to fall back and re-occupy their former position. That order was obeyed with alacrity, and thus failed the monstrous device by which it had been hoped access would have been opened to the now famous "outpost" of Richmond. The Federal loss was 4,000, of whom 1,900 were prisoners. That of the Confederates was given in detail thus: Mahone's division, 450; Elliott's South Carolina brigade, which was blown up by the mine, 300; and Ransom's, Clingman's and Wise's commands, 300.

OPERATIONS IN THE SHENANDOAH VALLEY.

We must now leave Grant engaged in the investment of Petersburg, and notice briefly the operations in the Shenandoah Valley. During the summer of 1864, several offensive movements were planned, and chief among them was Early's invasion of Maryland. After the retreat of Hunter from Lynchburg, the way was left open, and Early accordingly moved with his entire force — about 20,000—up the Valley, and driving Siegel from Martinsburg, occupied that town. A few days later, Early crossed the Potomac, entered Maryland, and halted at Frederick City. At Monocacy Bridge, four miles thence, he defeated and put to rout a considerable Federal force. Instead of pursuing them, he proceeded by rapid marches toward Washington and Baltimore, collecting the horses and cattle along his line of march. The Federal Capital was now in imminent peril, and it is claimed had Early improved the opportunity, he might have occupied the city. But instead of riding into Washington, he dispersed his army in detachments, which were sent about the country to destroy telegraph lines and intercept trains. Thus, perhaps, passed the great opportunity of 1864. Re-uniting his forces at Hagerstown, he re-crossed into Virginia, bringing with him 5,000 horses and 2,000 beef cattle. Martinsburg was re-occupied, and from thence he sent General John McCausland with a cavalry force into Pennsylvania. It penetrated as far as Chambersburg in that State. The town was fired and a considerable portion of it burned.

DESOLATION OF THE VALLEY.

On the 7th of August, Hunter resigned, and the command of the Federal force in the Valley was given to General Sheridan. He at once prepared for an aggressive campaign, but before any move was made he was visited by Grant (September 15th), and between the two the destruction of the section known as the "Garden of Virginia" was planned. The Commander-in-Chief then returned to his position at Petersburg.

THE BATTLE OF OPEQUAN CREEK.

On the 19th the two armies met at Opequan creek, and after a hard fought battle, lasting several hours, the Confederates were forced to retreat. The Federal loss was 4,990, of whom 653 were killed, 3,719 wounded, and 618 missing. That of the Confederates was 5,000. Early fell back twelve miles to Fishers Hill, where he was again attacked by superior numbers and compelled to retreat toward Staunton, and Sheridan proceeded to carry out Grant's orders respecting the devastation of the Valley. His cavalry spread over its entire extent, and in its wake destruction reigned supreme. Nowhere in the New World had such vandalism been witnessed. At the end of three weeks, Sheridan sent the following report to Washington:

"The whole country, from the Blue Ridge to the North Mountain, has been rendered untenable for a rebel army. I have destroyed over 2,000 barns filled with wheat and hay and farming implements, over 70 mills filled with flour and wheat. I have driven to the front of the army over 4,000 head of stock, have killed and issued to the troops not less than 3,000 sheep. A large number of horses have also been obtained."

BATTLE OF CEDAR CREEK.

After the battle of Fishers Hill it became evident that General Early had not a sufficient force with which to cope with Sheridan, and accordingly General Lee sent Kershaw's division to reinforce him. Sheridan, after having laid waste the Valley, rested his army on the south bank of Cedar Creek, a small stream which forms the boundary line between Shenandoah and Frederick counties, and repaired to Washington to consult with the Secretary of War with reference to the transfer of the 6th corps to that city.

On the night of the 18th of October, General Early determined to attack the Federal position during the absence of Sheridan, and under cover of the darkness, he marched his army out from Fishers Hill (to which place he had returned and taken position after being joined by Kershaw), and in order to flank the Federal lines, it was necessary to move the larger column through a narrow gap in the mountains, so narrow, in fact, that two men could not walk abreast. The marching, for more than seven miles over a broken country, along mountain sides and down hills so abrupt that horses could scarcely travel, occupied almost the entire night, and it was near daybreak before a position in front of the Federal lines was attained.

But all was upon time; everything had been conducted with the utmost secrecy, and not even a picket alarm had been given. Orders to attack were given, and with Payne's division in the lead, a charge across the creek was made, Sheridan's head-quarters being the objective point. The infantry followed rapidly on, Gordon's division following Payne, with that of Pegram in reserve. A terrible fire was opened from all points. It was a fearful surprise to the sleeping army, the 8th and 19th corps of which were entirely routed, and retreating left many hundreds slain in the camps; and 1,500 prisoners, 18 pieces of artillery, 2,000 stand of small arms, and several hundred wagons fell into the hands of the Confederates. Fully two thirds of Sheridan's army was in rapid retreat, but the 6th corps and the cavalry commanded by Generals Torbert, Merritt and Dwight had not yet been engaged. At 9 o'clock A. M. the field had been won, and had the victorious troops now pressed on and struck the 6th corps, Sheridan's army would have been involved in utter ruin. But instead, Early's force, for some unknown cause, halted on the field and allowed the Federals to form a new line near Middletown. At 10 o'clock A. M. Sheridan had completed his famous "Ride from Winchester," and at 3 o'clock P. M. assumed the offensive, and moving forward, vigorously and successfully assaulted Early. Gordon's division was the first to break, then followed Kershaw's, and later Ramseur's. Soon after, Wharton's and Pegram's lines gave way, and the field was soon covered with flying men. It was a shameful rout. Never before had the Confederate soldiery so behaved. Their loss was 3,500 killed and wounded, and 2,500 prisoners, while that of the Federals was 4,990, of whom 653 were killed, 3,719 wounded, and 618 missing.

AROUND PETERSBURG.

We must now return to the theater of war around Petersburg. On the 1st of August, Grant had 85,295 men present for duty. On the same day Lee's force numbered 54,751, reduced from 60,000 by his having sent Kershaw's brigade to Early in the Valley. On the 12th, Grant, believing that Lee had sent three divisions instead of one to the Valley, determined to assail Richmond, and for this purpose, Hancock's corps embarked on the James and landed at Deep Bottom, whence it advanced toward Richmond. But it was not long ere it was learned that three divisions had not gone to the assistance of Early. One important advantage was gained, however—Hancock's northward movement, which resulted in the

CAPTURE AND DESTRUCTION OF THE WELDON RAILROAD.

When General Lee became aware of the position of the Federals on the north bank of the James, he drew the troops heavily from Petersburg to the defense of Richmond, and on the 18th, the 5th corps under Warren moved south of Petersburg and struck the Weldon railroad only four miles south of the city. In doing this a gap was left open on his right and into it Lee at once thrust Mahone's division, which succeeded in forcing Wright farther south, and in capturing 2,000 prisoners, but it was finally obliged to fall back. The next day another serious engagement took place, but Warren held his position, and in three days succeeded in destroying seven miles of the road, but it cost him a loss of 4,543 men. From this date until the close of the year, a continued series of engagements, sorties, raids, advances and retreats took place, a recountal of which is not necessary to our plan, and would from their similarity of detail scarcely interest the reader. Therefore we proceed to the consideration of the momentous events of 1865, which was

THE BEGINNING OF THE END.

Winter put an end to all military operations, and both armies lay inactive awaiting the opening of the spring campaign, which commenced with the 25th of March, 1865. The first action was that of FORT STEDMAN or HARES HILL. At four o'clock on the morning of that day, all things being in readiness, a body of Confederate sharpshooters, 250 in number, with empty guns left their own works and stealthily moving across the intervening space, scaled the outer works of the enemy. It was to the Federals as great a surprise as would have been a clap of thunder from a noonday sky. They were driven from their batteries, and yet not a musket was fired. This movement was followed by that of several brigades which had been massed for the purpose. The Federals having recovered from the surprise occasioned by the daring adventure recited, now opened a murderous enfilading fire upon the assailants, and soon General Gordon found it judicious to retire. In the assault, the Confederates captured nine pieces of artillery, but being unable to remove them, they were disabled and left behind; also, 550 prisoners among whom was one brigadier-general and several field officers of lower rank.

This action seemed to arouse Grant to the realization that it was time to open the campaign, and on the 29th he began a heavy movement against the Southside railroad. Pouring forth 50,000 men, of whom 9,000 were cavalry, he succeeded after several reverses in the accomplishment of his object. Saturday night, April 1st, was a gloomy one for General Lee.

The Federal forces had now passed around to the south-west of his position, thus cutting off not only his source of supplies, but also his line of march southward, should he be compelled to abandon his works. Not only this, but three Federal corps lay before him ready to strike the Petersburg defenses at daylight.

The hour came, and at sunrise on that balmy Sabbath morning the attack was made from three separate points. The 6th corps went though first, at a point nearly opposite the western extremity of the city; a little farther west was the point of attack of the 24th corps; while to the east was that of the 9th corps, which succeeded in carrying Fort Mahone, one of the strongest defences of the city. Ord's and Humphrey's commands having carried the works in front of them, swung around to the right and joined Gibbon's division before Forts Alexander and Gregg: these were the strongest fortifications south of Petersburg, and with their reduction the way to the city would be opened. The assault was at once made, and Fort Alexander carried, but so determined was the resistance of Fort Gregg that Gibbon's columns were forced back, leaving the ground covered with the dead. Three furious charges were signally re-

TOMB OF EX-PRESIDENT MONROE,
Hollywood Cemetery, Richmond, Va.

pulsed, but at length the gallant garrison, with smoke-blackened faces from their blazing batteries, was forced to yield, and the works were carried.

At this moment, Generals Lee, Hill and Mahone were in Petersburg consulting upon their future movements. The terrible sounds of battle were coming nearer and nearer. "How is this, General?" said Lee to A. P. Hill. "Your men are giving way." Hill drew a rough coat over his uniform and mounting his horse, accompanied by a single orderly, dashed away to the front. In a ravine he rode into the Federal skirmish line, the sound of a dozen rifles instantly rang out upon the air, and the noble Hill, who had been foremost in so many victorious charges, fell to rise no more. (A sketch of his life will be found in the first volume of VIRGINIA AND VIRGINIANS.)

The day waned and with it the fortunes of the Confederate arms; the works were carried after thousands of men had fallen in their defence. But how different was the scene in Richmond, twenty-two miles away! It was a beautiful, balmy spring evening, and the people had gathered in their respective churches for worship. President Davis was seated in his pew in St. Paul's Church. A messenger walked briskly up the aisle and handed him a telegram: it was from General Lee, and in it he said: "Petersburg is lost to the Confederacy, and Richmond must be evacuated at once." The President arose immediately and left the church with a measured but nervous step. No one save himself knew the exact contents of that message, and yet every one in the assemblage intuitively felt that something of dread import had taken place at the front. Quivering lips passed the news from church to church, and the congregations were speedily dismissed; then the rumor was caught up in the streets and soon carried to the remote limits of the city.

EVACUATION OF RICHMOND.

Night passed away, and the day brought such a scene as had only been witnessed in the abandoned cities of the Old World. A government was preparing to move; wagons were hastily laden with boxes and trunks at the departments, and driven to the depot of the Richmond & Danville railroad. Thousands of citizens determined to follow the fortunes of the fugitive government, and as much as a hundred dollars in gold was offered for a conveyance. Night came again and brought with it a reign of terror. No human eyes in Richmond were closed in sleep that night. The city council convened and resolved to destroy all the liquor in the city, and at midnight the work of destruction began. Hundreds of barrels were poured into the gutters, but despite every effort the straggling soldiers secured a quantity of it, and from that moment law and order ceased to exist. Many stores were pillaged, the lawless marauders crashing windows and battering down doors, that they might grasp the coveted merchandise within. Wild cries of distress mingled with the yells of the pillagers rent the air and a livid pallor rested upon every face.

But the worst element of destruction had not yet appeared upon the scene, although it hovered near. General Ewell, then in charge of the city, now ordered the four principal tobacco warehouses in the city to be fired. Mayor Mayo, through a committee of citizens, remonstrated against the order, the execution of which placed the entire business portion of the city in jeopardy, but without avail. The torch was applied, and the rams of the Confederate navy lying in the James were blown up. Daylight dawned upon the awful scene. The beautiful city was a sea of fire; tongues of flame shot from block to block, and far in beneath the dense columns of smoke might be seen the figures of the rioters rushing amid the glare like demons to and fro, laden with plunder of every kind. It was a scene indeed that beggared description.

The victors were near. A short distance below the city, and on the north bank of the James, lay the division of General Godfrey Weitzel, and to his eye and ear the lurid flames and thundering explosions conveyed an assuring conviction. He knew that Richmond had been abandoned by the Confederate authorities. His martial bands filled the air with inspiring national strains, and as the day dawned orders were given to advance and occupy the city. As the sun arose long lines of cavalry—the 4th Massachusetts in advance—entered the city and filed along Main street. A body of fifty cavalrymen occupied the city square, and Lieutenant Johnson de Peyster ascended to the top of the Capitol building and unfurled the National flag. The dread scene deepened in awful intensity; the hissing of the conflagration, the sullen curses of the vanquished, the shouts of the victors, the screams of women and children united to form a very pandemonium. But at last, through the efforts of the soldiers and citizens, assisted by a favorable change of the wind, the flames were stayed. Martial law was proclaimed, the discordant elements stilled, and order once more reigned.

FROM RICHMOND TO APPOMATTOX COURT HOUSE.

It was a dark and moonless night when Lee withdrew the wreck of his shattered army from Petersburg and Richmond. Orders had been issued for the forces to unite at Chesterfield Court House, a point nearly midway between the two cities. From this point it was his intention, it appears, to reach Danville and form a junction with Johnston, who was then marching northward; but a terrible disappointment awaited the army at Amelia Court House. The orders of General Lee for the forwarding of supplies thither from Danville had been shamefully neglected, and with this bitter revelation all hope vanished; capitulation was inevitable to the sorrowful mind of Lee, as it was to his meager and starving army, the loved cause for which they had so heroically striven for four long and weary years must be relinquished. No orders were given relating to straggling, and of the 38,000 who started on the march, thousands in soulful mortification abandoned the ranks. Especially was this true of Virginians, who stopped at home rather than go on to participate in the final bitter surrender.

Grant's forces followed on in rapid pursuit, and at Jetersville, the cavalry under Sheridan, passed in front of the fugitive army. But now the soil of the "Old Dominion" so long reddened with the life-blood of her sons, is to bloom again; her hills and valleys which erst have quaked with the reverberation of arms are to be re-attuned to nature's peaceful music; the bugle blast of war is to be stilled; and her patriot sons, unsurpassed as soldiers, are equally to vindicate themselves as citizens. It was late on the evening of the 6th that several of the Confederate generals gathered around the bivouac fire, and then decided in view of the state of affairs to advise General Lee to surrender, but before their action was reported a correspondence was opened between Generals Lee and Grant, which resulted in an interview and arrangement of the terms of surrender. After the meeting, which occurred at the house of Wilmer McLean, in the little village of Appomattox Court House, Grant wrote as follows:

"APPOMATTOX COURT HOUSE, VIRGINIA, *April* 9, 1865.

"GENERAL—In accordance with the substance of my letter to you on the 8th inst., I propose to receive the surrender of the Army of Northern Virginia on the following terms, to wit: Rolls of all the officers and men to be made in duplicate, one copy to be given to an officer designated by me, the other to be retained by such officer or officers as you may designate. The officers to give their individual paroles not to take up arms against the government of the United States until properly exchanged, and each company or regimental commander to sign a like parole for the men of his command. The arms, artillery, and public property to be packed and stacked, and turned over to the officers appointed by me to receive them. This will not embrace the side arms of the officers nor their private horses or baggage. This done, each officer and man will be allowed to return to his home, not to be disturbed by the United States authority so long as they observe their paroles and the laws in force where they may reside.

"U. S. GRANT, Lieutenant-General.

"GENERAL R. E. LEE."

To this General Lee replied:

"HEAD-QUARTERS ARMY OF NORTHERN VIRGINIA, *April* 9, 1865.

"GENERAL—I received your letter of this date, containing the terms of the surrender of the Army of Northern Virginia as proposed by you. As they are substantially the same as those expressed in your letter of the 8th instant, they are accepted. I will proceed to designate the proper officer to carry the stipulations into effect.

"R. E. LEE, General.

"LIEUTENANT-GENERAL U. S. GRANT."

The futile struggle was ended. General Lee rejoined his ragged and shrunken army to bid it a sad farewell. In that memorable address he touchingly said: "Men! we have fought through the war together. I have done the best I could for you." And grandly indeed had the simple utterance been attested! It was a magnificent pageant from the Chickahominy to the final act at Appomattox Court House; sublime in its realization of valor, endurance, and patriotism. Freedom records no sacrifices surpassing it in magnitude. And the grand hero, Lee, re-illumining the lustrous diadem of his mother Virginia, is jointly enshrined in the reverential hearts of her sons with her Washington.

Crushingly overwhelmed, the starving army of Northern Virginia laid down its arms, but its pitiful fate only invested with mournful incense its heroism and sacrifices. Its achievements will increasingly command the admiration of the world during all time.

The blighting effects of the war remained. The prophecy of Howell Cobb, uttered in the Montgomery Convention, that the Gulf States need have no fears, for Virginia would be made the theater of war, had been terribly fulfilled. The iron hand was everywhere visible. Materially and socially she had been shaken to her center. As a helmless wreck, she was seemingly helpless amid furious elements. Her industrial system blasted, her manufactures wrecked, her wealth dissipated, her commerce destroyed, and her once bounteous fields, her sanctuaries and the homes of her people alike a spectacle of desolation. A funereal pall of darkest gloom overspread and all but paralyzed the present, whilst the dread uncertainty of the fateful future almost held hope even in chained abeyance. But the oft-tried and as nobly exemplified spirit of the Old Dominion again asserted itself. Her brave sons, accepting the stern ultimatum, girded themselves about with newly-born energies and united in the effort of reparation. Gloriously have they redeemed their misfortunes, and righteous is the result. With grandly waxing strength, marvelously developing natural resources and expanding wealth, her unapproachable geographical advantages are enforcing recognition. Disdaining the grinding shackles of arrogant and arid New England; endeared to the great South as the votive shrine upon which was sacrificed its best blood, Virginia is firmly grasping the scepter of manufacture, fast withering in the palsied hands of the late arrogant North.

GEOGRAPHICAL AND PHYSICAL VIEW.

The Virginias lie between north latitude 36° 30' and 39° 30', and 1° 36' east, and 6° 24' west longitude, and their boundaries are as follows: On the north, by Pennsylvania and Maryland; north-east and east, by Maryland and the Atlantic Ocean; south, by North Carolina and Tennessee; west and north-west, by Kentucky and Ohio, or by the Ohio river, which flows for a distance of 300 miles along its western boundary. A legal description of the dividing line, separating the two States, would read about as follows: Beginning at the mouth of Knox creek, a corner of the States of Kentucky, Virginia and West Virginia, and thence with a line of and including the counties of McDowell and Mercer, to the top of East River Mountain; thence with said ridge and with Peters Mountain to the Alleghany Mountains; thence with the top of the same to the Haystack Knob, a corner of Virginia and West Virginia; thence with the southern line of and including Pendleton county to the top of Shenandoah Mountains; thence with the same and Branch Mountain to a corner of Hardy and Rockingham counties; thence with lines of and including the counties of Hardy, Hampshire, Morgan, Berkeley, and Jefferson, to a point on the Maryland and Virginia line where the Potomac river intersects the Blue Ridge.

The States may be divided into four distinct physical regions: First, the tide-water region; second, the Piedmont region; third, the great valley region; and, fourth, the trans-Alleghany region.

The tide-water region embraces all that portion of the State lying between the coast and a line drawn through the cities of Petersburg, Richmond and Fredericksburg, which are situated near the lower falls of the Appomattox, the James and the Rappahannock rivers, respectively. This line extended would mark a point at which all the Atlantic rivers of Virginia leap from the granite base on which stands the whole Appalachian mountain system. Through this region flow many navigable rivers, and into it extend numerous coves and inlets, either from Chesapeake Bay or from the ocean; around them are extensive areas of swamp land. The surface is nearly level, the undulations being so gentle that the currents of the rivers are scarcely perceptible. The soil is moist and sandy, of an alluvial formation, closely resembling that of the Floridian peninsula. The climate during the winter is mild and pleasant, but during the summer it is sultry and malarious.

The Piedmont (foot of the mountains) region extends from the west-

SCENE ON THE UPPER POTOMAC.

ern limit of the former region to the summit of the Blue Ridge mountains, and extends entirely across the State from north to south. The soil, near the head of tide-water, is sandy, but as we approach the base of the mountains a clay soil of great fertility is found; and here, for the first time on the Atlantic coast, appear the primordial rocks, the disintegration of which has added much to the richness of the soil. Springs, with never-failing sources, gush out in every direction. Valuable minerals abound, and deposits of limestone sufficient to supply Christendom with lime for ages to come, lie at a short distance beneath the surface. Its climate is temperate throughout the year, and as healthy as any in the world.

The great valley region includes all the country lying between the Blue Ridge on the one side and the Alleghany on the other. It is known under the name of the Shenandoah Valley, and from the fertility of its soil has been called "The Garden of Virginia." It is the central part of the great valley which is co-extensive with the Alleghany range, that part of it south of Virginia being called the Cumberland Valley. Geologists trace it far north, even to the banks of the Mohawk river, in New York. They inform us that it belongs to the Silurian formation, which would place it directly on top of the Azoic and beneath the Devonian formations. There are several varieties of slate, sandstone and conglomerates; limestone also abounds. Many beautiful streams flow through the valley, but owing to the absence of springs the country is not well watered. The summer is cool and pleasant, but the winter is cold and damp.

The trans-Alleghany region embraces all the country lying between the Alleghany mountains and the Ohio river, and includes the entire State of West Virginia. To describe it would be to describe the State. In the east it is mountainous, while in the center are beautiful ranges of hills, the termini of the western spurs of the Alleghanies, and in the west lies the fertile region of the Ohio Valley, much of which, for its fertility, is not excelled on the continent. This entire region may be said to be one vast coal-field, its area being 23,000 square miles, of which 15,000 is underlaid with the richest veins of coal. Only three States outrank this region in the extent of its coal deposits, namely: Illinois, Iowa and Missouri.

Over this entire region stand, in almost primeval grandeur, vast forests, sufficient to furnish timber for the ship-yards of the world for years to come. Ages of the most active industry will not exhaust the coal and timber of this region. It is here that the traveler beholds the grandest scenery in America, and lofty mountains, craggy peaks, frowning precipices, rock-ribbed cañons, rushing torrents, and roaring cataracts meet the eye of the beholder.

www.ingramcontent.com/pod-product-compliance
Lightning Source LLC
Chambersburg PA
CBHW071237300426
44116CB00008B/1071